Praise for
ˌun·a·ˈbridged

"*Unabridged* is a whip-smart, entertaining, and thoughtful chronicle of the prospects for dictionaries at a time when Google—or, even more so, AI—might seem to be poised to take over all their functions."

—Ben Yagoda, author of *Gobsmacked! The British Invasion of American English*

"A captivating look at the inner life of dictionaries. For anyone who's ever had a favorite word."

—Mignon Fogarty, host of the *Grammar Girl* podcast

"Stefan Fatsis has written the book I have wanted to read for years: the untold story of the American Language and how it has been curated and developed by the editors at Merriam-Webster. But into this fascinating narrative Fatsis himself becomes part of the story as a rookie lexicographer working his way into the system, giving this book an extra dimension, charm, and wit. You find yourself cheering for Fatsis to score a definition like a Little League parent pulling for their kid."

—Paul Dickson, author of *The Dickson Baseball Dictionary* and *G.I. Jive: A Dictionary of Words at War*

"People have to decide what 'gets into the dictionary.' This witty book gives us a look into the Rooms Where It Happens."

—John McWhorter, author of *Nine Nasty Words* and *Pronoun Trouble*

"Right from the opening pages of *Unabridged*, you know you're in the hands of an author who's having an absolute blast discovering the story that unfolds before you. Read on and Fatsis's joy will quickly become your own."

—Drew Magary, author of *The Hike* and *The Postmortal*

ˌun·a·ˈbridged

Also by Stefan Fatsis

A Few Seconds of Panic

Word Freak

Wild and Outside

ˌun·a·ˈbridged

the thrill of (and threat to) the modern dictionary

stefan fatsis

Atlantic Monthly Press
New York

Copyright © 2025 by Stefan Fatsis
Dictionary space break illustration © Maisie Derlega

All rights reserved. No part of this book may be reproduced in any form or by any electronic or mechanical means, including information storage and retrieval systems, without permission in writing from the publisher, except by a reviewer, who may quote brief passages in a review. Scanning, uploading, and electronic distribution of this book or the facilitation of such without the permission of the publisher is prohibited. Please purchase only authorized electronic editions, and do not participate in or encourage electronic piracy of copyrighted materials. Your support of the author's rights is appreciated. Any member of educational institutions wishing to photocopy part or all of the work for classroom use, or anthology, should send inquiries to Grove Atlantic, 154 West 14th Street, New York, NY 10011 or permissions@groveatlantic.com.

Any use of this publication to train generative artificial intelligence ("AI") technologies is expressly prohibited. The author and publisher reserve all rights to license uses of this work for generative AI training and development of machine learning language models.

FIRST EDITION

Printed in the United States of America

The interior of this book was designed by Norman E. Tuttle of Alpha Design & Composition.
This book was set in 12-pt. Bembo with Gill Sans and Times New Roman at Alpha Design & Composition of Pittsfield, NH.

First Grove Atlantic hardcover edition: October 2025

Library of Congress Cataloging-in-Publication data is available for this title.

ISBN 978-0-8021-6582-4
eISBN 978-0-8021-6583-1

Atlantic Monthly Press
an imprint of Grove Atlantic
154 West 14th Street
New York, NY 10011

Distributed by Publishers Group West

groveatlantic.com

25 26 27 28   10 9 8 7 6 5 4 3 2 1

dedication

: a name and often a message prefixed to
a literary, musical, or artistic production
in tribute to a person or cause

For Chloe, who knows the words

contents

: the topics or matter treated in a written work

note : a brief comment or explanation	ix
introduction : a part of a book or treatise preliminary to the main portion	1
1 train : to teach so as to make fit, qualified, or proficient	11
2 history : a chronological record of significant events (such as those affecting a nation or institution) often including an explanation of their causes	24
3 business : a usually commercial or mercantile activity engaged in as a means of livelihood	48
4 define : to discover and set forth the meaning of (something, such as a word)	62
5 corpus : a collection of recorded utterances used as a basis for the descriptive analysis of a language	75
6 neologism : a new word, usage, or expression	91
7 slip : a small piece of paper	110
8 collection : an accumulation of objects gathered for study, comparison, or exhibition or as a hobby	135
9 slur : an insulting or disparaging remark or innuendo	157
10 pronoun : any of a small set of words in a language that are used as substitutes for nouns or noun phrases	181

11 entry : something entered: such as : a headword with its definition or identification — 201

12 social media : forms of electronic communication through which users create online communities to share information, ideas, personal messages, and other content — 216

13 news : material reported in a newspaper or news periodical or on a newscast — 234

14 artificial intelligence : the capability of computer systems or algorithms to imitate intelligent human behavior — 253

15 future : time that is to come; what is going to happen — 268

16 end : the point where something ceases to exist — 284

acknowledgments : things done or given in recognition of something received — 303

endnotes : notes placed at the end of the text — 309

bibliography : the works or a list of the works referred to in a text or consulted by the author in its production — 375

index : a list of items (such as topics or names) treated in a printed work that gives for each item the page number where it may be found — 381

note

: a brief comment or explanation

Dictionaries can be confusing—so many Websters! Here's a short explainer about names and titles in the pages ahead. Merriam-Webster Inc. traces its roots to Noah Webster Jr., the American revolutionary, politician, newspaper publisher, writer, author, educator, spelling reformer, and, most important, lexicographer, which is a fancy word for someone who writes or edits a dictionary. All things dictionary in the United States descend from Noah Webster—not, I should point out, his distant cousin Daniel Webster, the early nineteenth-century lawyer, congressman, and Secretary of State. Mix them up and risk embarrassment at your next lexicography party.

Noah Webster was born in 1758. His birthday, October 16, is National Dictionary Day, which he has to share with National Liqueur Day, Department Store Day, and, if it falls on a Wednesday, Hagfish Day. Webster published his first dictionary in 1806 and his first major dictionary in 1828. After Webster's death in 1843, the G. & C. Merriam Company, founded by brothers George and Charles Merriam, acquired the rights to the 1828 book, which was titled *An American Dictionary of the English Language*.

Merriam-Webster defines *unabridged* as "being the most complete of its class : not based on one larger." Noah Webster's 1828 dictionary is considered the first in a series of eight unabridged editions, followed by ones published in 1841, 1847, 1864, 1890, 1909, 1934, and 1961. The 1847 edition was the first to use *unabridged* as a formal descriptor, but only on the book's spine. The 1864 edition was the first to include it in the title, while the 1890 edition was the first to use the word *international*. The 1909 edition was named *Webster's New International Dictionary of the English Language*. The 1934 edition was *Webster's New International Dictionary of the English Language, Second Edition, Unabridged*, and the 1961 edition was *Webster's Third New International Dictionary of the English Language, Unabridged*—even though they are actually the third and fourth *international* editions, and seventh and eighth in the Noah Webster line. In the history of American dictionary publishing, marketing often trumped logic.

The 1934 and 1961 editions get some facetime in this book. I refer to them as *Webster's Second* and *Webster's Third*, or just the *Second* and the *Third*. They're also known in-house as W2 and W3. In addition, all of Merriam's print unabridgeds are sometimes called their publication year alone, as in "the 1828" or "the 1961." I also do that.

The online versions of Merriam's dictionaries play an even larger role here. The website originally based on the *Third* is officially named *Merriam-Webster Unabridged* and requires a subscription. I refer to that digital dictionary as the *Unabridged*. Merriam's free online dictionary, originally based on its abridged *Merriam-Webster's Collegiate Dictionary*, known as the *Collegiate*, is Merriam-Webster.com. I also call the website the OWL. Read on to learn why.

The G. & C. Merriam Company was renamed Merriam-Webster Inc. in 1982. For the sake of simplicity, and because people call it both, I refer to the company as Merriam or Merriam-Webster—but not Webster, because the big guy's name adorns non-Merriam dictionaries. In the early 1900s, federal courts ruled that "Webster" entered the public domain after the copyrights expired on Noah's earliest works.

A couple of additional style notes: As with the definition of *unabridged* above, words used in the text in connection with lexicography or the dictionary are italicized—except when illustrating a dictionary entry, in which case they are boldfaced, just like in a print dictionary, or an online one. Full dictionary entries—headword, part of speech, usage label, sense number, boldface colon, definition, etc.—are rendered as if in an ink-on-paper dictionary, because ink-on-paper dictionaries are cool. Same for the chapter titles, whose definitions are taken from Merriam-Webster.com.

Finally, there are a handful of footnotes and lots of endnotes—sources, sidebars, digressions, expositions, lagniappes, notebook dumps, rabbit holes, what have you. Whether you toggle back and forth from the text, read them chapter by chapter, or save them all for the end, I do hope that you will read them.

introduction

: a part of a book or treatise preliminary to
the main portion

I fell in love with the dictionary on my eleventh birthday. My big present that day in 1974 was *Webster's New World Dictionary of the American Language (Second College Edition, Deluxe Color Edition)*, published by the World Publishing Company of Cleveland, Ohio. I still have it, right over there, on a shelf in the corner, its spine bandaged like a battlefield wound. The hardcover is robin's-egg blue with gold lettering. The dust jacket disappeared decades ago but I can picture without googling its mosaic of full-color illustrations on glossy paper. I was obsessed with the drawings inside. The Concorde. The Car of the Future. The dude in a leisure suit gazing over the Astrodome. The mod chick in go-go boots and a Jane Jetson cape bestriding the "Trade Towers, N.Y.C.," which—more than two decades later, from the roof of my Brooklyn co-op—I would watch, in horror, collapse.

Forty years and three months after that tween celebration, I visited the offices of America's most famous dictionary publisher, Merriam-Webster Inc., in Springfield, Massachusetts. For the first time in more than half a century, the company was overhauling its foundational book, *Webster's Third New International Dictionary of the English Language, Unabridged*, and I wanted to write about it. The four-inch-thick, thirteen-and-a-half-pound, 2,700-plus-page doorstop sold in 1961 for $47.50—around $500 today, which says a lot about what it cost to produce a dictionary of that size and scope but also about how American society valued the work. The redo was an absurdly ambitious effort, too, but all of it online, because the print dictionary as a mass-market product was slowly dying if not dead.

Merriam estimated that a full edit and expansion of the pixelated *Unabridged* would take a couple of decades, at least, and then continue until every editor had relocated to that great reference library in the sky, because new words never stop coming and meanings never stop evolving. After writing a longform story about the project for the online magazine *Slate*, I asked Merriam's president and publisher, John Morse, if I could stick around as a sort of lexicographer-in-training slash journalist-in-residence to write a book. He said yes. I parked in the back and entered through the old loading dock. I had my own key.

For the next few years, I researched Merriam's dusty history and drafted definitions of words that were new or topical or weird or neglected or fun. This work made me a participant—an extremely minor one—in a human endeavor stretching back to the third millennium BCE, when ancient Sumerians created written lists of words, wedge-shaped marks of cuneiform script recorded on clay tablets. The Akkadians who conquered Sumer, ancient Greeks and Romans, Renaissance writers, German scholars, English philologists—all contributed to the still-evolving art and science of decoding the written word and explicating the endless shifts in language. (One guy I especially admired: Ambrosius Calepino, an Augustinian monk who spent thirty years compiling his 1502 Latin masterpiece, *Dictionarium*, and went blind doing it.)

The first centuries of word-collecting didn't produce dictionaries in the modern sense, alphabetical lists of headwords with definitions. Early lexicographers usually grouped words by subject, and their work was intended to assist scholars, not general readers. Like

Dylan going electric, the first monolingual dictionary in the English language changed everything. Robert Cawdrey's *A Table Alphabeticall*, published in 1604, was explicitly populist, and had an amazing subtitle:

> contayning and teaching the true writing, and understanding of hard usuall English words, borrowed from the Hebrew, Greeke, Latine, or French, &c.
>
> With the Interpretation thereof by plaine English words, gathered for the benefit & helpe of Ladies, Gentlewomen, or any other unskilfull persons.
>
> Whereby they may more easilie and better understand many hard English wordes, which they shall heare or read in Scriptures, Sermons, or else where, and also be made able to use the same aptly themselves.

Cawdrey's *Table* included about 2,500 words on 120 pages—from *abandon* ("cast away, or yeelde up, to leave or forsake") to *necromancie* ("blacke art, or conjuring, by calling upon spirits") to *zodiack* ("a circle in the heaven, wherein be placed the 12. signes, and in which the Sunne is mooved"). There were simple etymologies—*g* or *gr* for words derived from Greek, *fr* for French—but no pronunciations or quotations to chart historical development. The idea was to "helpe" society's "ignorant," Cawdrey wrote, "acquaint themselves with the plainest & best kind of speech." But he also wanted to assemble the many words entering English from literature, science, and the arts, or imported by "far journied gentlemen" who "pouder their talke with over-sea language."

From around that time onward, dictionary-makers would see themselves as Sisyphean stewards of language—documentarians, sense-makers of the babble below. In the preface to his 1755 *A Dictionary of the English Language*, Samuel Johnson labeled the lexicographer a "humble drudge." Johnson, whose full and public life was an uninterrupted quest for fame and immortality, whined about the "unhappy mortals" who toiled on dictionaries, "who can only hope to escape reproach, and even this negative recompence has been yet granted to very few."

Johnson aimed to rescue English from "the corruptions of ignorance, and caprices of innovation." It's hard to know whether he was erecting a straw man or preempting criticism—he was a complicated person, argumentative, melancholic, sex-obsessed, drunk—but he at least recognized that a dictionary was a snapshot of a language at a moment in time, not a declaration of cultural permanence. Able to produce "no example of a nation that has preserved their words and phrases from mutability," Johnson warned against the idea that the lexicographer "can embalm his language, and secure it from corruption and decay."

A half century or so later, Noah Webster debuted his first dictionary. One hundred fifty-five years after that came *Webster's Third*. When I arrived at Merriam, the job of the dictionary was firmly established: to identify words that appear consistently in professionally edited media over an unspecified but sustained time; to define them according to a bunch of rules that I learned and will explain as needed; and to publish them online. By the time I finished this book, it wasn't clear how much longer flesh-bone-and-blood lexicographers would be needed to chronicle the march of the English language.

The *Webster's New World Dictionary* I got for my birthday was my go-to reference through high school and college, and into my professional life as a reporter. And I didn't just love the pictures. I loved the words, too. The foreword by dictionary legend David B. Guralnik made language, and by extension lexicography, sound exciting, in

introduction 5

a man-on-the-moon kind of way.* "The first decades of the second half of the twentieth century," Guralnik wrote,

> have witnessed not only a population explosion, but an information explosion of unprecedented proportions. Rapid advances in the physical sciences and in technology are bringing with them countless new terms and new applications of established terms. Vast sociological and political upheavals have had lexical consequences, and the young of our land, both alienated and unalienated, have made full, vigorous contribution to the slang sector of the language.

"Unprecedented," "rapid," "countless," "vast," "vigorous." English in that turbulent era was—to use a word that Merriam-Webster says is "now stereotypically associated with the language of hippies in the 1960s and early 1970s"—pretty groovy. But so it was, I would learn, in every previous era. Cawdrey had new words from his "far journied gentlemen." Noah Webster started writing his first dictionary because of "almost insuperable difficulties . . . for explaining many new words, which recent discoveries in the physical sciences had introduced into use."

I checked my small dictionary collection to see how editors hyped their particular linguistic times. In the preface to *Webster's Third*—a copy of which lies open on the elegant wood and iron antique dictionary stand that was a wedding present from a childhood friend—editor in chief Philip B. Gove noted the "metabolic process of constant change" in English and the growth of vocabulary from the newfangled disciplines of "rocketry," "automation," "synthetics,"

---

*After the moon landing in July 1969, the dictionary's editors rushed to add the word *mascon*, "a concentration of very dense material beneath the surface of the moon," and a name to a biographical entry:

> **Armstrong 1. Louis,** 1900–71; U.S. jazz musician **2. Neil,** 1930– ; U.S. astronaut: first man to step on the moon

and "soil science." In 1966, the *Random House Dictionary of the English Language* credited the "remarkable explosion of knowledge" of the mid-twentieth century with flooding the language: computers and other "cybernetic machines," space exploration "by manned flight and by transmitted signal," and "innumerable other developments." The fifth edition of G. & C. Merriam's scaled-down *Webster's Collegiate Dictionary*, published in 1936, a leather-bound printing of which belonged to my immigrant father, hailed a language boom from "comparatively new fields of knowledge" like "Aviation and Radio."

My favorite in this category is a 1943 printing of Funk & Wagnalls' *College "Standard" Dictionary of the English Language* that my mother picked up for me at a yard sale. The unnamed author of the "Introductory" waxed about the "innate restlessness of the genius of our language, which through constant changes has inspired its comparison to the ebb and flow of the tide." Words were proliferating so fast, "some actually forged in the hot-houses of the advertising or the business world, and constantly being offered for recognition," that (apologies in advance for directly quoting this meandering bloat) "to-day it is not merely necessary to pick the verbal flowers that spring into being along the highroad of life—that would be a simple task—but one must cull with care and learn all that there is to learn about every one of these products of the *Via Verborum* before one can determine the quality of their title to admission to the dictionary."*

Pioneering as Webster, cheerleadery as Guralnik, restrained as Gove, purple as Funk, the editors of these books shared a common bond and commitment: gathering, curating, and elucidating the torrent of new words sprouting in their linguistic hothouses. But those braggy and highfalutin prefaces and introductories about the linguistic fecundity of the times were also come-ons to customers for dictionaries made of paper and cardboard. If you didn't have the latest lexicon with the most, newest, grooviest, scienciest words,

---

* *Via Verborum*: "the way of words," *via* in the Latin sense meaning a road.

you weren't prepared to confront the revolutionary epoch in which you lived.

For all their wonderment, the editors couldn't have fathomed today's via verborum. The word *internet*, short for *internetwork*, arrived the same year that my first dictionary was published. But *Internet* didn't get into the renamed *Merriam-Webster's Collegiate Dictionary*, the company's best-selling book, until 1997. The grandmommy and -daddy of lexicons, the *Oxford English Dictionary*, the *OED*, didn't add it until 2001. Today, the lowercase *internet*—"an electronic communications network that connects computer networks and organizational computer facilities around the world," according to Merriam—houses literally tens of *trillions* of words (in aggregate, natch).

As a place for people to manipulate, store, and spread words, and a garden for new ones, the internet has revolutionized language in ways that would have gobsmacked Guralnik when he edited my deluxe color birthday gift.

Does that mean culture is churning out more new words now than during those previous periods? The natural assumption: Of course it is! Consider the infinity pool of instantly accessible sources of speech and writing: the ubiquitous media, social and conventional, churning, churning, churning language 24-7-365, an HOV lane on which colloquialisms zoom from their rural hideaways to the big city. *Doomscrolling* one year, *cheugy* another, *rizz* the next. The way we communicate—globally and instantaneously, unconstrained by time or space or impediments physical or temporal—demonstrates indisputably that language change is extremely fast and incredibly pervasive.

But English-speakers have been cranking out new letter strings for things and ideas since they squatted on this continent four hundred years ago. The nation, H. L. Mencken wrote in 1919, "is producing new words every day, by trope, by agglutination, by the shedding of inflections, by the merging of parts of speech, and by sheer brilliance of imagination." Vast computer databases and connected internetworks have made it easier to discover new words, easier for them to bubble into popular awareness and sweep the country faster than you can say *on fleek*.

In the print age, RIP, the size of a dictionary was restrained by page limits imposed by editors or, in the case of larger, unabridged dictionaries, the constraints of bookbinderies. *Webster's Third* housed a total of about 465,000 words when it was published in 1961. The last full revision of the *Collegiate*, in 2003, had about 165,000. Merriam said that book included 10,000 new words and meanings, a thousand a year since the prior redo. When I started my reporting in 2014, Merriam was adding about twice as many words a year online. Maybe there were in fact more words to choose from. Or maybe dictionaries, unshackled by the old print handcuffs, were eagerer to enter—lexicography-speak for adding a term to a lexicon—more of the words that culture was imagining and agglutinating.

The catch is that there are fewer general-interest commercial dictionaries in America actively performing the art and craft of lexicography today than in a century. I was only vaguely aware of that, and the underlying story that the internet was disrupting the dictionary, when I heard that Merriam-Webster had undertaken its renovation of *Webster's Third*. The audacious project was a full-throated rebuke to the industry's slow decline.

We are in a golden age for the study and appreciation of words. One lexicographer called it a period of "meta awareness" of language. Dictionaries are more accessible than ever—on your laptop, held in your grubby little hand. More people use them than ever, and dictionary publishers possess the digital wherewithal to track that use like never before. There is more writing about language than ever, too. When journalists like William Safire and Edwin Newman made lay language criticism a thing in the 1970s, they were unicorns. Today you can't point a cursor without hitting a language column, podcast, or social media account. Stories abound about tech neologisms, pronouns, emoji, slivers of teen-talk or leetspeak that spread across social media and into the mainstream mouths of adults. And wordplay is booming, too; consider the daily wails about words included in or omitted from the *New York Times*'s Spelling Bee.

The first Trump years coalesced around words. Not just words that let Trump's opponents relievedly mock him, like *covfefe* or *bigly*. But words and phrases, new and old, that polluted our discourse and roiled our streets and brains—*racism, antisemitism, impeachment, shithole, fascism*. Two days after the 2020 presidential election, the most frequent lookups on Merriam's website were *fascism, coup, sycophant*, and *sedition*; the same list four years later included *suffrage, gaslighting, democracy, narcissist*, and, again, *fascism*. And in 2020 came a brand-new word—*covid*—that convulsed the planet. In our hyperloop of chaos, anger, frustration, panic, fear, and disbelief, we need words to explain what's happening before our eyes. They often aren't enough.

In Merriam I expected a quirky story about the mild-mannered drudges and the remaking of an oldfangled, singularly American institution seeded at the dawn of the republic, its trunk climbing through the nation's timeline, with new buds sprouting every day. For a few years, I watched it try to reinvent and reimagine itself as never before—burrowing my own wormhole among the words, leaving my footprint if not my byline in the sidewalk cement of the capital-D dictionary.

And when my time at Merriam was done, I wandered around the world of dictionaries and words for a few years more. I pilgrimaged to Oxford to soak in the history of the *OED* and lexicography, and to Greenwich Village to gawk at the most remarkable dictionary collection ever. I attended dictionary lectures and language conferences. I voted year after year for the Word of the Year. I even published an article in a scholarly journal called *Dictionaries* and delivered a talk about it at an online academic gathering.

The story of Merriam-Webster, I learned, is the story of American English and the story of the business of American English, too. The intersection of day-to-day culture and the ever-changing language. The gift and the challenge of the bottomless ocean of the internet. The demands of dictionary-making in the instant-gratification digital age. It's also the story of a quirky and charming subculture of word-lovers and obsessives, about language and its power to shape us, to influence us, to annoy and rouse us—to be preserved for eternity by a concept more than four millennia old.

Ever since receiving that *Webster's New World*, I had romanticized the dictionary. It was the guardian of that thing we hold most dear, the storage bin of our language, the spreadsheet of who we are as a people now and where we have been. Merriam-Webster was a towering, central figure in the history of American intellectual life. But it was also, I discovered, something more mundane: another early twenty-first-century digital media outfit battling to survive an increasingly bookless world—one overlorded by Google algorithms, social-media mentions, pageviews, and clicks—that had humbled plenty of iconic brands.

From the moment I walked under the alto-relievo* of a dictionary above Merriam's front door, I was mesmerized—by this cluttered repository of two hundred years of word-making, and by the work, all those thousands of words queuing up to be validated as members in full standing of English, like new citizens waiting to recite the National Oath of Allegiance. I had questions. How do words get into the dictionary? Where do they come from? Who decides what they mean? And how do we write and think about them? At a time when technology is reshaping the ways people conceive, use, share, and relate to one of the most basic features of our collective humanity—language—what does a dictionary even mean?

---

* Merriam-Webster.com's definition of *alto-relievo*: "a sculpture in high relief." Its definition of *high relief*: "sculptural relief in which at least half of the circumference of the modeled form projects."

1
train

: to teach so as to make fit, qualified, or proficient

When it opened in 1940, the headquarters of the G. & C. Merriam Company—a two-story, Georgian-style brick-and-stone rectangle modeled after the Old West Church in Boston, ninety miles to the east—was a monument to solidity and importance, the intellectual anchor of a city on the rise. "This fine building on the brow of the hill will stand as a milestone on our march of progress," Springfield's mayor declared at the groundbreaking ceremony. When I saw the building for the first time, in 2014, it looked like a drab elementary school in a neighborhood neglected by time and government alike. The drive there took me past a strip club near the fire department named the 5th Alarm Lounge. An editor would tell me she pulled a uey after leaving work one night to avoid gunfire.

But I fell instantly for the building's throwback charm. Broad central staircase and dowdy conference rooms. Aging carpet and creaky wooden doors. Walls painted sanitarium green and cafeteria yellow. A mishmash of stately wooden desks from the day the staff moved in and bland taupe cubicles circa 1990—not to mention a large oak table from a century or so before that. Google, or any other modern publishing company, this wasn't.

On my maiden visit as a reporter, John Morse greeted me in the lobby and gave me a tour. With a round face, empathetic eyes, and a rumpled appearance, Morse reminded me of Clarence the guardian angel in *It's a Wonderful Life*. I'd known him a long time; years earlier, I had written a book about competitive Scrabble, and Merriam publishes the official dictionary for the game.

On the first floor, in a glass case down an echoey hallway, Morse pointed to a copy of Noah Webster's first work of lexicography, *A Compendious Dictionary of the English Language*. (Another copy was choking in a copper box in the building's cornerstone.) Webster offered the slim collection to the new nation in 1806 for a buck fifty. Each of the book's 40,000 words received a brief definition, and there was little in the way of etymology or pronunciation. "You have to be a dictionary weenie to care about the *Compendious*," Morse said. Sitting nearby was Webster's monumental 1828 follow-up, *An American Dictionary of the English Language*. That book contained an astronomical 70,000 entries and made Webster Webster.

The second floor was home to the editorial staff—definers, etymologists, pronunciation editors, about forty people in all when I arrived—plus the most comprehensive extant repository of the history of American English: 16 million three-by-five slips of paper, known as citations, or "cits"—pronounced *cites*—with examples of word usage culled for more than a century from newspapers, magazines, academic publications, trade journals, contemporary fiction, advertisements, radio transcripts, television shows, annual reports, government reports, cereal boxes, photo captions, comic strips, seed catalogs, restaurant menus, car manuals, airline tickets—you name it—crammed into alphabetized drawers in rows of chest-high, brick- or tan-colored metal filing cabinets of varying sizes and styles that stretched around the editorial floor like dominoes.

"The essential value of the company is inside those drawers," a Merriam editor, Peter Sokolowski, told me. "It's irreplaceable." The files were supposed to be fireproof. But with no sprinkler system—an accidental soaking would cause irreparable damage to the paper—no one wanted to find out if that was true.

Fourteen months later, after Morse and Merriam agreed to let me embed with the dictionary, I returned to begin my training as a lexicographer. On my first day of "work," Morse handed me a three-ring binder with a knobby black cardboard cover of uncertain age titled "A Reading List for New Editors. Priority readings and suggested sequence." There was a twenty-page interview with *Third* editor in chief Philip Gove from a 1969 issue of an academic journal, *The English Record*, which I would read. There was an article from a 1966 issue of the academic journal *American Speech* titled "Gerund/Noun and Participle/Adjective" that listed twenty-one rules for gerunds and thirty-one for nouns, which I would not.

I carried my homework upstairs and went to see Stephen Perrault, the editor with the best title in this place or maybe any place—director of defining—and Madeline Novak, who ran editorial operations. Like Morse and many other Merriam employees, Perrault and Novak were lifers. Perrault was hired in 1979, Novak in 1980, and they were married in 1984. Tall, sandy haired, and soft-spoken, Perrault seemed like a gentle touch. We shared vocation and avocation: words and sports, though, as a sportswriter, my passions overlapped a bit more. Novak was cheerful and friendly and very much on task. She made the place go. Merriam had welcomed me in to document the work of the dictionary, but I immediately worried that I'd be a bug in the editorial software, a pain-in-the-ass reporter sucking up precious time required to manage the complexities of a project so ambitious it would require decades to complete.

Perrault and Novak showed me to my very own cubicle, which they had furnished with the final printing of the *Third*, from 2002, and the last edition of the *Collegiate*, the eleventh, a year later. (There were no plans for a twelfth edition.) On the short end of the L-shaped laminate desk sat a PC and a box of white, yellow, blue, and pink slips of paper, which, in pre-digital days, had color-coded purposes: white for citations, yellow for draft definitions, blue for production details, pink for miscellaneous notes. There was a coffee mug adorned with Merriam-Webster's familiar logo, blue letters spelling the company name inside a red circle. A few brightly colored pushpins were stuck in the drab rattan wall.

Perrault asked what I'd like to do at Merriam.

"I want to write definitions," I said.

"Definitions that actually get in the dictionary?"

"Yes."

"Yeah, we'll see."

In the time of the *Third*, and beyond, training editors was a formal process. New hires needed the right academic credentials—a master's or PhD in linguistics or philology was a bonus, though plenty of BA-onlies like me were hired as entry-level editorial assistants—plus six months of indoctrination before they could be, as Gove said, "left alone with a word." Step one for a new editor involved ingesting Gove's training manual, the ominously named Black Books: six black loose-leaf binders containing 616 pages of single-spaced memos.

The Black Books were Gove's manifesto. "We must see to it that a mid-twentieth-century dictionary gives evidence of having been written by editors who lived in the twentieth century," he wrote. But mostly they were a rulebook: dense, thickly paragraphed, impressively detailed, pedantic, picayune. "Adjectives" spanned seventy-six pages. "Etymologies" had 104 subdivisions. The section on "Sense Division" featured what looked like a math equation—$x : M$. Editors were instructed how to stamp those multicolored slips on which they pasted citations and typed up definitions: "with his name and date in the lower right margin; subsequent stampings by later handlers should appear in chronological order above or to the left of the final stamp." To mark texts for citations, they were told to use a No. 2 lead pencil or a red pencil. "Taboo: blue, purple, yellow." In the library quiet of the editorial floor, staffers even used the pink slips to ask each other to lunch.

Defining seemed to my green eyes to be part logic, part rules, part writing, part intuition, part style. But unlike what I did for a living, the goal of the definer was to put words together in a way that *didn't* make them stand out. Definitions don't get bylines; stylish ones don't win awards. The best definition is so clear, concise, and comprehensible as to feel obvious. You want the reader to think: Of course that's what that means. "You're trying to speak as the voice of the dictionary," Perrault said. "You have to learn that voice and learn to speak with it." And not be overawed by it. "You come to work here. Suddenly, you're the dictionary? You're writing the definition?" he said. "It's very intimidating."

Merriam hadn't foisted the Black Books on newbies for decades. After the *Third*, an editor named E. Ward Gilman created a trimmed-down, fifty-seven-page manual playfully titled "Studies in Lexicography as a Science and an Art: Style Book esp. for Copy Editors, Proofreaders, & Other Interested Editorial Folks." Its twelve pages of "helpful hints" included advice from Ludwig Wittgenstein: "Everything that can be thought at all can be thought clearly. Everything that can be said can be said clearly."

For new hires of old, there were worksheets and classes, months of practice, flailing efforts, and withering critiques. Today, the classes were no more, partly because, in the absence of a new big *Collegiate* to ramp up staffing every decade, hiring was sporadic. In any case, Perrault and Novak adored "Gil"—a real titan of the place, and of the field—but viewed lexicography more as learnable trade than philosophical quandary. "The best way to do it is to actually try it and I'll show you what you did wrong," Perrault said.

It didn't take long to settle in. I created one document for my own new words—a lot wound up being, surprise surprise, about sports—and another for draft definitions. I switched my font to Times New Roman to mimic the print dictionary. I got handy with the citation files. I added words and quickie definitions to the in-house New Words spreadsheet cataloging potential entries. The first time I opened the file, it contained 1,936 "new" words. I didn't lift my eyes for two hours.

"They're all interesting!" I said to one of my colleagues, associate editor Emily Brewster, who wore narrow black eyeglasses and had excellent posture. Brewster had a word-nerd following thanks to tweets about objectless prepositions, the history of *scuttlebutt*, and why people were looking up *popinjay*, as well as videos on flat adverbs and weird plurals. "You're in the right place," she replied. "There's no shortage of words that are interesting if you're interested in them. That's what's so great about this job. There's no shame in being interested in any word. It's all worth thinking about."

Some of my early finds were totally new words, some were new senses of existing ones: *bro shake*: "the grasping of the right hand with another's right hand at a 90-degree angle sometimes followed by a brief embrace," I wrote; *dogpile*: "a celebration in which participants dive on top of one another immediately after a victory"; *fluffer*: "1. a worker on the set of a pornographic movie who arouses a male actor in preparation for a scene 2. one who helps prepare a person or group for a performance or event 3. a sycophant." *Fluffer* had layers.

I found some of these words while "reading and marking." Merriam editors scoured an array of printed material for an hour or so a day in search of new words, or new or interesting usages of old words. For generations, a pool of typists turned the findings into citation slips. During peak prep for the *Third*, a half million new cits were created annually; in recent decades, they were entered into a database. Reading and marking was the oxygen of dictionary-making. Pre-internet, definers relied exclusively on in-house citations to unlock a word's meaning and illustrate it in print. The typists sat in a corner of the editorial floor not far from me, surrounded by colorful skyscrapers of print awaiting their attention. The last of them would be laid off while I was there.

I was excited to discuss my list of candidate words with Steve Perrault. And he was happy to discuss them back. Words were his life's work—spotting them, watching them emerge in the language, determining their worthiness for admission to the dictionary, choosing the order of the other words used to define them. Perrault was word judge, word jury, and word executioner. It's a subtle intellectual power, and this laconic* man in khakis and button-downs enjoyed the process by which he got to wield his expertise. Perrault was a master lexicographic diagnostician. When a definition walked into his office, he could immediately suggest a course of treatment.

We'd meet in a small conference room featuring a wall of floor-to-ceiling tan metal shelves holding the company's masterworks, from Noah Webster's 1841 in the upper left to the final printing of the *Third* in the lower right. (The 1806 and 1828 editions were too rare and fragile for open display.) I loved the cracked bindings and decaying paper; the kaleidoscope of brown, black, and maroon leather, and blue and orange jackets; the range of sizes from slim, multivolume editions in 1890 and 1909 to the Brobdingnagian *Webster's New International Dictionary, Second Edition, Unabridged*, of 1934. The Unabridged Room, as I thought of it, revealed the march of time, the English language, the dictionary business, and this company. It was instantly my favorite spot in the building. Others liked it, too. One day I walked in on an editor taking his regular postprandial nap.

Like newbies of old, I flailed and Perrault corrected, gently. He wondered if my attempted definition of *slewfoot*, a hockey term for kicking out the skates of another player from behind, should focus on committing the act or on the act itself, i.e., should I define the

---

* *Laconic* as defined in the first half of its Merriam definition ("using or involving the use of a minimum of words"), not the second ("concise to the point of seeming rude or mysterious"). Perrault was patient, welcoming, drolly funny, and nerdily sincere—or maybe sincerely nerdy; he once used the word *jeepers* in conversation, I think unironically.

verb or the noun first? Same with *headbutt*: verb first with noun as "undefined run-on" at the back end of the entry? Or vice versa? Does the headbutter have to headbutt another head, which my definition implied, because, as Perrault noted, "you could headbutt anything."

As for the finer points of grammar, I was no Strunk. My definition of *decleat*—when a football player hits another player so hard that the hit-ee leaves the ground—was for an intransitive verb, Perrault observed; there was no object. But *decleat* is a transitive verb—something is happening *to* someone. "So you're knocking someone off his feet by delivering a violent blow," he said. I could put the object in parentheses at the start of my definition: "to knock (an opponent)," Perrault typed. He noted that I wrote "his" feet. The definition needed to read "his or her" or avoid gender altogether.*

Perrault had more questions. Did *decleat* mean to literally knock off of one's feet or could it mean to knock over or just hit hard? Did it happen only in football? Or could it be applied in sports where players don't wear cleats? In fact, I'd encountered the word in an essay by Jason Collins, a National Basketball Association player who had come out. "Being gay certainly didn't affect how I played," Collins wrote. "I tipped rebounds to teammates, tried to de-cleat opponents with my screens, and I did my best to make life miserable for the opposing big."

"That's interesting," Perrault said. Then he noted that the article, posted on *The Players' Tribune*, where athletes told stories in their own words, hyphenated *decleat*. Which led to a discussion of how definers use databases to determine, based on frequency of usage, whether a headword should be a closed compound (*headbutt*), an open compound (*head butt*), or hyphenated (*head-butt*).

This was what I quickly came to love—the detective quality of lexicography: searching through scores of newspaper stories and book

---

* "Their feet" was not yet a consideration. That would change. See chapter 10 for a discussion of pronouns.

passages and databases for quality cits; composing short definitions and assembling backing data for New Words; pondering whether the noun or verb form of *headbutt* should go first—getting, to quote the title of a biography of James Murray, the first editor of the *OED*, caught in the web of words. I loved the feelings of abandonment, isolation, and discovery. The solitary hunt.

My editorial colleagues at Merriam were uniformly kind people who seemed to adore their work, and have lives outside of it. Perrault and Novak liked to garden, and one day left a small vase of beauty-berries on my desk because I had mentioned seeing BEAUTY-BERRY on the Scrabble word list. (Scrabblers notate words in all caps, not italics.) Emily Brewster and her husband owned a bar/restaurant/live music place in the little town of Turners Falls, Massachusetts. Neil Serven was a competitive candlepin bowler who wrote short stories. Peter Sokolowski was a freelance trumpeter who hosted a jazz show on public radio. Mark Stevens corresponded for years with, and eventually met, a prison inmate who had found a typo in a Merriam book. *The New Yorker* wrote about their relationship.

Pre-internet, the only public acknowledgment Merriam editors received for their work was in the front matter of the big books. The *Third* listed every editor's name, title, and academic credentials. The last edition of the *Collegiate* mentioned only names. On today's websites, you won't find any information about who's writing the definitions. For someone whose profession fostered a belief that every written word should appear under a boldface byline, the selfless anonymity of the dictionary felt oddly admirable.

The old joke was that a dictionary was out of date the second it was printed. That was no longer true. Updating the online dictionary never stopped. The best-case scenario was that the dictionary wouldn't be done until Earth was. That metaphysical reality of the macro slog was mind-blowing. The micro slog of the individual definition was how lexicographers stayed sane. Each word was its own puzzle, riddle, challenge, world. So little time, so many words.

At Perrault's recommendation, I read the front matter of the *Third* and the *Collegiate*. The latter was written by editor in chief Frederick C. Mish, who for years was a running character—"the rex of lex"—in William Safire's "On Language" column in the *New York Times Magazine* that I read faithfully growing up.

In a section on capitalization, Mish used *Dutch oven* as an example. I knew that a Dutch oven was a pot for cooking. But it also meant farting in bed and pulling the covers over another person's head. Everyone knew that, right? The farting sense, though, wasn't in the online *Collegiate* or the *Unabridged*, and there were no citation slips for it in the paper or electronic files. But the colloquial *Dutch oven* was all over the place online. I smoked out this dialogue from season 5, episode 4 of *The Sopranos*, "All Happy Families . . .":

A. J.: Oh, somebody hot-boxed us? I saw you close the window!
Blundetto: What's that?
A. J.: It's when you close all the windows and fart on purpose.
Blundetto: That's a Dutch oven.
Tony: In bed it's a Dutch oven.
A. J.: Well, what's a Dutch oven?
Artie: When you fart in bed with a woman and you force her head under the covers.
A. J.: That's awesome.

I made a note to investigate *hot-box* (or should it be *hotbox*?) and added *Dutch oven* to New Words: "the act of farting in an enclosed space (usually under bedcovers) and then forcibly trapping another person in it."

The *OED* added *fart* in 1895. The original noun definition read, "A breaking wind. Often in *let (let flee) a fart*." It was labeled "Not in decent use" and cited Geoffrey Chaucer's *The Miller's Tale*, circa

1386: "This Nicholas anoon leet fle a fart." Perrault told me he had read some of the digital citations I had created for *Dutch oven* and was skeptical. Then, the very next day, he walked to my cubicle brandishing a *Sports Illustrated* he had been reading and marking. In a profile of retired Green Bay Packers quarterback Brett Favre, Perrault found this:

> Favre grew up in Green Bay. Or tried to. He jumped on the backs of so many teammates after touchdowns that Holmgren threatened to fine him $5,000 for his next leap. He babysat Mariucci's children, but "after a while, they didn't want that anymore," Mariucci says. "He kept giving them the Dutch oven."

The lexicography gods had a sense of humor. Perrault still wasn't persuaded. "This is quite a tricky thing to define," he said, reading my draft. "You're going with 'the act of.' In its original uses and most of the uses I'm seeing, it's not referring to the act, it's referring to the place—the enclosed, farted-into area. In this particular example"— the quote about Favre—"'he kept giving them the Dutch oven,' talking about *giving* somebody the Dutch oven. That's kind of an idiom—he gave him the Dutch oven. 'Give' as in 'subjected them to,' not saying he put them into the Dutch oven. If we actually want to pursue that one further, that's going to be not so easy to deal with. It's got some issues. A lot more research is required."

We both laughed. Another day, reviewing a batch of words in the letter P, Perrault noticed that *pom-pom girl* was defined in *Webster's Third*, and now in the online *Unabridged*, like this: PICKUP, PROSTITUTE.* Wut? I asked Perrault if I could try to fix it. I spent days trapped inside Lexis, ProQuest, Google Books, Newspapers.com, and the citation files hunting for examples of *pom-pom girl* like a pig

---

*All-caps denotes a cross-reference to another entry in the dictionary.

sniffing for truffles, and then more days staring at the screen writing a definition, and second-guessing, and rewriting, and revising again.

You could blame the definition on the analog way that Merriam editors once collected information. Definers were at the mercy of the cits; they performed deductive guesswork based on tiny scraps of evidence. Now, a first usage or ideal illustrative quotation or additional sense could be one more click away. Digital meandering improved the process of defining words incalculably. It also could be crippling.

A handful of cits in the files* confirmed that *pom-pom girl* was a term for a prostitute in Japan and Korea during and after World War II. No Merriam editor had taken a citation for the cheerleader meaning. With a few (thousand) clicks, I was able to create a fuller picture. I traced *pom-pom girl* to the early 1900s, when for a couple of decades it referred to a stage performer in a dance, vaudeville, or burlesque troupe. I discovered that the football cheerer sense dated to at least 1940—five years earlier than the *OED*'s earliest citation date, thank you very much. And I watched as the word was adapted for metaphorical usage, first, as best as I could determine, in 1974 by the environmentalist and writer Edward Abbey, who described Tom Wolfe as a "pretentious fad-chaser and apologist for the techno-tyrants. That . . . fascist little fop: the pom-pom girl of American letters."

Pom-pom girl might seem like a silly word on which to cut your defining teeth. It wasn't new, or newsy, or the spawn of technology or social media. It wasn't going to get many clicks, so it wouldn't increase eyes on ads on the Merriam website. But *pom-pom girl* allowed me to recover, document, and preserve the forgotten past of a single lexical unit—and learn how to define. The journey took

---

*There are two sets of files. The Consolidated Files contain slips from around 1900 through the publication of the ninth edition of the *Collegiate* in 1983. After that, cits were collected digitally and, until 2010, printed and stored in a smaller, separate set of cabinets called the New Files. Today, definers consult the physical files only occasionally.

me to a high-school basketball game in Wisconsin in 1913 and a masquerade ball in Lake Placid, New York, in 1921; to wartime Japan and New Guinea; to novels by Peter Matthiessen and Terry Southern; to spring training with the 1962 New York Mets; to the invention of tufted vinyl cheer props in 1965.

Pom-pom girl was at once unexceptional and also perfect. It zigged through time, its meaning morphing along the way, from allusive and innocent to risqué and vulgar, and back to innocent again. It reflected the mystery, history, density, and poetry in every string of letters, and the need to capture all of it for time eternal. "Many a single word," the philologist and *OED* backer Richard Chenevix Trench wrote in 1851, "also is itself a concentrated poem, having stores of poetical thought and imagery laid up in it."

2

history

: a chronological record of significant events (such as those affecting a nation or institution) often including an explanation of their causes

In his long and rich public life, Noah Webster Jr. was arrogant, argumentative, snobby, and complicated. The sixth-generation American son of a Connecticut farmer and weaver, Webster was a revolutionary but later revered England. He thought those with little property or education shouldn't be allowed to vote because they might "yield their own opinions to the guidance of unprincipled leaders." In his 1828 dictionary, Webster's second sense of *people* was: "The vulgar; the mass of illiterate persons."

So Webster wasn't much for the common man. But when it came to language, he was a champion of the common word. "The business of the lexicographer is to collect, arrange, and define, as far as possible, *all* the words that belong to a language, and leave the author to select from them at his pleasure and according to his own taste and judgment," he wrote in response to a critic. Not *some* words or the *right* words. *All* the words *as far as possible*.

In the 1780s, a young Noah Webster—Yale College* graduate, failed lawyer, failed private-school operator—wrote a three-volume

---
*It became Yale University in 1887.

reference set for schoolchildren. The 120-page book, commonly known as the Blue-Back (or Blue-Backed) Speller for the color of its cover, was Webster's first manifesto on linguistic independence from England. In it he trashed British educational methods and endorsed a new American approach to spelling, pronunciation, and grammar. Webster was just twenty-four, but he styled himself as "the prophet of language to the American people."

The Blue-Back Speller would establish Webster's reputation as provocative and strident. It also was a huge success, staying in print for more than a century, selling millions of copies, and allowing Webster to begin work on what he believed was his calling: creating an American dictionary. "Sir, we must . . . have a Dictionary," one writer implored, "and to YOU we must look for this necessary work."

For years, Webster had jotted thoughts in the margins of Samuel Johnson's 1755 dictionary. But he was distracted by other matters. A New York City newspaper war with Alexander Hamilton. A growing family. A bout of yellow fever. A 700-plus-page *Brief History*, as its title began, of epidemics and pestilential diseases. Webster finally resigned as editor of a pro–Federalist Party daily paper in New York and moved to New Haven, Connecticut. For $2,066.66, he bought a two-story Georgian house formerly owned by Benedict Arnold. And then he embarked on what he labeled—in an ad in the back of a Connecticut newspaper in June 1800, above announcements of the death of a sailor and a reward for a lost cow with "a white face and large teats"—"a Dictionary of the American Language."

"It is found that a work of this kind is absolutely necessary, on account of differences between the American and the English language," Webster wrote. "New circumstances, new modes of life, new laws, new ideas of various kinds give rise to new words." From his years as a Revolution hanger-on and newsman, Webster already was perceived as insufferable and didactic. His proclamation was greeted with vitriol. Pro-America Republicans dumped on it because they disliked elitist, Europe-defending Federalists. Federalists dumped on it because the idea of an *American* language insulted the King's English. Webster couldn't win.

Webster's hot language takes didn't help his early reputation. He lent some support to a 1768 proposal by Benjamin Franklin to regularize spelling by replacing the letters C, J, Q, W, X, and Y with six new ones of Franklin's creation. And, like Franklin, he advocated for phonetic spelling, which he called a commonsense solution to America's urgent need for a proprietary language "distinct from all the world." In his 1790 *Collection of Essays and Fugitiv Writings*, Webster wrote that "if a gradual reform should not be made in our language, it will proov that we are less under the influence of reezon than our ancestors."

Webster's 1806 *Compendious Dictionary of the English Language* stuck to the usual twenty-six letters (reform was "impractical" and "not at all necessary," he concluded). And while Webster wimped out on *fugitiv*, *proov*, and *reezon*, he did offer some changes that matched spelling to pronunciation (*opake*, *soop*, *spunge*) and eliminated silent letters (*ake*, *determin*, *farewel*, *wo*). Those didn't catch on. But others did: *plough* into *plow*, *draught* into *draft*, *gaol* into *jail*, and *centinel* into *sentinel*.

Citing Latin phonetics, Webster bagged the *-k* at the end of words like *musick* and *publick* ("beyond measure absurd"). He dropped the *u* in words like *colour* and *honour*. He substituted *-er*, *-se*, and *-ize* endings in words like *theatre*, *defence*, and *realise*. He also included hundreds of words specific to the government, science, and life of the new country—*revolutionize, constitutional, presidency, dime, dollar, docket, alkaline, electrometer, vaccination*—and borrowings from Native American culture like *snowshoe*, *tomahawk*, and *skunk*.

The 432-page *Compendious* generated little income and was panned by critics—"the wildest innovator of an age of revolutions," one said acidly of Webster and his orthographic inventions. Even his own brother-in-law, Massachusetts legislator Thomas Dawes, quipped, "I ain't quite ripe for your orthography." But Webster was undeterred. In the book's twenty-one-page preface, and in subsequent letters and essays, he attacked Johnson's dictionary as sloppily written, error-filled, etymologically lacking, and loaded with "the lowest of all vulgar words." (Webster cribbed generously from Johnson, but never mind.) He wrote long rebuttals to his critics in newspapers and pamphlets, mounting the case for an American language. "New words will be formed, if found necessary or convenient, without a license from Englishmen," he said.

After packing the walls of his second-floor study with sand to muffle noise from his children, Webster sat at a table shaped like a donut and, from sunrise until four in the afternoon every day, worked on an expanded dictionary. Webster plowed through the letters A and B. Then one morning, he said, he was struck by the voice of God and fell to his knees. He turned his life over to strict Calvinist faith. Many of Webster's future definitions would be saturated with piousness. But the immediate effect was a bizarro ten-year detour into an erroneous hypothesis—based on a passage in Genesis beginning "And the whole earth was of one language, and of one speech"—that all languages descended from a single tongue, spoken by Adam and Eve before the Tower of Babel, that Webster called Chaldee. His manuscript, titled "Synopsis of Words in Twenty Languages," was never published.

Short of money, Webster in 1812 moved his family to Amherst, Massachusetts, into a house overlooking the town green and, eventually, the college he would help establish. He cut a new distribution deal for his speller and, in 1817, returned to the dictionary. "In the second story of his new home," his granddaughter Emily Ellsworth Fowler Ford wrote,

> Webster set up anew the large circular table he had used for some years in New Haven. Dictionaries and grammars of all obtainable languages were laid in successive order upon its surface. Webster

would take the word under investigation, and standing at the right end of the lexicographer's table, look it up in the first dictionary which lay at that end. He made a note, examined a grammar, considered some kindred word, and then passed to the next dictionary of some other tongue. He took each word through the twenty or thirty dictionaries, making notes of his discoveries, and passing around his table many times in the course of a day's labor of minute and careful study.

By 1821, Webster was into the letter H. In 1822, he moved the family back to New Haven, where two of his six daughters had married and settled. (Webster and his wife, Rebecca Greenleaf Webster, also had two sons, one of whom died in infancy.) This time Webster reinforced his study with double-paneled walls instead of sand. He reached R at the end of 1823. Webster spent the last year of the project in Paris and in Cambridge, England. In January 1825, his right thumb "almost exhausted," he composed the final entry:

ZYGOMAT′IC, *a*. [Gr. ζευγμα, a joining.] Pertaining to a bone of the head, called also *os jugale*, or cheek-bone, or to the bony arch under which the temporal muscle passes. The term *zygoma* is applied both to the bone and the arch.

"When I had come to the last word, I was seized with a trembling, which made it somewhat difficult to hold my pen steady for writing," Webster recounted. "The cause seems to have been the thought that I might not then live to finish the work, or the thought that I was so near the end of my labor. But I summoned strength to finish the last word, & then walking about the room, a few minutes, I recovered."

After two years of painstaking and contentious editing, the book was published in 1828 by a fellow Yale graduate, William Converse. When it rolled off of Hezekiah Howe's printing presses in New Haven, on the day before Thanksgiving, Webster was, at the age of seventy, an old man for his era. Many of his haters were dead, the political battles he had instigated were long forgotten, and his public profile was dimmed. His dogmatism had softened over a quarter century plus of personal and professional struggle. He had abandoned the self-aggrandizing notion that he would create a distinct American language, but not his more worthy and tenable faith in the idea of a distinctly American dictionary. "It is not only important, but, in a degree necessary," Webster wrote in the preface,

> that the people of this country, should have an *American Dictionary of the English Language*; for, although the body of the language is the same as in England, and it is desirable to perpetuate that sameness, yet some differences must exist. Language is the expression of ideas; and if the people of one country cannot preserve an identity of ideas, they cannot retain an identity of language.

The compromise was not only visible in the title but also in the book's content. Webster's dictionary contained a staggering 70,000 entries, 12,000 more than the most recent edition of Johnson. Webster still lifted from his nemesis, but he also claimed he had written nearly 40,000 definitions of words making their debut in a dictionary of English. The book featured 4,000 new scientific terms, like *phosphorescent*, *planetarium*, and *sulphate*. It legitimized the common language of everyday life: *savings-bank, fracas, glacier, explode*. It added *jeopardize*, which Webster called "a modern word used by respectable writers in America, but synonymous with jeopard and therefore useless."

There were words borrowed from Native American culture (*canoe,** *maiz, moose, persimmon*), the Dutch (*landscape*), and Mexico (*cajota*, "A Mexican animal resembling a wolf and a dog," presumably

---

* Webster's definition of *canoe* reveals how he may have felt about Native Americans: "A boat used by rude nations, formed of the body or trunk of a tree, excavated, by cutting or burning, into a suitable shape. Similar boats are now used by civilized men, for fishing and other purposes."

a coyote; *axolote*, "A water lizard found in the Mexican lake," today *axolotl**). It sanctioned entirely new American words like *boost* ("To lift or raise by pushing [*A common vulgar word in N. England*]"), *currency*, *fudge* ("a word of contempt"), *roundabout*, and, yes, *Americanize*. And while it quoted plenty of the Bible and dead Brits, it also cited Ben Franklin, Alexander Hamilton, George Washington, Washington Irving, and other American idols, those "pure models of genuine English."

The two-volume book of almost two thousand pages was a remarkable achievement. But it was far from perfect. Based on Webster's decade of bad research, the etymologies were, to put it mildly, terrible. Among his imagined linguistic connections, which seem based largely on related sounds: that *speak* was related to Italian (*spiccare*) and Ethiopian (*sabak*) and *establish* to Arabic (*nasaba*). Webster had largely abandoned his spelling crusade—the silent *e*, for instance, was back—but some "reforms" remained. *Tung*, the Old English spelling of *tongue*, had "own-place entry," that is, listed as a headword, not a variant spelling. *Controller* got the business sense definition of *comptroller*. *Cotemporary* was preferred to *contemporary* "for the sake of easier pronunciation and a more agreeable sound." And you can find Webster's evangelical fervor on just about every page. To illustrate the definition of *morality*, he wrote: "The system of *morality* to be gathered from the writings of ancient sages, falls very short of that delivered in the gospel."

But this time Webster's work was praised on both sides of the Atlantic—and he was celebrated as an American hero and, finally, as a language authority. His friend James Kent, a former chief justice of New York State's supreme court, compared the book to the Parthenon and the pyramids. "This Dictionary, and the language which it embodies, will also perish," Kent said in a speech at Yale.

---

* For these and more than a dozen other animals and plants, Webster cited a Mexican scholar, Francisco Javier Clavijero.

"But it will not be with the gorgeous palaces. It will go with the solemn temples and the great globe itself." As for Webster, his name would "dwell on the tongues of infants as soon as they have learned to lisp their earliest lessons."

Kent wasn't far off. Almost two hundred years after publication of *An American Dictionary*, Webster endures as one of America's most famous names and also its oldest brands, trailing only the likes of Baker's Chocolate, Remington firearms, Schaefer beer, Jim Beam whiskey, and Ticonderoga pencils, a group that sums up the nation pretty well.

Webster might have been a hero and eventually an immortal, but to the end of his corporeal life he remained a lousy businessman. Believing that his quarter century of labor justified jacking up the price, Webster charged twenty dollars for *An American Dictionary*—around $660 today. It took eight years to sell the first print run of 2,500 books. North of eighty, he supervised publication of a second edition in 1841. It featured fifteen pages of new entries that he wrote, including *aerodynamics* and *puritanically*. Webster died two years later and his heirs sold the remaining unbound sheets of the book to the J. S. & C. Adams company of Amherst.

Enter the Merriams. In 1831, three years after *An American Dictionary* dropped, brothers George and Charles moved to big-city Springfield from rural Worcester County to start a printing and publishing business. Their rules and "business maxims" cautioned employees not to stare at customers or toss change and encouraged them to maintain a "habitual suavity of manners." Their publishing repertoire included textbooks, Bibles, and hymnals. The industry was expanding thanks to the new technology of electroplating. Publishers could set type, create metal sheets with raised type from which to print the books, and then use the type for something else. That was ideal for printing and selling backlists. A dictionary fit the model.

At a trade show in New York in March 1844, George Merriam learned that J. S. & C. Adams was interested in selling the rights to Webster's dictionary. George immediately wrote to Charles from his hotel room. A man from the company named Adams would be returning to Amherst. George would try to persuade him to stop in Springfield to "talk over the p's & q's" of a sale. "Adams wont commit himself with others, till he confers with us," George reported. If a meeting could be arranged, George begged his brother to make a deal. "Half that book would probably be worth, <u>permanently</u>, more than any thing we have, or ever shall have else."

Whether Adams met with Charles in Springfield isn't known. But the brothers eventually closed a sale and moved quickly. In early 1845, they reprinted the book in a smaller royal octavo edition—eight text pages per sheet of paper, versus the original royal quarto, or four pages per sheet—and slashed the price to $10.50. The *Springfield Daily Republican* published a column of praise alongside an advertisement stacked with blurbs from the presidents of Yale, Amherst College, and Brown University, and assorted professors, judges, and clergymen. Webster's original 1828 edition, the local paper wrote, was "much less perfect and valuable than the present."

Next the Merriams hired Webster's son-in-law, Chauncey A. Goodrich, a Yale professor (of rhetoric, oratory, and pastoral theology), to prepare a full revision. Unlike Webster and other dictionary makers to date, Goodrich didn't work alone. He recruited a small group of scholars, mostly at Yale, who purged almost all of Webster's remaining orthographic and pronunciation eccentricities. The 1847 edition had 15,000 more entries than the 1828. But by shrinking the type size and whacking white space, the Merriams were able to condense Webster's two-volume set into one and slash the price even further, to six dollars. To bolster the brand name, they included a hagiographical, eight-page bio of Webster, whom the company praised in pamphlets, posters, media hits, and other promotional materials.

The brothers dissed rival dictionaries and curried favor with booksellers, politicians, government officials, and journalists. The president of the United States, James Knox Polk, endorsed the new edition, as did more than a hundred members of Congress, who wrote, "It is with pleasure that we greet this new and valuable contribution to American literature." The *Phrenological Journal and Magazine of Moral Science* advised readers to buy it: "If you are too poor, save the amount from off your back, to put it into your head."

But George and Charles knew the 1847 was a rush job. To subdue competitors—chiefly Joseph Worcester, who edited an abridgment of the 1828 and then authored several of his own books, triggering a long-running "War of the Dictionaries"—the brothers had to step things up. In a letter to the Merriams, Noah Porter, a Yale professor (of moral philosophy and metaphysics) who had assisted on the 1847, laid out "serious defects in Webster": the embarrassing word histories, sloppy internal structure in the definitions, an overall lack of comprehensiveness. Rattling off the names of Greek and Latin dictionaries dethroned by upstarts, Porter warned the brothers of "the hazard of finding yourselves superseded & displaced."

"The time has been when there was no reason to fear that a work superior to Webster... might be prepared by the diligence of scholars & the enterprise of American publishers," Porter wrote. "Those times have gone by."

The Merriams agreed to bankroll an overhaul. Porter agreed to lead it, and assembled the first lexicographic Dream Team. Starting at etymologies was Carl August Friedrich Mahn, a German scholar in the emerging field of philology, the study of the history of language and the historical connections among languages; Mahn would free the dictionary from Webster's Tower of Babel nonsense. Then came the Yalies. The chief defining editors were William Dwight Whitney, a Sanskrit professor who would later edit the massive *Century Dictionary and Cyclopedia*, and Daniel Gilman, the college's librarian and later president of the University of California and Johns Hopkins University.

Subject experts included geologist James Dana, whose surveys of Mount Shasta contributed to the California Gold Rush, and physicist and astronomer Chester Lyman, who helped discover that Venus had an atmosphere. The preface to the 1864 lists more than thirty contributors, a third of them Yale professors, all of them white men—though it does acknowledge unnamed "readers" who collected illustrative quotations, "not a few of the most faithful and judicious of whom were ladies." They included Porter's wife, Mary, and Gilman's sisters, Emily and Maria.

The etymologies were only the most glaring problem that Porter needed to address. He ordered editors to condense Webster's impressive but flaccid and repetitive definitions and arrange senses in the historical order of their use. He rewrote pronunciations to reflect modern phonetics and the differences in the way Americans spoke. He mandated a consistent style: Definitions of adverbs should start with "In a _____ manner"; of certain nouns with "The act of"; of words ending in *-bility* or *-ness* with "The quality of" or "The state of." Finally, to make room for more new entries, Porter mandated expulsion of "dependent & derivative" words, a polite way of saying that Webster needed an editor.

Webster's descendants weren't happy. In exchanges of lengthy letters, the two sides squabbled—over the family allowing another publisher to issue a dictionary under the Webster name, over the extent of the revisions, over editing demands by the Yalies.

The relationship between the Websters and the Merriams had been strained from the start. The family's goal was to preserve Noah's legacy and protect the copyright on his name and works. The Merriams' goal was to publish up-to-date books that made money. Only two family members worked on the project—the editor Chauncey Goodrich, who was married to Webster's daughter Frances, and Webster's son, William, who held a "sub-literary" position. But they were a giant pain, "sitting in judgment," Porter said, undoing edits to definitions, removing citations. Tensions ran so high that Porter threatened to quit. "I sincerely wish I could find some one who could take my place," he told the brothers, adding direly, "What seems to me a farce may turn out a tragedy for you."

I read about this drama in Yale University's Beinecke Rare Book and Manuscript Library, a white rectangle of light-filtering Vermont marble that houses the G. & C. Merriam Company archives for much of the nineteenth century. It was thrilling. I slowly deciphered the swooping penmanship on delicate paper. I swooned at the formal salutations like "I am truly yours" and old-timey words like *promptitude*. I marveled at the precise, leeward script of Henry Wadsworth Longfellow and the sloppy scrawl of President Rutherford B. Hayes on "Executive Mansion" letterhead thanking the publisher for courtesy copies of the big dictionary.

Mostly I came to admire the Merriam brothers. They bought the rights to Webster when the country was recovering from a financial panic and recession. They could be hard-asses to their employees and, like owners through time, were quick to let everyone know how much money they were bleeding.* But they also marketed the dictionary as it had never been marketed before. I read fawning letters sent (with free copies) to dignitaries around the world—Queen Victoria of England; King Kamehameha III of the Sandwich Islands; the president of the new nation of Liberia, J. J. Roberts. In return, the brothers asked for a few words of praise to use in promotions and advertisements.

---

* "It has involved an investment of more than twenty five thousand dollars before the first copy could be offered for sale," the brothers wrote to Chauncey Goodrich about the 1847 edition, "and it has been for three years such a source of anxiety, in various ways, as hardly any business inducements whatever would tempt us again to pass through." A few years later, they upped their spending estimate to "$40,000 at least," telling Goodrich they had "poured out our money like water . . . which we have not got back, and at the best may never do."

Springfield in 1864 had 22,000 people, seventeen churches, ten banks, and no hospital. Muddy, unpaved roads were lined with hitching posts for horses. Residents suffered from diphtheria, scarlet fever, and smallpox. But the Civil War was good for local industry, and the city boomed. Three-story brick buildings sprouted downtown, and a stretch of Main Street was paved in macadam. At the Springfield Armory—just down the street from Merriam's future home—more than 2,600 men cranked out a thousand rifled muskets a day, plus cannons, swords, and bayonets. Smith & Wesson struggled to meet orders for its .22 caliber pistol. The D. H. Brigham clothing company recruited seamstresses from across New England to fill orders for Union uniforms.

To entertain soldiers on the battlefield, a local lithographer named Milton Bradley, who had turned to games-making during the recession, busily manufactured a pocket-size version of his biggest hit, the Checkered Game of Life. Fifty trainloads of visitors descended on the city for its Fourth of July festival, which included a lecture by Ralph Waldo Emerson, a performance of *Hamlet* starring the soon-to-be-infamous John Wilkes Booth, and snake charmers, glassblowers, and a demonstration of laughing gas. "Still they come!" the *Springfield Daily Republican* said. "The amusement season holds on as tenaciously as ever."

But for the Merriams, the war meant higher taxes and the loss of the Southern market, making the decision to rebuild the dictionary even riskier. They hired staff not only in New Haven but also in Springfield and Boston, as many as seventy-five employees in all. "Such a book, of course, must have cost its publishers immensely, and the times, in one sense, are perilous for such an enterprise," the *Springfield Daily Union* wrote. In the archives at Yale, I found a handwritten sheet of paper titled "Time spent in editing Webster, ed. of 1864." The labor of the two dozen men who are listed—all of them working on the dictionary as a side gig—totaled 26.17 years. "The business guts of these guys," Merriam president John Morse told me with admiration bordering on bewilderment, "plowing their own money back into the company."

The brothers weren't just gutsy guys, they were pillars of the community. George was vice president of a group building the city's first library. Charles helped start a church, sat on the city council, and mounted a clothing drive for war refugees. Even their gardening was newsworthy; the *Daily Republican* noted that Charles had "raised some mammoth peaches this season," including one measuring eleven inches around. The brothers donated dictionaries to the winners of local spelling bees and sent a dozen to the Seneca Indians in New York, two for missionaries "and the rest for the dusky tribes themselves," the newspaper reported. A Springfield bookstore, Bridgman & Whitney, displayed in its window a copy the brothers planned to present to Union army hero Gen. Ulysses S. Grant.

The 1864 earned rave reviews and boffo sales. The book was 1,538 pages long and contained 114,000 entries, 30,000 more than the previous revision and 10,000 more than any dictionary to date, plus three thousand illustrations. Merriam bragged about the total number of print characters in the book—18,492,562, which was 24 percent more than an 1860 dictionary by rival Joseph Worcester, 30 percent more than the 1828, and more than six times as many as the Bible. The *Daily Republican* reported that more than 200,000 sheep "have been divested of their skins to cover Webster's large dictionary."

"Webster invents American lexicography," Morse said, "and the Merriams invent dictionary publishing."

New words came from the in-progress Civil War (*ambulance, drill-sergeant, six-shooter*), from a new mode of transportation (*locomotive, rail, freight-car*), from the unstinting march of modern life (*clothes-pin, Pound Cake*). As Noah Porter instructed, definitions were shorter and used simpler, more accessible prose. The entry for *settle* went from thirty-three senses in 1828 to thirteen in 1864. *Consider* and *dry* were both shaved from ten senses to four. Hundreds of Biblical quotations were excised in favor of contemporary writers. Webster's definition of *alone* was illustrated with lines from the books of Genesis, Psalms, and Mark; the 1864 included Genesis and Luke ("Man shall not live by bread *alone*") but also Franklin ("The citizens *alone* should be at the expense") and Samuel Taylor Coleridge ("*Alone* on a wide, wide sea"). Webster's definitions were still findable—touched up, pruned, reordered.

The 1864 looks like what we think of as a modern print dictionary. Though the first letter of each entry is capitalized (as it would be until *Webster's Second*), the rest of the word is lowercase. Subsenses are lettered and grouped semantically. Pronunciations include expanded character sets for phonetic spellings and tables of "differently pronounced words." Notes about usage are set off by drawings of a fist with a pointed finger.*

More important than how the pages looked was how the book was constructed: not from the whims and fancies of one man who injected personal biases, prejudices, peccadilloes, and inside jokes into his definitions, but from a rational, evidence-based, multilayered research and editing process involving dozens of subject experts and trained editors who applied precision and rigor to the definition of words.

In their blind devotion to Webster, most of that was lost on his descendants. In a letter to George and Charles, William Webster asked that his father's name be removed from the new dictionary, which "retains scarcely a single feature of his long popular work." The Merriams refused. They knew Webster's name evoked loyalty, among book-buyers and staffers. They were careful not to connect their editorial changes to deficiencies in the 1828. In the preface to the 1864, Noah Porter wrote that he believed the revisions "would be desired by Dr. Webster himself, were he now living, and fully

---

*This printer character was entered in the *Second* as a *fistnote*.

possessed of the principles which have been universally accepted by modern philologists and lexicographers." The editors, he said, were "studiously careful" to retain as much of Webster's wording as possible, "esteeming very highly" his "plain and clearly expressed definitions" and "preferring to err on the side of cautious reverence than on that of thoughtless innovation."

The changes to Webster's old dictionary didn't tarnish his legacy, they burnished it. "The name of its founder still rightly clings to it," the *Atlantic Monthly* wrote, "and the very height of the growing shadow lends something to the stature of the original personality which gave birth to this mighty thing."

George Merriam died in 1880, Charles in 1887. A capable, long-serving line of successors, mostly non–family members, updated the dictionary faithfully. But they also innovated and marketed. When the 1847 dictionary lost its copyright protection in 1889, they placed the words *Webster's* and *international* in the title of the 1890 edition, and added English words from Australia and Canada. They gave their new 1898 abridgment a savvily aspirational name, the *Collegiate*. And they advertised like crazy. One late nineteenth-century ad promised that the dictionary could do everything short of curing the common cold: "Best Help in Training Children to Become Intelligent. Conceded Superiority in Definitions. Best Represents Usage in Pronunciation and Orthography. Excels All Others in Etymology. Many Times More Sold Than Any Other. Latest and Best."

Merriam's persistence fended off competitors like *The Century Dictionary* and Funk & Wagnalls' *A Standard Dictionary of the American Language*, which debuted in the late 1800s and were revised in the 1910s before fading from the scene. And it set the stage for the company's biggest and most ambitious work ever: *Webster's Second*, published in 1934.

The *Second* was the doublewide of dictionaries, clocking in at 3,350 pages with, Merriam claimed, a record 600,000 entries, 12,000 illustrations, and 35,000 geographical names. A biographical appendix listed 13,000 people. Proper nouns abounded in the main text—given names; nicknames for people and places; Biblical figures; saints; art and literary titles; fictional characters; stars, constellations, and comets; districts and buildings; battles and treaties; legal cases; historical events; proverbs and sayings. "The greatest single volume ever published," Merriam boasted.

The *Second* was stuffed with lists of popes and dukes, and hundreds of illustrative quotations from the Bible, Shakespeare, and Dickens. But popular culture—a term itself dating to at least 1854—was considered unrefined. Viral celebrities like Mae West, Eugene O'Neill, and Babe Ruth weren't mentioned at all. And the book was priggishly didactic, brusquely dismissing usage that was, as the labels appended to entries declared, *incorrect*, *improper*, or *illiterate*.

The 1934 marked the apex of the dictionary as self-aggrandizing authority created by Great and Learned Men. That's how Merriam viewed itself, and how the public viewed Merriam—or at least how Merriam wanted the public to view it: that these stuffy, privileged white dudes, by virtue of their sex, race, class, and intellect, were authorities to be trusted. It was an echo chamber of elites: Merriam turned to America's thought leaders to work on its products and the thought leaders in turn endorsed Merriam. The *Second* was enhanced by 207 consulting editors, including the president of Johns Hopkins, the director of the Pennsylvania Museum of Art, the dean of Harvard Law School, "and scores of others of equal rank," a company history boasted.

It was important to Merriam to have one of these highly ranked gentlemen at the helm, even if only as a "symbol of scholarly respectability," as one historian put it. Noah Porter was president of Yale when he edited the 1890. The editor in chief of the 1909, William T. Harris, was a philosopher who headed the U.S. Office of Education.

William Allan Neilson, the chief of the 1934, was president of nearby Smith College, a philologist by training who visited Springfield every other Tuesday to attend editorial board meetings.

The creators of the *Second* believed the dictionary was a rulebook, a set of guidelines to regulate spelling, grammar, and pronunciation—to judge definitively whether a word was improper or incorrect—and a moderating force for decency and propriety in the world. It was, John Morse said, "the high-water mark of reference sources being magisterial documents that gentlemen of good education create for the general public—the high-water mark for the dictionary as an authoritative, authoritarian document."

The *Third* would bring a new philosophy. Its editor in chief, Philip Babcock Gove, had plenty of rank himself. Gove's ancestors arrived in the Massachusetts Bay Colony in 1647. The son of an osteopath, Gove grew up in Concord, New Hampshire, majored in philosophy at Dartmouth College, and earned a master's in English at Harvard University. For more than a decade, Gove taught English at New York University while completing a PhD at Columbia University. One possible dissertation topic was Samuel Johnson's use of illustrative quotations with definitions. Gove chose something else, but he researched and published papers about Johnson and other old dictionaries.

Nearly forty, with a wife and two children, Gove enlisted in the navy during World War II. Afterward, he decided to change careers. "I am not a linguist and have no claim to being a lexicographer," he wrote to the G. & C. Merriam Company. But, citing his research, he had "about as much knowledge as an outsider could acquire" about dictionaries. If a job were available, Gove said, he would like to apply, "because for several years I have wished that I were connected with the printing of Webster's dictionary."

Gove was hired as an assistant editor in 1946, as Merriam began staffing up for the *Third*. In 1950, the company recruited another figurehead as lead editor, W. Freeman Twaddell, a German professor at Brown. But after nine months in Springfield, Twaddell told his bosses that the company didn't need him or any other tweed-blazer outsider. "No one personage in scholarship combines high reputation and balanced versatility as the Merriam-Webster editorial staff does," he wrote in a memo. "The appearance of any one name on a title page as a warrant of quality is, from now on, unwise."

Twaddell stepped aside and Gove was promoted at a salary of $8,000. As an editor, he had come to believe that dictionaries should reflect the language, not dictate it—that they should be descriptive, not prescriptive. The *Third* would still be traditionally thorough—the project would take more than a decade, an editorial staff of seventy, 202 experts in fields from Māori etymology and pavement construction to colorimetry and knots, and 750 editor-years of work. (The cost: $3.5 million, or more than $37 million today.) But it represented a massive departure from its predecessor in substance and style, and triggered a cultural brouhaha that would have gobsmacked Noah, George, and Charles.

Thin and debonair, his narrow face accented with a suave mustache, Gove was blessed with the central trait required of a lexicographer: anality. He lived on a working farm twenty-five miles east of Springfield. But he was at his desk at 8 a.m. every day, even during snowstorms. He didn't like meetings. He socialized at work only during lunch in the basement cafeteria. He banned smoking and all but banned talking on the editorial floor.

Gove imposed what he saw as logistically, culturally, and lexicographically necessary changes to the unabridged dictionary. Every decision was dictated by space—the need to create as much of it as possible in order to cram new words into the finite boundaries of the printed book. Gove decreed that individual senses of words wouldn't be printed on separate lines but run together in a clump. Neither would the quotations used to illustrate meanings, which almost always were truncated. "I have declared violent war on all commas in definitions," Gove wrote in 1958; he later claimed the crackdown saved eighty pages. Most dramatically, he altered Merriam's defining style, outlawing the use of complete sentences and discouraging the use of clauses and series. The resulting single statement definition had to be "replaceable" or "substitutable"—able to be plugged into a sentence in place of the word it was defining.

Gove wasn't the first lexicographer to strive for straightforward definitions. But he was the first to mandate consistency through substitutability. It wasn't always possible; pesky parts of speech—adverbs, prepositions, conjunctions—made crafting standard entries tough. But as a general principle, Gove's replaceable definition changed lexicography.

All that space-saving, paradoxically, was intended to allow definitions to be as expansive as possible. Sometimes, the results were comical. Two of the *Third*'s most frequently mocked definitions were *door*, at seventy-two words, and, weighing in at ninety-one words, *hotel*. I mean, omg:

> a building of many rooms chiefly for overnight accommodation of transients and several floors served by elevators, usually with a large open street-level lobby containing easy chairs, with a variety of compartments for eating, drinking, dancing, exhibitions, and group meetings (as of salesmen or convention attendants), with shops having both inside and street-side entrances and offering for sale items (as clothes, gifts, candy, theater tickets, travel tickets) of particular interest to a traveler, or providing personal services (as hairdressing, shoe shining), and with telephone booths, writing tables and washrooms freely available

Try substituting that in a sentence: *After arriving in New York by train, she checked into a building of many rooms chiefly for overnight accommodation of transients and several floors served by elevators* . . . The entry for *oxygen* is an even more absurd 192 words: "a nonmetallic chiefly bivalent element that is normally a colorless odorless tasteless nonflammable diatomic gas slightly soluble in water, that is the most abundant of the elements on earth occurring uncombined in air to the extent . . ." Take a breath and chuckle. Plenty of Merriam editors, past and present, did. One summed up Gove's philosophy to me this way: "If this is unabridged, then, goddamn it, it's going to be unabridged."

Still, the *Third* couldn't be any bigger than the *Second*—a bookbinder couldn't handle more pages—so Gove eliminated almost all "nonlexical" encyclopedic matter and, he said, excised 250,000 "obsolete words" to make space for new terms from two world wars, one Cold War, technology, science, sports, politics, and pop culture; the book would contain a grand total of about 465,000 words.

Schooled in the modern field of structural linguistics, Gove believed that speech should guide usage, and that rigid rules obscured the reality of how people spoke and wrote. He replaced the *Second*'s subjective labels with the classifications *standard* and *nonstandard* and cut back on labeling words *slang*. The idea was to let notes and quotations illustrate a word's meaning. For that, Gove didn't want to depend on the writing and speech of dead white males alone. The *Third* welcomed crime writer Mickey Spillane and actress Ethel Merman, the latter illustrating (quite nicely) one sense of the transitive verb form of *drain*: "Matinee days are tough; two shows a day *drain* a girl."

It is this spirit of the mandate that amazed me—the desire and obligation to deconstruct and compartmentalize the language, to deposit every precious lexical bauble into its own delicate origami box. If you're going to try to define every word, you might as well try to lasso every star in the galaxy. There are just too many words, and new ones being created at a rate that far exceeds the capacity of a modestly staffed dictionary to determine what's out there and what's worth adding. When I asked John Morse about the absurdity of the mission, he quoted one of his predecessors: Lexicography is the art of the possible.

Publication of the *Third* in the fall of 1961 was Big News, covered as an important cultural milestone. Hanging in the Merriam lobby was a photo of President John F. Kennedy—sharp gray suit; white pocket square; dark, patterned tie—accepting a copy from Representative Edward Boland of Springfield, who had worked on Kennedy's campaign and would accompany the president on a historic June 1963 trip to Ireland. Kennedy looks pleased and, with a firm grip on the book, full of one of his favorite words, *vigor*.

Webster's Third triggered a culture war, in popular and especially highbrow media, that was launched by a poorly worded press release touting the appearance of *ain't* in the dictionary. But Gove, and in some instances the *Third* itself, did a lousy job of explaining that the inclusion of a particular word—that is, an acknowledgment of its existence—did not amount to an endorsement of the way it was used. Critics both liberal and conservative attacked the dictionary as an air-raid siren of social and linguistic decay. In a January 1962 essay with the overcooked title "Sabotage in Springfield," the writer Wilson Follett called the *Third* a "shock," "a scandal and a disaster," and "in many crucial particulars a very great calamity."

Follett was appalled that *hepcat* was included while the names of the apostles were omitted. Other critics railed (often wrongly) that scores of words—*finalize, irregardless, wise up*—were entered without a corrective ruler on the knuckles. The *New York Times* fulminated against the book's "permissiveness" and "informality," and implored Merriam to stop the presses and start over. "This development is disastrous because, intentionally or unintentionally, it serves to reinforce the notion that good English is whatever is popular," the paper harrumphed.

"It Ain't Right," *The New Republic* declared; "It 'Ain't' Good," said the Washington, DC, *Sunday Star*. ("Say It Ain't So," said *Science*.) "A Non-Word Deluge," *Life* magazine exaggerated. "Anarchy in Language," apocalypsed the *Chicago Sun-Times*. By far the longest denunciation was a March 1962 article in *The New Yorker* by Dwight

Macdonald, which concluded that the *Third* had "made a sop of the solid structure of English, and encouraged the language to eat up himself." Macdonald compared the *Third* to the end of the world.

Maybe the uproar reflected post-*Sputnik* insecurity, or a brewing battle between scientific-driven forms of knowledge and belle-lettristic ones, or worries that racial tensions and longhaired beatniks* would topple the old order. Or maybe it reflected concern that established institutions—among them the G. & C. Merriam Company and its dictionaries—could no longer be trusted. Whatever its origins, the furor was misguided, and the dictionary misrepresented. Critics frequently decried words and usages from the *Third* that were also in the *Second*. And no one complained about a new edition of the *Collegiate*, which was based entirely on the *Third*.

A competitor arrived in 1966, *The Random House Dictionary of the English Language: The Unabridged Edition*, which had been in the works for nearly two decades. In direct response to the *Third*, Houghton Mifflin in 1969 rolled out, at a cost of more than $4 million, *The American Heritage Dictionary of the English Language*, which called itself the "custodian of American tradition in language" in "these permissive times." The *American Heritage* touted a usage panel of more than a hundred editors, journalists, and professors, including Follett, Macdonald, and a dozen other critics of the *Third*. The debate dribbled into the next century. In a 2001 cri de coeur against what he viewed as permissive usage, David Foster Wallace attacked the "notoriously liberal" *Third*—and repeated mistakes made by Gove's critics, writing that the dictionary "included such terms as *heighth* and *irregardless* without any monitory labels on them." In fact, the former was labeled *chiefly dialectal* and the latter *nonstandard*.

The outrage and competition failed to topple Merriam from its perch atop American lexicography; its brand name was strong enough

---

* *Beatnik* was new in the *Third*, defined as "a usually young and artistic person who rejects the mores of conventional society."

to withstand the turmoil, which generated month after month of free publicity. The *Third* sold well—50,000 or so copies a year for several years—and lexicographers and linguists mostly praised it. Readers liked it, too. "I think that those who are finding fault with your new dictionary are making much ado about nothing," a man from Ohio wrote to Merriam. "Usage makes language."

Still, Gove was deeply wounded by the attacks, and he spent the next decade defending the *Third*. He also assisted with early planning for the *Fourth* that everyone assumed was inevitable. And he did some nuts-and-bolts lexicography for the new editions of the *Collegiate*, defining some scatological and racially insensitive terms, a subject that interested him (and also perhaps in retaliation for Merriam's president, over Gove's objection, striking *fuck* from the galleys of the *Third*; more on that later).

Gove died at home of a heart attack in 1972. He was seventy.

3

business

: a usually commercial or mercantile activity engaged in as a means of livelihood

In 1988, Merriam's then president, William Llewellyn, wrote a seventy-page memo labeled C-O-N-F-I-D-E-N-T-I-A-L, detailing plans for a new edition of the company's signature work. *Webster's Fourth New International Dictionary, Unabridged* would be "the dictionary of record for the 21st century," he declared. It would contain 50,000 new terms—*bodice-ripper, chimichanga, ghetto blaster, high five, Jazzercize, minivan, power lunch, sabermetrics, sound bite, trail mix*—bringing the total to half a million and growing the book by three hundred pages.

Existing entries would be revised. Poorly attested ones would be axed. Quotations would be added from the six million citations collected since publication of the *Third*, from Jimmy Carter, Julia Child, Noam Chomsky, and hundreds of other people whose last names didn't begin with C. Without a new *New International* on the company's timeline, Llewellyn wrote, Merriam "will quickly be just another dictionary publisher and before long, not even the biggest one."

Llewellyn estimated that the *Fourth* would take nine years and cost nearly $7 million to produce—the equivalent of around two years of after-tax earnings. The *Fourth* would generate a total profit of $2.8 million on sales of 40,000 units in its first two years, and about $900,000 a year after that, he said. It wasn't "an investment to warm the heart of a Harvard M.B.A. perhaps." But it was "an opportunity and a responsibility" essential to Merriam's history and mission. The unabridged dictionary "is what makes Merriam Merriam and is what fosters the sales success of our other books," Llewellyn wrote.

The action at the time, though, was in the lucrative market for "college" dictionaries—your classic hardcover desktop source, cheaper and with far fewer entries than an unabridged book. Merriam was moving more than a million copies a year of the ninth edition of the *Collegiate*, published in 1983. By the fall of 1988, a few months after Llewellyn wrote his memo, that book had been parked on the *New York Times* bestseller list for 155 weeks; Merriam boasted that the *Collegiate* was the top-selling hardcover book in American history, except for the Bible. But competition was mounting. Simon & Schuster, Houghton Mifflin, and Random House were preparing new college dictionaries of their own. A new unabridged would have been business folly. Over and over, the *Fourth* was kicked down the road.

Llewellyn turned out to be wrong about what would happen if Merriam didn't revise the *Third*. Random House abandoned dictionaries in the early 2000s. My beloved *Webster's New World* cycled through corporate owners until a fifth and likely final edition appeared in 2014, sixty-three years after the first. When I started work on this book, the *American Heritage* had a full-time staff of four, down from double digits just a few years earlier. By the time I finished, it had none. Merriam had done just fine without a *Fourth*.

Llewellyn couldn't imagine the demise of the print dictionary. "The age of the book has certainly not passed away . . . nor do we expect it to," he wrote. But he did predict that commercial uses would emerge for "machine readable information." By the mid-1990s, when the internet was still a dusty frontier town called the World Wide Web with fewer than 25,000 sites, electronic versions of out-of-print dictionaries—"loose nukes," John Morse called them—began turning up online. The 1963 edition of the *Collegiate*, which had been licensed to government agencies and universities. A 1913 printing of an unabridged. In June 1995, Merriam tried to secure the URL dictionary.com. Two tech entrepreneurs, Brian Kariger and Daniel Fierro, had grabbed it, along with thesaurus.com and reference.com, just six weeks earlier.

Merriam faced a choice that would determine its future: Should it license the *Collegiate* database to outsiders for use online or venture on its own into the uncharted depths of cyberspace? Merriam decided to put the dictionary up, for free. "The gamble that we took is: Do people use their dictionaries or not?" Morse said. If the print dictionary was a desk ornament people cracked only occasionally, then they wouldn't use the website. And if they didn't use the website, Merriam wouldn't generate the traffic that advertisers demanded in exchange for their business.

It's a weird reality of the analog world that a company wouldn't have a grasp on whether consumers who bought its product actually used its product, and how often. That was dictionary publishing. The dictionary was as ubiquitous as a spatula; even if you never made pancakes, you had one. In some homes the dictionary was dog-eared, in others it was a dust magnet. What was the percentage of each? Who knew. But almost from the start, traffic to Merriam's website was substantial. When a server was stolen and Merriam had to revert to an older version of the site, sympathy emails poured in. "Everything we wanted people to feel about dictionaries, in fact they did," Morse said.

In the first few years of the internet, users would type "dictionary" into Excite or AltaVista and the search engines would spit out Dictionary.com.* Then users searched for a specific word plus "definition."

---

*Dictionary.com went live in 1998. It first loaded several public-domain dictionaries and later cut licensing deals for the *American Heritage* and Random House's unabridged.

As new sites came on the scene and search algorithms became more sophisticated, "definition" became superfluous. The battle shifted from who had the best URL to whose links rose to the top of the Google results page. Emerging victorious in search—not writing the best definitions or marketing the most authoritative books—was Merriam-Webster's biggest modern competitive priority.

When I talked to Morse about the subject, Merriam hadn't entered *SEO*—the abbreviation for search engine optimization—into the dictionary. (It eventually did.) SEO is a cat-and-mouse game, a quest to decipher how Google's omnipotent and opaque algorithms crawl millions of websites, spitting out content that best matches and is most relevant to a user's query. It's central to the work of every online company chasing users, advertisers, subscribers, and sales. Google tweaks its formula and companies adjust. Google is the Road Runner—*beep! beep!*—and websites are Wile E. Coyote, scheming ways to catch his prey, usually getting crushed by an anvil instead.

Google's algorithms evaluate a complex network of factors. Is a website's content substantive? Are words on a page directly connected to a search? Is the site updated frequently? Does it offer a variety of media—text, images, video? Do visitors stick around? Does the site link to reliable sources? Are advertisements distracting? Is the site mobile-friendly? When Google tinkers with how it measures those variables, rankings go up or down, the number of visitors and pageviews do the same, and the fortunes of businesses rise and fall. Morse called it "a bit of a zero-sum game."

Morse's digital focus contrasted with his analog surroundings. His desk was piled with papers. He took notes on yellow legal pads. His office included two leather-backed chairs for visitors, and shelves jammed end to end with Merriam titles—the march of the *Collegiate* through time occupied a prime spot—and hundreds of non-Merriam word books, too.

During one of my visits, Morse swiveled to his desktop computer and googled one of Merriam's most frequently looked-up words:

paradigm. A Google box with a definition appeared first. That was becoming problematic for dictionary publishers; Google licensed a database from Oxford Languages, publisher of the *OED*, and for most users that was plenty. Merriam's programmers were powerless to stop that. A company called Paradigm was second on the Google results page. Dictionary.com's entry for the word was third. Morse clicked on it.

For about a year, Dictionary.com had been climbing in the search rankings and Merriam had been falling. Morse thought he knew why: Dictionary.com had a new page design packed with content and updated frequently. For *paradigm*, the website showed a map of the world with a dot marking the origin of *paradigm*. "You probably sort of knew where Latin and Greek were spoken, but they put this up. And I guarantee that helped their Google ranking." There were old etymologies and randomly generated illustrative quotations that didn't help explain the meaning. "But it's content," Morse said. Finally, the website offered *paradigm*'s "difficulty index" (above 50 percent), related words (*paradigm shift*, *paradigmatic*), and the point value of its letters in Scrabble (fourteen) and *Words with Friends* (sixteen).

Did all of that help a reader better understand *paradigm*? No, but that wasn't the goal. The goal was for Google's bots to trip over the word as frequently as possible. The new paradigm for *paradigm* was redundancy. Merriam's free website had just undergone a redesign, in part to make it more attractive to Google. The more *paradigm* appeared on a page, the better it looked to Google's indiscriminating binary code. This made sense for an encyclopedia—a good article about Abraham Lincoln would include the word "Lincoln" a lot—but not for a dictionary.

The idea of the dictionary as reactive business makes more sense when viewed as the latest iteration of a familiar story in American lexicography and life. Noah Webster competed to get his books into every school district in the young country. His successors competed to get the best shelf placement in bookstores. Now they were competing to persuade Google to put Merriam at the top of a search result.

Compared to Dictionary.com, which was owned in the mid- to late 2010s by the online giant Ask.com, Merriam faced a technological disadvantage. But it held its own. After that day in Morse's office, I googled each of the top twenty words on Merriam's list of all-time lookups. Merriam-Webster.com was the first dictionary hit for thirteen. (It was the first dictionary hit for *paradigm* in 2025.) The declines, though, were real: a year-over-year drop of more than 30 percent in monthly visits to the free desktop site, which correlated almost directly to a drop in revenue. The main culprit was Merriam's slippage in SERP, or search engine results page, after Google implemented one of its periodic algorithm updates. Morse couldn't be sure what irked the Google bots, but the bots were irked, and so were the suits.

Morse's bosses at Merriam's parent company, Chicago-based Encyclopædia Britannica Inc., forced him into what had been unprecedented for the dictionary publisher: layoffs. A first round near the end of 2015 slashed eleven people. Three laid-off editors had worked at Merriam for 130 years combined. Also gone were the four typists, two "daters" (who hunted the first usages of words), and a synonymist (who, as the word implied, worked on the thesaurus). To save money, and stave off more job reductions, Morse, Steve Perrault, and Madeline Novak lowered their paid hours to twenty a week. Their loyalty to Merriam as an institution, and to lexicography and its future, felt noble and selfless.

When I arrived soon after the layoffs, Perrault looked shaken. The editorial floor was never a frat party; there already were plenty of empty desks because Merriam didn't need to ramp up staff to produce a print *Collegiate* anymore, and the silence was always profound. But now there were even more empty desks, and the quiet felt leaden, ominous. "It's creepy in here now," an editor said.

The typists' space hadn't been touched since their departures. I picked up two boxes of slips from a green shelf, the first starting with *Dan* and ending with *dank* and the second ranging from *darn* to *davenner*. The typists had been transferring paper citations from the 1960s, '70s, and early '80s into the database, in alphabetical order; after thirteen years, they were up to *da-*. I flipped through a few: *dart-gunning* (William Safire, *New York Times*, 1976), *data-diddling* (Gina Kolata, *Smithsonian*, 1982), *darshan* (John Updike, *New Yorker*, 1972), *dasher* (*Springfield Union*, 1973). That last cit was stamped COPELAND SEP '73. Robert Copeland was one of the veteran editors who had been laid off.

The preservation of this kind of artisanal dictionary work was one of Merriam's charms, and its decline was depressing. That hit home when another veteran lexicographer, Jim Lowe, put down his red pencil after nearly half a century. Lowe was a legend—even to me, because he edited the first *Official Scrabble Players Dictionary*, published in 1978, and four editions that followed. He worked on crossword puzzle dictionaries, mass market dictionaries, four editions of the decennial *Collegiate*, and dozens of other books. His was the embodiment of a lexicographer's life—inquisitive, patient, tireless, methodical, uncomplaining—and of the old way of doing the job.

Lowe was feted at a holiday potluck lunch. I'd been told that Merriam retirees received a sheet-cake sendoff. Morse knew Lowe wouldn't want a fuss. The food was arranged on red and green tablecloths atop a citation-files cabinet and a work table normally covered with old page proofs. Morse offered a toast. "How many of you remember what you were doing on February fifth, 1968?" he asked. "How many of you were *alive* on February fifth, 1968? That was the day Jim Lowe was hired."

There was laughter and applause. From an ancient index-card box, I grabbed a pencil and some blue slips to take notes. It may sound paradoxical, but like some lexicographers of a certain generation,

Lowe was a man of few words. He described being hired long ago, and finding the work to his liking.

"So I stayed and stayed and stayed and stayed," he said, sweetly. "I was always thrilled to find a new word we didn't have. I'll probably still do that."

"Send 'em in," Steve Perrault replied.

"I hope for a bright future for the company and for all of you," Lowe said.

Someone whispered that this was more than Lowe had said in all his years at Merriam combined.

"Jim, we are in your debt," Morse said.

Encyclopædia Britannica was first published in Edinburgh, Scotland, in 1768. When Noah Webster began work on what would become *An American Dictionary*, the third edition of Britannica was one of his go-to references, along with Samuel Johnson's dictionary and a Latin-English one. When Britannica in 1964 announced a deal to buy the G. & C. Merriam Company for $14 million, the *New York Times* put the news on page one. It was, the newspaper reported, a union of "two of the oldest and most distinguished reference works in the English language."

Steady Merriam was a boon to Britannica. The encyclopedia was a bigger-revenue business—those thick sets of leather-bound books weren't cheap—but an inconsistent one. While the profit margin on a set was high, people didn't fork over cash to the salesman upfront; they paid in installments. That meant that, especially in good years, when the company persuaded lots of people to buy its books, Britannica could find itself with more expenses, from making and delivering encyclopedias, than revenue. Merriam, by contrast, collected payment for its books in full. Its income helped smooth over Britannica's cash-flow bumps.

Even before the internet rendered obsolete the idea of a generic and static research source, the encyclopedia had begun to decline. By the 1990s, if you were going to spend a thousand bucks on something for your kid, it was more likely to be a desktop computer than a three-foot-long, thirty-two-volume set of books stuffed with facts in alphabetical order. In 1964, Britannica was selling upward of 175,000 encyclopedias a year. In 1990, the number was still more than 100,000. But in the next half decade—which saw the rise of the internet and the debut of Microsoft's CD-ROM encyclopedia, Encarta—Britannica's annual sales plummeted by around 80 percent.

The company was controlled by a not-for-profit foundation established by then owner William Benton, an advertising executive, university administrator, and U.S. senator; its sole beneficiary was the University of Chicago. Losses mounting, the foundation in 1995 put Britannica up for sale. An investor group led by Jacob E. Safra, a scion of a billionaire Swiss-Lebanese banking family, acquired the distressed publisher for around $130 million. That was less than half of book value. Jacqui Safra, the story went, loved the encyclopedia as a child. He called Britannica "the crown jewel of accumulated knowledge."

The *Times* wrote that Britannica "fell behind in the computer age." And that was five years before Wikipedia, which Britannica executives saw not as a grand experiment to agglomerate human knowledge—an idea dating to the third century BCE and the ancient libraries of Alexandria and Pergamum—but as a doomed fad. A former top Britannica editor compared someone using Wikipedia to visiting a public restroom: "It may be obviously dirty, so that he knows to exercise great care, or it may seem fairly clean, so that he may be lulled into a false sense of security. What he certainly does not know is who has used the facilities before him."

The problem for Britannica was that everyone needs to go, and sometimes in a hurry. The company pivoted to selling pricey online subscriptions to libraries, colleges, and universities, which previously had bought a new set of books every few years. But it couldn't win over consumers. Britannica was scholarly, but Wikipedia was free. Crowdsourcing might be imperfect, but, as Wikipedia matured and entries were edited and fortified, it proved more reliable than critics had feared. The journal *Nature* published a comparative analysis concluding that the differences in accuracy between a few dozen entries in Britannica and Wikipedia were "not particularly great." In 2012, Britannica finally stopped printing books.

In the *Harvard Business Review* the next year, Britannica president Jorge Cauz wrote that Wikipedia helped the company "sharpen" its business strategy. Britannica hired dozens of editors and writers and paid scores of academics to rewrite and refresh the encyclopedia's online articles. Cauz said advertising revenue on Britannica's consumer websites had increased 70 percent over three years, to around $13 million. (He didn't note that Merriam accounted for around half of the total.)

When Britannica's tailspin had begun in the early '90s, it used profits from the dictionary to support non-dictionary operations. Now, more than two decades later, it was doing the same thing again. In a different corporate structure, Merriam's woes might not have necessitated layoffs. Its total workforce was down to around sixty total, all but a handful working in the tatterdemalion but fully owned building in Springfield. Merriam was about as lean as a media company could be. Britannica, by contrast, employed around five hundred people worldwide and was headquartered in a historic, century-old building with a three-story clocktower on the downtown Chicago riverfront.

Safra bought Britannica because he loved the encyclopedia. In more than two decades, he hadn't visited Merriam. So when it came time to cut, Merriam had to cut. John Morse was able to preserve everyone whose full-time job was defining words. But the layoffs, he said, "tore at the heart of what goes on here."

Media companies were especially vulnerable at the time (and would remain so). Private equity vultures were slashing print and digital news operations. Flashy publishing startups were laying off hundreds of workers. Merriam was different, a niche business with a minuscule staff and a primary task that could be supplemented by "content"—blog posts, listicles, videos, quizzes, puzzles—that could generate cred and drive eyeballs, though also stretch editors, who would rather be defining. ("I didn't get into lexicography to become famous or anything," Merriam's Emily Brewster said.)

Morse's cuts shaved enough to meet Britannica's demands. SEO tweaks and a social-media offensive inched traffic and revenue higher. The *Washington Post* labeled Merriam a "winner" of a 2016 Clinton-Trump presidential debate, and the *New York Times* featured Merriam's debate-tweeting on the front page of its website.

But the temporary downturn led to a major editorial casualty: the revision of the online *Unabridged*. For a while, the project made sense. Adding thousands of entries would bring the old dictionary into the new age and create a storehouse of words that Merriam could exploit for future ventures. But when the click deficit persisted, the subscription-based *Unabridged* felt like an extravagance. Bulking up the lexicography on the free site—more and beefier definitions; additional illustrative quotations; new supplemental information notes, aka SINs, that explain a word's history—would goose the bots, serve more readers, and boost the bottom line.

I loved that Merriam had been willing to pursue its institutional and intellectual holy grail; that's what attracted me to its story in the first place. But, Morse acknowledged, the company didn't do enough to justify the quixotic venture. It didn't dress up the *Unabridged* website. It didn't use the thousands of fun and timely new entries, and new-and-improved old ones, to lure users behind the paywall. Despite the editorial commitment to the *Unabridged*, subscriptions didn't increase. Between mainstream and social media, "we got an awful lot of attention," Morse said, "but we weren't set up to catch it." It was just too easy to get words for free.

Morse said he wasn't disappointed; most staffers never thought they'd work on Merriam's iconic dictionary and, for a few years, they did. But after a second round of job cuts nine months after the first—including one editor who had defined hundreds of music terms and another who managed the 20,000 or so monthly reader emails—Morse was mad. Now sixty-five, he was planning to retire in a year or two, once the dictionary had long-term strategic and succession plans in place. He spoke his mind. There were consultants and phone calls and a visit by some suits to Springfield. And then Morse was informed that he would be retiring—not in two years but in two weeks, on the date of his twentieth anniversary as publisher.

Britannica's president told the Merriam staff in a six-paragraph email. Jorge Cauz praised Morse's "dedication, industry knowledge, and well-placed optimism." He announced that Lisa Schneider, who ran Merriam's digital operations, would be the new publisher of Merriam-Webster Inc. "Please join me in thanking John Morse for his long and valuable career at Merriam-Webster and for his strong influence on its future," Cauz wrote.

The perfunctory farewell didn't put Morse's career into context. He was hired to write definitions for the *Collegiate* and supervise other projects. He was never director of defining or editor in chief of the print books, and, at thirty-five years, his career at the company wasn't as long as some of the editors he was forced to can. But Morse was only the second president in Merriam history with substantial editorial experience, someone who could speak as fluently about the Consolidated Files as about a consolidated financial statement.

The announcement stunned the editorial staff. "Yes, these have been stressful times," Steve Perrault wrote when I offered my condolences, "though at this point I think I'm getting a little numb. But it's certainly hard to imagine this place without John." Others were less charitable. They saw Morse as a casualty of an intramural battle. "We are being sucked down by this dead whale," one staffer said, referring to the encyclopedia. That Britannica was upending Merriam's history as an unsexy but stable workplace angered people, too.

There was a farewell lunch at a German restaurant with a receiving line and a waterfall of tears. The next day, employees gathered in a first-floor conference room to reminisce. There was no sheet cake. "I think they knew I would walk out a day early if they did that," Morse said.

For its centennial in 1947, Merriam commissioned a company history titled *Noah's Ark, New England Yankees, and the Endless Quest*. It was written by Robert Keith Leavitt, a former New York adman whose author credits included a biography of the Pennsylvania Salt Manufacturing Company. *Noah's Ark* was a grandiose bit of apple polishing. But even at its haughtiest, it got Merriam's mission right. "A never-ending adventure, a ceaseless seining of the endless river of words," Leavitt wrote. "The lexicographer—if he is to do an honest and thorough job of recording authentic usage and keeping his record up to date—can afford no letup, no breathing spell in his constant watch upon the flow of words."

The growing fear was that Merriam would let up, and then wind up like other dictionaries not named Oxford, with a makeshift editorial staff focused on creating clickable content while lexicography was reduced to defining a small batch of trendy words for an occasional press release. If that happened, it would mark the end of the legacy of Noah Webster and of the Merriam brothers, George and Charles. Because, as Webster wrote in the 1828, a dictionary should be judged by "the copiousness of its vocabulary."

A few days after Morse was whacked, I called to check in. He was enjoying a morning coffee on his back deck on a blue-sky fall day. He was already busy with volunteer and board work. He was planning to join a Merriam field trip to Noah Webster's birth house in West Hartford, Connecticut. Morse told me that part of the conversation with Britannica involved creating a cost-efficient corporate structure in which Merriam reported more directly to its parent. "Having a lexicographer run the company was atypical," he said.

Morse was sanguine about the future of the dictionary, and of Merriam. There was so much to do to make the online lexicon more thorough, responsive, and beautiful. So many people around the world who wanted to learn American English and needed apps on their smartphones to do it. Morse loved the dictionary and the business of the dictionary. He wasn't willing to throw in the towel on it, even if the company to which he had devoted his career had thrown it in on him.

4
define

: to discover and set forth the meaning of
(something, such as a word)

For generations, Merriam had seemed immune to the vicissitudes and chaos of corporate America. There were no restructurings or sudden strategic pivots. No mergers, buyouts, or management purges. No headlines, no drama. Merriam adapted to changes confronting its core businesses the way its lexicographers defined words: calmly, quietly, rationally, methodically.

That's what happened after the generational *Unabridged* revision was scuttled. The project's final Release—Merriam lingo for a periodic batch of words added online—included 1,400 new entries and 700 new senses of existing terms. It was the usual fun mix of trendy, serious, and newsworthy: *Bitcoin, meet-cute, FOMO, microlending, hella, TMI, dox, revenge porn,* and a new sense of the transitive verb *verse*, "to compete against or oppose (a person or team)," as in "the Power is *versing* the Rangers." In the end, a total of more than 12,500 new entries and 3,000 new senses of existing entries were added to the *Unabridged*.

The *Unabridged* website wasn't shut down, just put in amber. Everyone seamlessly pivoted to working on the free site, which staffers had taken to calling the OWL, for Online Webster's Lexicon—and because an actual owl had for a time perched outside the office windows. Director of defining Steve Perrault combed the *Unabridged* additions to decide what to port over. It wouldn't be everything; the OWL used *Collegiate*-style definitions, which were more concise, with fewer quotations and etymological matter. Editing down the more expansive *Unabridged* entries would require person-hours that, with a staff working less in aggregate and generating more non-defining content, Perrault couldn't afford.

I was bummed about the change but, weirdly, no one else seemed terribly upset. The layoffs, yes. But the switch in websites, not so much. The romance of working on the ninth generation of Noah Webster's unabridged—his great-great-great-great-great-great grand dictionary—was no match for the relief of still being allowed to define words, no matter where those definitions would be consumed. "There's so much work to be done on the dictionary," Perrault said when we met in the Unabridged Room. "But there are things obviously that are completely outside our control. So all we can do is just take it one day at a time." He sounded like an athlete at a postgame news conference: We gotta read and mark within ourselves and define 110 percent.

Perrault knew that the previous twenty years had been great for the dictionary. The freedom from the tyranny of space. The tools to perform broader, deeper, and more accurate research. The ability to better understand what readers want and respond accordingly. But there was also a sense of loss for a less complicated time, when you edited the college dictionary every ten years and completed other projects in between. No one had imagined that people would stop buying print dictionaries. Now lexicography was, Perrault said, a "constant process of adaptation and change," including and perhaps especially business change.

I asked whether he would devote any resources to the *Unabridged*—maybe have editors draft two versions of entries, one for each database, or assign one definer to the *Unabridged* to maintain a token flow of words into the big online book. No, he said, the shift was total. But there was one possible exception.

"Well, *you* could do that," he said. "You could consider what you're doing to be for the *Unabridged*."

If I was going to keep writing definitions, I wanted to write fat, full, complex ones. If they never made the *Unabridged*, if Perrault whacked them down to fit the OWL, it didn't matter. I ran the idea past John Morse (this was months before he was early retired).

"I can be Noah. I can be Samuel," I said.

"We'll find you an attic someplace," Morse said. "You can wear a hair shirt."

"Put on a wig in the morning," I replied. "Call me in forty years. See if I'm still there."

My Merriam colleagues cranked out definitions as if they were getting paid by the entry. For me, completing even one was like flipping over a Volkswagen. Each word looked so simple—I'd written 100,000-word books; how hard could a three-line definition be?—but turned out to be impossibly complicated. Sometimes the challenge was crafting the definition itself. Sometimes it was compiling and evaluating the evidence.

There were some definite clunkers in my garage, words I knew wouldn't crack Merriam's code. *Assholic* looked like it could be an undefined run-on at the end of the entry for *asshole*. Hits for *hatespeak* (which would not be entered) paled next to *hate speech* (which would). Social justice warriors weren't marching against the *pigmentocracy*. Actual lexicographers don't form attachments to the letter strings they're investigating. I had trouble breaking up with my words. When I saw *Backpfeifengesicht* used to refer to Republican senator Ted Cruz and then to Martin Shkreli, the "pharma bro" convicted of securities fraud, I was a teenager in love. What a fantastic borrowing from German! I defined *Backpfeifengesicht* as "a face that deserves to be slapped or punched." In my note for Perrault, I wrote:

Almost always glossed,* except by Ted Cruz's college roommate, who tweeted: "When I met Ted in 1988, I had no word to describe him, but only because I didn't speak German. Thank you, Germans, for 'Backpfeifengesicht.'"

Flagging relative obscurities like *Backpfeifengesicht* was my own little test of modern lexicography. With every rabbit hole I burrowed down and every draft definition I produced, denying perfectly cromulent words entry into a dictionary without any page limits seemed shortsighted. Merriam grew nimbler during my time inside 47 Federal Street. While most New Words still stood with the hoi polloi behind the velvet rope, some were admitted with a wink and a smile. I was trying to figure out how to persuade the bouncer to let me in with a couple of hot words on my arm.

Perrault nixed *Backpfeifengesicht*. My list included a second set of words that didn't boast overwhelming evidence but felt like plausible entries in the dictionary-eat-dictionary online age. These were my NCAA-expands-the-basketball-tournament-again words, words that said, "Are you not entertained by these letters in this sequence?" and also, "It's a bottomless lexicon. Just push the button."

I defined *hairography* as "rapid choreographed movement of hair in a performance (as in a music routine or video)." Only seventy hits in the news database Nexis, but a robust internet presence—and it was the title of an episode of the hit TV show *Glee*, which my then teenage daughter loved. I discovered that the non-coffee sense of *jamoke*—"an unsophisticated or unintelligent man : BUFFOON," I wrote—dated to 1946 and appeared three hundred times in Nexis.

---

* **gloss** *noun* | **a** : a brief explanation (as in the margin or between the lines of a text) of a difficult or obscure word or expression

How could Perrault pass on *headbutt*, for which there were more than five thousand Nexis cits in the previous year alone? Certainly that met the Merriam standard of "widespread" and "sustained" use. The noun *meetup*. A much-needed revision of *redshirt* and the new sports term *medical redshirt*. And what about *fluffer*, the pornography sense of which had more than four thousand hits in Google News, one hundred fifty in Nexis, and dated, according to the *Routledge Dictionary of American Slang*, to 1977?

While I respected the Merriam process, I also copped to a selfish, subjective quest to scribble my initials on the language. Sure, I wanted to get something, anything, into the dictionary. But there was one word in particular whose entry would let me die in peace: *sportocrat*. I first saw it in 1997 in the *Wall Street Journal*, where I worked at the time. In a story about Nike tempering its ugly-American ways to gain credibility and market share in the staider climes of international sports, my colleague Roger Thurow wrote that Nike chairman Phil Knight "shudders at the thought of kowtowing to the 'sportocrats,' as he calls them, and dreads ever becoming one himself. 'That would be my ultimate nightmare,' he says."

Sportocrat dripped with contempt for the elitist prigs who squired the International Olympic Committee and soccer's governing body, FIFA, the *sports aristocrats* who ruled international athletics as if it were a hereditary trust. If you tweaked the spelling slightly, thinking *bureaucrat*, the word carried a taint of the officious. "Nike relished being the in-your-face outsider who offended the 'sporteaucrats'—the gray-haired men in blazers who control international sports," I had written in my own *Journal* story about Nike trying to break through at soccer's World Cup.

I found a letter written to an Australian newspaper around the same time: "Three cheers for the Sydney cab driver who introduced the Olympic sportocrat to the delights of our rail system." My colleagues at *Slate* used both *sportocrat* and *sporteaucrat*. *Sports Illustrated* referred to FIFA as "a cartel of sportocrats." *Surfing Life* asked why the sport should "go scrabbling after the good graces of a bunch of European sportocrats." A story about the IOC recognizing the governing body for Ultimate Frisbee captured the word exquisitely: "Ultimate belongs to the people, not the sportocrats of Lausanne."

The spread of *sportocrat* was modest but genuine, reflecting the way words slowly gain acceptance. *Sportocrat* was at least twenty years old and counting. It had a linguistic toehold among sportswriters of a certain sensibility. It had appeared online and in big-name print publications. It was out there, its use was consistent, and its meanings were several. Perrault, though, was skeptical. There were more than five thousand hits for *sportocrat* on Google, but just thirty-five on Google News and a couple dozen on Nexis. He also was wary because I personally had championed the word. Anonymous, unpretentious, data-based Merriam-Webster was no place for lexicographic nepo babies.*

Still, like a parent who doesn't play favorites with a brood of children, Perrault respected each of my draft entries whether it stood a prayer of making the database or not. While I favored the officious context of the *sporteaucrat* spelling over the years, Perrault noted the *plutocrat* connotation, which led me to reevaluate the *autocrat*, *technocrat*, and *aristocrat* implications. Lookups revealed the *-ocrat* ending surpassing *-eaucrat* to an extent that I considered dropping the latter from my definition. Perrault said to make sure to include the suggestion of privilege or venality, which I did.

Merriam admirably maintained that resisting the urge to drop every possible letter string into the database remained not just the historically faithful but intellectually and professionally right thing to do. But I couldn't help thinking that if I'd sent the same batch

---

* I confess to desperately wanting to be quoted in the dictionary myself. But that would have violated a Govian rule: no illustrative quotations from Merriam staff.

of drafts to Oxford, most of them would have found their way in. In one update in 2017, Oxford's free online dictionary (which in a few years would itself be a victim of dictionary retrenchment) added a few entries that felt solid, like *drunk-dial*, and a lot of stuff the staying power of which seemed questionable at the time: the portmanteau words *haterade* (*hate* + *Gatorade*) and *funtastic*; the pronunciation derivative *biatch*.* Of forty-six newies touted in an Oxford press release, just two already were in the OWL: *lovefest* and *unsee*.

Indeed, some of my words—*pigmentocracy, headbutt, meetup, redshirt* (including a new, non-college-sports sense meaning to delay the start of a child's formal education to gain an advantage), *medical redshirt*, and, yes, the porno sense of *fluffer*—were in Oxford's free site when I drafted them. In lexicography, though, no editor is sprinting to a definer's desk waving the competition and screaming, "WHY DON'T WE HAVE THIS?" There's a shoulder-shrug of reality—the art of the possible—and a certitude in trusting the process. Merriam had a finite number of definers devoting a shrinking number of hours to defining an ever-growing number of words, and it had its standards. If *fluffer* didn't clear the height line of the amusement park ride of the dictionary—if Perrault decided that other words were more deserving of the five minutes or two hours of his zero-sum editing time—then *fluffer* had to wait until it did.

But that height line was getting lower and lower, and that carried competitive consequences. Oxford had the resources to fully serve both strains of modern lexicography: high-mindedly revising the *OED*, finish date whenever, while also casually recognizing media-friendly buzzwords that helped generate headlines, like this one, from *Time* magazine's website: "Oxford Dictionary Proves It's Totally With It By Adding 'Squad Goals,' 'Yas' and 'Drunk Text.'"

---

* What did I know: The main *OED* added *haterade* and *biatch*, dating them to 1983 and 1986, respectively, within a year.

Squad goals—"Used in reference to a person or thing seen as a model to aspire to or emulate, especially with one's friends (often as a hashtag in social media)"—might have had the lexicographic half-life of hydrogen-7 (really short). But, as Katherine Connor Martin, then Oxford's head of U.S. dictionaries, told me, people were trying to look it up, and it was better to give them an answer instead of a 404 error. Plus, illustrating the definition with a quotation—"this photo is the best case of squad goals we've ever seen"—from a BuzzFeed article about Britney Spears eating hamburgers with supermodel friends after filming a music video was *chef's kiss* (which Merriam would enter in 2023).

The speed of information processing and distribution online—and the highly self-referential nature of social media—meant that words bubbled up and spread and then stuck (or didn't) faster than ever. For instance, the phrase *on fleek*, which Merriam defined as "perfectly done : exactly right : EXCELLENT," quickly went from a six-second Vine video by Chicago teen Kayla Newman, using the name Peaches Monroee, to marketing tweets by IHOP ("Pancakes on fleek") and JetBlue ("Our fleet's on fleek"), to the title of a Cardi B song—and then into plenty of dictionaries.

Martin mentioned one of her faves: *vajazzle*. She thought it was an amusing fad word that would quickly vanish. Then a "woman of advanced years" told her she came across it in the British celebrity magazine *Hello!* and wondered what it meant. Martin dated it to 2010. The free Oxford added it in 2012: "Adorn the pubic area (of a woman) with crystals, glitter, or other decoration." Into the next decade *vajazzle* was still shining brightly. "This Is the Most Compelling Vajazzle I've Ever Seen," read a headline on the website Jezebel in 2024.

Oxford's approach to its free dictionary was different than its approach to the *OED*. The former was a lively commercial dictionary. The latter was a scholarly, "historical" dictionary. "The *OED* is telling the history of the word," Martin said, "so it tends to make sense to wait until it has a history." The unofficial length of time was about a decade, but technology created exceptions for words including *podcast, crowdsourcing,* and the verb *google.* Those became so ubiquitous so fast that even if no one were to use any of them ever again, they still would belong in the historical lexicographic record. The free site could take a less temporal approach. "If people want information about a word and we have information about it, then we want to provide that information," Martin said.

If Oxford's servers noticed that a lot of people were looking up a word, and the word did in fact exist—meaning it was likely in Oxford's version of the New Words database—and there was enough evidence to create an entry, and the usage appeared settled, "there's no reason to wait at all," Martin said. Hello, *vajazzle*! Dictionary.com had a similar philosophy. "We don't have any strict rule about timing," an editor tweeted. "We'll add something if enough people are interested in looking it up, and that interest is ongoing."

Entering words into a dictionary isn't the American League batting race. There's no minimum number of plate appearances required to qualify. Plus, dictionaries should occasionally have fun. I'd like to think fun inspired my dictionary colleagues to enter two words made up by writers for *The Simpsons.* They were used in a documentary celebrating Springfield's bicentennial and its founder, Jebediah Springfield:

> **Pioneer boy [Bart]:** Mr. Springfield, how can I hope to achieve such greatness?
> **Jebediah Springfield:** A noble spirit embiggens the smallest man.
> **Edna Krabappel:** [watching the movie] Embiggens? Hm. I never heard that word before I moved to Springfield.
> **Ms. Hoover:** I don't know why. It's a perfectly cromulent word.

The free Oxford online dictionary entered both *embiggen* and *cromulent* in 2017. Merriam lifted the rope for *embiggen* in May 2018. The *OED* added both three months later, and Merriam finally added *cromulent* in 2023.*

I called *Simpsons* writer Dan Greaney, who came up with *embiggen*. It happened during season 7 of the show. The staff was sitting on couches collectively crafting the script, Greaney remembered. Dressed in a red flannel shirt, one of the showrunners,† Bill Oakley, typed on a laptop as writers suggested lines. Oakley challenged everyone to invent a couple of nonce words. Greaney was working on a Springfield town motto that would appear on a plaque.

"I was trying to say something lofty in a frontiersy way that was suitable for a guy in a coonskin cap," he said. "It was the whole phrase that popped into my mind"—*A noble spirit embiggens the smallest man.* "It was a short enough little fragment that it could get into the spot. At that point I hadn't been there very long, so just getting anything in the script was very satisfying."

Greaney admitted that he was bummed when a single, century-plus-older instance of *embiggen* was discovered, via Google Books, long after "Lisa the Iconoclast" aired. The word appeared in 1884 in an obscure British journal, *Notes and Queries: A Medium of Intercommunication for Literary Men, General Readers, Etc.* The journal looks like a nineteenth-century Twitter—disconnected ideas, thoughtlets, and replies—set in type. In the August 16 issue, a C. A. Ward of Haverstock Hill responded to a Mr. Walford about the impossibility of deciding what noun or adjective should be turned into a verb "when the many-mouthed beast takes it into its head to make one."

---

* The OWL defined *cromulent* as "ACCEPTABLE, SATISFACTORY" and *embiggen* as "to make bigger or more expansive : ENLARGE, EXPAND." It labeled both words *informal* + *humorous*.
† Merriam: "a person who oversees the writing and production of each episode of a television series and has ultimate managerial and creative control over the series."

Cricket has its slang; football has its slang; and lawn tennis has its genteel slang. But fresh slang coming up destroys old slang, and it is this we must look to, and not to grammarians, to rid the dictionaries of the jargon that 'neweth every day.' Are there not, however, barbarous verbs in all languages?

C. A. Ward then dropped a Greek word he said would roughly translate to *embiggen*, adding, "if we may invent an English parallel as ugly."

I assured Greaney that his "independent re-formation," as the OED described it, wasn't tainted; no one would think a Hollywood comedy writer was ripping off *Notes and Queries: A Medium of Intercommunication for Literary Men, General Readers, Etc.* "I will confess that as a young person I had the ambition to get a word into the dictionary," Greaney said. "So I've accomplished one of a certain number of stupid things I hoped to do." He was genuinely honored that Merriam had endorsed his word, because "Merriam-Webster means it's in American English." He was also glad that *embiggen* got in before *cromulent*, which was coined by his fellow show writer David X. Cohen. "He's a noble spirit," Greaney said. "I'm the smallest man."

My own efforts to get into the dictionary were complicated, if not quite ignoble. Steve Perrault was among the smartest, most careful, most engaging and supportive editors with whom I've ever worked. He also could be quick to dismiss words with which he wasn't familiar—at least ones suggested by me. Which was fair. I wasn't a lexicographer. I didn't deserve to jump the queue. My decisions on what to define were more subjective and professionally ill-informed than any other editor's. I wanted words that were interesting to write about, not just deserving of entry. And my meager contributions no doubt would have required more of Perrault's extremely limited time than they were worth.

Despite all the data-gathering about usage, it all felt so subjective. The final *Unabridged* Release shortly after the revision was halted, and the final press release highlighting some of its entries, included *waggle dance*. The word, defined as "a series of figure-eight movements performed by a bee to indicate the direction and abundance of a distant food source," wasn't shipped over to the OWL. The OED had it, dated to 1952, and so did Dictionary.com, imported from its licensed source, the old Random House unabridged.

I interrupted John Morse's retirement one day to ask about *waggle dance*. He framed it in business terms. The word carried opportunity costs. Merriam couldn't and shouldn't, he said, ignore trendy buzzwords and internet slang—or a cool science term like *waggle dance*. But not at the expense of the stuff that people looked up a lot. "What I do worry about in pursuit of getting *waggle dance* in the dictionary is you don't have a full definition of *esoteric* or *ubiquitous*," he said. A former chief editor of the OED, John Simpson, made a similar point about dictionaries highlighting faddish updates in press releases. "It didn't worry me that aspects of language could be transient," Simpson wrote, "but I did worry that concentrating principally on new words trivialised what we could and should be doing."

After the OED added *embiggen* and *cromulent*, the linguist Geoffrey Nunberg took a swat on social media. "Priorities are priorities," he tweeted. "But if the editors get a moment, they might revisit 'diversity' (last revised 1897), 'demagogue' (1895), 'elite' (1891), 'insensitive' (1891) & 'slur' (1912) etc. & reassert their foregone claim to serious cultural relevance. O tempora o Murray!"* Nunberg, a University of California, Berkeley, professor known for his NPR language commentary, was making a lexical point. *Embiggen* was arguably self-explanatory. *Cromulent* was almost entirely associated with *The Simpsons*. Readers searching for a dictionary definition of those words probably were doing so to see if a dictionary had added them,

---

*Nunberg was playing off OED editor James Murray and the Latin phrase *o tempora! o mores!*, a quotation from Cicero that the OWL defined as "oh, the times! oh, the customs! —used as an exclamation of despair at prevailing social or political norms."

not because they wanted to know what they mean. In other words, definers might have more important things to do lexicographically.

Morse thought they also might have more important things to do commercially. "What about the seven-hundredth-most-looked-up word?" he said. "What happens when the seven-hundredth-most-looked-up word gets used by Trump tomorrow?" he said. "What people look up is what matters. That's where the tonnage is."

The problem was that typing the unrevised seven-hundredth-most-looked-up word into a Google search bar would still produce an actual, existing Merriam definition, imperfect though it might be if last updated in 2003 or 1961 (which is certainly better than 1912 or 1897). Typing "fluffer," however, would reveal a Dictionary.com or *OED* entry, on which a reader might click. My personal authorial disappointment notwithstanding, even if an entry for *fluffer* didn't yield many clicks, they were clicks that Merriam didn't get, eyeballs that didn't linger on its website, who knows how many dollar-sign-spinning pageviews that slipped away.

5

corpus

: a collection of recorded utterances used as
a basis for the descriptive analysis of a language

In the early 1990s, Orin Hargraves answered an ad for a lexicographer placed in the English newspaper *The Guardian*. He got the job, and later freelanced for British, American, and German publishers. Merriam once told him that, if he wanted a full-time gig, he'd have to move to Springfield. No dice. Hargraves was a volunteer cook and caretaker at a Buddhist retreat near Baltimore and didn't want to leave his teacher, Sayamagyi Daw Mya Thwin, better known as Mother Sayamagyi.

Over lunch at a dictionary conference, I asked Hargraves if there was a parallel between lexicography and meditation. "The common element," he said, "is the need to return constantly to a repetitive and sometimes monotonous task—keeping the mind focused on the breath, or on the task of defining, while attempting to exclude distracting thoughts that would lead the mind down some other path and away from concentration." He added, "Being a meditator has certainly made me a better lexicographer, though the reverse is probably not true."

In the cozy culture of dictionaries beyond Merriam, Hargraves was known less for his Buddhism than for his expertise as a computational lexicographer. That's just what it sounds like, someone who applies analytical software to giant datasets of language to deliver insights into the meaning and use of words. Hargraves got into it by chance, when he was hired in the mid-aughts to work on the grandly named Preposition Project, which collected and described the properties of more than three hundred prepositional phrases for use in natural language processing, a branch of artificial intelligence focused on making computers understand and apply human language. He then worked on a lexical database called VerbNet at the University of Colorado Boulder, where he moved after leaving the Maryland retreat when Mother Sayamagyi stopped teaching.

When VerbNet's funding dried up, Hargraves returned with his new skills to freelance lexicography and became a fan of a program called Sketch Engine created by two British lexicographers. By applying search parameters and churning through every example in a corpus—a curated collection of text—Sketch Engine could develop insta-profiles of words, phrases, grammatical patterns, and collocations.* How does a word behave in conjunction with other words? How does it relate grammatically to other words? How does it reflect regional characteristics? Analytical software began revolutionizing dictionary-writing.

"In the old-fashioned way, you're called on to use your intuition a lot more because of the dearth of evidence," Hargraves said. "If your intuition is really well-formed, you'll be right sometimes. But you'll be wrong many times, because evidence often contradicts what you think. A good example is the verb *cause*. Give me a definition of what the verb *cause* means."

"To force something to happen," I said.

"That's what everybody says. But if you look at the citational evidence of the verb *cause*, it means to make something *bad* happen.

---

* collocation *noun* : the act or result of placing or arranging together *specifically* : a noticeable arrangement or conjoining of linguistic elements (such as words)

You never say 'cause happiness' or 'cause joy'—you say 'cause disaster.' This is something that your intuition will just not tell you. You have to look at the evidence."

Corpora aren't new. In the 1960s, two linguistics professors at Brown, Henry Kučera and W. Nelson Francis, assembled a million-word corpus consisting of five hundred samples of text of about two thousand words apiece taken from printed matter published in 1961 across fifteen genres. The idea was to create a giant database with which to identify patterns in language—from the frequency that individual letters appeared in print, to the placement of particular words next to one another, to esoteric linguistic investigations into principles of grammar.

The categories for the corpus were chosen at a 1963 conference at the university: Informative Prose (Press: Reportage; Press: Editorial; Religion; Skills and Hobbies; Popular Lore; Belles Lettres, Biography, Memoirs; Learned; Miscellaneous) and Imaginative Prose (General Fiction; Mystery and Detective Fiction; Adventure and Western Fiction; Romance and Love Story; Humor). Verse was excluded because "it presents special linguistic problems different from those of prose," Francis and Kučera wrote. Drama, "the imaginative re-creation of spoken discourse, rather than true written discourse," also was out. Fiction couldn't include more than half spoken dialogue. How much of each category to include was determined by data in a monthly journal, *Lexicon Book Publishing Record*. "Samples were chosen for their representative quality," the authors noted, "rather than for any subjectively determined excellence."

The Brown University Standard Corpus of Present-Day American English was a landmark in what would be called computational linguistics. After the professors published a paper in 1967, the editors of the new *American Heritage Dictionary of the English Language* asked them to make another million-word corpus for the dictionary's proprietary use. That was a quick and innovative way for the fromscratch *AHD* to build a database of citations, and to generate word frequencies and other statistical insights for the dictionary.

In the 1970s, a group of linguists in England and Norway replicated the Brown corpus—same genres, same number of samples, same year, different sources. Academics in Australia, New Zealand, India, and other English-speaking countries mimicked the mimicking. As computing power grew, so did corpora. In the 1980s, the 60-million-word COBUILD corpus, a joint project between a British dictionary publisher (Collins) and university (Birmingham) was used to create a learner's dictionary. In the early 1990s, a consortium of English publishers and academics, with funding from the British government, produced the 100-million-word British National Corpus.

After Brown, though, the United States took a back seat in corpus innovation. An attempt by American academics in the early 2000s to create a red, white, and blue version of the British corpus flopped because they were unable to obtain copyright permission from publishers to access material. As a result, an unrepresentative sampling of text came from sources like transcripts of *Buffy the Vampire Slayer*.

Mark Davies, a linguistics professor at Brigham Young University, decided to make his own corpus. Davies collected 20 million words from each year back to 1990, mining text from five main categories (spoken, fiction, popular magazines, newspapers, and academic texts) and fifteen subcategories (magazines, gardening, religion, African American affairs, et al.) to create the Corpus of Contemporary American English, or COCA. (Three more categories were later added: TV and movie subtitles, blogs, other web pages.)

Davies skirted copyright infringement by collecting only a portion of the data. For every two hundred words of text, he replaced ten words with an @ sign. "It's ruined for reading the article, but for linguists ninety-five percent of the data is there," he told me. Through the magic of "relational databases," the information is arranged into subject categories, tagged and marked by part of speech, and converted into a quickly searchable format. I asked Davies how he accessed the text. "I know where to get the data," he said. "I can't tell you where I get the data."

At its last update, COCA contained more than a billion words. Davies also made corpora for news (20 billion words and counting), early English books (755 million), Supreme Court opinions (130 million), American soap operas (100 million), TV shows from 1950 to 2000 (75,000 shows, 325 million words), and movies from 1930 to the present (25,000 films, 200 million words). A coronavirus corpus compiled from January 2020 through December 2022 "designed to be the definitive record of the social, cultural, and economic impact of" COVID-19 contained nearly 1.5 billion words.

Davies's iWeb corpus—his children told him the *i-* morpheme was played out but he ran with it anyway—collected 14 billion words from half a million URLs from 100,000 different websites and allowed users to target searches. "People can come in and say, 'I want to search your fourteen billion words but I only want to search for, say, solar-power websites,'" Davies said. "So they can create a solar-power corpus in three or four seconds that will have, who knows, ten million words. They're searching only about solar power or bread-making or whatever."

In addition to routine lexicography, corpora are deployed in all sorts of cool ways. Data scientists analyzed Donald Trump's tweets to determine which were written on his Android and which on a staffer's iPhone. An academic used Davies's Corpus of Founding Era American English (138 million words) and Corpus of Early Modern English (1.3 billion) to show that Supreme Court Justice Antonin Scalia wrongly argued, in the 2008 case *District of Columbia v. Heller*, that the Second Amendment phrase *bear arms* is not a military term alone.

Citation-based lexicography relies on human intuition and expertise to evaluate words in isolation. Corpus-based lexicography exploits the power of computing to sift through billions of words and identify patterns of linguistic behavior. Is a *chaise longue* a chair or a sofa? How have smartphones and dating apps altered the frequency of use of *swipe*? Which is more British and which more American, *home in* or *hone in*? You could write perfectly passable entries for these words and phrases the old-fashioned way. But the word techies maintained that the research wouldn't be as thorough or accurate in the absence of analytical tools.

Wendalyn Nichols, an editor at the British dictionary publisher Cambridge University Press, told me that corpora allow definers to go "from evidence to definition, rather than from what you thought a word meant to finding examples." The tools made definers better language sleuths. "You can see patterns all of a sudden—tease out the differences between *ramshackle* and *rundown*," she said.

They're useful for non-definition content, too. In 2018, former CIA director John Brennan told Trump on the site then known as Twitter: "Your kakistocracy is collapsing after its lamentable journey." Oxford's Katherine Connor Martin posted a graph using Sketch Engine showing the monthly frequency of *kakistocracy* in a corpus of almost 30 billion words amassed from online news articles from around the world. Merriam, by contrast, reported that searches for *kakistocracy*—"government by the worst people"—rose 13,700 percent. Oxford's tweet was about how the word was being used. Merriam's was about people's curiosity about it.

Oxford was into corpora and analytics. At the publisher's New York offices, Martin showed me her gizmos. Oxford definers relied primarily on two in-house corpora: the Oxford English Corpus, a carefully balanced collection of more than 2.5 billion words from mostly edited sources from around the English-speaking world, and the Oxford New Monitor Corpus, a more freewheeling collection of text from thousands of internet feeds of recently published material that yielded about 150 million words a month and totaled more than 10 billion words.

My go-to research tool at Merriam was the database Nexis, which is huge but skews toward newspapers. Corpora, by contrast, are created to provide variety: newspapers, magazines, and nonfiction books; academic texts and trade journals; novels; advertisements and other popular ephemera. They also can be structured to examine words in the context of time. The Oxford English Corpus was synchronic, providing a snapshot of the language during a fixed period. The New Monitor Corpus was diachronic, reflecting month-to-month changes. "That allows us to see if the use of a word is spiking in this sample of vocabulary on the internet," Martin said. "And therefore, does this seem like a word we ought to add soon because people are saying it a lot."

Instead of an Excel spreadsheet containing a couple thousand New Words, Oxford boasted a database with tens of thousands of candidate entries. Editors could do more than write a few notes in a cell. They could upload documentary evidence like photos and videos. They could see who was working on what word, and then suggest ideas, add links and comments, and track drafts. Martin opened it up. "Poor Jessie," she said, referring to a colleague, "stuck with *bro-country*."

I mentioned that I had been working on a couple of *bro* words myself: *bro hug* and *bro-shake*. "*Bro* is huge!" Martin replied, confiding that a full-on *bro* revision for the *OED* was about to drop. "It's a hard one. It's often in blends. If *bro* is ever combined with another word that has the O sound in it, it tends to become a portmanteau." Like *bromance* (which in neological time was old; Oxford's online dictionary added it in 2010 and Merriam followed a year later).

I asked Martin to use Sketch Engine to create a profile of *bro*—a brofile! In the New Monitor Corpus, she searched for "bro modifier noun." We were looking for "gramrels"—grammatical relationships. The software displayed words most associated with *bro*. "And hey, look at that!" Martin exclaimed. *Hug* was tops not only in overall frequency but in statistical significance—that is, how much a word is associated with another word relative to the average English word.

To borrow from the baseball sabermetrics term VORP, for Value Over Replacement Player (which I had been meaning to add to New Words), you could call this Value Over Replacement Word. Martin said the sketch disproved her suspicion that *bro hug* should be entered as a combining form at *bro*. It deserved own-place entry. She changed the search parameters to yield results for *bro* modifying a noun or *bro* as the object of a verb. She asked the software to collect examples of *bro* following "full of." "Full of horny bros," I read. The world contained a surprising—unsurprising?—number of parties and bars full of horny bros.

Martin then searched for *bro* as a modifier in order of frequency. *Bro-country* went to the top. It was more common than *bro hug* but had a weaker statistical association because *country* is associated with a lot of words while *hug* is not. "And, hey," Martin said, "*bro-code, bro-culture, bro-science*." But no *bro-shake*.

My own Merriam-style research confirmed that *bro-shake* was marginal. But the corpus software could have helped me better situate *bro hug* in the pantheon of compound *bro* words, and to decide which merited entry. Instead of defining *bro hug* (Nexis showed a strong preference for the open compound) and the far less qualified *bro-shake*, I could have done a full, and I'll show myself out now, broverhaul.*

In 2010, a group of scholars at Harvard and the Massachusetts Institute of Technology performed a quantitative analysis of Google's database of 5.2 million digitized books, which included 361 billion words in English. They estimated that the English lexicon included more than a million unique words and cross-referenced that with words in *Webster's Third* and the *American Heritage Dictionary*. In a

---

* Oxford would enter *bro-country* in the free dictionary but not the *OED*. "A style of country music influenced by hip-hop, rock, and R & B, and featuring male vocalists singing lyrics celebrating themes such as drinking, women, and pickup trucks."

paper published in the magazine *Science*, the researchers concluded that 52 percent of the English lexicon consisted of "lexical 'dark matter' undocumented in standard references."

That 52 percent figure was evidence mostly that printed works contain a lot of typos. But the *Science* paper did reveal how digital tools could detect "low-frequency words" that lexicographers might miss and produce a more accurate assessment of current usage, "to reduce the lag between changes in the lexicon and changes in the dictionary." The findings raised some existential questions to which I kept returning. In the internet age, what's the point of selective lexicography? Do we really need an *Unabridged* or *OED* to tell us whether a word is a word? Or is our new ability to type a string of letters into a search engine and instantly see how often and in what context it's been used an adequate substitute? Absent the old space constraints, why should Merriam or anyone else get to pin a ribbon on a word? Are dictionary editors clinging to the twin totems of curation and authority like the residents of a South Pacific atoll refusing to leave despite climate change submerging their homes forever?

"Human opinion on whether something is a word is worthless," Erin McKean said. "Because if they're discussing it, it's a word."

I met up with McKean at a workspace for developers in San Francisco. It was a tech-boom archetype and on-the-nose contrast to Merriam's headquarters at 47 Federal Street: upholstered cubes, polished concrete floors, bike storage, fresh tulips, catered lunches, and conference rooms with names like Gauge (decorated with old water meters) and Wrench (decorated with wrenches). McKean once headed U.S. dictionaries for Oxford—the NPR program *Talk of the Nation* called her "America's lexicographical sweetheart" (cringe)— but grew disillusioned with conventional dictionary-making. Now, in an online project called Wordnik, she was attempting to marry her defining chops with a new life as a programmer.

After delivering a TED Talk in 2007 about the digital transformation of the dictionary, McKean was approached by Silicon Valley venture capitalist Roger McNamee, an early investor in Facebook. McNamee was taken with McKean's sermon about how dictionaries had outlived their role as linguistic gatekeepers and how dictionary makers weren't exploiting the infinite capacity of the web. When McKean walked off the stage, McNamee told her there was a business in a norm-busting lexicon.

They talked for a year. Other investors joined, McKean teamed up with lexicographer Grant Barrett and computational linguist Orión Montoya, and Wordnik was born. McKean envisioned the site as a response to a question she heard constantly: Why isn't this word in the dictionary? Instead of explaining why words are left out, she believed, dictionaries should be in the business of getting them in. That led to Wordnik's motto: All the Words. It was aspirational but also a rejection of the limited nature of conventional dictionaries, which McKean came to feel were good mostly for telling readers what words are in conventional dictionaries—that is, for validating the way people tend to think about the authenticity of words—and didn't do enough to reveal the munificent glories of an ever-changing language.

"The problem is that when you've defined yourself as an authority, you can only do things that bolster your authority," she told me in San Francisco. "And the less rooted in facts your authority is, the harder you have to work to maintain it—and the fewer edge cases you can allow. You always have to ask the question, 'Why not?' And the answer to that 'Why not?' is that, for them, it doesn't fit with our picture of ourselves as an authority."

McKean compared it to a parent telling a child "because I said so":

No one ever wins an argument with "because I said so." And the further we get into a world where everything is measurable, the less persuasive "because I said so" becomes. So when a new edition of the *Collegiate* came out in the sixties, there were—what?—a hundred people in the world who had access to the Brown Corpus?

And that was just a million words. It would have taken an individual months to track the citations for any word that was added to any of those new editions. You had to take their word for it. Now, new lists of words come out, anyone with access to Google can go count the number of Google hits that something gets, and come up with a perfectly plausible list of words that have the exact same frequency and pattern counts in English that weren't in [the dictionary]. And you're like, what is the difference here?

McKean believed there was little difference. To her, the gatekeeper model of lexicography was out of step with technology, and with the notion that words should be celebrated, not judged.

"The thing that I think is the hardest to understand is that I don't think you can become a lexicographer unless you love words," she said. "And I think if you really love something, you want to share it. Listen to this band, you've got to see this movie, you've got to read this book—you've got to see this word. Are they like dragons on their hoards? They don't want to give them up? How could you learn a word like *Zugunruhe*"—a German word she had just come across meaning a migratory restlessness in birds—"and not want to share it with people? I have to limit how many times I tweet in a day about 'look at this cool word I just learned.' Because they're amazing, and each one is so perfect in what it does. Things don't become words unless they're useful to somebody somewhere."

All the Words meant a dictionary shouldn't discriminate, cull, omit, ignore, reject. Of course, there aren't enough lexicographers alive to define all the words. "You can write villanelles with more ease than you can write Merriam definitions," McKean said.* So

---

*Merriam's definition of *villanelle* shows why it's hard to write one:

villanelle *noun* **:** a chiefly French verse form running on two rhymes and consisting typically of five tercets and a quatrain in which the first and third lines of the opening tercet recur alternately at the end of the other tercets and together as the last two lines of the quatrain if definitions were preventing dictionaries from including all the words, she thought, maybe the problem wasn't the words—maybe the problem was the definitions. Maybe they were expendable.

"I certainly don't think that Merriam and Oxford should stop writing definitions," she said. "But what about the conservatively hundreds of thousands, probably over a million words that don't have definitions now and aren't likely to have definitions soon? Do we just ignore them? Do we pretend they're not there? We've all assumed that the definition is the best way to convey little packages of meaning. I'm not sure it is. There are very few other four-hundred-year-old technologies that we still use."

Another big-shot Wordnik backer, Steve Anderson, the first investor in Instagram, told McKean that automobile engineers had determined that a joystick was a better tool to steer a car than a steering wheel, but you couldn't suddenly put joysticks in cars because people would freak out. Definitions were the steering wheels of the dictionary entry. But no one's life would be endangered if they were to disappear. So McKean came up with a new model: "free-range definitions." Computers would collect words and then mine the web for example sentences that give readers a clear understanding of how a word is used, and how they should use it. That would doubtless be better than crowdsourcing definitions, the MO of Urban Dictionary and Wiktionary, because untrained human lexicographers aren't assiduously combing citations to parse meaning, they're just making them up.

Wordnik needed to give users some conventional information—and give servers something to crawl through. It licensed the latest editions of the *American Heritage* and *Roget's Thesaurus*. It paid $100,000 to keyboard the century-old *Century Dictionary*. It uploaded the GNU Collaborative International Dictionary of English, an adapted online version of the 1913 printing of Merriam's unabridged. And it drew from Wiktionary and a database at Princeton, Wordnet.

To find example sentences, Wordnik accessed the mammoth collection of text in the public-domain Project Gutenberg. It pulled from the nonprofit digital library Internet Archive. It subscribed to a service that scraped blogs, and it cut deals with newspapers, magazines, and publishers. And it scanned Twitter. After a few years, Wordnik was good at painting insta-portraits of conventional words—words for which definitions existed within its storehouse. For example, Wordnik's Word of the Day one day was *picaroon*, meaning a pirate or rogue. Its definitions came from the above-mentioned sources. Examples came from Washington Irving, Daniel Defoe, and some self-published books. While they weren't as precise as sentences curated by a human editor, they were enough to put *picaroon* into context.

That was all innovative and interesting, lexicographically. But as Silicon Valley startups go, Wordnik flopped. When it became clear within a few years that the site wasn't going to be an ad-driven commercial smash that upended the traditional dictionary, McKean's investors turned it over to her. She raised operating money through grants and converted it to a nonprofit. Wordnik became an engineering experiment and a labor of love.

Since Wordnik wasn't achieving the goal of all the words, McKean devised a campaign that generated publicity: a million new words. Hundreds of thousands of "missing words" were already on Wordnik's servers. Users had searched for more than three million different character strings that yielded no instant information. A lot of them were typos, full sentences, gobbledygook. Wordnik hired a data consulting firm, Summer.ai, that used machine learning and natural language processing tools I don't pretend to remotely understand— elastic search, trigrams, Lambda, vectorization, HTML parsing, language detection—to isolate likely words and collect examples of their use in text that could be added to Wordnik.

The programmers separated candidate words (*frappul, bialya, conquistar, quaestuary, outsnark, zyxnoid*) from junk (*kryogenkryokonitekryoscopy, naaaaa, shit my pt says*). That pared the list to about 1.8 million strings. Further refinement brought it down to around 997,000. Then, using the application programming interface, or API, for the search engine Bing, Summer.ai collected examples of usage, differentiating between sentences that seemed to define the word and those that just used it. If the sentence met certain inputted parameters for a "free-range definition," into the database it went. The effort ended well short of a million new words, but still generated a lot of newbies.

At the same time, McKean added words by hand. During the pandemic, she loaded coronavirus words and example sentences. One day she told me about spotting a Japanese word, *tsukuroi*, in the *New York Times*, which a reporter defined as "the art of repair." McKean posted a comment and a link, giving the word a dictionary existence if not a full-blown definition. *Tsukuroi* was validated. Wordnik's very engaged users entered thousands of words themselves.

McKean then focused on structuring and coding the Wordnik data—the dictionary definitions, synonyms and antonyms, example sentences—to sell to word-game makers, language and educational app developers, and people who wanted to make social-media bots. That helped pay the monthly cost of the servers with something left over for McKean, who took a job at IBM and then one at Google.

Through the years, Wordnik built a small but passionate community that indulged its linguistic obsessions with like-minded souls. Users compiled lists of new or favorite or weird words that sounded like *Jeopardy!* categories—Fictional Beasties, The Roaring Twenties, Never for Sale on Craigslist. One user, vendingmachine, had "looked up 16328 words, created 64 lists, listed 3619 words, written 1399 comments, added 3 tags, and loved 354 words." Another, hugovk—Hugo van Kemenade, a Finn who discovered the first known use of *selfie*—wrote a script that searched Twitter for the phrase "X is my new favorite word" and added whatever X was to a list, which totaled almost 27,000 words on the day I checked. (Some additions: *fucupcakes*, *floetry*, and *cinnamontography*.) A Wordnik blog series, "Five interesting words from . . ." featured "interesting words from interesting books."

In the mid-2020s, more than a decade after its founding, Wordnik's software was delivering example sentences for *defined* words, from aggregated source material and from social media. But if you looked up a new, *undefined* word that had been added by McKean or a volunteer, Wordnik didn't automatically locate examples. That had proved harder to achieve.

For one thing, McKean was caretaking Wordnik largely by herself, ten or twelve hours a week in her spare time. But the bigger challenge was an engineering one. Wordnik needed to search mountains of relevant text—news outlets, blogs, books, and much more—and pluck out reliable and relevant information. Artificial intelligence was making that harder. Sources once freely available to humanities projects like Wordnik were erecting digital roadblocks; while Wordnik linked to sources, AI voraciously consumed text as training material for bots without credit. Plus, writing generated via AI itself isn't writing generated by a human. Wordnik would have to program servers to distinguish between good and bad content, which wouldn't be easy, or cheap.

McKean believed that Wordnik someday would be able to instantly process a word typed into its search box and, whether it was already in its database or not, deliver jewel-box sentences that allowed sentient readers to understand what that word meant. (And add it to the database, too.) Every hapax legomenon* used somewhere by someone to express some comprehensible idea, thought, description, or sentiment would get its own room in this sprawling linguistic apartment complex.

"That's still the dream," McKean told me at the end of 2024. "I still think it's a pretty good dream."

---

*The first definition on Wordnik of *hapax legomenon* is from the fifth edition of the *American Heritage*, published in 2011: "A word or form that occurs only once in the recorded corpus of a given language."

In the meantime, she managed Wordnik's quotidian technical programming issues and updated the lexicon manually. Here are a few recent additions, with quotes from the linked sources. *Prebunking*: "warning people that they might be intentionally misled, then showing them a mild form of misinformation." *Greenhushing*: "a company's refusal to publicize (environmental, social, and governance) information." *Misergonia*: "the eye-gougingly deep irritation triggered by certain aspects of office life." *Divorce regret*: self-explanatory.

"Maybe we don't need hundred-thousand-dollar marketing campaigns or staffs of a hundred people, and maybe we don't need all of the apparatus that the twentieth century told us we needed," McKean said. "Maybe we just need a bunch of servers and a small group of people who like to do this as a hobby."

6
neologism
: a new word, usage, or expression

How are all of those words that Wordnik wanted to scoop into its online net created? And how do their meanings evolve? Ask a linguist and you'll get sciencey-sounding terms like "semasiological change" and "onomasiological change."* Together they cover most types of word-formation. Subsets of the former include: generalization (for instance, *blog* expanding from a personal internet diary to a full-on website to, more recently, an individual entry on a blog or website); specialization (*hacker* narrowing from a talented programmer to a talented and devious one); and metaphor (*virus* adding a computer meaning to its biological one). The latter has more categories: compounding (*weblog*), truncation (*blog*), blending (*vlog*), morphological derivation (*blogger*), and borrowing (*μπλογκ*, which is *blog* in Greek).

I borrowed all of that information, including the examples (except for the Greek spelling of *blog*), from an academic paper by linguist Jack Grieve. To study word formation in social media, Grieve, a professor at the University of Birmingham in England, in the mid-2010s

---

*The former is rooted in the Greek *semasia*, or meaning, as in *semantics*, and the latter in the Greek *onoma*, or name.

created a corpus from posts on Twitter. It contained nearly nine billion words from 980 million tweets written by seven million users across the United States over one year. After some heavy-duty data crunching, Grieve and two colleagues identified twenty-nine "emerging word forms" that had grown substantially in use over that time, and also mapped how they spread regionally.

As you might expect, the list was largely slang. Grieve broke the emerging words into "semantic domains." The profanity and insult category included *fuckboy* or *fuckboi*, which Oxford's free online dictionary defined as "a weak or contemptible man" and "a man who has many casual sexual partners," and *gmfu*, for "got me fucked up," meaning made to feel out of sorts. From social media came *celfie* or *celfi*, a spin on *selfie*; *notifs*, for online notifications; and *faved*, the verb form meaning to like something, usually on social media. Drugs offered *xan*, short for Xanax or other benzodiazepines, and *tookah*, for marijuana.

There was truncation (*notifs*; *xan*; *famo*, from *family*; *faved*, from *favorited*), compounding (*fuckboy*; the smushed-together *amirite*), and blending (*brazy*, from the B in the Los Angeles gang the Bloods plus *crazy*—to avoid the C, which was associated with a rival gang, the Crips). Grieve created a separate list of words that already had appeared in a mainstream dictionary (he used Merriam's OWL) but had undergone old-fashioned semasiological change, including *joggers* (jogging pants), *slay* (to succeed), *squad* (a group of friends), and *unbothered* (happily oblivious).

The papers resulting from the corpus—titled "Analyzing Lexical Emergence in Modern American English Online" and "Mapping Lexical Innovation on American Social Media"—explained how social media reshapes the native tongue, and how words zoom into the popular consciousness. A few words in the study dated to the early 2000s, most to the 2010s. Grieve tracked how the new forms trended on Google and when they were added to Urban Dictionary, and cross-referenced the definitions there with how they were used on Twitter. The words in all likelihood were spoken before they made it online, a linguistic fact that can make pinpointing the Big Bang of individual neologisms tricky.

Mapping and tracking the emergence and evolution of new words seemed to me like it should be a fertile area of study. But Grieve, who is Canadian, told me that the field of sociolinguistics—which Oxford defines as "the study of language in relation to social factors, including differences of regional, class, and occupational dialect, gender differences, and bilingualism"—was less interested in changes in "lexis," or the words themselves, than in grammar or speech. Word change can be slow and mysterious, hard to nail down even with giant corpora and computational software.

Two years after the first data analysis, Grieve went back and examined a slightly expanded set of words from the study, fifty-four in all, to see what had become of the rising neologisms. More than half had declined in usage since the first go-round. *Unbae*, to break up with—*bae* meaning "sweetheart" or "baby"—had dropped from 148 occurrences per million words to just four. *Unbae* had its fifteen minutes but was unlikely to endure. *Brazy* looked like a better candidate for longevity, rising from 1,745 to 10,723 occurrences per million. Three years later, it merited an entry in Dictionary.com as "hip-hop slang . . . popularized by members or affiliates of the Los Angeles-based gang the Bloods."

What predicted the success of a word? Grieve analyzed staying power based on length; part of speech; "word formation process" (acronym, creative spelling, or standard word formation like compounds, blends, borrowings, etc.); and whether it marked a new meaning altogether. Words that offered new meanings—*balayage*, a type of hair-color highlighting; *cosplay*, dressing up as a fictional character; *gainz*, weight gain specifically through exercise—tended to rise in usage more than words in other categories.

Shorter words also were more likely to stick (because social media favors shorthand and English favors brevity*), as were ones that could be used across spoken and written contexts. Survival of the fittest was lexical as well as biological, Grieve concluded, quoting Charles Darwin: "The survival or preservation of certain favoured words in the struggle for existence is natural selection."

Grieve did his study just once. Data collection was a pain, funding was challenging, and Twitter had made it harder to identify the location of tweets, which was essential to charting the spread of the words. The big dictionary makers, Oxford and Merriam, didn't ask to work with him. "Not a lot of payoff to continue," he said.

Another academic effort used an even broader computational sweep to identify new words and examine why they succeed or fail. This one was led by Hans-Jörg Schmid, the chair of modern English linguistics at Ludwig Maximilian University in Munich. Schmid is German but studied English; "I don't know anything about German grammar and stuff," he joked. Like Grieve, Schmid said academic linguistics gave short shrift to word formation, favoring more identifiable processes like speech formation and diffusion. "It's a fringe topic," he said. "They think it's not real linguistics because there's no generalizations. You can't make predictions about what the next [new] word will be. But you can predict the next word in a sentence."

Schmid started compiling examples of word formation in the mid-2000s—*Aga saga*, a genre of British novels set in middle-class homes that might own an Aga brand stove; *she pee*, a urinal for women. Schmid and his colleagues began scraping words from Google and writing code to analyze them. They named their data-miner NeoCrawler, because it was *crawl*ing the internet for *neo*logisms. They named the tool used to identify new letter strings Discoverer.

---

*Most words used by English speakers are one or two syllables long. "We're not Germans," Indiana University English professor and dictionary historian Michael Adams told me.

The computational work wasn't simple; there's a lot of lexical noise and junk on the internet—typos, misspellings, inadvertent compounds, bad hyphenations. A sampling from one day (May 23, 2018) of one newspaper (Britain's *The Sun*) yielded *coolbox, non-VIPs, chef-level, li-ttle, mega-mansion, gin-flavoured,* and *unfollowing*. Which were new-word candidates worthy of further observation and which weren't? Discoverer was programmed to make assessments, and then researchers manually determined whether a word was a Candidate or Garbage. *Overtourism*: Candidate. *The-lives-of-Grenfell-tower*: Garbage. Candidates were added to the NeoCrawler database for further analysis.

Schmid's group identified 958 neologisms from more than 2.6 million web pages and then tracked their spread every week. Almost 80 percent of the new words were nouns, with compounds and blends accounting for two-thirds—numbers that lined up with additions to the *OED* between 1950 and 2010, the researchers found. Even in the internet age, language creation was predictable.

Thanks to the size of its database and the precision of its analyzer, Schmid's decade-long project was successful in mapping the growth of new words. Within a few years, you could find all of NeoCrawler's top twenty-five most frequent words in a Merriam, Oxford, or Dictionary.com database, including *Trumpism, blockchain, dumpster fire, internet of things, chatbot, upskill, virtue signalling,* and *glamping*. Some median-frequency words had broken through to lexicons, too, including the 2016 Twitter creation *Milkshake Duck*, for something or someone that becomes popular but quickly turns out to be worthy of hatred, and *buildering*, or climbing tall buildings. Even some of NeoCrawler's lowest-frequency nominees—*monthiversary, cyberoffensive, meatmare*—would show growth potential.

Understanding the rate and quality of the diffusion of words—not just how frequently they show up but where and in what context—is important to understanding shifts in the language. A new physical thing, a scientific discovery, some popular phenomenon—all can slingshot a word. Other words can be stymied by the tenor of public debate, or the lack of it. Donald Trump tried to counter the spread of *alt-right* as a pejorative with the parallel construction *alt-left*. But it didn't gain traction, maybe because it was derivative, or because what Trump was attempting to name didn't exist.

Despite mainframe data crunching, why some words take off and others don't remains partly a mystery. An "extra-linguistic event" might push terms into prominence or permanence—think covid words or *bankster*, a nineteenth-century portmanteau of *banker* and *gangster* that spread anew after the financial crisis in 2008. An in-group, usually young people, might create a word to establish some facet of identity, only for the idea to vanish like a puff of mist from a vape pen, or for the in-group to age out. A technology or a trend may endure or crash. "The vast majority of words are just not successful," Schmid said.

Schmid's and Grieve's linguistic data-gathering demonstrated the breadth of change in modern English, largely because of technology. Going viral isn't a new phenomenon—every generation has its catchphrases and in-words, some of which survive, most of which don't—but the speed and universality accelerated everything. "Newspapers and TV stations and radio stations were the only way to contribute to diffusion," Schmid said. Now, a teenager on TikTok is as likely to invent a word as a writer for *Saturday Night Live*.

"We don't have comparative data from the past," Grieve said, "but it seems to me that language is changing relatively quickly just because there's so many more ways for regular people to disseminate language change."

These academic studies amounted to a digital early warning system for words. By flagging new terms to monitor, they could be put to practical use by commercial lexicographers. I found a much older analog method in the quarterly academic journal *American Speech*, which filled a set of shelves not far from my cubicle at Merriam.

American Speech was founded in 1925 at the suggestion of the newspaper columnist, satirist, and language buff H. L. Mencken. In his book *The American Language*, Mencken said the way Americans treat English reflects who we are as a people: unconcerned with rules and traditions, open to change, characterized by "restlessness, that impatience of forms, that disdain of the dead hand." America, he wrote, "shows its character in a constant experimentation, a wide hospitality to novelty, a steady reaching out for new and vivid forms. No other tongue of modern times admits foreign words and phrases more readily; none is more careless of precedents; none shows a greater fecundity and originality of fancy."

But Mencken was also a cynic. This is the guy who wrote, "No one in this world . . . has ever lost money by underestimating the intelligence of the great masses of the plain people." So his admiration for America's word spirit came with some side-eye. There was a "prodigality" in the nation's linguistic "leap in the dark," he wrote. Neologisms like *rubber-neck*, *has-been*, and *lame-duck** showed "the grotesque humor of the country, and the delight in devastating opprobriums, and the acute feeling for the succinct and savory." Verbs like *itemize* and *burglarize* were formed "by torturing nouns with harsh affixes." Adjectives like *scary*, *classy*, and *tasty* were created by "shading down suffixes to a barbaric simplicity."

For his language research, Mencken leaned on a University of Nebraska linguist named Louise Pound, one of the first scholars to study American English. Pound and two other academics created *American Speech*. The new journal was published by the American Dialect Society, which was founded in 1899 as a place for studiers

---

*Mencken used a hyphen in all three words. Merriam today enters *rubberneck* as a closed compound and *lame duck* as an open compound. *Has-been* is still hyphenated.

and lovers of American English to convene. *American Speech* was designed to be mostly, as its title indicated, about speech.

The exception was a column by a linguist at Washburn College in Topeka, Kansas, named Dwight L. Bolinger. Instead of looking at language through the fashionable field of phonology, the study of sounds, Bolinger had been writing, for a small journal called *Words*, about new words that people were using in the moment. His column was originally called "The Living Language" and later renamed "Among the New Words." In 1941, he moved it to *American Speech*.

"Among the New Words" treated emerging words—and more than eight decades later still does—as worthy of full lexicographic attention, with robust, citation-heavy entries, today replete with links, screenshots, GIFs, memes, and videos. For language obsessives, it reads like pulp fiction. I dug up Bolinger's first column. Most of its new words would endure: *blacktop, bra, burp, curvaceous, front, fuddy-duddy, G-string, lay an egg, leg up, prototype, quisling,* and the product of another tortured noun, *winterize*. Others would fade from use, like the noun *Corrigan*, which Bolinger defined as "something done backwards; one who so acts, etc.," after Douglas "Wrong Way" Corrigan, an aviator who in 1938 flew to Ireland when he was supposed to go to California. *Quisle* (to act as a traitor) and *sitzkrieg* (inactive warfare, or an inactive war) also didn't catch on.

But endurance wasn't the point. "Among the New Words" wasn't evaluating the dictionary worthiness of a word. It was the first draft of language history. Instead of writing down a new word on an index card, sliding it into a drawer, and waiting to see what happened, Bolinger (who would go on to teach at Southern Cal, Colorado, Harvard, and Stanford) was exposing new words and expressions to sunlight. "Often the styles and the ideas are transitory," he wrote, "so that they leave no mark upon the dictionary," which he called "that solemn repository."

neologism

For a fiftieth-anniversary book, one of Bolinger's successors, John Algeo, with assistance from his wife, Adele, who coedited "Among the New Words" with him, cataloged every word in the column's history. The first alphabetical entry is a World War II term, *AA*, an antiaircraft gun, and the last is the functional shift—noun to adjective—*zippered*, from the same period. (Both would be entered in *Webster's Third*.) Reading the index of Algeo's book is like looking at an old minor-league baseball roster and seeing who made The Show* and who didn't—in this case, not just into the dictionary but into the culture.

Mencken would have been psyched that *blenderize* (1982), *capsulize* (1954), and *jumboize* (1960) didn't stick. *Autocide* (1964), death by automobile, didn't either, even though Ralph Nader's exposé *Unsafe at Any Speed* was published a year later. "Among the New Words" had just one citation for *checkbook baseball* (1976)—a short-lived term at the dawn of player free agency that was likely a spinoff of *checkbook journalism*, which appeared in the same issue. *Gas guzzler* (1979), yes; *fringe parking* (1950)—"vehicular parking on the outskirts of a city's business district"—no.

Newsworthy was word-worthy in 1941. I would have guessed that *acquaintance rape* and *date rape* (1989), *shoo-in* (1950), *rehab* (1982), *cutting edge* and *mover and shaker* (1985), and *couch potato* (1988) were older. By contrast, there's something about *letter bomb* (1971), *quackupuncture* (1974), *bed-hop* (1979), and *theme park* (1972) that feel very seventies. I was unsurprised that *designated homer* (1974, a home run hit by a designated hitter), *duckwich* (1943), and *tenigue* (1954, *ten*sion plus fat*igue*) flopped. And also that people aren't living in a *quadminium* (1972) or riding a *helibus* (1954).

Our current anti-science, anti-intellectual age could benefit from a revival of *thobber* (1959), "a person who prefers guess-work

---

* The ninth sense of *show* in Merriam is "*often capitalized* : the major leagues in baseball—used with *the*".

to investigation and reinforces his beliefs by reasserting them frequently."*

Saddened that so many lovely neologisms were hidden from public view, Allan Metcalf had an idea. "I was thinking that *Time* magazine has its Person of the Year," Metcalf told me, "and why can't we do for words what *Time* did for people?" In 1990, members of the American Dialect Society selected the first Word of the Year: *bushlips*, defined as "insincere political rhetoric," referring to President George H. W. Bush's broken 1988 campaign promise, "Read my lips: No new taxes."

Metcalf, an English professor at MacMurray College in Jacksonville, Illinois, for more than forty years, assumed that the language pros of the dialect society would nominate words "headed straight for our everyday vocabulary and secure places in the dictionaries." Instead they promoted a bunch of faddish stuff, like *technostupidity* ("loss of ability through dependence on machines") and *potty parity* ("equalization of toilet facilities for the sexes"). Metcalf misjudged human behavior. Lexicography was sober research committed quietly and alone. Word of the Year was a key party. You couldn't be sure who you'd go home with.

To guard against another loser winning—like *bushlips*, which barely lasted a news cycle—WOTY leaders refined their thinking. The lexicographer and WOTY regular David Barnhart, a son of the prolific twentieth-century dictionary-maker Clarence Barnhart, established criteria: Was the word completely new? Had it been used before in other contexts? Was it "a major focus of human activity

---

* *Thob* was coined in a 1926 book by a prep school English teacher and writer named Charles Henshaw Ward. "Here you will see a display of the remarkable ways in which we all *think* out the *opinion* that pleases us and then *believe* it," Ward wrote in *Thobbing: A Seat at the Circus of the Intellect*. "The initial letters of the three words form a much-needed verb, to *thob*." For more, see the endnotes.

or behavior" in the previous year? Did it have staying potential? The Word of the Year could be brand new or newly popular. But it had to have been used widely and reflect the zeitgeist of the annum gone by.

Looking at the WOTY winners from a distance, you might nod in recognition of a specific event (*chad*, 2000; *bailout*, 2008), cringe at terminology that dates you (*World Wide Web*, 1995), or wonder what the hell people were thinking (*to pluto*, a verb meaning to demote, as in what happened to Pluto when it was reclassified from full-fledged to dwarf planet, 2006). That's the genius of Word of the Year. The public is a sucker for media-driven argument engines. It's a short walk from "LeBron is better than Jordan!" to "They should have picked *rizz*!" As a culture we are forever searching for ways to make sense of our big, complicated, confusing world. By turns serious, innocuous, meaningful, and entertaining, Word of the Year neatly boxed up 365 days in a single, simple term. It was media catnip and hot-take gold.

Dictionaries picked up the idea. *Webster's New World* was the first to crown a WOTY—*shapeshifter* in 1996. Merriam and Oxford joined in 2003 and 2004, naming, respectively, *democracy* and *chav*, the latter a British term the OED defined as "a young person of a type characterized by brash and loutish behaviour and the wearing of designer-style clothes (esp. sportswear); usually with connotations of a low social status." The publishers tried to elbow each other out for newsiness and media hits. *Webster's New World* was the Iowa caucuses of WOTY, releasing its Word of the Year in the fall. To juice web traffic, Merriam let users pick its winner in 2006 (*truthiness*) and 2007 (*w00t*). In 2015, Oxford selected an emoji, "Face with Tears of Joy," and Merriam went with a suffix, *-ism*. Edgy!

Over the years, a WOTY science emerged. Sexy buzzwords, often ephemeral, were the most obvious path to attention. But the big publishers eventually opted for an empirical approach, choosing news-driven words that readers were looking up more than they had before. In 2016, for instance, Dictionary.com said lookups for its winner, *xenophobia*, spiked 938 percent the day after the United Kingdom voted to leave the European Union, with "hundreds of users looking up the term each hour." Oxford Dictionaries reported that its WOTY, *post-truth*, was based partly on a jump in the "frequency of word use" in one of its corpora. Merriam reported that total lookups for its winner, *surreal*, increased by about 80 percent over the previous year.

By the 2020s, there were more than a dozen Words of the Year in English and WOTY season ran from late fall to early January. The originator of the brand, the American Dialect Society, crowned a champion last. The group held its annual conference in conjunction with that of the Linguistic Society of America, where academics delivered papers with titles like "On the unavailability of argument ellipsis in Kaqchikel" and talks on "A phonetic and pragmatic analysis of *um* and *uh* in spontaneous conversation." A session called "Five-Minute Linguist" helped ivory-tower types pitch their research to mainstream media. There were meetings of the Society for Pidgin and Creole Linguistics and the Society for the Study of the Indigenous Languages of the Americas. One year I attended a fascinating talk titled "Wayyy longgg: orthotactics and phonology in lengthening on Twitter" that examined how users lengthened words for emphasis. To the authors' surprise, they did it by extending the last letter of a word, not the stressed one.

But WOTY was the hot ticket. To people who study words for a living, selecting a single one to represent an entire year is a serious undertaking. It's about the sharp lines of language and usage, how society adopts and spreads new terminology, and, increasingly, the dramatic ways that social media influences the way we write, talk, and interact. The job of evaluating the trendiest "lexical items"—it is noted annually that a nominee need not be a single word but can be a phrase or compound that behaves as a single unit—for developments and distinctions in style, manner, and cultural context is so weighty that it takes two days to pick a winner (nominations one night, final vote the next).

I participated in almost a decade's worth of WOTY votes, online during the pandemic and IRL before and after. I checked my journalistic objectivity at the door and did my linguistic civic duty. Every year, the same pattern emerged. A few words would totally surprise, some product of Gen Z or online culture that had bypassed middle-aged me. Others would reveal themselves, in enthusiastic nominations by audience members, to be more widespread and consequential than imagined. Recency bias was common. Months or years later, nominees that in the moment seemed ready to catapult to glory (and commercial dictionaries) were felled by the unpredictable currents of writing, speaking, and media. Others seemed obscure at the time and stayed that way. In 2015, forty-two people picked *ammosexual*—"someone who loves firearms in a fetishistic manner"—as the Word of the Year. WTF?

That year, only one of more than forty nominees in nine categories had anything to do with Donald Trump (*schlonged*). The winner was *they* used as a gender-neutral singular pronoun, particularly as a "nonbinary identifier." Trumpian words dominated in 2016, 2017, and 2018. By 2019, Trump was all but forgotten, linguistically; the WOTY Final Four—*(my) pronouns* (the winner), *ok boomer, cancel,* and *Karen*—had nothing to do with him. The 2020 vote was dominated by the pandemic; 2021 was a mash-up of our national nightmares: Trump's January 6 *insurrection* was the champ, beating out *vax/vaxx*. The suffix *-ussy* wore the crown in 2022.

On the first weekend of 2024, I joined more than three hundred linguists, lexicographers, students, writers and editors, and other random word-lovers—ten times as many as voted on *bushlips* thirty-four years earlier—in a ginormous Sheraton ballroom in midtown Manhattan to select the 2023 champ. The American Dialect Society received 199 online nominations from librarians, software engineers, a retired fighter pilot, an Australian podcaster, and others, plus a bunch more in person. The year's big topics were well represented: the Barbie movie, the Israel-Hamas war, artificial intelligence. And there was the usual large scoop of TikTok/Instagram/YouTube/texting language coined and deployed by the youngs; I was totally unaware of the animated web series *Skibidi Toilet*, which, per Wikipedia, "follows a war between human-headed toilets and humanoid characters with electronic devices for heads."

As a sports guy, I was pleased to hear a paean to *tush push*, defined by the organizers as "quarterback sneak for short yardage perfected by the Philadelphia Eagles (also called the *brotherly shove*)." Even more pleasing was that the paean was paeaned by eminent octogenarian linguist Dennis Preston. Preston lauded *tush push* for its Yiddish roots, its engaging rhyme, and its quick ubiquity—coined in January 2023, firmly established in football vernacular by the fall—and he noted the potential for expansion; Pop Warner leagues could call it "tushy pushy," he said to laughter from the crowd.

"I recommend it very highly to overcome the decades-long ignoring of sports terminology by this very Word of the Year event," he said. I high-fived Preston after his stem-winder, but, alas, *tush push* didn't even win the Most Creative Word of the Year category, which went to the *Barbie*-ism *Kenaissance*. The WOTY eggheads, as Preston articulated, have never stanned for sports.

Concerns were raised that nominees *delulu* (short for *delusion*, "as in *delulu is the solulu* [delusion is the solution"]) and *hallucination* ("A.I.-generated response containing false information presented as factual") were offensive. "Not everyone cares about how language reflects views of mental health and ableism and stuff, and there's another conversation to be had about policing language versus actually dismantling ableism," one speaker said, "but it has been discussed significantly online among folks who are attentive to those things that for some people *delulu* seems like it's making fun of the actual reality of delusions as a way of being cute."

Every year WOTY strays, or sprints, into the polemical and political. Every year someone wants the voters to Make a Statement that would correct popular opinion about the worst humans and developments of the year. The impulse is usually well-meaning; sometimes the politics fits, sometimes nominators try to shoehorn it in, and sometimes they attempt to sit on the suitcase to get it to close, suggesting words that might have reflected the year, or a part of it, but didn't come close to gaining the linguistic traction that would merit the honor.

At the Sheraton, one prominent linguist, Sonja Lanehart of the University of Arizona, endorsed *context*—the word used by the presidents of Harvard, MIT, and the University of Pennsylvania when asked by a gotcha-seeking Republican member of Congress whether calls for the genocide of Jews would violate university rules of conduct.

"We are a linguistic organization, and words have been weaponized in a way that I feel we need to address," Lanehart said. "*Context* was one of those things, and part of that is context is missing and our voice is missing in particular in some of these debates. We have words like *genocide, antisemitism, woke*—various words that are being weaponized in ways to subvert what they are trying to accomplish, and it diminishes all of us. And if we can't stand for something as a linguistic organization in this particular time, I don't know when we would."

Another linguist, Nicole Holliday, then an assistant professor at Pomona College, took the mic. "This is my thirteenth Word of the Year vote," she told the room. "We have been arguing about the politics of this organization and the kind of statement that we want to make every single year, and I don't think that we will ever all get on the same page about that. But I also think we should be really thoughtful about what our mission is here, whether it's to make a statement that's apart from language or intrinsically connected to the way that humans used the English language in the previous year."

It felt like the room was exhausted by politics. Enter *babygirl*.

"I had always had this feeling about seeing certain men in my life and I had no word for it," a speaker said about the Informal Word of the Year nominee, defined as "older male fictional character or celebrity seen as emotionally damaged, helpless, or vulnerable." "I had no idea how to describe this baby-girl-ness that these men had but now I do. I look at them with their dorky little sweaters and their sloppy little haircuts and I say, he is *babygirl*." Someone else lauded the utility of *(derogatory)*, which WOTY defined as "parenthetical comment humorously appended after a word that might not be expected to be derogatory": "My friend group and I use it to differentiate the Sean in our group and the Sean that is my ex."

Then, in the Most Useful/Most Likely to Succeed category, came debate over a word that the *New York Times* didn't print in its write-up of the event: *cunty*, "having an audaciously exceptional appearance or attitude." Like other taboo words including *bitch* and the n-word, recent usage of *cunt* and *cunt*-related terms reflected both reclamation and appropriation.

Women and queer people repurposed what started nine hundred years ago as a technical term and morphed into a misogynistic slur; *cunty* was entered by the *OED* in 2014 as "despicable; highly unpleasant; extremely annoying." The WOTY sense of the word—as with another online nominee, *serve cunt*—was appropriated from Black trans communities and drag ballroom culture in the 1990s, where it originated. When Beyoncé sampled the 1996 song "Cunty (The Feeling)" by drag queen, musician, and designer Kevin Aviance on her 2022 song "Pure/Honey," the word went mainstream, "eliminating its misogynistic meaning and positioning it as something aspirational," *Rolling Stone* wrote. *Cunty* now meant *campy*.

"I'm Talia Sherman, Brown University, and I would like to speak on behalf of *cunty*." Sherman, a sophomore linguistics major, already had made a splash at the WOTY mic with an impassioned manifesto for *FAFO*, short for *fuck around and find out*. "This lady is extraaaaaaa!" Grant Barrett, a lexicographer, host of the public-radio show *A Way with Words*, and WOTY-vote commentator, typed onscreen. Sherman was even more animated about this c-word.

"I feel like we took the *-y* and added it on and that was a whole semantic shift, worldwide movement, earthquake, elevation, change," Sherman said, her pace accelerating. "Because *cunt* is a word that's been used to denigrate women, to put women down. It is a pejorative term, to make fun of women's genitalia, just everything that we hate about this entire, like"—here Sherman made a guttural sound of disgust that I can't figure out how to render in type—"everything, all the sexism, all the misogyny comes through in that word. And yet we are taking it and we are elevating it and making it different and I appreciate that." The room filled with smiles and laughter. "And now I can say *cunty* and I don't feel like a misogynist, like a self-hating woman, and that's great. And someone the other day texted me and said you're giving power to *cunt*, and I feel like once we give power to *cunty*, then we can actually reclaim *cunt* and we can say"—here her voice rose like a politician's or a preacher's—"yes, she was a feckless"—pause—"and, and yeah."

"Okay! Thank you!" said WOTY emcee Ben Zimmer, a linguist, lexicographer, *Wall Street Journal* language columnist, and chair of the American Dialect Society's New Words Committee. "Last comment before the voting! Go ahead."

"I just want to second her, because for so long *cunt* and *dick* have been these opposites and *dick* is not a bad word and *cunt* is the worst word you can say and now I can get up here and say *cunty* in front of a thousand people," the speaker said. "It's important."

That drew applause, too, but it wasn't the last comment.

"If we're applying this in ways that we think are sort of like extra-feminist and stuff, that's kind of appropriating," said Dominique Canning, a linguistics PhD candidate at the University of Michigan. "We're reapplying a word that has existed in a community for a long time to mean something—and it's not specifically about having or being a cunt. Don't make it cis. Like, don't do that." Canning said the definition was inadequate, and that it should attribute the term to ballroom culture. The moderators obliged with an edit: "having an audaciously exceptional appearance or displaying fierce femininity (from LGBTQ ballroom culture)."

In the end, *cunty* didn't win the category; *(derogatory)* did. The overall WOTY winner straddled the line between serious and fun: *enshittification*, which the *Times* did print. It was coined by the writer Cory Doctorow in a November 2022 blog post to mean a gradual deterioration in the quality of internet platforms like Facebook, Twitter, and TikTok. In May 2023, NPR's *On the Media* aired a three-part conversation with Doctorow about the word, and the experiences it addressed. In December, *enshittification* was entered by Dictionary.com. That's a rapid ascent.

Topping *babygirl, ceasefire, context, girlie, Kenaissance, let (someone) cook*, the artificial intelligence term *stochastic parrot*, and, in a runoff, *(derogatory), enshittification* was a worthy WOTY, capturing the growing frustration in this particular year with internet subservience and AI overlords. It was structurally simple but creative—the redundancy of the *en-* prefix ("cause to be," according to Merriam) and *-ify* suffix ("invest with the attributes of : make similar to") gave it memorable lexical oomph—and it had the potential to grow beyond its narrow definition, as words do.

On the blog *Strong Language*, which is about swearing, Nancy Friedman wrote that *enshittify* and *enshittification* "are primed for neologistic success." Friedman cited the FUDGE factors established by WOTY founder Allan Metcalf: frequency of use, unobtrusiveness, diversity of users and situations, generation of other forms and meanings, and endurance of the concept. "By those criteria, Doctorow's inventions strike me as pretty fucking FUDGE-y," Friedman wrote. *Enshittification* had a chance to do what most new words fail to do: live on.

7
slip
: a small piece of paper

Lexicography's digital doohickeys and what they enabled were fascinating and indispensable and fun. But what I cherished most about my all-access pass to Merriam-Webster was the paper.

I loved rooting around in the Consolidated Files, stumbling on a yellowed snippet of a 1974 *New York Times* story by McCandlish Phillips—a reporter who once revealed that a Ku Klux Klansman had been an Orthodox Jew—that used the phrase *Dashing Dan*. Or extracting from a basement file a 1928 card with comments from an editor named Loveridge about an illustration to accompany *green turtle* ("Head very poor, claws on hind flippers over-accentuated"). Or finding in a metal cabinet a 1956 contract to pay an Ohio State University marketing professor $150 to define 652 business terms, from *general store* to *window display*. Or encountering a wall of boxes filled with words typed in reverse order.* When I did any of that—which I did a lot—I was awed by the mightiness of this thing.

But my infatuation with this musty and sweet-smelling history—tens of thousands of pounds of cards and books and sheets of paper

---

*See the endnotes for an explanation of the Backward Index.

crammed inside drawers, stacked in stairwells, smushed into creaky filing cabinets in the dungeon—wasn't just sentimental. Merriam didn't need the paper to practice modern lexicography. Definers rarely made the trip to the Consolidated Files. But the paper—especially the slips—was more than a reliquary. It was a living, breathing portal into the history of American words. It was indispensable to charting and understanding the story of American English.

Merriam didn't invent the citation slip. Samuel Johnson collected about 150,000 quotations for his 40,000 headwords. When James Murray took over in 1879 as editor of the OED, the creators of the then two-decades-old project already had amassed about two million citations, or quotation slips, as they are known at Oxford. From the outset, readers were instructed to send submissions on four-by-six-inch slips, "written out with its quotation and the full reference on a separate half-sheet of note-paper, *lengthwise, and on one side of the paper only.*" But contributors posted much more: book and newspaper extracts stuck on torn-off bits of envelopes or the backs of theater bulletins.

The slips arrived at the Scriptorium, as Murray jokingly called the specially built, corrugated shed where he and his staff made the dictionary, in boxes and sacks and even a bassinet; "a hamper of I's," one worker said. They were sorted—by Murray's eleven children, among others—and filed in specially designed bookcases containing more than a thousand pigeonholes and, as the number of slips swelled, on bookshelves. By the time the first edition was published, in 1928, the OED had amassed more than five million.

At Merriam, slips were used to make the 1864. "Paper to be written on one side so as to be cut up into slips so that all the quotations for each word may be gathered readily together & be before the eye of the definer at once," editor Noah Porter explained. Alas, I didn't find any slips from that era in the Merriam papers at Yale. After Porter's death in 1892, the Merriams brought the dictionary north from New Haven. The oldest three-by-fives in Springfield date to the first book created there, *Webster's New International Dictionary*, published in 1909. Citations were handwritten on light blue slips and stamped with an inch-high numeral 1. A blue slip pops up in the Consolidated every quarter inch or so. When *Webster's Second* was published in 1934, the files held 1,665,000 cits. New ones for that book were stamped with a big 2.

Philip Gove went at it more systematically than his predecessors. Gove told editors to read for up to two hours a day and mark words from anything and everything. The intent was to portray "language as it is," not as it was rendered by a hunched-over editor drafting a stilted sentence fragment with a pencil. Under Gove, editors collected about 80,000 cits a month, or nearly a million a year, bulging the files to about 10 million when the *Third* was published. The pace slackened after the big book was done, but editors kept precise track. Merriam's 1976 in-house annual report noted that "208,646 citations were added to the files during the year, bringing the total number of citations to 12,275,742."

The current 16 million number excluded slips with existing definitions cut from dictionaries, new draft definitions, cross-references, and editor comments and questions. There certainly had been a lot more. Before the move to 47 Federal Street in 1940, editors likely culled and tossed cits that had been rejected again and again. John Morse once tried to check the total by counting the number of cits per inch and then multiplying that number by the length of a drawer and then by the total number of drawers. His estimate was pretty close.

The Consolidated is a mosaic of colors and inks and fonts and papers and stamps. You can easily discern the period from the style. Elegant, flowing, fountain-pen cursive in the late nineteenth and early twentieth centuries. The evolution of manual and then electric typewriter fonts. There are carefully scissored quotations from newspapers and magazines, curt and precise and visually evocative of the dates typed beneath them.

The files are a century-long scrapbooking project. Full-page clippings folded one, two, three, four times, like a kid stuffing a school note into their back pocket. Black-and-white photostats that began appearing in the 1950s, when Gove instructed editors to take multiple citations from single passages, especially for common words, to avoid the tendency to flag unusual words while ignoring run-of-the-mill ones. Early computer printouts with truncated tails on the g, j, p, q, and y, which reminded me of an annoyed college professor who, on a paper I submitted in the 1980s, underlined every last one.

The aesthetics make the cit files a work of art. Their content makes them an irreplicable and irreplaceable archive of American English. The cards hold forensic clues to how identically trained curators compiled and adjudged the quotidian changes in the language for more than a hundred years. USED FOR SCHL DICT 4. REJECTED FOR 9 COLL. USED FOR CII.* Those all-caps distinctions weren't mere editorial and business judgments on what belonged in a dictionary. They were clinical assessments of the state of American English and American culture (and Merriam-Webster) on any given day. Every physical detail about a card—the ink, the typewriter, the publication font, the handwriting, the glue, the stamp, the type of paper—provided context about the word it chronicled and the time in which it was chronicled, about the way information about the language was conveyed, curated, and preserved.

On January 22, 1959, Philip Gove wrote to an executive named Art Lerps at R. R. Donnelley & Sons of Chicago, the printer for *Webster's Third*, with an urgent, confidential request. He asked Lerps

---

* C and COLL in those notations stand for *Collegiate*, SCHL DICT for *School Dictionary*, and the numerals for the editions.

to print five copies of galley proof number g267 and, during his next visit to Springfield, "give them to me privately or, if anyone else is present, without identifying comment." If Lerps wouldn't be in Chicago before visiting Merriam, Gove asked him to have the proofs mailed to his home on Old Patrick Road in Warren, Massachusetts, "without calling the matter to anyone else's attention through correspondence."

Gove's covert operation was part of a plan to persuade his bosses not to remove *fuck* (verb and noun) and *fuck up* (transitive verb) from the pages of the upcoming dictionary. Gove had composed the *fuck* definitions himself. His scrawly, part-print, part-cursive handwriting is preserved in the Consolidated Files on the yellow slips called "buffs," for their color.* The draft of *fuck up* is in the handwriting of etymologist Charles R. Sleeth.† Five of the six senses for the two words are labeled *considered obscene and usu. unprintable*; the sixth sense—"CHEAT, DOUBLECROSS"—isn't, perhaps because it wasn't sexual or, more likely, because Gove didn't want to repeat the long monitory label three times in a single sense. The drafts are stamped between April and October 1958 and accompanied by Sleeth's handwritten etymologies.

Gove didn't define many words for the *Third*, but *fuck* was a big deal. He had a personal interest in taboo language but, more important, he was a descriptivist. *Fuck* hadn't appeared in a general English dictionary since 1795, but there was, to put it mildly, sufficient evidence supporting inclusion, so it qualified. Gove also worried that excluding one four-letter word would draw attention to it, especially because reviewers, like preadolescents, would be looking to see which were in and which weren't. He hoped that galley g267—one column of type running from *fuchsia* through

---

* buff *noun* 3 a : a moderate orange yellow 3 b : a light to moderate yellow

† Sleeth was a Rhodes Scholar, Princeton PhD, and English professor who worked at Merriam for a decade before returning to academia. He wrote a book titled *Studies in Christ and Satan*.

fuegian, with the entries in question sandwiched between *fuchsite* and *fucoid*—would allay concerns. "I believe," Gove wrote,

> that an unabridged dictionary for adults who are intelligent enough to understand our definitions generally should not omit this common word regardless of its taboo status and that no responsible and mature person should object to the way it is covered. I believe further that anyone who first becomes aware of the proposed coverage by seeing the definitions in print is perhaps more likely to accept them than if he hears rumors about them beforehand or if he has to deal with the abstract question of whether or not the word should be included. That is to say, laid away in their alphabetical place amidst a few hundred thousand words, the definitions, marked "usually considered unprintable," are harmless, but if singled out for prurient publicity and sniggering allusion they can make disproportionate trouble.

Gove explained to Lerps the "wider" considerations that were "primarily commercial rather than linguistic or moral." He admitted that he couldn't act with "the usual independence of an editor in chief" because "such independence is only a trust which I enjoy as long as I don't abuse it." He said that Merriam's president, Gordon J. Gallan, would have to decide whether the company's board of directors should weigh in on the matter.

If these informative steps can be taken by presenting the result in its entirety—that is, as the definitions will look to the eye—I believe the final decision to include or omit, whichever, has a fair chance of being a wise decision. But if I write a regular letter that is read by half a dozen or so who handle correspondence, I fear that talk will start, half-informed opinions will get aired, sides will be taken and it may then be too late for calm and mature deliberation. I have little doubt that if the finished book gets into the hands of the public with no advance rumors and with no long waiting period of expectant curiosity, there may be no serious objections, or at least none strong enough to force us to retreat pusillanimously to withdrawing books and making plate changes.

This may all sound silly to you. The definitions as you can see them now in galley proof have gone through this office without any special handling from initial written query to several members of the staff to final copy, needless to say with no attempt to keep them from anybody's knowledge—and no one to my knowledge has murmured loudly although some do think the taboo should be respected by omission. I hope I've made myself clear, and I'm sure you will co-operate, whatever your own view.

Art Lerps may have been bewildered by Gove's lengthy confessional. After all, the editor in chief presumably could have just ordered the galley pages without relaying his every thought to the printer. Or maybe Gove was covering his bases; the last thing he needed was objection from the company that owned the ink. (*Fuck* indeed was a topic of conversation at Donnelley—"betting on its chances of survival was lively in the composing room," historian Herbert C. Morton wrote.)

Lerps replied immediately. He was at Donnelley's office outside of New York City but would be back in Chicago in a few days and would "personally and unobtrusively take care of the five galley proofs you requested." He would complete the clandestine assignment with a visit to Springfield the following week or, if Gove wanted the pages sooner, mail them to his house. "I understand your position and agree that the final decision to include or omit 'usually considered unprintable' words can best be made by seeing them properly defined in type and in their alphabetical position among the other words," Lerps wrote.

Gove's gambit failed. On February 4, Gallan wrote a brief "Memorandum for Dr. Gove":

Please delete the following completely:
   fuck . . . vb
   fuck . . . n
   fuck up vt

While recognizing the widespread usage of these terms in vulgar and sometimes colloquial speech, it is my judgment that their inclusion would be misinterpreted to the extent so as to seriously affect the sale of 3d Ed.

Would it be practical to submit to me, in manuscript form, those entries which, in your judgment of social sensitivities, many users of the Dictionary might consider morally objectionable?

Gove's letter to Lerps fills a critical gap in the story of *fuck*'s removal from *Webster's Third*. It's a window into the editor's thinking on an issue that would irritate him until his death, and reflects the lengths to which he went to defend his editorial principles. It's an important piece of paper, one that was hidden along with Lerps's response in a manila folder labeled OBSCENE TERMS in a filing cabinet in the Merriam basement and serendipitously discovered by Merriam editor Peter Sokolowski and language writer Ben Zimmer in 2024, sixty-five years after it was written. The Gallan memo also was unearthed randomly in the basement, by Lindsay Rose Russell, a University of Illinois English professor who was researching a book about women lexicographers. The slips on which Gove and Sleeth composed the entries—with straight and squiggly cross-outs, edits, underlines, parentheses, brackets, and stamps—were in their proper place in the Consolidated Files.

We don't know what went down between Gove and Gallan, whether there was a face-to-face where Gove presented the galleys and made his case. It's also not clear how much Gove pushed back on Gallan's decision. A few months later, a federal judge in New York, Frederick van Pelt Bryan, overturned a thirty-year obscenity ban in the United States of D. H. Lawrence's novel *Lady Chatterley's Lover*. In an undated note, stored among his papers at the University of Wyoming, Gove wrote that *fuck* had been "legal to print since July 21, 1959." Did Gove bring up the court ruling in one last attempt to persuade Gallan to restore *fuck*? Or was he just hoarding grist? Other memos tucked away inside Merriam might hold the answers.

We do know that no other "morally objectionable" words were removed from the *Third*; all the biggies are in there. We also know that Gove was right: Leaving out one "usually unprintable" word was a publicity magnet. Reviewers accused Merriam—and Gove personally—of cowardliness and hypocrisy (though usually without mentioning the offending word itself). "Why this residual prudishness?" Columbia linguist Mario Pei wrote in the *New York Times Book Review*. "Should not a dictionary based on usage face the facts of life?" Others noted the *Third*'s *fuck*lessness, too: the *Miami Herald*; a conference of the American Ethnological Society; the *Manchester Guardian Weekly*; Dwight Macdonald's *New Yorker* screed; and *Hungarian Studies in English*, which wrote that the *Third*'s editors "have had the moral courage to break with musty Victorian taboos and have included some of the oldest words of the language (except, regrettably, one)."

Gove was so resentful of the public heat that for years he kept a file of mentions of the omission. He handwrote them on white slips as if they were citations. "Peevish, stubborn Yankee," said Kory Stamper, a Merriam editor for nearly two decades, who unearthed and shared with me that file from Gove's papers at Wyoming. I wondered if Gove periodically opened the *Third* to page 917, stared at the rightmost column where *fuck* and *fuck up* should have been, and growled.

Gove's revenge: personally shepherding *fuck* and other profanities into future books. In 1971, during preparation of the eighth edition of the *Collegiate*, Gove questioned the editors' initial decision to omit *fuck*-related entries. His discussion about the topic with an editor, Robert Copeland, is preserved on pink slips in the Consolidated Files (the ~ symbol represents the word itself, a common dictionary notation*):

> **Gove:** Perhaps the decision to exclude compounds and collocations shd be reconsidered in light of the no. of cits we have for these terms (and especially because many of these terms are not s.e. [self-explanatory], e.g., fuck up, ~ off, ~ around, ~ over).
> **Copeland:** I concur, especially with fuck up and maybe fuck around. I would think fuck up a must since it isn't s.e. Also fuck over in C8 should prob have the usage note above the use as a meaningless intensive

The effort to expand the oeuvre was thwarted by editor H. Bosley Woolf. "HBW's advice: Omit ~ *around*, ~ *off*, ~ *over*, ~ *up*," Gove wrote on a slip. But the debate wasn't finished. Another editor, E. Ward Gilman, looked at Gove's draft entry and decided it was lacking, especially compared to that of the *Third*'s challenger, the *American Heritage Dictionary*, which had entered *fuck* in the book's debut edition in 1969. Gilman wrote on a pink:

> PBG's C8 treatment of this is considerably played down—it is even less complete than the AHD coverage. If we're going to bother with it at all, I should think we'd want at least a moderately thorough treatment: specifically . . .

---

* The ~ mark was used in definitions in place of the headword on subsequent reference, usually to save space in print. It follows the second sense of Merriam's definition of *tilde*: "the mark used to indicate negation in logic and the geometric relation 'is similar to' in mathematics."

1) the meaningless intensive is in the -ing form only; our note should say so.
2) ~ up + ~ off (the former in AHD) should be covered.
3) sense of vt = cheat, screw, gyp, swindle <they -ed me out of $100> (0 AHD) + = interfere with, meddle (in AHD) should be treated.
4) senses of n = 1) partner (in AHD) and = damn, hoot <don't give a ~> (0 AHD) should be covered*

The f-word got into the eighth *Collegiate*, which was published in 1973. Unlike his reaction to Gallan big-footing him in the *Third*, Gove didn't appear upset that he was overruled on *fuck around*, *fuck off*, *fuck over*, and *fuck up*. And he didn't seem eager for a longer entry than what he had composed. "Since when do we model our dicts on the likes of AHD?" Gove wrote next to Gilman's note. At the top of the slip, he scribbled "Closed" and stamped the date, March 23, 1972.

Gove didn't live to see the addition of *fuck*, *fucked-up*, *fuck off*, *fuckoff*, *fuck over*, *fuck up*, and *fuckup* to the Addenda to the *Third*. Only *fuck over* still isn't in the OWL. *Fuck all* was added to the online *Unabridged*. *Fuck around* remained, as of this writing, on the outside looking in.

Examining these slips, letters, and memos is a historical exercise; they add facts to our understanding of the evolution of language. But it's also a very personal one. I was eavesdropping on a multigenerational, intraoffice conversation. It was as if Gove and Copeland and Gilman and the other Merriam editors I came to know by their stamps and handwriting and three-letter initials were sitting around the table in the Unabridged Room hashing out what to do about *fuck* or *ain't* or

---

* "(0 AHD)" meant that particular sense was not covered by the *American Heritage Dictionary*.

pragmatic—like the 1919 Black Sox emerging from that Iowa cornfield. These were real people making critical decisions about the way words are depicted. The slips let me join the discussion all these years later.

Sometimes the conversations lasted decades. On June 28, 1930, a Merriam special editor for grammar named A. D. Sheffield recommended saving four lines of print in the *Second*'s entry for *preposition* by deleting an explanation that a preposition "may follow (in position) its object." An assistant editor with the last name Thomas replied in gorgeous, right-leaning red ink: "There is still abroad in the land a good deal of schoolmasterly feeling that such locutions are a bit off-color, as violating the etymology of *pre*position. I should retain the statement." Thomas wrote that twenty-nine years later, on September 17, 1959.

A conversation about how to label *irregardless* also lasted decades. Merriam dated the first use of the word to 1847 and reported that it was "popularized in dialectal speech" in the early 1900s. Commentators began calling it out as improper as early as 1927. "The most frequently repeated remark about it is that 'there is no such word,'" a note in the *irregardless* entry in the OWL reads. "There is such a word, however. It is still used primarily in speech, although it can be found from time to time in edited prose. Its reputation has not risen over the years, and it is still a long way from general acceptance."

Merriam books have entered *irregardless* for generations. There's also evidence in the Consolidated Files, extracted and promoted by Kory Stamper like a county-fair preacher spreading the gospel, that *irregardless* isn't just a bastard form of *regardless*, it's a word in its own right—an intensified form of the root word that enjoyed a dialectal minute in the South in the late nineteenth century. Stamper laid out her findings in a revised usage note, explaining that while the *ir-* prefix normally expresses negation, in this case "it appears to function as an intensifier." The note cites similar, "while rare," words including *irremediless* for *remediless*, *irresistless* for *resistless*, and *irrelentlessly* for *relentlessly*.

I did my own spelunk into the Files, hauling the short stack of *irregardless* slips back to my desk. I was looking for debate: Did Merriam just willy-nilly include one of the most notorious words in English? How kid were the gloves worn by editors when debating how the entry should look? Did they have strong feelings about it?

They did. On page 1312, *Webster's Second* labeled *irregardless* as *Erron. or Humorous, U.S.* Six years later, in 1940, on a single white slip, editors argued about that. Harold Bender, the *Second*'s chief etymologist, suggested that the entry include an etymology—*irrespective* + *regardless*—and lose the second part of its label. "It is Erron. as to linguistic history, but it is not Humorous," Bender wrote. "It is good Colloq. Americana. I have heard & seen it many years."

For evidence, Bender quoted a popular—and racy; the unmarried main character has an abortion—recent bestseller, *Kitty Foyle*, by Christopher Morley: "But she can take things in her stride, irregardless of what's happened." Senior general definer John Bethel, however, wasn't impressed with the etymologist's incursion into the field of usage labels. "I see no reason, yet, to change," Bethel wrote. "Certainly *Kitty Foyle* is no well of English undefiled—or even Colloq. if I hear right." The *Humorous* label stuck in later printings of the *Second*.*

But opinions changed. As part of his purge of monitory labels, Philip Gove wrote in the explanatory notes for the *Third* that *nonstandard* would be "used for a very small number of words that can hardly stand without some status label but are too widely current in reputable context to be labeled" *substandard*. If you were going to include it at all—and its frequency of use demanded its inclusion in an unabridged dictionary—*irregardless* needed to be flagged. But how?

In 1958, as the book's deadlines bore down, two renowned editors—H. Bosley Woolf and Mairé Weir Kay, known in-house as Miss Kay—took up the debate. "Irregardless of our changing staff,"

---

*I asked John Morse to decode the turf war. "I think I share Bender's opinion on this matter, but this really isn't his area of responsibility, so Bethel pushes back."

Kay wrote cheekily on a pink on December 11, "yours seems to be as near a 'usage desk' as is currently available—does this seem an appropriate place for a substand label?" On the flip side of the slip, Woolf replied, "I don't think substand is quite right, for irregardless is used by people who would never dream of using twicet, throwed, hisself, etc. And of course it isn't slang. PBG"—Philip B. Gove—"suggests the OCCASIONAL use of nonstand, and this seems to me to be a proper place for it."

The following June, another editor, reviewing the entry, noted that there was "no such label in style file as nonstand." They clearly hadn't read the earlier notes. "It is not generally acceptable," a senior editor, Anne Driscoll, replied, "but PBG approved it for this and one or two other entries."

When the *Third* was being condensed into the seventh edition of the *Collegiate*, an editor noted that *irregardless* had been deleted during preparation of the abridged book but was used in the front matter as an example of a few words that "are disapproved by many but that have some currency in reputable contexts." Should it be restored? the editor asked. Gove replied in red pencil: "Yes, pls. Should be as in 3d."

Irregardless would never leave a Merriam dictionary again. Because it was a word, and these slips of paper helped explain why.

It would be much harder, and in some cases impossible, to do this kind of research about other American commercial dictionaries.

The citation slips used to make the landmark *American Heritage Dictionary* in the 1960s were locked away in a storage facility in Orlando, Florida. Thirty-one cabinets stuffed with slips compiled by editors at Random House for its dictionaries were in a warehouse, too. Editors who once worked for those publishers didn't know how to gain access to the material. Oxford in the early 2000s pulled the plug on the last two planned volumes of the acclaimed

Historical Dictionary of American Slang, originally published by Random House. The book's three-by-five cards were handwritten by its editor, University of Tennessee lecturer Jonathan Lighter, who had been collecting examples of slang for three decades. Ben Zimmer, who was an editor at Oxford at the time, shipped the slips to a storage facility. "It was sad," he said. "I assume they're still gathering dust wherever I sent them."

The cits for the *Webster's New World Dictionary* of my youth, dating to the book's first edition in 1951, weren't even that fortunate. When the dictionary's operations in Cleveland were shuttered, fifty years later, most of its correspondence and archival material was sent to the offices of parent company John Wiley & Sons Inc. in Hoboken, New Jersey. The slips, I learned, were thrown away.

Here's a happier story, at least as slips go. The *Dictionary of American Regional English* was one of America's grandest lexicography projects. That effort to chronicle the country's local wordways began in 1963 and officially ended in 2017, when the National Endowment for the Humanities rejected a last-ditch grant application. In between, *DARE* charted more than 60,000 words and phrases, from *a* to *zydeco*, with stops at *bobbasheely*, *caflummux*, *pudjicky*, and *whoopensocker*. Six print volumes were published between 1985 and 2013. *DARE* amassed enough paper to fill eight rooms at the University of Wisconsin, where it was based.

The archive included the results of foundational interviews conducted between 1965 and 1970. Eighty fieldworkers traveled the country in dark green Dodge vans nicknamed Word Wagons. Using reel-to-reel tape recorders, they talked to 2,777 people in 1,002 communities who provided a total of 2.3 million answers to, initially, 1,847 questions grouped into forty-one categories, from weather to utensils to money to body parts to family relationships to exclamations. Once the fieldwork was done, *DARE* editors relied on traditional lexicographic sources and methods, collecting hundreds of thousands of four-by-six citation slips.

The day I called, outgoing editor Joan Houston Hall was sorting, organizing, labeling, and boxing a half century of paper—150 boxes with who knew how many to go. The university, Hall said, was never a major financial supporter of *DARE*. But it provided office space and agreed to preserve *DARE*'s papers. The collection hadn't been digitized. Hall once looked into scanning just the questionnaires, but *DARE* couldn't afford the $40,000 cost.

Hall was relieved that Wisconsin would store everything. She was compiling a catalog specific enough to be helpful to researchers. "If anybody really wanted to know how a dictionary is created from scratch," she said, "this would be a good place to do it."

You can find the slips that helped produce the *Oxford English Dictionary* in the late 1800s and early 1900s in the basement of the headquarters of Oxford University Press in the picturesque English city on the River Thames. To reach them, an editor named Peter Gilliver led me down a warren of halls and clicked us through doorways like we were heading for a secure room in the bowels of MI5 headquarters.

Ruddy-faced with bright blue eyes and neatly parted gray hair, Gilliver joined the editorial staff of the *OED* in 1987. In addition to his daily defining work, he authored a 600-plus-page history, *The Making of the Oxford English Dictionary*. Gilliver researched and wrote the book over fifteen years, one-fifth of the time it took to produce the first edition of the *OED*.

Gilliver was a charming tour guide. We chatted about the history of the *OED*, about the quirks of its founding as a historical dictionary, about its relationship with Merriam through the decades. From 1968 to 1977, the *OED* sent quotation slips of American words to Springfield to cross-reference against Merriam's citation files for antedatings and other information. The collaboration ended after the BBC interviewed the *OED* editor at the time, Robert Burchfield, about *Webster's Third*. The network titled the segment "An Enemy of Good Language?" Burchfield criticized the American language, not the dictionary, but then–Merriam president William Llewelyn got a secondhand report, fired off an irate letter, and scotched the partnership.

Gilliver paused in a hallway to show me photos from a dinner in 1928 celebrating the *OED*'s publication. England's prime minister, Stanley Baldwin, was in attendance, as was a onetime editorial assistant named J. R. R. Tolkien, whose time at the dictionary influenced the inventive language in his fantasy novels *The Hobbit* and *The Lord of the Rings*. Guests dined on smoked salmon, caviar, mock turtle soup, lamb, and lobster. For the next five years, the staff produced a supplement with updates. And then, from 1933 to 1957, English-language lexicography at Oxford stopped, possibly from exhaustion after a seventy-year slog. "I don't think they could bear to think about it," Gilliver said.

As of the time I visited in 2019, almost half of the entries in the second edition of the *OED*, published in print thirty years earlier, had been revised online. Those fat books in tiny type combined the first edition and subsequent additions but did not update the old stuff. Unlike Merriam, which had scrapped the online revision of its own unabridged opus, the *Third*, Oxford was devoted first and foremost to its signature masterpiece, the *OED*.

"I may not be there to see the completion of it," Gilliver said of the redo, "but that is the thing we have to do—finish the revision." When that happens, the *OED* won't stop for two and a half decades like it did a century earlier, because that's not how lexicography works anymore. "If only people would stop changing the language," Gilliver joked.*

---

* As of January 2025, more than 54 percent of the second edition had been revised, Gilliver told me.

The *OED* is housed in a modern wing of Oxford University Press, squeezed among centuries-old buildings made of the yellowish Headington limestone from nearby quarries used at the university as far back as 1307. In an outdoor quadrangle, dozens of bicycles were parked around a droopy old willow. Gilliver explained that Murray and his staff never worked here. Half toiled in the Scriptorium on Murray's property and half at the Old Ashmolean, a university building in the center of town. The place felt like a college campus, and functioned like one, too. It offered a knitting club, an orchestra, and sports teams organized by OUP Amalgamated Athletic Clubs. Gilliver was a former chair of the Oxford Bach Choir. "I think there are a lot of frustrated creatives here," he said.

The *OED*'s open-plan editorial floor was at the time home to about sixty lexicographers, plus half as many technical support staff. There were no Merriam-like unwritten rules about noise, but it was pretty quiet. We stopped at Gilliver's desk. He and another editor were working on a batch of existing entries starting with *serv-* that included 544 senses in all. Eighteen were done. The assembly-line performance target was thirty senses per week; *serv-* should take a couple of months. (A magnet on Gilliver's desk read, HOW WILL YOU KNOW YOU HAVE FINISHED?)

Next up in the spreadsheet on Gilliver's screen was *servage*, an obsolete word with meanings related to *servitude, slavery,* or *serfdom.* According to the existing *OED* entry, *servage* was used predominantly in the Middle English period (roughly the twelfth through fifteenth centuries), with a few outlier citations, including one from a book by the nineteenth-century English economist and philosopher John Stuart Mill. Gilliver had rewritten, reordered, and antedated its senses, and even found and used a quotation from a 2003 book, *Slavery in the Twentieth Century,* by Suzanne Miers, a historian at Ohio University.

In a small room adjacent to the editorial floor, Gilliver showed me filing cabinets with quotation slips collected from 1957, when work began on a second supplement, until the rise of electronic citations in the early 1990s. Readers still sent in, and the *OED* still filed, the occasional paper slip. The really old stuff, though, was what I came to see. The brightly lit basement held the DNA of the *OED*: millions of slips, galleys, fascicles,* books, photos, and other evidence of a century and a half of dictionary-making.

Gilliver and archivist Beverley McCulloch had pulled a sampling for me. (Unlike Merriam, the *OED* employs an archivist.) The original 1857 proposal from the Philological Society of London for a *Lexicon totius Anglicitatis*—a complete glossary of the English language. The "LIST OF BOOKS, &c.," ordered alphabetically and by time period ("First Period: A.D. 1250 to 1526"), read for quotations by staff, academics, and members of the public. First-edition page proofs marked in black ink and red pencil.

Gilliver and McCulloch showed me an index of words researched for the *OED* by Dr. William Chester Minor, the American surgeon incarcerated for murder in an English insane asylum whose story is the subject of Simon Winchester's book *The Professor and the Madman*. (Minor also defined words for the 1864.) And the public plea issued by Murray in 1885 for extra quotations for specific words. "The main body of material is amply sufficient for purposes of historical illustration," he wrote, "but for the special needs here carefully examined into and noted down, special search and watchfulness on the part of all friends of the Dictionary will render most important aid." *Barmaid* needed citations before 1772; *barkingly* after 1608.

The storage room was protected by flood alarms and fire doors. An emergency rescue firm was on call. The biggest threat to the oldest material, though, was the way it was originally stored. The quotation slips from the first edition were stacked unevenly in bundles of a couple hundred apiece, strangled by twine and stuffed

---

* "A part, number, 'livraison' (of a work published by instalments)," per the *OED*'s unrevised entry. "One of the divisions of a book published in parts," in Merriam's simpler phrasing.

every which way in metal or cardboard boxes jammed in row after row of sliding gray metal shelves. McCulloch had embarked on what would be a many-years-long project: marching through the old boxes alphabetically, snipping off fraying string, restacking slips neatly, placing them in mustard-colored, acid-free folders secured with unbleached cotton tying tape. We opened a folder marked ENDANGER–ENDFULL. The quotation on the top slip, crumpled, creased, and torn, was from a 1770 letter by the pseudonymous Junius, a critic of the government of King George III. Sure enough, it was used in the entry for the word.

A small wooden tray with quotation slips, editors' notes, and entries from other dictionaries invariably sat on the desks of OED definers. Unlike at Merriam, the old paper was essential for revising and expanding the dictionary's march-of-time entries. To get a sense of how the OED slips differed from the Merriam cits, I asked McCulloch if I could examine some old ones. I couldn't settle on a specific word to investigate, so I used an online coin flipper to pick a range. The winner: words starting with *snoa* to *snof*. I parked myself in the OED's small library, and McCulloch delivered two boxes, SNIGGLE–SOFT and SNAK–SNU.* Since the OED was assembled alphabetically, those slips were gathered mostly in the early 1900s.

God knows who the last person to look at them was. I counted eighteen bundles wedged haphazardly in each of the two S boxes. I gently perused hundreds of slips, admiring the looping longhand of the OED's volunteer contributors. I paused at the first quotation for *snirt*, from 1724: "Now let her snirt, and fyk her fill." (Paging Philip Gove! But *snirt* and *fyk*, I learned, were Scottish words meaning, respectively, to snicker and to fidget.) The slips for *snoach*—"To snuffle; to breathe or speak through the nose, etc."; most recent quotation: 1888—were missing. *Snob* took up about half a stack.

---

*The boxes overlapped alphabetically because the slips in SNIGGLE–SOFT were used by editors in drafting definitions while the slips in SNAK–SNU were not.

I discovered that the spelling of *snitch'em's*, an old English card game, on the quotation slip didn't match the spelling in the headword at the top of the slip and in the *OED* itself—*snitch'ems*. I pointed out the discrepancy to Gilliver. In those days, he said, fact-checking every slip turned in by volunteer contributors, known as "readers," was impossible. Editors used their best judgment. It was crazy easy for us to check, though. I typed the first eight words of the quotation ("this game may be ranked among the fairest") into Google Books and the source, a 1798 issue of *The Sporting Magazine*, popped up. Two apostrophes. "That's a correction I can make," Gilliver said.

McCulloch wanted me to see older slips. She delivered a box labeled ASSIZE–ATTRIBUTION holding six of the bow-tied mustard folders. These words were in "Part II" of what was originally titled *A New English Dictionary on Historical Principles*. Part I stretched from *a* to *ant* and was published in 1884. Part II continued from *ant* to *batten* and was published a year later. Some of these slips likely dated to the 1850s or '60s.

I untied the folder ASSUMPTION–ASTONISH and felt the fragile weight of history. The corners of the top slip, marked 849 in the *OED*'s slip-numbering system, were folded over, the top and bottom centers torn where the string once choked a bundle. On it I read the handwritten entry for the second sense of *assumption*, "The action of taking for or upon oneself." Slip 851 was a quotation for that sense, from Horace Walpole's 1768 book *Historic Doubts on the Life and Reign of King Richard the Third*.

The *OED*'s second edition was a mash-up of the first edition, the second supplement—published in four volumes from 1972 to 1986 and incorporating the 1933 supplement—and five thousand additional new words or senses. Its twenty volumes housed 291,500 entries illustrated with 2.4 million quotations on 21,730 paper pages filled with 59 million words. The printed books seem a ridiculous anachronism now. A friend offered to give me a second edition and, as much as I like the sound of pages whooshing, I declined. The *OED* website told me the set weighs 137.72 pounds. I wasn't going to drag that around for the rest of my life.

I asked Gilliver in an email whether the old slips should be preserved, in either paper or digital form.

"Of course," he replied:

> Thinking about the slips generated in the course of the lexicography that's going on now, it's easy to think that preserving them is less important, since the bulk of our work is done electronically, and is being preserved by the rather different means that are needed for data held in that form. But really I suppose there's no difference between the newest slips and the ones created over a century and a half ago. Today's "current" materials will become "historical" in due course, and will therefore be of interest to future historians.

Still, Gilliver was cautious. Oxford had discussed digitizing the quotation slips. But that was ultimately a business and logistical decision.

"Whether we would consider throwing away the slips once they've been scanned, I wouldn't like to say, as it's a very hypothetical question, but I can see that it would be easier to contemplate storing them in some less readily accessible place."

I say scan everything, upload everything, make it searchable, use it as content—and save the originals. The physical cards aren't just a bulwark against disasters in the cloud. They have a visual and tactile power that transports whoever holds them to the date stamped thereon. And they offer a full, safeguarded record of the important business of lexicography. Every dictionary maker had its own styles and rules, and every slip might help unlock some unknown mystery about meaning, etymology, or usage, or the way humans cataloged words on paper. The slips are mileposts in the history of language, an index of the minds of the people who created them.

Among commercial dictionaries in America, Merriam's slips were 16 million three-by-five sentinels of the nation's linguistic legacy. John Morse had strong feelings about what should happen to the slips.

"What should happen to them, what should happen to all the company records, what should happen to all the editorial files, what should happen to the books." (Morse reminded me that many of the books read and marked for the *Third* were stored in the basement.) "If you had all the money in the world, you ought to start the American museum of dictionary-making and house it at 47 Federal Street and bring in an archivist. That's what ought to happen. But there isn't a lot of money to make an American museum of lexicography."

There was value in all of the material, and you didn't know where or when it would turn up. Rummaging through some old desks that were about to be junked, Kory Stamper discovered a cache of correspondence from the 1930s between Merriam and the National Bureau of Standards about defining colors. She kept it, and was fascinated. And wound up writing a book about the subject. The book you are holding (or reading digitally) couldn't have been written without the paper archives, either. Plenty of other titles benefited from visits to Merriam's dusty corners, as well as academic and journalistic dives into individual words and company history. "There's just so much hiding in these files," Stamper said.

There's a larger-scale parallel to Merriam's cits. Around the time the Merriam brothers were publishing the 1864, libraries began replacing bound book catalogs with cards. The system lasted more than a century. In the 1980s, libraries began converting their card catalogs to electronic databases. Tens of millions of physical cards—filling countless blond-wood drawers with elegant brass handles occupying acres of floor space—were unceremoniously destroyed. Sometimes they were *ceremoniously* destroyed; hundreds of cards from the University of Maryland, Baltimore's Health Sciences Library were attached by their guide holes to red and blue balloons and sent heavenward, or at least toward New Jersey. An official at one college pointed a gun at a card catalog and "shot" it. No one was remorseful.

The writer Nicholson Baker reported those examples in a 1994 *New Yorker* article titled "Discards." At a time when electronic databases were slow and error-riddled, Baker argued that cards were easy to find and simpler to read than a halting scroll of onscreen text. Thanks to "the irreplaceable intelligence of the librarians who worked on them," card catalogs steered users where they wanted to go more efficiently than digital replacements, often delivering more and better information. Their destruction was a "national paroxysm of shortsightedness and anti-intellectualism," he said.

Baker was writing at the first light of the internet, and there's little debate about the efficacy of the online library catalog today. But information often was lost in transition from paper to pixel—such as, Baker pointed out, the original price of a book, the date of acquisition, and the initials of the cataloger. Stories died, too. When a Cornell University librarian said the school's cards "have to be burned," Baker described how Vladimir Nabokov scrolled manually through the Slavic Literature trays at Cornell while translating *Eugene Onegin*. Card catalogs were a "large, conveniently packaged core sample" of the history of the library, Baker wrote, not to mention human knowledge.

As with the Merriam cits, library cards also could be beautiful—written in "library hand" penmanship designed by Melvil Dewey and Thomas Edison in the late 1800s; typed on manual Remingtons and IBM Selectrics; updated and corrected in red pencil and black ink. The Library of Congress published a book with images from its cards—"Salinger, Jerome David, (b. in New York, 1919; residence, Westport Conn.; writes short stories for the New Yorker; his first novel)." An Oregon artist painted reclaimed cards with related images. (The card for HICKOCK, RICHARD EUGENE, one of the killers in Truman Capote's *In Cold Blood*, was decorated with red splotches.)

A Massachusetts librarian asked authors to inscribe their cards with a message. "I love card catalogues, / but I only wish / mine were more dogeared!" the poet Billy Collins wrote.

At Merriam, Kory Stamper once proposed applying for a National Endowment for the Humanities grant to digitize the slips and partner with a university linguistics program to link them to entries, but the idea stalled. Google engineer Jon Orwant, who ran the Google Books project, told me that scanning the slips wouldn't be hard; Google could design a machine. I connected him with Merriam but that didn't go anywhere, either. And while Britannica owner Jacqui Safra once telephoned John Morse to inquire about using the old slips in new ways, the company didn't have the money or ambition to digitize 16 million of them.

Stamper's fear, and mine, was that, at some point in the possibly not-too-distant future, Britannica or whoever owned Merriam would sell 47 Federal Street and downsize to a smaller space. If that happened, a university might want to acquire the whole caboodle—slips, books, records. But there was a nonzero chance one wouldn't, and Merriam would break up its history, donating some of it to a library, selling some of it to private collectors, tossing a few boxes to the Smithsonian. And dumpstering the rest.

Even John Morse thought that was possible.

"This is an incredible repository of information about the language and information about dictionary-making and information about the institution that really preserved Webster's dictionary project longer than any dictionary project you can think of in the English-speaking world," he said. "On the other hand, let's face it, dictionaries come and go. I think at some point you just have to assume that civilization moves on and not all of its artifacts are preserved. You can't keep the entire historical record. I'm not happy about that."

8

collection

: something collected *especially* : an accumulation of objects gathered for study, comparison, or exhibition or as a hobby

Madeline Kripke collected books. And manuscripts, pamphlets, photographs, posters, letters, marketing manuals, advertisements, cigar boxes, newspaper and magazine articles, school workbooks, catalogs, bibliographies, lockets, matchbooks, and much, much more. Almost all of the material was about dictionaries and language. And most of it was crammed into a 1,200-square-foot loft with twelve-foot ceilings on the seventh floor of a neoclassical factory building on Perry Street in Manhattan's Greenwich Village, where, before it was converted to pricey condos in the 1980s, the Italian-language daily newspaper *Il Progresso* was printed.

I had heard a lot about Kripke's collection. Even without the scores of packed boxes in storage lockers around the city, my word friends said it was the biggest private collection of its kind, and one of the biggest of any kind—a must-see for dictionary scholars, reporters, lovers, obsessives. "Her collection is so far and away better than everything out there. Every library in the world, every collection in the world—hers blows it away," said the lexicographer and author

Jesse Sheidlower, who like other dictionary people pilgrimaged to Perry Street many times.

But the collection wasn't just big, I was told, it was important—and so was its curator, a towering figure of modern lexicography, one of the most fascinating people you'll ever meet. Near the end of 2015, I sent Kripke an introductory email with references, explained my reporting on Merriam, and said I'd be in New York the following week. Could I visit?

Kripke wrote back two days later. "You're welcome to come see my collection, though at this point my place is more untidy than ever since I've been having some physical difficulties for the last few months and am coping less well with general management," she replied. "That said, I'd still be happy to show you what I can."

Kripke said she was "unusually busy" because she had begun rehabbing an ailing hip "and on top of that I'm in the midst of a complex transfer of about 500 cartons of books from an old warehouse to a new one. And both tasks—which I've been unable to ignore or postpone—are fairly gargantuan." She praised my magazine story about the *Unabridged* in *Slate* ("a very interesting—even an impressive—read"), noting that her own recent focus "has been almost exclusively on the dictionary's history in minute detail." She concluded, "I look forward to meeting you and showing you some things if our schedules permit."

The next week, Kripke buzzed me up and opened the door. Nothing anyone had said prepared me for what I saw.

Kripke's books filled custom-made floor-to-ceiling shelves with glass fronts. They obscured counters, packed cupboards, spilled from banker's boxes, teetered on the steps of library ladders, towered from almost every plank of hardwood floor. She estimated that the apartment contained 20,000 books. Plus, she said, there were thousands more in those cartons in not one but three different storage facilities. "Everywhere you go, you're going to knock something over," Kripke said. It reminded me of the Sagrada Familia, Antoni

Gaudí's religious masterwork in Barcelona: riotously enormous and seemingly haphazard but carefully crafted and slyly cohesive. And also unfinished.

Kripke was eager to show off—and I was eager to see—the cache of nineteenth-century Merriam-Webster documents she had acquired at auction, sight unseen, contents unknown. She escorted me from the tiny table where she perused, annotated, transcribed, and cataloged to the rear of the flat. We treaded a path the width of one shovel after a blizzard, books lining the way instead of snowbanks. To the left was Kripke's doorless bedroom, which featured a Bruce Springsteen poster from his album *Born in the U.S.A.* ("Someone gave it to me. I love him. He's great.") A wall of books occupied half of a queen-size bed. Kripke slept on the other half. I hoped my gasp wasn't audible.

A wisp of a woman with short gray hair and wire-rimmed glasses, Kripke when I met her looked older than her seventy-two years. She was from Nebraska but was a New York archetype: smart, brash, tough, and combative, subsisting on Chinese takeout and a mediocre diner a few blocks away. (One frequent dictionary guest said he never saw her prepare so much as a cup of tea.) Kripke had ailments, including the deteriorating hip that made navigating her labyrinthine apartment even more challenging. She would need surgery and then, she worried, a walker, which would necessitate packing up some books to—only temporarily, she insisted—clear a wider lane.

For Hanukkah when Kripke was ten years old, her parents, Myer and Dorothy, gave her the sixth edition of Merriam's *Collegiate*, published in 1949. The dictionary unlocked the world. With it, Linnie, as she was known in her family, could read any book, at any level, and look up whatever she didn't understand. In a notebook each night, she recorded every unfamiliar word she had encountered that day. The next day, she reviewed the previous day's words. And at the end of the week, she reviewed them all at once. She remembered reading *The Frogs* by Aristophanes that year, with her dictionary as a constant companion. "You could open up a page and learn something right there, or you could intentionally open to a certain page and learn something," she said. "I just thought of it as a book of little stories—that each word contained a little story."

Kripke grew up in Omaha, in a house of intellectuals. Myer, the son of a scrap-metal and glass dealer, was the rabbi at Beth El Synagogue. Dorothy wrote children's books about Judaism, some of which became bestsellers. Kripke's preternaturally brilliant older brother, Saul, would become one of the great American philosophers of the twentieth century. As a teenager, Kripke chafed at being the rabbi's daughter and the genius's sister. She enrolled at Barnard College in New York and embraced the 1960s. "I was a bona fide hippie," she said. "I took all the drugs and slept with everybody and, you know, had a great time."

After earning a bachelor's degree in English, and then a master's in Anglo-Saxon across Broadway at Columbia, Kripke worked as a welfare case officer and trained in the new field of computers. One day, a job interview at the old telephone company Ma Bell was postponed. "I was all dressed up, dolled up in a dress and nylons and heels and makeup and lipstick and the whole thing. And I said, 'I'm not going to be all dolled up and waste my day.'" Kripke opened the *New York Times* want ads, saw one that looked interesting, called, and went straight in. She got the job, as a children's books editor at the publisher E. P. Dutton.

Kripke loved the work, but after three years she was laid off. She then freelanced as a copy editor and proofreader. Since different publishers favored different dictionaries, she filled a couple of shelves with reference books. "It dawned on me that they were really what I was interested in," Kripke said. "I don't know why." As she bought more dictionaries—usually from a store in the Flatiron Building called the Reference Book Center—she began to learn about dictionaries, peruse their bibliographies and indexes, and buy books that appealed. Then she found work in a rare-books store in the Village.

In the early 1970s, Kripke read about a notorious book by the language scholar Allen Walker Read titled *Lexical Evidence from Folk Epigraphy in Western North America: A Glossarial Study of the Low Element in the English Vocabulary.* During a trip to the western United States and Canada in 1928, Read recorded vulgar slang from bathroom stalls and wrote an eighty-three-page scholarly tract about what he had found. Prudish American publishers wouldn't touch it. Read self-published seventy-five copies in Paris.

By the time she got wind of Read's book, Kripke had amassed around three hundred dictionaries and other references. But *Lexical Evidence* sparked new curiosities: older books, and slang. A buyer friend placed an ad for her in a trade publication, *AB Bookman's Weekly*. Kripke paid $20 for a photocopy of Read's work and thought she was ripped off. Her friend suggested asking Read himself about acquiring an original. She found him in the Manhattan phonebook and arranged a meeting. Between the call and the meet-up, she realized that Read, by then an English professor at Columbia, "was this eminent personage—and I was this stumblebum." To demonstrate her seriousness, Kripke made a list of all of the language books in her library. She and Read became friends, and he became her lexicography mentor.

Kripke's collection soon overwhelmed the 350-square-foot, $70-a-month, rent-controlled walkup on West Eleventh Street where she lived for more than three decades before moving to the Perry Street condo a few blocks away. As the freelancing declined—for a time Kripke ghostwrote romance novels—the book-buying (and a little bookselling, to pay bills) accelerated. Kripke came to know every rare-books dealer, every auction house, every academic, lexicographer, and word-lover. She could be ruthless in pursuit of a title, and occasionally fell out with a dealer who in her estimation did her wrong, or a collector who acquired something she wanted.

Kripke's tastes and desires grew specific, eclectic, and expensive, and her knowledge grew as vast as her sprawling library. She didn't buy all of this stuff just to have it, though, the way some collectors do. She was an expert in the material, regaling guests with the backstory of whatever she extracted from a shelf, cabinet, or pile. "All the dealers loved her. They saw a dollar sign marching in," said Barbara Minsky, an artist and one of Kripke's close friends. "But they also saw someone who was elegantly knowledgable about every detail imaginable about everything she bought."

Like the first edition of the 1502 dictionary by the Italian monk Ambrosio Calepino that, Kripke explained, was updated and reprinted for three centuries. Or an original copy of Noah Webster's 1828. Or *A Dictionarie in English and Latin for Children* from 1602. Or a stack of late eighteenth- and early nineteenth-century volumes of the racy *National Police Gazette*. "It's very rare," Kripke said, turning pages with excitement and care. "It's chock full of slang. It's full of pugilism and sports and weightlifters and girls with petticoat skirts above their head—the *National Enquirer* of its time."

"For her, everything was a joy—these were no commodities," Tom Dalzell told me. A slang expert and author, and a prominent San Francisco labor union lawyer, Dalzell also had a large collection, though not anywhere near the size of Kripke's. "She loved showing. She loved finding something to sell you," he said. "It was a big, beautiful universe for her that was not just 'How much did this go for the last time it was up for auction?'"

Minsky put it to me this way: "She had this grin on her face. She'd look at you. Her eyes were dancing. She enjoyed it so much and she enjoyed sharing it. It gave pleasure to her to amuse you, to amuse me, to amuse anyone she brought into her lair."

Kripke began tours of the apartment by extracting a small flashlight from a pocket and wielding the beam across the dim room like a pointer. Here was the start of my guided tour:

> I have books on American English here and the shelf below and stuff that's stacked up in front of it is of the same subject matter. Then I have slang from all different languages here and here in groupings of Russian and Irish and from Argentina. And then I have, up on the top shelf, the ones about bad words because I didn't want to, you know, put them smack in front of somebody. These two shelves are criminal-gang terms, modern books with glossaries, most of them. I think there are a couple of them here that are, you know, runoffs from the top shelf.
>
> Then over here I have a lot more of the same kind of stuff, but a little bit earlier and not so modern. This shelf and that shelf I have a lot more, uh, mostly slang. Not all of it—there are some spellers and stuff, some vintage things, I mean, [circa] 1800 spellers. But then this shelf right here where I'm pointing is slang from sixteenth, seventeenth—not many sixteenths, one or two that are actually sixteenth century—seventeenth, eighteenth, nineteenth. And the ones below it the same. Then over here the top shelf is mostly French books and their slang. Those two books at the end are fashioned to have a chain go through them, and there are books of prostitutes' slang and sex workers' slang.
>
> Then below that I have professions—you know, train workers, oil workers, racetrack touts. More and more French books on the third shelf down. Then on the fourth shelf a lot of hippie and psychedelic. The next two shelves, this shelf and that shelf, are mostly cowboy and various services, military services—the Army, Navy, Air Force, flyers' slang. The stuff that's the oilfields and the racetracks, that's more like jargon rather than slang.
>
> But that's sort of the lay of the land.

The lay of the land segued to specific terrain. For me, that meant the Merriam-Webster documents. In the mid-2000s, Kripke got a call from some newbie ephemera dealers who had found her name in the membership directory of the Ephemera Society of America. Along with dictionaries, spellers, and word books, Kripke on a whim had added to her list of interests the history of the G. & C. Merriam Company. The society had never been a fruitful source; Kripke would go to its convention and find nothing relevant.

Until now. The dealers told Kripke they had been hired by descendants of Homer Merriam to sell his personal papers. Homer was an important figure in the company's history. He joined his oldest brothers, George and Charles, in Springfield in 1855, about a decade after they had acquired the rights to Webster's dictionary. He took over as president after their deaths, oversaw the publication of the 1890 unabridged and the 1898 *Collegiate*, and hired able and loyal executives who would run Merriam into the 1920s.

Kripke took a train to Connecticut to meet the dealers. She thought she had an agreement to buy the entire archive, and they settled on a price. But then rogue lots emerged, she said, from the dealer and the family, who may have realized belatedly that the material had more value than they realized. Kripke sighed and bought as much as she could. But she didn't like it, claiming (without specifics) that the original dealers and Homer's descendants had "stooped to dirty pool."

Homer's papers—dozens of boxes—had been stored in a barn in New Hampshire, and they smelled like it. Kripke deodorized the files and got to work. She erected stacks on the living-room floor (back when there was space on the living-room floor). Correspondence with printers and publishers and engravers here. Financial spreadsheets there. Advertisements. Photographs and postcards. Letters from customers. Legal briefs. Pamphlets and articles about the "War of the Dictionaries" between the Merriams and rival publisher Joseph Worcester. Prospectuses, catalogs, and ad campaigns for the landmark editions published in the late nineteenth and early twentieth centuries. The stacks were transferred into boxes, the contents of the boxes sorted into folders, the material in each folder arranged chronologically.

Shoeboxes housed literally thousands of letters. Some hadn't been touched in 150 years. Kripke first taught herself to decipher nineteenth-century handwriting. ("Some of the worst offenders were George and Charles," she said. "Homer had beautiful handwriting. Very legible.") Then she read every letter, transcribed the ones she considered historically or commercially valuable—as best she could; long dashes indicated where she couldn't make out a word or phrase—and appended notes for an assistant, who typed everything up.

On her desktop computer, Kripke opened a spreadsheet listing all of the Merriam documents. One by one, she clicked on them. She knew something about every minor character—the professor who wrote paleontology definitions; the drunk Polish royalist who revised etymologies; the missionary in Udupiddy, Ceylon (now Sri Lanka), to whom the brothers sent a dictionary.

Kripke had some favorites. One was that March 1844 letter in which George wrote to Charles about the opportunity to buy the unbound sheets of Webster's dictionary. ("Half that book would probably be worth, permanently, more than any thing we have, or ever shall have.") Kripke discovered it among the thousands of papers in the Homer archives—a puzzle piece that solved the mystery of how the Merriams came to acquire America's greatest reference work, and then usher in corporate dictionary publishing in the United States. Kripke dubbed it "The Aha Letter," and the name stuck.

Kripke suspected that Homer's family and dealers had extracted from his papers correspondence that might have stand-alone value—like the letters I had read in the Beinecke Library at Yale, to and from presidents and dignitaries. But one had fallen through the cracks and into her hands: a neat and polite April 1849 letter to the Merriam brothers from a Brooklyn newspaperman named Walter Whitman.

Before composing his most famous works of poetry, Walt Whitman edited several newspapers and wrote hundreds of features, editorials, and reviews. At the time the founder and editor of an antislavery weekly, the *Brooklyn Freeman*, Whitman told the Merriams that he had "published one long notice (written by me)" about their first Webster's dictionary, the 1847, and two shorter ones but had not received a courtesy copy. "If convenient, upon receipt of this, I wish you would envelope a Dictionary and put on it my address," he wrote, six years before the publication of *Leaves of Grass*. He requested a book bound in top-of-the-line Russia leather, "black, or some other dark color."

Kripke gently removed the letter from a box. It was encased in a plastic sleeve adorned with a yellow Post-it. "This was history," she said.

Kripke spent more than $100,000 on Homer Merriam's papers. A 1619 dictionary in her collection was valued at $60,000 and her 1828 Webster at $16,500. She paid $27,650 for a 1633 edition of a rare grammar book, *The English Schoolmaster* by Edward Coote. *The Scoundrel's Dictionary* (1754) and *The Swell's Night Guide Through the Metropolis* (1841) cost more than $13,000 apiece. The 1502 Calepino: $12,000. *Cab Calloway's Cat-o-Logue* (1938): $7,500. I neglected to ask how much she paid for a ledger written by Noah Webster detailing his expenses on the 1828 dictionary. "Sort of a pride and joy item," she said.

The collection comprised perhaps thousands of individual purchases. They weren't all four- and five-figure line items—in the early years, her priciest acquisitions were a few hundred bucks apiece, tops. But overall? No one disputed that over the previous five decades,

Kripke had spent more than a million dollars buying books and other stuff about words.

Kripke didn't volunteer the source of her wealth. She told me offhandedly that her parents helped her buy the loft apartment, as if she was a recent college grad getting settled in the big city. But the story of Kripke's money wasn't a secret. It dated to the early 1960s in Omaha, when a woman who lived a couple of blocks away read one of Kripke's mother's books, *Let's Talk About God*, and invited the author over. Dorothy and Myer Kripke immediately hit it off with Susie Buffett and her husband.

Warren Buffett was in his early thirties and doing well investing for modestly wealthy clients. The Kripkes had inherited some money on both sides of their family and had saved some of their own. Dorothy encouraged Myer to ask their new friend Warren to invest for them, too. "He doesn't want the kind of money we have," the rabbi demurred. After a few years, though, he relented. The Kripkes' $67,000 was around three times less than what Buffett's typical clients entrusted with him, but he said yes. "I wasn't admitting many people in the 1960s," Buffett told the *New York Times*. "But I liked Myer. I wanted people who, if it went bad, we could still be friends."

Over thirty years, the Kripkes' modest investment grew to an astonishing $25 million. "Like an atomic bomb," Rabbi Kripke told another reporter. The Kripkes' story was in the news because they were donating $7 million to the Jewish Theological Seminary in Manhattan to help rebuild a tower that had been destroyed in a fire. Dorothy Karp and Myer Kripke had met in a class at the seminary and, in 1937, a week after Myer was ordained, were married in a courtyard below it.

The Kripkes lived frugally. They never moved from their three-bedroom rental apartment in Omaha, and never bought a fancy car or clothes that weren't on sale. They planned to donate the bulk of their money (the seminary would get another $8 million) and they gave some to their children. The money allowed Madeline

Kripke, by the late 1990s, to be a full-time collector and to buy the Village loft and fill it with her passion. After Myer died in 2014 at the age of 100, price was no obstacle in his daughter's pursuits.

Kripke was fully aware of the breadth and quality of her collection—and that she needed to figure out what would happen to it after she died. She talked about that in dictionary circles for at least two decades, and publicly when asked. "If I magically had my druthers," she told a journalist in 2013, "I could just buy a building and declare it the Dictionary Library or the Lexicography Museum, and have an institution carry it on." Over the years she flirted with one university or another. Her brother had established the Saul Kripke Center at the City University of New York to house his vast array of philosophical and mathematical work. A Madeline Kripke Center could have done the same for her vast array of lexicographical material.

But Madeline Kripke delayed and delayed—and collected and collected, and worked with a rotating cast of assistants to perform the Sisyphean task of cataloging it all. She stopped inviting friends over; the only people allowed in the apartment were her amanuenses and dictionary-curious people like me. "She was online all the time buying. She would say, 'I spent five thousand on a book today, Barbara,'" her friend Barbara Minsky said. "I rarely saw her. She really threw away everybody."

Then came covid. On April 25, 2020, six weeks to the day after the World Health Organization declared the pandemic, Kripke died in one of the hospitals that made New York the gruesome epicenter of a global crisis. News of her death spread on Twitter. "Oh, god, no," Jesse Sheidlower wrote. "This is a tragedy, on many levels," said another admirer, Merriam editor Ammon Shea. "She was an amazing person and kind and generous in sharing with fellow lexicographers," John Morse commented. "It is hard to imagine a world without her."

The *Times* published a lengthy obituary. The headline called Kripke the "doyenne of dictionaries." The cause of death was reported as the coronavirus and complications of pneumonia. A remembrance in the journal of the Dictionary Society of North America described her as "the greatest collector of dictionaries, primarily those of slang, that the world has known, and very likely will ever know." She was seventy-six. Admirers gathered to memorialize her on Zoom.

Kripke died without a will. Her brother became the administrator of her estate. Nearing eighty himself, Saul Kripke was engaged with compiling, editing, and cataloging his own lifetime of brilliance; he was the enfant terrible of philosophy, one of the most prolific philosophers of all time, much of his work unpublished. The siblings had a complicated relationship, which Madeline Kripke made clear whenever Saul's name came up. But upon his sister's death, Saul set any animosity aside. "Whatever their relationship was previously," Jesse Sheidlower said, "he was aware of the importance of this as a scholarly thing."

It was impossible to appraise the monetary value of Kripke's collection with pinpoint accuracy. At her death, Kripke and her assistants had cataloged around six thousand items in a spreadsheet that ran to 1,909 pages and 726,982 words, and that was only a third or so of the trove. The easiest and most profitable course would have been to hire a dealer to sell everything, book by book, item by item. Instead, Saul convened some of Kripke's lexicography colleagues—Sheidlower, Dalzell, Shea, slang dictionary editor Jonathon Green, Indiana University English professor and dictionary historian Michael Adams. Saul asked the group for advice: What is the collection worth? What options do I have to dispose of it? The panel agreed that not only would Kripke have wanted her collection to remain intact and publicly accessible, but selling it off in lots would diminish not only its scholarly value but her legacy.

The participants kept their deliberations secret, preventing collectors from swooping in to contact other family members with offers. Three universities were interested: Michigan, where Kripke had been close with a venerable language scholar; Stanford, which had a substantial dictionary collection and a lexicography research program; and Indiana, which had recently acquired nine tons of material from the family of twentieth-century American dictionary-maker Clarence Barnhart and also held the papers of the slang lexicographer Eric Partridge, a first edition of the *OED* in fascicles, and a first edition of Samuel Johnson's dictionary, plus dictionaries related to at least six hundred different languages.

According to people involved in the process, Michigan was hoping to receive the collection as a gift, while Stanford wouldn't guarantee keeping it whole. That gave Indiana the inside track. Adams recused himself from the advisory panel and prepared a pitch promising that the collection would welcome public use. A coffee-table book, seminars about the history of dictionaries and English, colloquiums and conferences about slang and Merriam-Webster, on-campus exhibits, a retrospective on Kripke's life—Adams had a long list of ideas. "I just tried to make it clear that, if the collection came to Indiana, it wouldn't gather dust in a storage facility," he said.

Indiana, a public institution, didn't have millions lying around for acquisitions; its stately but modest Lilly Library for rare books and special collections is no slouch but, financially, Harvard's Houghton Library or Princeton's Firestone Library it ain't. Still, the Lilly recently had received a million-dollar donation earmarked for a special purchase. The universities were asked for two sealed bids, one for the Merriam-Webster documents and one for everything else. Stanford offered the most money, I was told. But the family accepted the offer that ensured the collection wouldn't be dispersed: Indiana, which bid a total of $780,000. It would cost an additional $70,000 to pack and ship the material from Greenwich Village to Bloomington. Kripke's lifework had a new home.

collection

In June 2021, more than a year after Kripke's death, Indiana library staff made a site visit to her apartment. The stacks had grown since I'd visited. Photos revealed the refrigerator now topped with dictionaries—a century old? two? three?—that climbed to the ceiling. Kripke's tiny desk was under siege from a Jenga tower of documents. The guest bathroom, relatively clear when I had been there, was now home to old boxes and new acquisitions still shrouded in brown wrapping paper.

Amid the clutter it was easy to miss the grandeur in plain sight, the order that existed in Kripke's beautiful mind, if not on her floors and walls and countertops and cabinets. You could see that rough design in a photo from that day the Indiana librarians visited—one section of the custom cherry bookshelves built when Kripke moved into the converted factory building two decades earlier.

It's a tiny sliver of the collection, exactly a hundred books and pamphlets on four shelves each a couple of feet long, part of the wall that she described for me on her flashlight tour. There were some of Kripke's greatest joys—books about the language and culture of tramps, hobos, and the unhoused, Americans down on their luck. *Four Years in the Underbrush: Adventures as a Working Woman* (anonymous, 1921); *The Milk and Honey Route: A Handbook for Hobos by Hobos* (Dean Stiff, 1931); *The Hobo's Hornbook: a Repertory for a Gutter Jongleur* (George Milburn, 1930).

Kripke had lined up a few favored pamphlets face out, protected in plastic sleeves. *An Earnest Plea for the Homeless Men and Boys of Bowery* (1905), about the Bowery Mission in New York, founded in 1867. *Tramp Jokes: Recitations and Monologues* (1908). (A sample: "Jack Feedem—Would you really 'hustle' if a job should be offered you? Tired Thomson—Would I! Why, I'd run a mile widout stopping!") And *The Hobo Philosopher or the Modern Diogenes* (Roger Payne, 1928). Each had cultural and historical value; each told a story about places, people, and times. Kripke would have been delighted to relate them all to you.

Moving trucks weren't allowed on cobblestoned Perry Street, so, in November 2021, Kripke's apartment was emptied one vanload at a time. The boxes were shuttled across the Hudson River to a warehouse in New Jersey and reloaded into two semis for the 750-mile journey to Indiana. They arrived in December and made a reverse commute: unloaded at the university's main storage facility, shuttled by vans to the main campus, and deposited for inventory on the highest floor of the Herman B. Wells Library, a modernist structure made of Indiana limestone that looks like two boxes lying side by side, one five stories high and one ten.*

In the end, Kripke's apartment filled 856 white banker's boxes. More than half of them—490—contained fewer than twenty-five items. Another 174 held more than twenty-five. Documents, ephemera, and letters filled 170. The rest were miscellaneous or unknown. A cluttered back room housed the several hundred boxes from Kripke's storage units in Manhattan, contents also miscellaneous and unknown.

I visited the collection's new home in the fall of 2022. Most of Kripke's apartment boxes were stacked three and four high on wooden pallets. Others were slotted in cubbies lining a wall. Seven pallets, out of a total of sixty, had been unpacked, their contents arranged unscientifically on metal shelves: *Lexicography and the OED*; *Every Goy's Guide to Common Jewish Expressions*; *A Wife's Guide to Baseball* by Hall of Fame pitcher Bob Gibson's then wife, Charline.

The ultimate goal: a searchable online database of every item in the Kripke Collection, as it was now known, carefully tagged with identifying metadata. Erika Dowell, the Lilly Library's associate director and curator of modern books and manuscripts, said the

---

*There wasn't room in the grander Lilly Library to store and sort Kripke's boxes, but the Lilly would be the place for exhibitions of the collection.

process was slow and tedious. Each box had to be opened, inventoried using bibliographic software called Zotero, repacked and relabeled, and sent to Indiana's main storage facility. The books were easy; more painstakingly, tens of thousands of documents comprising hundreds of thousands of pieces of paper would have to be examined and sorted. The project would likely take a revolving-door team of part-time catalogers and archivists, mostly graduate students, a decade or more to complete.

"It feels kind of overwhelming," I said to Dowell.

"Oh, yeah," she replied. "It does."

Indiana's Michael Adams wore a trim gray beard and rimless glasses. He talked quickly and stepped lively. At academic conferences only, he donned a dark suit and bow tie. Adams specializes in the history of English, with a subspecialty in dictionaries. He had edited *American Speech*, headed the Dictionary Society of North America, and helped compile a dictionary of Middle English; he authored books about slang in *Buffy the Vampire Slayer*, profanity, and invented languages like Klingon and Tolkien's Quenya and Sindarin. He was working on a biography of Allen Walker Read, Kripke's mentor.

Like Kripke, Adams took joy in the linguistically seemingly mundane. Like Kripke, he was insatiably curious. Like Kripke, he believed that every book or pamphlet or photo or advertisement or trinket contained a story that was worth sharing.

Adams met Kripke at the dictionary society's biennial conference in 1997. She was a founding member of the group, in 1975, and attended every meeting until her health began to wane. Adams never traveled to Kripke's apartment. But they had long talks about her latest acquisitions and interests. Kripke emailed photos of items she knew Adams would appreciate, or covet. One was a specially bound edition of the short-lived *Dictionary of American English on Historical Principles* inscribed in faux medievalist type for King George VI and his royal consort, Queen Elizabeth, when they visited the United States in 1939. Only a handful were produced—one for the royal couple, one for President Roosevelt, one apiece for the book's British editors. Kripke teased Adams about which copy she might own.

And now he was the caretaker of Kripke's legacy—"a once-in-a-lifetime or -career acquisition," he said. Adams couldn't believe his good luck. "I manage to serve lexicography, my friend, and Indiana University all at the same time. What an opportunity." He revered Kripke's respect for lexicography and the ferocity of her appetites. "What Madeline understood that I think way too few people understand is that dictionaries, every single one of them, are windows on a culture," Adams told me. "She just saw them connected to the lives of people in ways that other people don't. They see them as dusty tomes or doorstops or booster seats at home, or tools to get things done. She saw them as emblems of human aspiration and endeavor."

When I met Adams in the tenth-floor room turned over to the collection, he was measuring an oversize, hollow replica of *Webster's Third*—twenty by fifteen by six inches—used to market the book. Adams was planning to blog about random finds from the Kripke boxes. The replica would be the subject of one of his first posts. I recognized the item from Perry Street. Kripke kept it on her fireplace mantel. Adams had seen it in the photos taken on the site visit. And then it happened to be in one of the first boxes he unlidded.

Like a kid on Christmas morning is a tired simile, but the only thing missing for its application here was wrapping paper. Before my arrival, Adams already had found a stack of holiday cards written by the lexicographer Eric Partridge from 1938 to 1977 (Box 352) and a small plastic box containing more than a hundred postcards exchanged between Robert Burchfield, the chief editor of the second supplement to the *Oxford English Dictionary*, the volumes published from 1972 to 1986, and a contributor named Wilfred Granville, who supplied cits and comments for entries from *bloke* to *man-hours* to *beef chit*, meaning "menu" (Box 346).

We kept hunting. A collection of Merriam-Webster advertisements, with an attached note written by Kripke. A pile of U.S. government-issued World War II foreign-language phrasebooks. A set of school dictionaries from 1929. Sheafs of 1970s puzzle paperbacks. One box contained big-ticket items, including a 1720 dictionary, *The New World of Words: Or, Universal English Dictionary*, which had more than 47,000 entries, and *Vocabulario Italiano & Inglese, a Dictionary of Italian and English*, a 1659 book with a bookplate identifying it as part of the collection of Steve Demakopoulos, an economist who collected dictionaries, especially ones in or about modern Greek. In a nearby box we found a book written by Demakopoulos, *Do You Speak Greek?*, with an inscription: "Dear Madeline, The Greek language in all its beauty, which you well know, thanking you for all the books you found for me."

From Box 166 Adams extracted a soft, puffy pink plastic dictionary, like a baby book. On the cover, a ponytailed teenage girl sits atop volumes labeled WEBSTER'S and DICTIONARY. She is pointing at a book in her other hand—presumably that very book—and laughing. DIG THESE DEFINITIONS! is written across the top.

Adams would later discover that the book was part of a line of products aimed at teen girls, and connect it to other books in Kripke's collection that we unearthed that same day—a 1962 glossary of teen slang based on the TV show *The Many Lives of Dobie Gillis* and an autographed copy of *Steve Allen's Bop Fables*, a 1955 book in which the comedian reimagines children's stories for the hip new times. "When she collected them, long after she lived through the cultural change they represent," Adams would write, "she saw them in context and took them seriously, not as foam on the top of more serious cultural matters."

Adams left to teach a class and I spent a few more hours rummaging. If this were a movie, a rapid-cut montage would whiz before your eyes. An *"Assemble-It-Yourself" Edition (15 Sections and a Two-Part Binder)* of a non-Merriam-Webster's unabridged from the 1950s. Issues of the saucy *Snatch Sampler* magazine by Robert Crumb and other illustrators published in 1977. ("We really like drawing dirty cartoons!" they wrote. "It helps us get rid of pent-up anxieties and repressions and all that kind of stuff. . . . We hope you enjoy lookin' at 'em as much as we enjoy drawin' 'em!!") An issue of *Pennsylvania Magazine* edited by Thomas Paine from 1776. *OED* fascicles and full sets. A film canister labeled "Porn (late '30s?)." The childhood spelling records of George S. Merriam, son of founding brother George. A 1966 issue of the men's magazine *Mr.* with a feature on "The Hippie's Lexicon." Probably the world's most extensive collection of the tiny, very (very) graphic comic booklets known as Tijuana bibles, which peaked in popularity in the 1930s. I had never seen one before. Hoo-boy!

As someone familiar with obsessive passions, I felt like I understood Kripke's vacuum-cleaner approach. She was consumed by one thing. She dedicated her life to it. She let nothing and no one distract her. Everything else fell away. That's how it is for GOATs, I thought, and, in her highly circumscribed world, Kripke was the undisputed GOAT.*

She was also like a swarm of desert locusts devouring everything in their path—ruthless, single-minded, insatiable. Yes, she could lecture with expert specificity about what filled her apartment, and her acquisitions had genuine monetary and, more important, historical value. But she knew what she had become. "She did not confuse herself with a normal person—she was aware of her own craziness," Tom Dalzell said. "But she always had someone who was crazier that she could tell you about." Still, there were boxes she didn't even know existed, items that she had purchased because they were listed on eBay or in a rare-books catalog but never found time to inspect and consume.

Before leaving Bloomington, I spent a couple of hours with the head of the Lilly Library, Joel Silver, who had greenlit the Kripke

---

*I would later draft a definition for *GOAT*, also *G.O.A.T.*, "greatest of all time."

acquisition. Silver, a scholar of rare books and an expert in special collections, had lived his forty-year career at the library. With abundant pride, he escorted me inside a small, temperature-controlled (low sixties) room behind a bank-vault dial lock where the Lilly's "best, scarcest, and most expensive" holdings lived.

This movie montage should move more slowly, documentary style: George Washington's letter accepting the presidency; one of the twenty-six extant copies of the first printing of the Declaration of Independence; Thomas Jefferson's markups on the Bill of Rights. The earliest known manuscript of "Auld Lang Syne," included by Scottish poet Robert Burns in a letter to a friend. Ian Fleming's corrected typescripts for his James Bond novels. First editions of everything from Joseph Smith's *The Book of Mormon* to Edward Gibbon's *The History of the Decline and Fall of the Roman Empire* to Adam Smith's *The Wealth of Nations* to Karl Marx's *Das Kapital*. WITH COMPLIMENTS OF A. LINCOLN, reads the inscription on a first edition of the Lincoln-Douglas debates.

"Have you ever held an Oscar?" Silver asked. I hadn't. I donned white cotton archival gloves and hoisted John Ford's 1941 Best Director Academy Award for *The Grapes of Wrath*. (Oscar is heavy!) I turned the pages of a first edition of Johnson's 1755 dictionary, and of the plan for his work that Johnson had prepared for the Earl of Chesterfield, "One of His Majesty's Principal Secretaries of State," eight years before, and of the handwritten manuscripts of Eric Partridge's *A Dictionary of the Underworld*, written three hundred years later. I suspected a copy of that would turn up in one of the Kripke boxes.

Kripke's stash was the biggest acquisition in sheer volume (and one of the most expensive) that the Lilly Library had made since Silver arrived in the 1980s. Technically, it complemented the university's existing holdings, giving Indiana a foam finger of bragging rights as the lexicography capital of North America. The overwhelming majority of the material might not be Historically Important— signed by Honest Abe or presented onstage in Hollywood. But in those public-university rooms, or in Kripke's apartment, it was easy to understand that history didn't judge or discriminate. You could find value in it all—in a Noah Webster letter from 1806 (also in the climate-controlled vault) or a pink plastic novelty item from the 1950s.

Kripke's ultimate gift was letting others smell and touch and read in the original what she had gathered, meticulously and haphazardly, and figure out for themselves what it contributed to our collective culture. "There's something about the originals and being in the presence of the originals, studying them, handling them, that you can't get in any other way," Silver said before we exited the room. "It's not just what is contained in these books. It's the container itself that transmits knowledge."

Madeline Kripke, rest in peace, left the world a lot of containers.

9
slur

: an insulting or disparaging remark or innuendo

 mustard-colored filing cabinet in the Merriam basement bore a typewritten label in a slot across the front:

CORRESPONDENCE

N-WORD

SQUAW

The cabinet's drawers were packed so tightly I had to wriggle the folders to pull them out. A few concerned a 2004 letter-writing campaign about *squaw*. The 2003 edition of the *Collegiate* defined the word as "an American Indian woman" and "WOMAN, WIFE" and labeled the senses, respectively, *now often offensive* and *usually disparaging*. A Native American group in Idaho, the Women of Color Alliance, complained that Merriam's definition was "incomplete" and did not "encompass the pain and damage in the history of this word as a racial slur." It added that the word originally was a disparaging term for female genitalia.

Merriam replied to the group that *squaw* derived from a Massachusett word meaning "woman" and that the genitalia story came from a 1973 book and was unsubstantiated. "There has in fact never been any evidence put forward to support this derivation," an editor wrote. The episode received little or no media attention.

The same couldn't be said for the rest of the drawer. In September 1997, an African American affairs magazine, *Emerge*, published a brief item about two women from Michigan offended by Merriam's definition of the n-word* as "a black person" or "a member of any dark-skinned race." Delphine Abraham, a computer technician from Ypsilanti, said she was shocked to discover how the word was defined. She called Merriam and spoke to John Morse and launched a petition drive against the company. Kathryn Williams, the curator of an African American history museum in Flint, said she was outraged after speaking to a young person and finding the entry. She called the NAACP, which organized a protest campaign. The women argued that Merriam's definition of the word implied that every Black person was one.

The company received scores of angry letters, all of them preserved in the folders in the basement. I sat down at a long table in the unused former cafeteria and read them. They are blunt and passionate and often profane. One was from Williams, the museum curator. "What gives you the right to define an entire race of people?" she wrote. "The word is used as a racist and oppressive term and by you putting this word in your dictionary . . . Merriam-Webster is promoting racism and oppression." Like many other correspondents, Williams said the word to her meant "an ignorant person." She asked Merriam to devise a "neutral" definition—or, if it couldn't, to excise the word entirely.

Merriam responded to every letter, fax, and phone call, more than two thousand in all. The company abhorred the use of this racial slur and wasn't being racist, John Morse told correspondents. He said

---

*The word and the shortened *n-word* appear several times in this chapter. I've chosen to spell out the full word only in historical quotations.

that the *Emerge* story purposefully omitted the usage note explaining just how offensive Merriam judged the word—"perhaps the most offensive and inflammatory racial slur in English," the note said. He said there was no published evidence for the meaning "an ignorant person." And he explained that Merriam did not invent words, it merely defined them based on published evidence.

"To remove the word from the dictionary," Morse wrote, "would simply mislead people by creating the false impression that racial slurs are no longer part of our culture, and that, tragically, is not the case."

The dictionary was rational, as the dictionary always was. But the mail kept coming, and so did media attention. Merriam announced it would consult with outside "scholars and educators" about all offensive terms. The result was a new policy: For more than two hundred words deemed *offensive*, the italicized warning label would be moved to the front of the entry, before the definition. The layout reordering didn't satisfy Merriam's critics—with reason, because the definitions themselves would remain unchanged. "The only thing they are planning to do is switch the words around," Delphine Abraham said. The NAACP threatened to investigate Merriam's hiring practices (the company didn't employ any Black editors at the time).

No amount of clinical instruction on the dispassionate process of dictionary-making could elide the reality: The definition of the n-word or any other toxic word was by nature political. How words are received by those who write, speak, and read them is, in the end, a personal consideration. Everyone will never be satisfied, nor can they be. White people can't understand how the word could sting a Black person's ears, or what it might feel like to see it in print.

In the first sentence of chapter 1 of his 2002 book about the n-word, which employed it as a one-word title, Harvard Law School professor

Randall Kennedy asked rhetorically how it should be defined. Kennedy didn't attempt to play lexicographer. His 148-page book explores the word's every application, alteration, and reclamation, and quotes hundreds of examples of its use. Still, in recounting the episode at Merriam, Kennedy, who is Black, landed on the publisher's side. The campaign against the definition was "misguided," he wrote. The dictionary "defined the term adequately."

The entry didn't then and still doesn't explore the word's every nuance—as a term of bigotry or endearment, of familiarity or contempt, of brute force or offhanded banter. Instead, Merriam flashed the reddest light possible, recognized the word's broad sources (the usage note, which first appeared in the 1993 *Collegiate*, said that Joseph Conrad, Mark Twain, and Charles Dickens had used it in their writing), noted "use by and among blacks is not always intended or taken as offensive," and left it at that.

But the word was perennially one of the most looked up on the Merriam website. And it had skirted revision during the online *Unabridged* project, which had an unmet goal of updating the 10,000 most-searched words. It might have been uncomfortable, but answering society's thorniest linguistic questions was part of the mission of the modern dictionary.

I asked University of Arizona linguistics professor Sonja Lanehart about Merriam's definition. Lanehart, who is Black, edited *The Oxford Handbook of African American Language*. She said her main complaint was the lack of explication of the dialectal differences. "For this particular word, in order to do it justice, I think the dictionary has to get these different nuances, in the same way they would with anything else," Lanehart said. "I think it's a cop-out just to say it's the most offensive term. Why? In what context? It's probably one of the most *contested* terms. It's an extremely offensive term in certain contexts. But it's not in every context.

"I think we're processing toward the end of the debate between older generations and younger generations—'You don't know your history, you shouldn't use that word' sort of thing. And even processing through 'Oh well, they're just doing reclamation, they're embracing something that had been negative and now they're making it a positive thing.' It's more complicated than just those easy labels that we want to put on what it is."

The word derives from the Latin word *niger*, meaning "black." The earliest known published use in English is from 1574. In America, it's from 1619, when colonist John Rolfe wrote in his diary: "About the last of August came in a dutch man of warre that sold us twenty Negars." The word was spelled variously—every vowel except O shows up in early renderings—and historians describe early usage as neutral and descriptive. The *OED* records the first derogatory use in 1775 in a British ballad during the Revolutionary War. But it probably was a pejorative earlier. Ignatius Sancho, a child of enslaved parents who after their deaths became an intellectual and writer in England, wrote in 1766 that he was "one of those whom the vulgar and illiberal call '*Negurs*.'"

In his 1828 dictionary, Noah Webster didn't include any spelling as a slur. At the entry for *Negro*, however, he made a parenthetical comment: "It is remarkable that our common people retain the exact Latin pronunciation of this word, *neger*." In the Unabridged Room one morning, I deshelved each edition of the big book. The word didn't appear in Webster's revised 1841 edition or the first Merriam edition in 1847 or a new printing in 1859. Other vulgarities were omitted, too. I finally found it in the 1864, defined as "A negro;—in derision or depreciation."

The word would never leave a Merriam unabridged again—though definers would tinker with the entry as if defusing a bomb. In 1909, editors added the descriptive "now usually contemptuous." *Contemptuous* ("manifesting or expressing contempt or disdain," per the 1909 definition) was stronger than *depreciative* (disparaging or belittling). Perhaps some long-gone cits for that edition showed an increase in hateful usage. But in *Webster's Second* in 1934, the word was downgraded to "usually derogatory"—*derogatory* bearing the softer meaning "expressive of a low opinion : DISPARAGING." The entry carried no warning. It was a citizen of American speech, the definition implied, a common form of address. That the word was *colloquial* was the worst Merriam had to say.

In a linear foot of slips in the Consolidated Files, I found an excerpt from a three-page typewritten letter to Merriam written on May 1, 1944, by "Lieut. Milton C. Wright (a negro)," as the editor who filed the slip identified him. Wright wrote:

> Since your work has such a phenomenal educational and informative value, to avoid dissemination of a term which is the bane of colored folk the world over it would be a most humanitarian gesture on your part to exclude the word or term altogether or at least to so treat it in defining it that its usage would constitute a serious ignominy and disgrace to the user.

I was awed and saddened. Awed because of the strength it must have taken for Lieutenant Wright to confront the certainly white gatekeepers at this certainly white institution about the most toxic, dehumanizing word in the language, the word with the power to stab him like a bayonet to the gut. Saddened because of the flattery, deference, and restraint he demonstrated in order to be heard at all.

But Lieutenant Wright was in fact heard. His letter appears, at least in part, to have prompted an associate editor, Edward F. Oakes, to examine the entry. Oakes is pictured in the front matter of the *Second* with his colleagues, with a suave mustache and an El Capitan of hair hurtling skyward from his forehead. On October 16, 1944, Oakes typed his thoughts onto three slips.

The first listed how Merriam and its competitors had handled the word since 1909. Funk & Wagnalls: "A word once in good use but now vulgar and opprobrious." Thorndike: "Word used in an unfriendly way." Winston: "Now usually a contemptuous or vulgar term." Oakes clinically recorded the *Second*'s "favorite labels for insulting appellations." *Yid* (Jewish), *hunky* (Central or Eastern European), *guinea* (Italian), *harp* (Irish), *squarehead* (German or Scandinavian), *spiggoty* (Spanish American), and *dinge* (Black) were merely *slang*. *Kike* (Jewish), *wop* (Italian), and *greaser* (Mexican) were *derogatory*. *Dago* (Italian or Spanish) and *skibby* (Japanese) were used *in contempt*.

On the second slip, Oakes wrote,

Full account of the usage seems something like this

—used mostly by whites, commonly in illiterate speech and in the speech of all classes in some localities, either as an emotionally colorless assertion of class superiority by the speaker over dark-skinned people or as an expression of contempt, or insolence, or wanton insult; also occasionally by Negroes, as formerly by both white owners and slaves, in familiar or affectionate style of speech

Superiority, contempt, insolence, insult. Oakes's thoughts seem progressive for 1944, as I'd come to expect from academic, neutral Merriam. I appreciated the effort to better reflect the gravity of the entry. On the third slip, Oakes suggested possible revisions:

1. —chiefly in vulgar or class-conscious speech. A Base Word.
2. —in illiterate speech or contemptuous superiority. Objectionable.
3. —used to emphasize racial distinction. Banned from Good Usage.
4. —usually in illiterate speech or disdainful reference.
5. —an offensive term, in illiterate use or in haughty contempt.
6. —Disparaging & Usually Contemptuous or Illiterate.
7. —Substandard Word, Usually Abusive or Illiterate.
8. —Offensive, Chiefly Illiterate or Contemptuous.

9.—ineligible for use except in rude or insulting speech.
10. —Offensive Usage.

"None of the 10 revisions is quite accurate," he concluded, "but any one ought to partially appease the plaints like Lt. Wright's."

Oakes stamped the slip with his initials, E. F. O., and then asked two other senior definers, John Bethel and Lucius Holt, to weigh in on what might be better "for meeting the demand of colored folk that this word be stigmatized in the Dict." Oakes noted that another editor, Edward Fuchs, favored option seven: *Substandard Word, Usually Abusive or Illiterate*. Bethel responded that he and Holt agreed that "literacy" had nothing to do with it. "One can hardly brand the educated white South as illiterate because of this locution," he wrote. His suggestion was a simple "objectionable, and usually contemptuous" or "an objectionable word, now usually used contemptuously."

Merriam did update the entry in 1947, to "(*A substandard term*) A Negro; — often used familiarly, now chiefly contemptuously." The revision squeezed some of Oakes's sixty-word summation into the one line of text available in the new printing. *Contemptuous* was a step up from *disparaging. Familiarly* implied it was sometimes used in an acceptable way. But if the objective was merely to "appease the plaints like Lt. Wright's" and meet "the demand of colored folk," then maybe Merriam was no more progressive than the rest of the country. Maybe the multi-degreed empiricists on Merriam's staff—the four abovementioned editors had PhDs from Harvard, Yale, and the University of Chicago—couldn't shed the innate racial biases of their privileged northern white lives, and of American life generally.

More than a decade later, as work on the *Third* lumbered toward conclusion, an editor named Ed Gates examined a bunch of citations. Gates was a relatively new general definer at the time, so it's doubtful he would have been entrusted with such a sensitive entry. He might have given it a first look, though.

Times were changing. The date stamped on the cits that Gates perused is May 7, 1959. I looked at that day's *New York Times*. Page 22 carried three stories: a Black civil rights leader saying, after the acquittal of a white man for attempting to rape a Black woman in Monroe, North Carolina, that Black people "must even be willing to kill if necessary" if the courts cannot protect them; parents protesting the firing of teachers in Little Rock, Arkansas, by school board members opposed to court-ordered desegregation; and the indictment of four white men for the gang rape of a Black college student in Tallahassee, Florida. Maybe Gates read the *Times* that morning. Maybe it shaped his thinking about race in America and his task for the day. I wished I could go back and ask him.

Deciphering stamps on a stack of cits is like reading the future in a deck of tarot cards. The slips can't tell us Ed Gates's state of mind, his political leanings, or his opinions on the civil rights movement. But they can tell us what he determined was useful in assessing a particular word. In addition to the letter from Lieutenant Wright, Gates marked a 1936 article in *American Speech* by a linguist who wrote that, "whatever the undertones," the pronunciation of "Negro" in East Texas as the slur was "a means of keeping the Black man in his place." And also an excerpt from a 1945 United States government manual, *Guide to Command of Negro Naval Personnel*, which stated that "Negroes prefer to be referred to in their individual capacities as Americans without racial designation." The word in question, it said, "is especially hated and it has no place in the Naval vocabulary."

Ultimately, the word's treatment in the *Third* rested with editor in chief Philip Gove. Gove had tried to clean up the chopped salad of monitory labels that declared that *yid* was *slang* but *kike* was *derogatory*. Those terms must have created more questions in readers' minds than clarity. Gove's breakthrough was replacing the multifarious labels on many racial, ethnic, and religious slurs with a single term: *offensive*.

So the word was defined in the *Third* with two senses: "negro" and "a member of any dark-skinned race." Both senses were *usu. taken to be offensive*. One problem was that "taken" put the onus of the offense on the target of the slur, not on the user. Another was the frequency of the perceived act. While the dictionary said that the n-word itself was *usually* taken to be offensive, it decided that *jigaboo* was only *often* taken that way.

Merriam didn't survey Black people and tally the results. We can safely conclude that, hearing the words spat offhandedly from the lips or typing fingers of white people seeking to diminish their humanity, Black people always considered them offensive.

I performed a similar exercise for another slur: *redskin*. I wasn't alone at the time in believing that the then name of the National Football League team in Washington, DC, was racist, and that its continued existence therefore made *redskin* the most widely used racial slur in print. It boggled the mind that the team had gotten away with propagating the slur for so long. Could Merriam's slips and entries explain why the word retained a patina of acceptability?

Redskin in both the *Unabridged* and the OWL was defined as "a North American Indian" with a label—*usually offensive*—that gave the NFL team's then owner, Dan Snyder, room to claim, as he had done, that the name wasn't racist. (Only *usually* offensive! Not *always!*) But the last time Merriam had updated *redskin*, for its 2009 *Learner's Dictionary*, it upgraded the label to something more definitive—*informal + offensive*—and appended a note: "The word *redskin* is very offensive and should be avoided." That wasn't quite as strong as the note in the same book at the entry for the n-word—"This is one of the most offensive words in English. Do not use this word."—but it was strong nonetheless.

In 2005, a scholar at the Smithsonian Institution's National Museum of Natural History published a paper asserting that *redskin* had benign origins. He traced the word to phrases used by Native Americans to describe differences in skin color with colonists, which were translated by French-speaking arrivals in the 1760s to *peau-rouge* and then into English. In the early 1800s, *redskin* was used by white people and, in translation, Native Americans alike. "I turn to all, red skins and white skins, and challenge an accusation against me," Black Thunder, chief of the Meskwaki, said at a War of 1812 treaty conference.

But as violence against American Indians became government policy, *redskin* as used in newspapers and literature assumed a derogatory sense, framed in stories about savage Indians and righteous white Americans. In the first edition of the *Collegiate* in 1898, *redskin* was labeled "often contemptuous." In the unabridged editions of 1909 and 1934, the label disappeared. What happened? In the first half of the twentieth century, Native Americans, increasingly perceived as a dying race instead of as foes on the frontier, faded from mainstream consciousness except as mythologized caricatures in pop culture: Wild West shows; cigar store Indians; *The Lone Ranger*; John Ford movies like *Drums Along the Mohawk* and *Stagecoach*; advertisements using words like *wampum* and *heap-big*; and sports mascots, like Chief Noc-a-Homa of Major League Baseball's Atlanta Braves.

The aforementioned NFL team was founded in 1932 in Boston, where it played for a few years before moving to the capital, and originally was named the Braves. Owner George Preston Marshall changed the name in 1933 to avoid confusion with the city's baseball team of the same name. He chose the new name to avoid having to change the logo. (Marshall was an avowed segregationist and the last NFL owner to sign African American players, in 1962, and then only after President John F. Kennedy threatened to evict the team from its home stadium on federal land.)

To the white purveyors of popular culture, Native American stereotyping appeared harmless. Which means that the uses of *redskin* in the sources read by Merriam editors were seen as harmless, too. The word was used as a synonym for "American Indian" for so long and with deeply embedded casualness that it might have been unrecognizable as offensive to the people who dispassionately collected samples and drafted definitions from them. That was white culture failing to recognize how the people being defined—Native Americans—viewed the word doing the defining—*redskin*. The nickname of a sports team wouldn't have raised an eyebrow.

The oldest *redskin* slips in the Consolidated Files were compiled for *Webster's Second*. "This is like one of those Redskin stories where the noble savages carry off a girl and the honest backwoodsman with his incomparable knowledge follows the track," reads a typed quotation from the 1913 Joseph Conrad novel *Chance*. For the next four decades, citations for *redskin*—from children's textbooks and magazines, and mainstream publications—portray the word as a common derogation. A 1959 slip quotes the literary critic Philip Rahv describing two types of American writer: the *paleface* and the *redskin*. Of the half dozen or so cits referencing Rahv's categories, from places like the highbrow *Times Literary Supplement* and *Saturday Review*, none judges them explicitly offensive.

Historically, dictionaries have been all over the map on the word. In 2002, a University of Iowa linguist, Robert S. Wachal, examined the treatment of twenty-six ethnic slurs, from *bohunk* (for a Bohemian) to *wop* (Italian), in twenty-five dictionaries dating to the eighteenth century. *Redskin* displayed the greatest range: from no label in a handful of books to "not the preferred term," "a common appellation," "informal," "offensive," "derogatory and racially offensive," "often disparaging," and "taboo and dated."

Online databases helped me track the evolution of the word's usage. But without the material that other dictionary publishers had locked up or thrown out, I couldn't track the evolution of the definition—how it progressed from inoffensive to kinda offensive to officially offensive, with some back-and-forth in between.

In the citation files I found a clue on a slip added in 1945, a line from W. Somerset Maugham's novel *The Razor's Edge*: "'. . . is that poor Larry still among the Redskins?' For that was the disrespectful way in which she was accustomed to refer to the inhabitants of God's Own Country." I didn't find a record of correspondence among editors, but that might have been enough to justify adding *usu. taken to be offensive* to the entry in the *Third*. Philip Gove didn't appear to weigh in on what to do about the label in subsequent abridgments of the big book. A series of buffs—the yellow slips for draft definitions—for dictionaries published in the 1960s and early '70s don't mention any offensive connotation, and the label disappeared again.

But then the culture, and Merriam, shifted. In 1968, students at Dartmouth College demanded that the school to drop its mascot, an undergraduate dressed in Native American costume. "I've often wondered to myself if the people who owned these teams ever stopped to think what goes through the mind of a 10-year-old Indian kid on a reservation in North Dakota when he picks up a sports page and reads a headline, 'Redskins Scalp Chiefs'?" a Dartmouth student, Bill Yellowtail, told the *New York Times* in a 1971 story about the successful campaign and the growing opposition to Native nicknames and mascots.*

The next year, Washington newspapers published stories in which Native leaders complained about the football team's name, comparing its use to other slurs. The team's president, the white (and white-shoe) lawyer Edward Bennett Williams, met with Native groups but

---

*Yellowtail would serve in the Montana state senate and work for the Environmental Protection Agency.

dismissed any concerns. "This is getting silly," he said. "Suppose blacks get together and demanded Cleveland's football team stopped calling itself the Browns, or ornithologists insisted that Baltimore was demeaning to birds because the name is the Orioles."

Here's where the transitory slips of paper in Merriam's files demonstrate their indispensable value. Almost every cit I've used here is electronically discoverable today. The pinks—the editors' notes—are not. Someone pasted on a slip the definition of *redskin* from a 1973 Macmillan dictionary with a "considered offensive" label. Then, in March 1977, two editors, Mairé Weir Kay—Miss Kay—and Dan Hopkins, had a conversation about how to treat *redskin* (and *paleface*) in the fourth edition of Merriam's *School Dictionary*.

"This sounds like an offensive term to me," Kay wrote. "Couldn't it be excluded as a smear word," she asked, citing slurs for Jewish, Italian, and Black people. Hopkins replied that there was "significant difference in intent in the redskin/paleface pair as compared to" the other words. "I'm inclined to agree that they can be dropped w/out real harm (obviously, both must go if either does)."

I found in the files a letter from Joyce C. Brunette of Washington, DC, received by Merriam on December 6, 1977, and typed on two sides of a white card, that would have supplied editors with additional evidence:

> You give the meaning of the word *redskin* as an American Indian. Those of us who are of American Indian descent resent being referred to as redskins just as Jews resent being called kikes or hebes, Blacks resent being called nigger or coon or burrhead, Italians resent being called wop or dago, Irish people resent being called micks; and so on. You have taken cognizance of the feelings of Jews, Blacks, etc., by giving the meaning of terms like kike, nigger, etc., as abusive; and yet with the ugly word redskin you simply indicate the meaning as being American Indian. It may be

what you call us and this is racist. We do not refer to ourselves as redskins any more than a Jew refers to himself as a kike. So please make the next edition of the dictionary non-racist and indicate that the meaning of the word redskin is abusive and insulting. Thank you.

The next year, Kay and E. Ward Gilman resumed the conversation about removing *redskin* from the children's dictionary. It wasn't the n-word, Gilman wrote, "but . . . it is hardly a term of praise or even neutrality." Replied Kay: "It is not a needed term so I'd drop it if it can be felt as offensive." "*Can be felt as* offensive" is materially different from "*is* offensive," but impressions of the word were shifting.

Two more pieces of info were added to the files in 1980: a chart clipped from an issue of *Maledicta*, an academic journal about offensive language, showing *redskin* to be a more familiar slur than *cracker*, *redneck*, or *whitey*, which were labeled *offensive* or *disparaging*; and a letter to Merriam from Bert M. Samqua, associate editor of the *Alligator Times*, a newspaper published by the Seminole Tribe of Florida. Samqua praised Merriam's dictionaries. But he said that the definition of *redskin* was "not only demeaning, but not even a true description."

He went on to shame Merriam by throwing back its own definitions of *red*:

Are all, if any, Indians actually 'red'? If so in what sense—color (: the color of blood or of the ruby) or the endorsement of a radical social or political change (: communist). I suppose with some interpretation you could use "in the red" because we as a people definitely were in loss (i.e. one continent). If you are to use this word at all you should explain that this could be considered both a slang expression, and usually taken to be offensive.

There's a stamp on the slip: USED FOR 9 COL, the 1983 edition of the *Collegiate*, where the word was labeled *usu. taken to be offensive*. It would take the Washington football team thirty-seven more years to change its name to the Commanders. But not because every dictionary, including the OWL, had by then agreed that *redskin* is straight-up *offensive*, or because the team had been the target of decades of protests and lawsuits. It dropped the name because sponsors including FedEx, Amazon, Target, and Walmart threatened to abandon the team if it didn't.

Lexicographers can only document change in language. What the public does with the language is out of their hands.

I placed the foot of slips for the n-word from the Consolidated Files into an ancient Muriel Corona cigar box. Another eight inches of slips for the word itself and related terms from the New Files—the cabinets holding the last pre-electronic citations—went into a box of similar vintage from Mailmaster, a stationery company in Attleboro Falls, Massachusetts.

The slips were a testament to the manner in which the word was used and treated in print by the 1970s: casual use by Black Americans—as a term of affection; as an intra-racial putdown; to refer to the oppression of white society—and also as a slur. There are dozens of citations. Reggie Jackson, quoted by Roy Blount Jr., in *Sports Illustrated* in 1974. James Baldwin in the *New York Times Book Review* in 1976. Sammy Davis Jr. in 1971, on a slip handwritten by Philip Gove, who heard him on a Boston television station. The comedian Redd Foxx in a *Rolling Stone* interview in 1973.

A 1971 slip cites the frequency of the word (12) in the million-word Brown Corpus. There's a description of Elvis Presley by the Black writer Margo Jefferson in 1973. A quote from a Black character, Detective Ron Harris, on the sitcom *Barney Miller* in 1981. A line from the 1929 poem "Message From Abroad" by Allen Tate. A quote from Miles Davis about backing out of the Newport Jazz Festival in 1972. A quote from the first page of Dan Jenkins's football novel *Semi-Tough* that same year. Truman Capote, Ralph Ellison, James Jones, Richard Wright, Henry Miller, Erskine Caldwell. A parade of twentieth-century literary lights.

And Muhammad Ali everywhere—praising Jack Johnson, the first Black heavyweight champion, in a Pete Hamill story in *Life* in 1968; dissing rival George Foreman in the *New York Times* in 1974 and in *Sports Illustrated* in 1976; uttering his trademark rhymes ("I'm just another nigger trying to get bigger"). "He really used it in any kind of pointed way," the journalist Robert Lipsyte, who covered Ali in the 1960s, told me. "He was kind of feeding off of that."

But I also found in the slips a twenty-five-year-old David Duke, in *Harper's Weekly* magazine, telling a crowd at a Ku Klux Klan rally in 1975 that he was excited to be there—"because there's not one nigger."

Merriam updated the n-word entry for the next edition of its *Collegiate* dictionary, in 1983. For the first time, it added a quotation to illustrate the word. It was from the California congressman Ron Dellums, and it was used for a figurative, third sense of the word, "a member of a class or group of people who are systematically subjected to discrimination and unfair treatment." The quote was truncated and the word, capitalized in the print source, was lowercased in the entry.

The slip for the citation is a pasted cutout from a story by Hunter S. Thompson in *Rolling Stone* on March 2, 1972, titled "Fear and Loathing in New Hampshire." The slip bears three stamps: DOHERTY FEB 24 '75, 6000 WORDS, and USED FOR ADDENDA 1976. The last two mean the quotation was to be included in an addenda section in a new printing of *Webster's Third* in 1976, which was spun off as a separate book, *6,000 Words*. Here's the full citation:

> Ron Dellums, the Black Congressman from Berkeley, calls it "the Nigger vote." But he wasn't talking about skin pigment.

"It's time for somebody to lead all of America's Niggers," he said at the Capitol Hill press conference when Shirley Chisholm announced she was running for President. "And by this I mean the Young, the Black, the Brown, the Women, the Poor—all the people who feel left out of the political process. If we can put the Nigger Vote together, we can bring about some real change in this country."

Dellums used the word for dramatic effect as part of a riff in speech after speech. In March 1972, he told a gathering of liberal Democrats in Oakland that the word referred to anyone "whose lifestyle is limited by others, whose very role in society is defined by others, whose justice and freedom and opportunity is limited by others." At a rally for a New Jersey congressional candidate that May, he used it more than a dozen times, calling for a coalition of all the people he said fell under the word's umbrella to "get some of this oppression and injustice off our backs."

Dellums's sense was supported by other contemporaneous usage I read in Merriam's files. There are cits from the 1960s into the '80s equating gay people, Irish people, young people, and even baton twirlers with the slur against Black people. (Not in the files: Yoko Ono, in a 1969 interview with a British magazine saying, "woman is the nigger of the world," which became the title of a 1972 song with John Lennon that drew Dellums's attention.) "Anybody can be a nigger, you know. Now it's the young white kid with long hair," said the Black comedian Dick Gregory, whose 1964 autobiography used the slur as its title, intending both to shock readers and to reclaim the word and neuter its power.

The first two senses in the entry when I first looked at it in 2015— "a black person" and "a member of any dark-skinned race"—were preceded by a monitory label: *usually disparaging + offensive*. The entry noted exceptions for in-group use and the Dellums sense. "Its use by and among blacks is not always intended or taken as offensive, but, except in sense 3, it is otherwise a word expressive of racial hatred and bigotry," the usage note read.

The entry didn't seem modern, broad, or detailed. It lacked the depth of the treatment in the OED, the *Historical Dictionary of American Slang*, and the *Dictionary of American Regional English*. It was inadequate and, in its inadequacy, misleading. The sense illustrated by the Dellums quote wasn't the only alternate meaning of the word, and, in minimizing its potency by applying it to other groups, it felt outdated.

I asked director of defining Steve Perrault about the entry. Revising it could cause a public outcry; certain sensitive words always did. And I—fiftysomething white guy and non-staff, amateur lexicographer—certainly shouldn't be the one to review and rewrite the meaning of "perhaps the most offensive and inflammatory racial slur in English." Perrault didn't think this was an urgent project. The entry had caused no fuss for years.

The slips I gathered were examined for the last few *Collegiate* editions and the print unabridged Addenda. Dating to the late 1950s, they reflected the word's disturbingly robust life in American culture and language. Some were for obsolete terms for inanimate objects based on racist imaging. Others were explicitly racist slang.

And some reflected early efforts to take ownership of the word against its history, to hurl it back like a hissing grenade or transform it into something prideful. In 1971, a Black undergraduate at Columbia was quoted saying that Black students "will absolutely refuse the white man's benevolent offer of a 32nd niggership at General Motors." A 1973 biography of Mick Jagger cited the "marvellous niggerisation of white kids who were sick to death of the fucking Lindy Hop and Matt Monroe and Pat Boone."

None of these spinoffs made any of Merriam's dictionaries. Until the turn of the century, Merriam stuck with just the main word. It tinkered only to add the Dellums sense and quotation in 1983 and, in response to the letter-writing campaign a decade and a half later, to move the warning label to the start of the entry, for this and the other two hundred or so words deemed *offensive*.

Merriam also added the usage note, which, I discovered in the Consolidated Files, was suggested and drafted by Steve Perrault. "The formulaic 'usu. taken to be offensive' hardly seems an adequate reflection of the violent emotions associated with this word," Perrault wrote on a pink slip in 1991. "A paragraph discussing its history and current status in greater detail would do the job much better, and would prob also eliminate many—if not all—of the angry letters we get about our treatment of it."

In 1999, an editor for the first time addressed the offshoot *nigga*. On a pink, Karen Wilkinson wrote that she entered it as a cross-reference at the entry for the word ending *-er*, "but I'm not really sure that this adequately covers it." She said the word ending *-a* "is currently used almost exclusively by and among blacks as either a term of affection or a neutral form of address," whereas the epithet "is more often rendered" with the *-er* ending. "Is some sort of usage note needed," Wilkinson asked. Two and a half years later, editor in chief Frederick Mish replied in red pencil: "Yes."

Wilkinson was correct about the need for distinction. A decade earlier, a Black reporter for the *Philadelphia Inquirer*, Terry Johnson, explained that the spelling differences demonstrated how Black and white people employed the words—in-group affection vs. slur. But nothing is simple when it comes to hate words, and the *-a* ending could be unholstered as an epithet, too. Karen Russell, the daughter of Boston Celtics legend Bill Russell, wrote in 1987 about growing up outside of the city where her father won eleven National Basketball Association championships. One night, she said, the family returned from a long weekend to discover that their house had been robbed, with the *-a* ending spray-painted on the walls.

That word was added to the last unabridged addendum in 2002, defined as "used chiefly among Afro-Americans; usu. taken to be offensive when used by others." But there was little chance readers would ever see it. It appeared in that printed book—a hundred or so pages of post-1961 entries—next to the heart medication *nifedipine*, and nowhere else. It wasn't added to the last print edition of the *Collegiate*, the following year. It wasn't added to the online *Unabridged*. Perrault told me it needed a better definition plus a usage note.

The word certainly merited entry. There were thousands of examples in print, many thanks to the rise of hip-hop music. In one database I searched, usage in the 1990s increased one hundredfold from the 1980s. Merriam editor Emily Brewster had tracked the word's growth for years and in 2019 drafted an entry for the OWL, with plurals ending in both *-s* and *-z*.

There was a major change this time: no formulaic *usu. taken to be offensive*. The first sense began with *offensive; see usage paragraph below*. Instead of a boldface colon, the flashing sign that the definition is nigh, there was an em dash: "—used as a pronunciation spelling of" the n-word. A second sense was labeled *sometimes offensive* and also dispensed with a proper definition: "—used by some black people to refer to themselves or to another black person in a neutral or positive way."

Brewster's usage note did the heavy lifting, explaining that the word originated as "a variant of the infamous racial slur"; noting the divergence of the two forms since the late twentieth century; mentioning its prevalence in hip-hop; and concluding that, despite the music's cross-cultural appeal, use "in any context" by a person who isn't Black is "considered highly offensive."

I asked Brewster about the approach. "Defining by usage note is especially helpful for emphasizing that the definition is describing how the word behaves in the language," she said. "With offensive words, the word's function is often the kernel of its meaning; the word is a vehicle for belittling, disparaging, insulting, etc., and doesn't have much meaning beyond that."

A paragraph of actual sentences could better explicate the varied uses, intents, and nuances. All those letter writers in the 1990s were right: The dictionary didn't need to define the word as "a black person"—it needed to define it as a slur. The rest was details. Not only was this a sensible way of handling explosive terms, it was an admission that the standard Govian model sometimes needed to be tossed aside.

The cits from the New Files would have been used for the last few *Collegiate* editions and print unabridged addenda. I sorted them into stacks of possible senses. I made eight for the -*er* ending and six for the -*a* ending. That didn't compare with the treatment in other dictionaries. The *OED*'s entry for the main word included fifteen noun and verb senses and subsenses "referring to people," plus sixty more "other senses," phrases, and compounds. The word filled ten pages in the *Historical Dictionary of American Slang*, loaded with illustrative quotations.

Those were clinical, historical approaches. Their thoroughness was numbing, as if an avalanche of examples and sober academic analysis somehow nullified the word's power. Merriam, by contrast, tiptoed around the complexity of usage, partly to avoid filling another filing cabinet or inbox folder with angry mail, snail and e-. Before Merriam disabled the function, there were more than a thousand comments beneath the online entry for the word, most of them toxic and ignorant and vile.

On the one hand, the lexicographer, even the white lexicographer, theoretically possesses the critical distance to do what Randall Kennedy suggested, to distill the meaning of even the most toxic racial slur to a few words in a dictionary. People who write definitions are, after all, historians; the linguist John McWhorter, who is Black, has noted that the word didn't attain "outright taboo status"—in which the context in which it is used doesn't matter—until the early 2000s.* On the other hand, how could I—or any white lexicographer—presume to really know that I could get the nuance right, that, in examining the word like thin slices of a brain on a glass plate under a microscope, I could accurately portray its linguistic wholeness?

"If you could choose one word to represent the centuries of bondage, the decades of terrorism, the long days of mass rape, the totality of white violence that birthed the black race in America, it would be 'nigger,'" the Black author and cultural critic Ta-Nehisi Coates wrote. The reclamation of the word by Black people for Black people, Coates argued, "confounds our very notions of power." The word was cinched to America's history of enslavement and bigotry and hatred and violence. But it was also embedded in a vibrant and spreading culture. "'Nigger' is the border, the signpost that reminds us that the old crimes don't disappear," Coates wrote. "It tells white people that, for all their guns and all their gold, there will always be places they can never go."

I decided not to go there lexicographically myself, to try to tackle the definition. I didn't ask Steve Perrault about the word again. Then one day, not long before the pandemic, I checked the Merriam website.

The entry for the -*er* ending had taken the same form that Brewster had used for -*a*. Readers were immediately told the word is *offensive* and steered to a usage note below that Perrault had rewritten and expanded; Conrad, Twain, and Dickens were gone. The first sense had changed from "a black person" to "—used as an insulting and contemptuous term for a Black person." The sense illustrated by the Dellums quote—"a member of a class or group of people who are systematically subjected to discrimination and

---

*In his 2021 book *Nine Nasty Words*, McWhorter admired the word's diversity. It isn't "just 'a slur,'" he wrote. "It is profanity, and profanity of a dazzling range of shades, in a way that reveals it, in all of its menace, filth, scorn, teasing, warmth, love, and interracial outreach, as one of English's words most—of all things—marvelous."

unfair treatment"—was now "rarely used and is itself likely to be found offensive" because the word's overall offensiveness "has grown to such an extent in recent decades." A new, second note dismissed the assertion that helped fuel the 1990s letter-writing campaign, that the word meant "an ignorant person."

Perrault told me this was the first slur to be redrafted this way. "All of these revisions and additions were quietly done," he said.

The partial quotation from Ron Dellums remained. It was still the only example of the use of this word in this dictionary.

10

pronoun

: any of a small set of words in a language that are used as substitutes for nouns or noun phrases

In 1884, an Erie, Pennsylvania, lawyer and church-music composer named Charles Crozat Converse proposed a new word to solve a lingering problem: the absence of a gender-neutral third-person singular personal pronoun. In the literary magazine *The Critic*, Converse announced that after years of "much digging among word-roots of various kinds" and after having "essayed numberless English word clippings," he had created "a certain lingual abbreviation and compound" which would be easier to remember than an entirely new word because "the memory is not taxed by any novelty of word-essence, but simply by that of its form." He announced his new word with a flourish, writing that:

> by cutting off the last two letters of the English word *that* and the last letter of the word *one*, and uniting their remaining letters in their original sequence in these two words, I produced that word now proposed for the needed pronoun—to wit,
>
> THON ;
>
> to the *th* in which I would give the same sound as in *they*.

Converse was trying to solve two problems: number and gender. The number problem is applying a plural pronoun to a singular antecedent—using *they* or *their* to refer to singular indefinite pronouns like *anyone, someone,* or *everyone,* or to gender-nonspecific antecedents like *a player, my friend,* or *Chris*. If you were taught in school, as I was, and worked in newsrooms with strict style manuals, as I did, then you were convinced, as I was, that the number problem was an actual problem, that singular *they* was factually wrong and also visually and aurally disturbing. Same with the gender problem—the longstanding embrace of the generic *he*, that is, using *he* or *his* when the gender of the antecedent is unknown. Even in our overwhelmingly patriarchal history, some language mavens were aware of, and troubled by, the dissonance.

People have been carrying on about pronouns for centuries. A 1659 rant by a Quaker writer against the use of singular *you* periodically makes the linguistic rounds. (Yes, *you* once was exclusively plural; *thou* was the singular; not by accident do we say *you are*.) In 1971, a group of Harvard linguistics faculty and staff argued against a proposal to bar the use of "masculine pronouns" to refer to people both masculine and non-masculine, asserting that the generic *he* is "simply a feature of grammar" and that there "is really no cause for anxiety or pronoun-envy on the part of those seeking such changes." In 2008, Yale computer scientist David Gelernter railed against "arrogant ideologues" and "language rapists" who are "recasting English into heavy artillery to defend the borders of the New Feminist state"—all because speakers and writers were, through repeated usage, diminishing acceptance of the generic *he*.

Gelernter used as a shield the finger-waggingly prescriptive *Elements of Style* by the English professor William Strunk Jr. (who wrote the original text in 1918) and the writer E. B. White (a student of Strunk's at Cornell, who revised the book in 1959). On the subject of the generic *he*, the book was, as you might expect given when it was written, fussily sexist. Even in the third edition in 1979,

White asserted that the generic *he* is "a simple, practical convention rooted in the beginning of the English language," that it has "lost all suggestion of maleness in these circumstances," and that it "has no pejorative connotation" and "is never incorrect."

As with pretty much every other language bugaboo, history would like a word. Using *they/their/them/themselves* with a singular antecedent of unspecified gender goes back centuries. The *OED* dates first use to 1375 in the Middle English translation of a French romance novel, *William of Palerne*, aka *William and the Werewolf*. Jane Austen deployed singular *they* more than seventy-five times, according to a comprehensive Austen website, the Republic of Pemberley. (One example from *Pride and Prejudice* (1813): "The venison was roasted to a turn—and everybody said they never saw so fat a haunch.") Shakespeare wrote in *A Comedy of Errors* (1623): "There's not a man I meet but doth salute me / As if I were their well-acquainted friend." Other singular-*they*-ers include Chaucer, Dickens, Trollope, Whitman, Wilde, Joyce, Kipling, Fitzgerald, Dos Passos, Auden, cummings, Woolf, and Orwell. Noah Webster left a bunch of singular *they*s in his 1833 revision of the King James Version of the Bible: "So likewise shall my heavenly Father do to you, if ye from your hearts forgive not every one his brother their trespasses."

Singular *they* was perfectly acceptable until a bunch of eighteenth-century grammarians declared it wasn't. "The *Masculine Person* answers to the *general Name*, which comprehends both *Male* and *Female*; as, *any Person who knows what he says*," Ann Fisher wrote in her 1745 bestseller, *A New Grammar With Exercises in Bad English*. Other grammarians said, "in all languages, the masculine gender is considered the most worthy" and "the masculine Sex is the superior and more excellent." In an 1875 issue of *The American Bibliopolist*, someone writing under the byline S. S. S. imagined the creation of *she*: born from *he* "except the prefix of a line symbolic of grace and beauty . . . [t]aking the most perfectly curved letter of the alphabet to convey this idea."

But rules deemed inviolable begin to look dumb in no small part because scolds say they are inviolable; history renders conventions untenable and squishy. Singular *they* not only abounds in everyday speech, it sounds fine. In written form, it's less nakedly sexist than *he*; it's less clunky than *he or she*, *s/he*, or alternating *he* and *she*; and it appears frequently in popular writing. If you're complaining that singular *they* is wrong because of schoolbook rules of agreement, well—breaking news—masculine *he* referring to indefinite antecedents is ungrammatical, too.

There have been holdouts, but media have gradually come around. John McIntyre, a copy editor at the *Baltimore Sun*, wrote that in the year after he started allowing singular *they* into the paper in 2015, not a single reader complained. The *Washington Post* dropped its ban that same year. The Associated Press conceded in 2017, permitting singular *they/them/their* "in limited cases . . . when alternative wording is overly awkward or clumsy." *Webster's Third* acknowledged the singular, and Merriam's free site noted that the use of *they, their, them*, and *themselves* "as pronouns of indefinite gender and indefinite number is well established in speech and writing, even in literary and formal contexts."

In short, *they* is fine.

If anyone has spent more time researching the quest for a gender-neutral third-person singular pronoun than Dennis Baron, I'd like to know who they are.

Baron is a professor emeritus of English at the University of Illinois Urbana-Champaign. In 1981, he wrote a definitive tract in *American Speech*, "The Epicene Pronoun: The Word That Failed."* In 2020, he published a book, *What's Your Pronoun? Beyond He and She*, which catalogs more than 200 gender-neutral or nonbinary pronouns,

---

* **epicene** *adjective, of a noun* **:** having but one form to indicate either sex

starting with *one* in 1770 by a usage critic named Robert Baker and ending with singular *them* used in a 2018 Super Bowl ad for Coca-Cola. (The chronology fills a sixty-page appendix in Baron's book.)

Baron has chronicled tempestuous back-and-forths in local newspapers and national magazines, demonstrating the prominence and passion the topic has evoked in public life. In 1851, the British philosopher John Stuart Mill, Baron discovered, called the absence of a gender-neutral pronoun "more than a defect in language; tending greatly to prolong the almost universal habit, of thinking and speaking of one-half the human species as the whole." In 1868, a *Boston Recorder* reader observed that it's easier to add "a hundred new nouns and adjectives, and fifty new verbs" than one pronoun.

In the next decade, a Philadelphia philologist "wishing to steer clear of all sexual partiality" proposed adoption of the French pronoun *le*. The head of the West Georgia Agricultural and Mechanical College suggested *se*, *sis*, and *sim*, a spin on the Latin pronoun *se*. A writer in a Nebraska newspaper recalled "some linguistic genius" suggesting *um*. "Perhaps 'um' is as good a word as any other. If any person is dissatisfied with the language as it now stands, we should recommend um to adopt it." Someone else proposed *E*, to match *I*.

Charles Converse fancied himself the Alexander Cartwright of pronouns, with *thon* the equivalent of the baseball founder's ninety-foot basepaths. "Note its literal and euphonic resemblance to the other pronouns," he gushed, "and that its final consonant has a neutral savor significant of its purport." Since the "acknowledgment" of the need for a new pronoun is "universal," he went on, "any argument in advocacy of it clearly would be a work of supererogation." I had to look up that sixteenth-century word—"the act of performing more than is required by duty, obligation, or need"—but it only confirms Converse's certitude.

Converse's proposal in 1884 prompted a national conversation. The *New-York Commercial Advertiser* reported that "one or two newspapers" had used another invented pronoun, *hiser*, a combination of *his* and *her*. More followed: the Latin *unus* and *talis*. *Ip* and *ips*; *hersh* and *herm*; *ir, iro*, and *im*; *hor, hors*, and *horself*, pronounced "like the first syllable of the word horror." In 1885, a young Michigan linguistics graduate, Fred Newton, who would go on to great heights in the field, backed singular *they, their*, and *them*—but respelled as *tha, thare*, and *thon*. A correspondent in *The Writer: A Monthly Magazine for Literary Workers* proposed *e/es/em*: "We may be sure that some such impersonal pronoun will eventually come. I say, 'Let "em" come.'"

Then a dictionary legitimized the battle. In 1897, Isaac K. Funk, who put the Funk in Funk & Wagnalls, added *thon* to the second edition of his book. Funk understood that pronouns form a "closed lexical class," meaning the barrier for entry is nearly insurmountable compared to nouns and adjectives. But he also believed there was a "great need" for a solution to the gender problem, kept tabs on suggestions, and used the power vested in him as the editor in chief of *A Standard Dictionary of the English Language* to do something about it. Invented pronouns, "like Wagner's music, are better than they sound," Funk conceded. But *thon* "is fairly well formed, and by analogy it fits in with thee, thou, this, and that. It is easily managed by the tongue, and supplies a long-felt want. Why not give it a trial?"

One reason was that early twentieth-century humans were sexist. In 1912, Chicago's public schools superintendent, Ella Flagg Young, invented the "duo-personal pronouns" *he'er, him'er, his'er*, and *his'er's*; MAKES PRINCIPALS GASP, the *Chicago Tribune* wrote about a speech she delivered. In response, the male schools superintendent of St. Louis declared the masculine pronoun "more euphonic" because men are "better attuned to the laws of harmony, and of cadence." The editor of *Harper's Weekly* declared apocalyptically: "When 'man' ceases to include women we shall cease to need a language, and won't care any more about pronouns."

The use of *he* in laws and other government documents, in England and America, was conveniently used to exclude women from voting and other facets of public life. U.S. suffragist Susan B.

Anthony gave speeches about pronouns, noting the hypocrisy of cherry-picking the application of *he*; if *he* referred only to men, Anthony said, women shouldn't have to pay taxes or be punished for violating the law. ("If a wife commits murder let the husband be hung for it.") The passage in 1920 of the Nineteenth Amendment to the Constitution didn't settle the grammatical disagreement. Its wording doesn't include any pronouns at all.

Some people felt, however, that the amendment did attach the right to an inclusive pronoun. Dennis Baron discovered that the Mississippi state senate, citing "the exigencies of the times on account of woman's new political freedom," proposed three new legal pronouns in the state: *hesh* ("pronounced with a long e as in the word feet"), *himer* ("with the short sound of i on the first syllable"), and *hiser* (short i, the s pronounced z). The bill failed by one vote. The *Sacramento Bee* took action. "HIR" WILL BE THE BEE'S WORD FOR "HE OR SHE," the newspaper's editorial page declared.

The *Bee* detailed the usual reasons for a gender-neutral pronoun—to avoid clunkiness, to improve specificity, "not to slight the female sex." And then it lowered the boom, simultaneously defenestrating language schoolmarms while demonstrating a rational understanding of how language works. "People live who, doubtless, will raise their hands in holy horror at the temerity that would coin such a word," the *Bee* said. "Yet, were it not for words manufactured to serve a vital purpose since the language was formed, we should yet be limited to the few score syllables of our cave-dwelling ancestors. Necessity is the mother of invention in language as in mechanics." The *Bee* used *hir* in its pages into the 1940s (though, judging by my search of its online archives, inconsistently).

Through world wars and second-wave feminism, writers kept denouncing the absence of a sexless pronoun—whether for nitpicky grammatical reasons or sexual-equality ones—and enthusiastically creating their own. *Su* (1921), *ha/hez/hem* (1927), *she/shis/shim* (1934), *heesh* (1942), *che/chis/chim* (1951), *ve/vis/ver* (1970), *tey/term/tem* (1972), *ey/eir/em* (1975), *ho/hom/hos* (1976), *sheehy* (1978), *one* (1979), *ala/alum/alis* (1989). There was a 1974 endorsement of *ne/nis/nim* on grounds that *n* is "roughly halfway" between *h* and *s*. And a 1975 suggestion of a blend of *he or she* and *it*: *h'orsh'it*.

The pronouns all shared this: Not a single one gained traction in popular speech or print. "The problem with the invented forms is that they look like invented forms," Baron told me. "People aren't sure how to pronounce them. They look different. They stick out like a sore thumb."

The singular-pronoun gender dilemma for centuries was rooted primarily in an assumption: that gender is binary. Debate centered on whether *he* is sexually all-inclusive and whether *he/she* and *he or she* are awk constructions leading down a garbled, twisting path. ("Everyone should do his or her best in whatever situations he or she finds himself or herself in," Merriam's Emily Brewster said in a video on the topic.) The other problem with the grammatical contortions around *he* and *she*—the more modern problem—is different: Third-person singular pronouns in English don't account for people who don't identify as either male or female.

This is one of Merriam's most popular tweets ever:

People keep
1) saying they don't know what 'genderqueer' means
    then
2) asking why we added it to the dictionary

Genderqueer joined the OWL in 2016, defined as "of, relating to, or being a person whose gender identity cannot be categorized as solely male or female." (Other terms used by people whose gender identity is neither masculine nor feminine include *agender*, *bigender*, and *gender-fluid*, all which Merriam has entered.) The *OED*'s definition is more expansive, giving agency to the individual who "does not subscribe to conventional gender distinctions, but identifies with neither, both, or a combination of male and female genders." It dates the first use of *genderqueer* to 1995, from *In Your Face*, a newsletter edited by a transgender activist, Riki Wilchins: "It's about all of us who are genderqueer: diesel dykes and stone butches, leatherqueens and radical fairies."

Language adjusts to meet societal change. Words are created to fill a void. While trans people have existed forever, English grammar hasn't met the needs of a person who "cannot be categorized as" or "does not subscribe to." As transgender awareness and visibility grew in the early twenty-first century, the lack of a nonbinary pronoun became even more glaring. "People use pronouns to do social work," Kirby Conrod, an assistant professor of linguistics at Swarthmore College, who is transgender, told me. "People are using *he* or *she* to render an opinion. In the case of trans people, they really do have an ideological flavor to them."

That's because pronouns are considered in linguistics as "placeholders" and, Conrod explained, in this framework the "difference between gendered pronouns is some sort of static physical quality of the person it's referring to." That's a "very sexist view of gender. Old-school linguistics assumes gender is an automatic thing that comes out of nowhere, where we need to think about how gender is constructed socially and how individuals move within the system of gender." *They* is the adjustment that Conrod personally chose to deal with their place in this system. The word felt natural and was easier for others to comprehend than an invented "neopronoun." "People have adopted it and are comfortable with it," Conrod said. "They don't have to pause before saying it."

The American Dialect Society recognized *they* as the 2015 Word of the Year, specifying its "newer usage as an identifier for someone who may identify as 'non-binary' in gender terms." Brewster proposed it for the *Unabridged* that same year. In 2019, Steve Perrault revised the *they* entry, adding a subsense in the OWL, "used to refer to a single person whose gender identity is nonbinary." Perrault also rewrote a usage note. "It's all just part of the familiar process of trying to create entries that accurately describe the past and present uses of English words," he told me.

Merriam's addition generated thousands of media hits—news stories, praise from socially progressive sources, condemnations from conservative Christians convinced they had totally unmasked a conspiracy inside 47 Federal Street. "'Trans' cultists and their dogmatist friends" were behind linguistic changes like nonbinary *they*, said an antigay, antiabortion, "pro-family" group. A right-wing blogger said "the leftists who run Merriam-Webster" were pushing "a political agenda." He included a screenshot showing Merriam's tweet about *they* and, unintentionally no doubt, the tweet directly above it—about the addition to the OWL of *deep state*.

Interest ran so high that Merriam crowned *they* its 2019 Word of the Year. Sure, it was four years after the bleeding-edge American Dialect Society. (In 2020, the group picked *singular "they"* as the Word of the Decade.) But Merriam, as it does, grounded its decision in data, not zeitgeists. It added the new *they* sense in September of that year, and the subsequent media attention triggered a tsunami of lookups. The company said the decision was based on searches from January to September only. In those months, *they* curiosity tripled over the same period the previous year, shooting up from the 400–500 range on the top-10,000 list of frequently looked-up words to 100–200. There were the usual event-related spikes—a nonbinary fashion model was in the news, a congresswoman said her daughter used the pronoun—but the surge reflected general interest.

I mentioned to Brewster that, before September, people looking for a nonbinary sense of *they* in Merriam would have been chasing ghosts. "Well," she replied in an email, dictionary users aren't a monolith, of course, so I assume some were searching to see if we'd added it yet; others were looking to prove to themselves or someone else that it *wasn't* a legitimate use; some were likely looking at the ages-old indefinite pronoun use, which is, I believe, fading fast and causing consternation to those who still feel strongly about it. There are actually multiple reasons for people to be looking up *they*. It really is in an incredible state of flux, which is remarkable for a pronoun.

They's leg up was that it already was part of the language; even for apolitical grammar fussbudgets, using *they* in this new context was comprehensible, and its adoption was gradual and organic. In 2018, Kirby Conrod, the Swarthmore linguist, conducted an online survey of 884 people about singular *they*. While respondents of all ages generally accepted uses of singular *they* with generic antecedents ("Every student tries to write their essay perfectly"), they were less tolerant of *they* used with proper names. The younger the respondent, however, the greater the acceptance of nonbinary *they*. The inflection point: people born between 1980 and 1985. "Younger people rated it as fine, older people rated it as sounding weird," Conrod said. "That's language change in progress." Change was happening among people who identify as nonbinary, too. According to the Gender Census, a nonacademic online survey of people "whose gender doesn't tidily fit into the female/male binary," the percentage of respondents over age fifty who said they would be comfortable using *they* as a personal pronoun rose to around 70 percent in 2024 from 40 percent in 2020.

Neopronouns were showing up more, too. In 2019, more than twenty colleges and universities—among them Harvard, Colgate, Vanderbilt, and the universities of Alabama, Colorado, Iowa, Kentucky, Michigan, and Vermont—allowed students to choose a personal pronoun for their academic records. Five years later, the number of schools had increased to nearly three hundred. Those sorts of official moves resulted in a gender-neutral pronoun smorgasbord, from *air* to *e* to *hir* to *xe* to *ze*.

The last two sent my Scrabble nerve-endings atingle. New high-scoring, strategy-shifting two-letter X and Z words? Heck yes! It turned out that Brewster had added *ze* to New Words in 2015, defining it as "that person—used as a gender-neutral pronoun," with a citation from *The New Yorker*. ("It's time to realize that not everybody who identifies as transgender has made, or can make, or even needs to make, a social and medical transition to living full-time in the gender with which we identify," Stephanie Burt wrote. "That's a standard, even a boring, thing to say in a crowd of queer-identified twentysomethings, some of whom take pronouns like 'they' and 'ze'; but not on TV, and not in the culture at large.") But time passed and Brewster wasn't racing to draft an entry.

Ze mostly appeared in stories *about* gender-neutral pronouns, not as a substitute for a gendered pronoun. By Merriam standards, that didn't cut it. I wondered whether those parameters needed to shift. You might not hear *ze* on *All Things Considered* or read it unglossed in the *New York Times*. But it was being used in some published texts—particularly in queer-studies journals and science-fiction novels—and was being written about in mainstream outlets. If as a result people were increasingly aware of its existence, that seemed validating. Brewster was happy to let me chase *ze*.

According to Dennis Baron's list, *ze* dates to the late nineteenth century. A proto-*ze* was *zyhe*, proposed in 1885 by George Washington Eveleth, a homeopath and prolific letter writer obsessed with Edgar Allan Poe (they had a long correspondence). "The Anglo-Saxon for *he* was *he*," Eveleth wrote. "The Danish for *she* was *zy*. Unite the two, thus: *zyhe* for the nominative; possessive, *zyhe's*; objective, *zyhem*." He wanted his word pronounced *zah-ee*. Three years later, in a Philadelphia newspaper, *ze* was credited to a botanist and mathematician named Joshua Hoopes. *Zie* popped up in a Chicago paper a few years later.

Ze and its relatives didn't resurface until the 1970s, when the rise of the feminist and gay and lesbian movements sparked new interest in pronouns. In the early days of the internet, *ze* et al. were adopted by some online communities. "Se/hir/se is in regular active use on the newsgroup alt.sex.bondage, a rich source of specialized language forms," John Cowan, a linguist, programmer, and constructed language (*conlang**) creator, reported in a Usenet group in 1992. Around that time, *ze* and *hir* also were used in online transgender and transsexual forums. And, according to trans writer, educator, and activist Willy Wilkinson, *ze* was the pronoun of choice in the San Francisco trans community.

More recently, as the topic of transgender identity and rights began receiving significant public attention, the words started popping up in mainstream sources, too. A staunch proponent was the trans activist Leslie Feinberg, whose 1996 book, *Transgender Warriors: Making History from Joan of Arc to Dennis Rodman*, contains one of the earliest known *ze* cits. "I don't have a personal stake in whether the trans liberation movement results in a new third pronoun, or gender-neutral pronouns, like the ones, such as ze (she/he) and hir (her/his), being experimented with in cyberspace," Feinberg wrote. "It is not the words in and of themselves that are important to me—it's our lives." Feinberg started using *ze* and *hir* but didn't object to others using *she* and *her* to describe hir/her. In its 2014 obituary, the *New York Times* referred to Feinberg as *she*. A remembrance of Feinberg in *The Atlantic* read, "Ze leaves behind hir partner ... and hir chosen family."

Transgender writer Kate Bornstein used *ze* in a 1996 novel, *Nearly Roadkill*, and in *My Gender Workbook*, in 1998. The latter was

---

* **conlang** *noun* : an invented language intended for human communication that has planned and cohesive phonological, grammatical, and syntactical systems

published by the academic house Routledge and reviewed in mainstream media, which noted the use of the genderless pronoun. *The Lives of Transgender People*, a 2011 academic study by Genny Beemyn and Susan Rankin, used *ze* and *hir*. In a 2016 essay, two professors of medieval history, Ruth Mazo Karras of the University of Minnesota and Tom Linkinen of the University of Turku in Finland, dealt with the ambiguous gender of a cross-dressing fourteenth-century prostitute named John/Eleanor Rykener by using *ze/hir/hirself.*

Ze and *hir* appear in a bunch of science fiction. They're in the 2011 novel *Up Against It* by Laura J. Mixon, writing under the pseudonym M. J. Locke ("Jane had seen images but had never met Obyx in the flesh. She had expected hir to be strange, but had not been prepared for how beautiful ze would be."). And in *The Girl Must Die*, a memoir by Erika Lopez, a cartoonist, performance artist, and novelist ("Ze changed hir name to one of those New Testament names, and re-fashioned hirself into a soft, puffy, half-finished hermaphrodite nicknamed The Pop n' Fresh Doe").

I asked some of the authors why they chose *ze*. Genny Beemyn, who is transgender, personally used *ze/hir* for several years after reading Leslie Feinberg's work before switching to *they/them* because it was "a simpler way to go." "It's not language most people have in their vocabularies," Beemyn, the director of the Stonewall Center, an LGBTQ resource at the University of Massachusetts, said of alternative nonbinary pronouns. "Trying to teach people new words is hard." Similarly, Ruth Mazo Karras said that in 2015, when she and her coauthor wrote their article, *ze* "seemed to me the most likely that would become standard." Afterward, Karras changed her mind. "If I were doing it now, I would probably just use *they*. It now seems to me that *they* is the most likely to become standard."

Laura Mixon told me she first thought about gender and pronouns as a teenager in the early 1970s after reading science-fiction writer Ursula K. Le Guin's *The Left Hand of Darkness*. "I fell in love with the book and the way it challenged gender norms," Mixon wrote in an email, "but it never occurred to me that there was an alternative way to think about pronouns till I read an article challenging LeGuin's use of *he* for the Gethens"—the "ambisexual"* inhabitants of the planet Gethen. "The way pronouns affect our sense of our identities—as well as our relationships to each other and the world—has been of great interest to me ever since." When Mixon began writing *Up Against It* in the early 2000s, she wanted a non-gendered pronoun for her nonbinary Viridians. "I looked up the assorted pronouns that have been used either in fiction or by NB"—nonbinary—"people in the lgbtq+ community, and settled on the ones that 'sounded right' to my ear, for purposes of the story."

Words follow culture. They don't impose their use. Consider *Latinx*, which Merriam dated to 2007 and entered in 2018, defined as "of, relating to, or marked by Latin American heritage" and "a gender-neutral alternative to Latina or Latino." Despite a push for its use, particularly by left-leaning groups, the word was largely shunned. "Why is the Term 'Latinx' Such a Loser Among Hispanic Voters?" a column in *Los Angeles Magazine* asked. A *Miami Herald* editorial was headlined, "The 'Latinx community' doesn't want to be called 'Latinx.' Just drop it, progressives." In a 2024 survey by the Pew Research Center, 75 percent of Latinos who had heard the term said it shouldn't be used to describe Hispanic or Latino people. Emerging in its place as a gender-inclusive term in both Spanish and English: *Latine*, thought to have originated in Spanish-speaking LGBTQ+ communities.

Similarly, decreeing that *ze* is officially "a word" won't make people adopt it. The appearance of prescription is a guaranteed fail, which largely accounted for the snark and hostility I found when searching "ze pronoun" on social media. Adoption grows out of behavior, and acceptance is needed for that. Because new pronouns

---

* ambisexual *adjective* : BISEXUAL: such as a : having, showing, or involving feelings of sexual attraction for both sexes b : having qualities or characteristics associated with both sexes : sexually ambiguous

have proved difficult for human brains to process, *ze* was an unlikely candidate for widespread usage. Especially as, in the late 2010s and early 2020s, singular *they* gained sanction. In the Gender Census, no individual neopronoun had an endorsement rate above 10 percent—*xe* came the closest—and *ze/hir* declined from 13 percent in 2015 to just 3.2 percent in 2024 (though *ze/zir* registered five percent). In any case, not a ton of love.

Enshrinement in Merriam, however, depends simply on Merriam. Even if the citations made a good case, adding *ze* carried political consequences, just as the inclusion of nonbinary *they* did. An official endorsement of a neopronoun promoted by transgender people would no doubt be seen as further evidence that Merriam was a "liberal" dictionary, especially during a second Trump administration hostile to transgender people and rights. Merriam would be on the receiving end of frothing emails, causing unwanted hassle inside the old brick building in Springfield. But so what. While dictionaries are in the business of validating words, not social change, sometimes the act of validating words validates change, too.

Merriam's updates of *marriage, racism,* and, in 2022, *female*—adding the sense "having a gender identity that is the opposite of male," the key part being gender identity, "a person's internal sense of being male, female, some combination of male and female, or neither male nor female"—elicited outrage from social conservatives. But that didn't deny the reality that meanings evolve based on patterns of usage by human beings, and that lexicographers are charged with recording that evolution. When Merriam one day revises its entries for *she* or *woman* to be trans-inclusive, right-wing commentators will rage, but the decision will be empirically and socially grounded. Similarly, if Merriam adds *ze*, I trust it will have concluded that the word's historical use, despite a lack of widespread daily use, is worthy of documenting.

The semantics of word meanings have real-world consequences beyond a few lines in a lexicon or a game of Scrabble. Judges and lawyers routinely quote dictionaries—sometimes wrongly or misleadingly—to justify or refute arguments. Consider a 2023 Florida law barring trans and nonbinary educators from using their preferred pronouns in the classroom. When trans math teacher Katie Wood and nonbinary science teacher AV Schwandes sued the state in federal court, lawyers for Florida cherry-picked from dictionary entries to assert that a person's pronouns must align with their sex assigned at birth. (The state ordered Wood to refer to herself in school as Teacher Wood.)

The Linguistic Society of America—the academic group that cohosts the Word of the Year vote—filed an amicus brief calling out "a selective and misleading recitation of dictionary definitions." The LSA described how "more up-to-date, comprehensive dictionaries than those Florida cites" show that he and she are about more than biology; it noted that the *OED*'s entry for *woman* included an illustrative quotation using the phrase "trans woman," and that the definition of *female* in Merriam-Webster included the aforementioned gender identity. Entering *ze* might play a similar role in some case someday.

More fundamentally, pronouns and their validation as words with fluctuating meanings matter because of what they represent to their users—"a sense of agency and autonomy and freedom and expression," Kirby Conrod, the Swarthmore linguist, said. "That goes beyond, 'Don't misgender me' but 'See me in some specific way.' And that's important.'" Dua Saleh, a Sudanese American singer, tweeted in 2020, "I love the pronouns that I use they/them/theirs & he/him/his but I've also been referring to myself with the neopronouns xe/xyr/xim." In an interview, Saleh elaborated. "I just like the neopronouns. I feel like they fit me better, not all the time, but they're just fitting. There's an element where I'm just like, 'Oh, this sounds really nice.' Or it sounds nice coming out of my mouth or hearing other people saying it."

I didn't investigate only *ze*. I spent hours database-hunting other individual pronouns that popped up frequently in college lists, in news stories, and on LGBTQ websites: *ze, hir, xe, xem, xyr, ve, ey, sie, zie, zim, zir.*

It was no contest: *ze, hir,* and *xe* topped the charts. The journalistic hits almost universally were stories *about* the words. About transgender people using them. About colleges offering them. About the backlash to colleges offering them. About media mulling how to handle them. And, from the right, reliably overwrought condemnations and laments about the death of language and the perversion of culture. *Ze* and its companions took a long ride on the Fox News culture war outrage machine. But there also were signs of change where you'd expect them, among young people. The University of Texas student newspaper used *ze* and *hir* as pronouns for an administrator without explaining what they meant.

Despite such occasional finds, and solid overall numbers in the databases, the Merriam questions lingered. Did *ze* show sustained usage over time? Or, like the other invented pronouns, was I witnessing a blip that would be forgotten as *they* gained acceptance? Was *ze*'s limited use in speech and writing as an actual pronoun disqualifying? Or was it more widespread than sources might indicate? Bronwyn Bjorkman, an assistant professor of linguistics at Queen's University in Canada who has studied how people use singular *they*, noted on Twitter (where her profile read "she/her/her, but surely they/them/their is the future") that an online knitting board she belonged to used *zie/hir/hir* "as a default gender neutral form, to anonymize students/colleagues."

I offered Steve Perrault my evidence.

"The issue with the pronouns themselves is that most of the examples we've seen for them to this point have not really been evidence of their use so much as evidence of people talking about or proposing their use," he wrote:

I suspect we're still a very long way from seeing something like *ze* used in place of 'he or she' in, say, a widely read news article with the expectation that English-speakers will actually know that it's something other than a typographical error.

But of course that doesn't mean that these words don't merit inclusion in the dictionary, since they're obviously out there, are gaining more use, and are of interest to people. They're highly look-up-able. Our normal approach would be to judge each on its own merits and enter or not enter it according to the evidence.

I took that as a go and drafted entries for *ze*, *xe*, and *hir*, including *zie* as an alternate spelling of *ze* and *zir* as an alternate spelling of *hir*. I gave Perrault a truckload of illustrative quotations from an assortment of newspapers, books, and even a play, a 2014 drama by Taylor Mac titled *Hir*. With editing help from Emily Brewster, I drafted entries for *gender-neutral pronoun* and *nonbinary pronoun*, illustrating them with quotations from a book by former *New Yorker* copy editor Mary Norris, from the LGBTQ newspaper *The Advocate*, and from publications in England and Canada. I also wrote a usage note for *gender-neutral pronoun* that attempted to distill seven centuries into seven sentences.

I was hopeful. Dictionary.com added *ze* in 2016. The *OED* followed with *ze* in 2018, using a first citation date of 1864, and *hir* in 2019, quoting the *Sacramento Bee*'s announcement a century earlier. I believed the three pronouns I defined deserved entry on their lexical merits—as Perrault said, they're out there. But as of 2025, they hadn't been added.

Still, thinking and learning about *ze* pushed me to the belief that there are times when The Dictionary benefits from flexibility, when it's okay to welcome a word that might just fall short of its ingrained standards—or might change those standards. Merriam in fact entered a gender-neutral pronoun once—Charles Crozat Converse's *thon*, defined in *Webster's Second* as: "A proposed genderless pronoun of the third person." (Alas, I couldn't find any citation slips for *thon* in the Consolidated Files.) When it was time to trim the *Second* for the slimmer *Third*, *thon* was among the quarter million words to hit the cutting-room floor.

A better and more recent comparison was a word that joined the *Unabridged* in 2016: *Mx.*, "*chiefly British* : used as a gender-neutral title of courtesy." Brewster had added *Mx.* to New Words less than a year earlier, and, even though the honorific dates to the late 1970s, by Merriam standards it took a quick path from identification by an editor to entry into the dictionary. (The *OED* and Dictionary.com already had entered *Mx.*) As with *ze*, *Mx.* wasn't used a lot on its own. The vast majority of stories I read in Nexis were *about* the honorific itself (and there were fewer than for *ze*). But it was gaining as an acceptable term in official domains; in Britain, *Mx.* was among suggested titles for driver's licenses and other government documents, and at banks and universities. "Once you're on the form someone uses to get a passport, you're a certifiably established member of the language," Brewster said.

A dropdown menu of proffered titles for a driver's license is arguably more official than a Harvard first-year choosing from among a bunch of pronouns for hiser campus documents. But how much more official? If young Americans were growing up comfortable with the idea that gender isn't binary, and maybe not so important to who they are, and didn't blanch at heretofore heterodox ways of denoting gender, why shouldn't American English reflect that? Or why shouldn't the signature American dictionary? If defining a particular word made it easier for a dictionary reader to understand and navigate the evolving language of contemporary life, why not include it?

11

entry

: something entered: such as : a headword with its definition or identification

Climbing the stairs to my cubicle, I liked to imagine the Merriam editorial department as it would have looked after the building's grand opening in 1940. Photographs helped. A row of modern metal desks, a dictionary stand on every one. Straight-back wooden chairs. Lights in the shape of inverted umbrellas dangling from the ceiling—"the most modern electrical equipment on the market," the *Springfield Daily Republican* marveled. With its tidy bookshelves and stately card cabinets, the spare and antiseptic second floor looked like a library reading room.

A decade and a half later, Merriam was staffed up for *Webster's Third*. One row of desks became two. The flat seats were replaced by banker's chairs on wheels. The place looked lived-in: metastasizing stacks of paper, an invasion of citation cabinets, new rows of books atop surfaces not intended to store them. I imagined men in dark suits and starched white shirts hunched over pinks and blues, and women editors, too—for the times, modern Merriam was progressive in its hiring. Some editors wore green eyeshades to reduce the strain of staring at all that tiny type. Dictionary pages turning, pencils scratching, drawers sliding; heels clacking and wheels squeaking on the slick linoleum floor: a cone of silence.

The back stairwell that I climbed after entering by the loading dock was slathered with scuffed and chipping pastel yellow paint. Two ceiling tiles were missing. Books and cabinets from the building's earliest days oozed onto the second-floor landing. On one shelf I found a 1913 school dictionary. On another a random assortment from the 2000s: rhyming, crossword puzzle, large print, medical. A seven-foot-tall green metal cabinet preserved thousands of slips pertaining to the production of *Webster's Third*. For some unknown reason there was a refrigerator on the landing, too.

If I came in through the front, beneath the sculpted dictionary, John Morse (when he still worked there) would answer the doorbell; there was no receptionist anymore. From there, the scavenger hunt was even more entertaining. A black rotary phone sat on a drop-leaf table in the lobby. An elaborate display case from the 1904 World's Fair preserved in time. I marched up the broad central stairwell and turned right. Against the wall was an actual phone booth. In it hung a painting of a house by the ocean: *Kelsey '76, New Harbor, Me.* There was an old teal desk chair and a log sheet. Eighteen calls were placed in the previous year. Which meant that, a couple of decades into the twenty-first century, Merriam-Webster staffers sometimes talked on a corded phone in a booth. They dutifully recorded the number dialed, their initials, and whether the call was B for business or P for personal. "Please keep your feet off the wall," a handwritten reminder said.

Onward toward my desk. The first to forty-seventh printings of *A Pronouncing Dictionary of American English* (1944). Red etymological filing cabinets, 117 drawers in all. An 1855 printing of the Merriams' first revision of Webster open on a stand. An original 1928 *OED* with a warning: DO NOT REMOVE FROM THE SHELF. Open copies of the 1864, 1890, 1909, and 1934 unabridgeds, facing skyward like sunbathers. One day I stopped at a cabinet holding slips used to elucidate pronunciations. I slid open a drawer labeled AE TO AIZ and removed a random pink: "*aforesaid afôreśaid* Pres. J. F. Kennedy taped in a CBS-TV documentary on him 11 Nov. 1973"; "*again* [ə gern] Arlene Blanchard OK City bombing survivor MSNBC 6/11/01." The sweep of history on little paper rectangles.

I passed a framed photograph on a wall titled *Anniversary Picnic, Orient Springs, May 9, 1931*. Several dozen Merriam employees posed on a hill in a park about an hour north of Springfield. Everyone had signed their names. Robert C. Munroe added "editor." The staff would have been deep into preparing the *Second* for publication—letters of the alphabet completed, page proofs readied, deadlines approaching like a cop car's flashing lights in the rearview mirror. I wondered if the weekend retreat was attended excitedly or grudgingly. If the staff chatted nonstop to compensate for the weekday silence. I wondered if they liked their work.

I unpacked my laptop and dropped a power cable through a gap between the desktop and the cubicle wall. One morning not long after the layoffs, but before Morse's departure, I greeted Steve Perrault. He told me he was doing mundane stuff like preparing data files for the switch from the *Unabridged* to the OWL. He couldn't get used to the name—and I couldn't either, because it was also shorthand for Scrabble's Official Word List—or to the new order of things, the missing persons. He seemed unnerved.

But I had words, and a company's history, to research. Here's how one day went. I visited the basement, reading memos from editors to consultants on the *Third* and admiring slips of artwork that illustrated definitions in that book. A few lost hours later, I came up for air, literally, because I was wheezing from the dust and dank. I helped Emily Brewster write a blog post about a new sense of *liftoff* that I had spotted (and would later define as "the initial raising of interest rates by a government central bank after a period of no change"). She identified another sense absent from the existing entry, something generally going up, and wondered whether a sense of the market or economy lifting off preceded the interest-rate sense. "That's the rabbit hole," she said.

I listened to the sound of Merriam-Webster: the buzz of the lights, the etymologist in the next cubicle breathing, a hissing radiator, traffic on Federal Street, the thrum of a server, my growling stomach, a rookie definer in a nearby cubicle turning a page, the etymologist scrolling his mouse, the etymologist exhaling, my stomach again. Seventy-five years earlier, the local paper had touted the "serenity and permanence" of the building, and it was right.

At 8:20 p.m., I was hungry and tired and ready to go when I was gripped by panic: If John Morse is gone, I'll trip the alarm. But he was inevitably the last employee in the building. Before leaving he walked the second floor like a department store security guard at closing time making sure no one was hiding in Beds and Bedding. I found him in his office tinkering with a plan for a small dictionary for the India market. I said I really should stay. My visits were infrequent, and there was so much to do, so many cits to pull from the Consolidated Files, so many definitions to draft. As he often did, with reason, Morse quoted the late editor Frederick Mish—"a trip to the citation file is a humbling experience"—and sent me back upstairs.

I was happy to be there. I loved the tactile experience of flicking through a cit drawer, the musky smell of the old paper, those handsome gradations of color and fade in the clippings and slips. And, most of all, the nervous anticipation and frisson of delight upon seeing a word—*my* word—typed in the upper left-hand corner of a white three-by-five.

I stopped first to search for *smashmouth*. I considered myself a *smashmouth*-ologist, having once written a page-one story in the *Wall Street Journal* about the growing use of the football term in nonfootball settings. I'd dated it to at least 1984, and quoted an NFL Hall of Famer saying he'd heard it in the early 1970s. I'd also reported that before it meant an aggressive style of football—facemask-to-facemask, in the trenches, grinding it out—it was slang for kissing. The cards in the Consolidated, though, skipped from *smashment* (from an 1889 short story by Rudyard Kipling) to *smashnosed* (from Nelson Algren's 1950 novel *The Man with the Golden Arm*: "'Ain't nothin' on *my* record but drunk 'n fightin',' the smashnosed vet with the buffalo-colored eyes was reminding the captain"). *Smashmouth* turned up in the New Files, though, including a cit from my *Journal* story. Cool.

Another one of my targets, *dogpile*, dated to at least 1921. I found two citations in the Consolidated Files, from 1945 ("two boys ran out in front of each sophomore group . . . In a moment there were five big dogpiles on the field") and 1955 ("There wasn't any of this fancy stuff about the game [football] then—just straight power with a dog-pile at the end of every play"). I loaded a quarter inch of slips for *redshirt* into a box. *Joggle* was on my hit list, too. It was entered as a verb meaning to shake or jostle. Missing was the portmanteau sense describing the action of people who run the New York City Marathon while tossing bowling pins in the air: to juggle while running (*joggle* = *jog* + *juggle*). I did find a slip with a pasted-on cutout from page 23 of *The New Yorker* of July 3, 1954, stamped GATES DEC 2 '58—a poem by Ogden Nash.

At fifty-one
I would not boggle,
Except that when I jog
I joggle.

The next morning, I pinned a photocopy of the poem to my cubicle wall and showed editor Peter Sokolowski, who was walking by. "Oh, Ed Gates!" he exclaimed. "He was one of the founders of DSNA—the Dictionary Society of North America. He became an academic."

I told Peter I was sad to return the *joggle* card to its drawer. No one might ever see it again.

"But," he said cheerily, "you know where it is!"

I was determined to get into the dictionary. The best path, I knew, wouldn't be through sparely used words like *Backpfeifengesicht*. I needed to home in on serious terms in the current cultural stew. In the Consolidated Files, I found nothing for *safe space*, which I had added to New Words, and just a couple of slips from the 1970s for *microaggression*; Emily Brewster let me take over drafting entries. I was psyched to be handling these trendy and important terms.

Safe space was, thanks to campus kerfuffles nationwide, having a moment. But it dated to at least the 1970s. "I hate more than anything encroachments on my safe space. Phones ringing. Doorbells ringing. A still room is where the magic happens," the writer Thomas Tryon was quoted as saying in a 1974 profile in the *Philadelphia Inquirer*. *Safe space* appeared in progressive outlets as a twist on older terms like *safe haven* and *safe harbor*. Early cits came from the women's movement (a classified ad in a 1976 issue of the feminist journal *Off Our Backs* read, "Anyone interested in creating a safe space to be mad?") and the personal-growth movement (a college professor in 1977 asked students to sign a pledge to "commit myself to creating a safe space for learning").

Dating *safe space* reflected one of the tangles of deciphering meaning from words on a page written long ago. The 1970s feel fresh to me—bowl cuts, tie-dyed jeans, Matchbox cars, Sting-Ray bikes, *The Mary Tyler Moore Show*—but its "new" words are covered with lunar dust now: one stray citation of a word that might not mean what it would come to mean, a momentary detour in the arc of a word's life. Trolling databases, it's easy to believe you're seeing something that you're not. One day I thought I had antedated the baseball sense of *cheese*, meaning fastball, to 1891 from 1905, which would have been sweet. Then I realized the newspaper snippet was, thanks to a glitch, actually from 1945.

In the case of *safe space*, the tricky part was inflection. Did early users intend *safe space* as a distinct compound noun, with the stress on *safe*? Or was it a phrase in which *safe* modified *space*, with the stress on *space*? Did the classified ad from the women's magazine refer to a specific place called a "safe space" where one could be mad, or a space where one could be mad that happened to be safe? The author of the Thomas Tryon piece, Dorothy Storck, used the lexical unit again in 1981 in a story about a road rage case in Philly. "We have all—yes—imagined ourselves leaping out of our safe space and pounding the one blocking our way." How did Storck intend for that to sound?

The first seemingly explicit citation I found was in a 1981 Associated Press story about a school for troubled rich kids. The AP wrote that the school's aim was "to create what [its founder] calls 'a safe space' where kids feel secure enough to risk behaving in new ways." The phrase was used in the lesbian and gay community in the 1980s and '90s, on and off of college campuses. Two decades later, *safe space* cemented itself in the latest culture wars as a place where a person could avoid uncomfortable ideas or debate. I tried to nimbly stuff all potential spins into my draft: "a place (as on a college campus) intended to be free of bias, conflict, criticism, or potentially threatening actions, ideas, or conversations."

Microaggression was climbing the usage charts, too. The two slips in the Consolidated Files, wedged between *micro-aggregation* and *microalgae*, came from *The Black Collegian* magazine in 1973 and '74. The cits were a couple of aesthetic beauties, pasted clippings surrounded by multicolored stamps and typewriting. The 1974 clip had a bright yellow background with *micro-aggression* underlined in thick red marker. Both bore the stamp of shame: REJECTED FOR 9 COLL, REJECTED FOR C10, REJECTED FOR C11.

The writers of the articles borrowed *micro-aggression* from a Harvard professor of education and psychiatry, Chester Pierce. The earliest known print citation of the word is a newspaper story about an October 1969 speech by Pierce at Vassar College. Pierce, who was Black, was quoted as saying that the American education system "permits generation after generation of black children to grow up to be second class citizens, meaning that it accommodates them to political reality . . . and makes them passive, docile, accepting."

> This is done, according to Dr. Pierce, by visiting on the child an accumulation of micro-aggressions, little put-downs and demeaning oversights which make a black person constantly on the defensive, unable to assume the offensive in any situation, even to fear to initiate conversation with a white person.

Pierce explained the term further in a 1970 book, *The Black Seventies*:

> Even though any single negotiation of offense can in justice be considered of itself to be relatively innocuous, the cumulative effect to the victim and to the victimizer is of an unimaginable magnitude. Hence, the therapist is obliged to pose the idea that offensive mechanisms are usually a *micro-aggression*, as opposed to a gross, dramatic, obvious *macro-aggression* such as lynching.

Pierce's use stuck among Black scholars. Over time the meaning expanded to behavior directed at other groups, including children, women, gays, and lesbians. It took two decades for the word to enter the academic mainstream and three to gain popular use. Along the way it lost its hyphen.

I tracked *microaggression*'s rise in ProQuest, a database that included a solid balance of scholarly and mainstream sources. It was virtually invisible through the 1980s and '90s before spreading among academics in the 2000s. Psychiatry and education professors hosted forums about the phenomenon and used the word in interviews. "Well, *microaggression* is where . . . you're a person of color in line and a Caucasian person cuts in front of you without even acknowledging your existence," one academic said in a 2010 NPR segment about the racial profiling of travelers. "Or if you're an African American and you're driving a nice Lexus, a white policeman pulls you over and doesn't ask for your driver's license or registration, but says, 'Where did you get this car?' Like, if you're a person of color, you can't own a nice automobile."

What propelled *microaggression* into the mainstream, though, was a conservative backlash to public articulations of perceived slights—such as when students of color at UCLA complained about, among other things, a professor correcting their speech. Episodes like that contributed to a right-wing feedback loop of exasperation and mockery. "A '*microaggression*,' in case you're not up on the jargon, is a trivial offense that, for ideological reasons, others are expected to take very seriously," a white male *Wall Street Journal* editorial page writer opined.

The cumulative effect of this breathless offense-taking was not to undermine the concept of *microaggression*, but to propel the term to popular understanding. Database hits for *microaggression* more than doubled in 2015 from the year before, and in newspapers and magazines they more than tripled. In the print dictionary era, a word like *microaggression* would have been bypassed until establishing cultural permanence. The boom year might have been a spike; let's give it time. But in the speedier online dictionary, *microaggression* seemed like an obvious entry. It had become a familiar word, one liberals might endorse as a valid recognition of the reality of human interaction in a bigoted world and conservatives might describe as a made-up term of social grievance.

Writing dictionary definitions reminded me of the scene in *Moneyball* where Oakland Athletics general manager Billy Beane (Brad Pitt) turns to one of his coaches, Ron Washington (Brent Jennings), to help persuade catcher Scott Hatteberg (Chris Pratt) to play first base. "It's not that hard, Scott. Tell him, Wash," Beane says. "It's incredibly hard," Washington replies. Defining *microaggression* was like playing first base. I had to explain a complicated, tentacled idea while avoiding any whiff of partisan ideology—and also interpret a phenomenon that, as a white male, I had never experienced. My illustrative quotations had to avoid tilting one way or another—they weren't supposed to be political at all.

I think I pulled off the latter, quoting articles in *The Atlantic, New York Times,* and *National Review.* The former was trickier. To craft a definition, I read, studied, compared, and labored for days before settling on this mouthful: "a brief comment or action that expresses a subtle and often unconscious or unintentional prejudice, denigration, or insult toward a member of a minority or less privileged group."

But I had doubts. Did the comment have to be "brief"? Was it *always* "subtle" or "unconscious" or "unintentional"? What role did the speaker's intent and the recipient's reaction play? How do you interpret intent? Did intent matter anyway? If the recipient considered a comment to be offensive, was it by definition offensive? This was the lexicographer's dilemma. They are instructed to set aside biases, use data, be thorough, logical, and impartial—but there's a reason no bylines, avatars, or teeny headshots sit next to entries in the dictionary. Objectivity is an illusion best served anonymously.

I did my best and sent the draft to Steve Perrault. More than a year later, an email arrived. "You'll be thrilled (?) to know that a couple of your proposed new terms—*safe space* and *microaggression*—are being added to the OWL," Perrault wrote.

The question mark was unneeded. Perrault shared his edits. *Safe space* would be sailing in as written. *Microaggression* got a workup. Perrault axed "brief," affirmed my other interpretations, and tidied my rambling, comma-filled prose. His final version: "a comment or action that subtly and often unconsciously or unintentionally expresses a prejudiced attitude toward a member of a marginalized group (such as a racial minority)." A few years later, after the 2020 killings of George Floyd and Breonna Taylor by police in Minneapolis and Louisville, respectively, and lots of reading and reflection, I wondered whether "subtly and often unconsciously or unintentionally" excuses the underlying behavior. A microaggression is whatever its recipient says it is.

In the moment, though, I was preoccupied with my accomplishment. I wrote something that was worthy of entry in the dictionary. I documented the march of the English language. I extracted and elucidated meaning from a row of squiggles and lines. As John Morse once said of the work done every day on the editorial floor, I created some knowledge.

Alt-right was another word hurled by the times into universal consciousness. The combining form *alt*, short for alternative, had been around for years. Merriam dated *alt-rock* to 1982. *Alt*'s desired effect is to lend edgy hipness to whatever it's attached to, with a touch of digital culture, from the prefix *alt* on Usenet newsgroups from the early days of the internet. *Alt-right* made its debut in mid-2009 in a headline on a right-wing website: "Economism in the Alt Right." But it didn't break out from neo-Nazi chat rooms and the private emails of its adherents until 2015, when it was used by white nationalist Richard Spencer.

Spencer, known for wearing a "fashy"* haircut and getting punched in the head during an on-camera interview while spouting racist blather on a street corner, claimed coauthorship of the parent form *alternative right*. He was quoted using *alt-right* in a *Washington Post* story about another right-wing neologism. "'#Cuckservative'

---

*I added *fashy* to New Words, defining it as "a hair style with the hair cut short on the sides and back and longer on top worn by young adherents of white nationalism."

is a full-scale revolt, by Identitarians and what I've called the 'alt Right,' against the Republican Party and conservative movement," Spencer told reporter David Weigel.

I added *cuckservative* to New Words. But *alt-right* was more promising, lexicographically speaking. There were just a handful more examples that year; it was so obscure that even Rush Limbaugh told a caller to his radio show that he hadn't heard of it. It limped along in 2016—five hits in January, none in February, nine in March, ten in April. In May, a story about photos of Taylor Swift being used on right-wing message boards boosted the number to around forty. Momentum built in July when right-wing provocateur Milo Yiannopoulos was banned from Twitter and Donald Trump retweeted an antisemitic meme about Hillary Clinton. With forty-nine mentions between the first and seventeenth, August shaped up as another ho-hum month. The following day, Trump appointed Steve Bannon, the head of Breitbart News, as his campaign chair. "The Breitbart alt-right just took over the GOP," read a headline on a *Washington Post* story.

And then *alt-right* took over the language. For the rest of the month, Nexis recorded a thousand mentions. September: 1,280. October: 900. November (the election): 5,800. December: 2,200. January 2017: 1,740. February: 2,560. As the Trumpies settled in to attempt to govern, the focus on the political fringe abated, and *alt-right* mentions dropped every month, falling to 750 in July. Then, in August, white nationalists rioted in Charlottesville, Virginia, and Trump praised "both sides" and triggered an *alt-right* wave: a record 7,400 Nexis hits.

Language corpora, newspaper databases, Merriam's in-house lookup feature—all allow linguists and lexicographers to deconstruct how people use and interact with words. A more obscure bonus is the ability to pinpoint when a word or phrase takes off. Dating first use is discrete, a eureka moment, a discovery. Tracing a word's evolution and identifying precisely when it tips the seesaw into broad awareness is a more forensic task. Tracking *alt-right* was like watching a time-lapse image of a disease spreading. I could freeze on the split second the rogue cells conquered the vital organ.

I knew that *alt-right*'s fifteen minutes could expire at any time—after the midterms, after Trump was gone, after the happy day when the racist, anti-immigrant, antisemitic, antigay, tiki-torch-carrying, frog-memeing trolls stopped polluting America's discourse. But I also knew that it could stick around. My personal distaste for alt-right ideas and behaviors was separate from my job of determining whether *alt-right* should go in the dictionary. And it sure looked like it was used enough in edited media over an extended time to merit inclusion, and it also looked like what it stood for wasn't leaving anytime soon.

When I discovered that *alt-right* wasn't in New Words, I added it and got to work. On the one hand, *alt-right* didn't appear in mainstream outlets before mid-2015. In print dictionary times, the word would have lingered in the card files and maybe, eventually—in six, eight, ten years—been entered in the *Collegiate*. On the other hand, it was everywhere now. I decided, therefore, that it belonged.

My New Words draft was a wordy jumble: "a far-right political ideology often labeled racist or antisemitic that eschews mainstream conservative politics and advocates extreme positions on issues such as race, gender, sexual identity, and immigration." I read Oxford's definition and the Southern Poverty Law Center's. I scanned hundreds of mentions online and plowed through scores of articles, searching like a Torah scholar for substance and nuance. I replaced "eschews" with "rejects." I mulled how to describe the alt-right. Was it an "ideology"? A "grouping"? A "movement"? Since its "members" lived largely on the internet—Breitbart, 4chan, the Daily Stormer—I added "online," and then removed it and then added it again. I asked myself: Should I shift "racist" and "antisemitic" to the end of the definition? Should I delete the generic groupings? Were its proponents "white nationalists"? Were they "fascists"?

After a dozen drafts, more citation research, watching videos of an alt-right conference at which attendees gave Nazi salutes, and yet more citation research, I finally settled on this:

>alt-right *also* alt right *noun* : a far-right political grouping that rejects mainstream conservative politics and promotes mainly through online media positions characterized as white nationalist, anti-semitic, racist, sexist, and homophobic

I noted that *alt-right* registered 66 million hits on Google and 238,000 on Google News, and more than three thousand on Nexis. "Whether it sticks as a political term is obviously unclear," I wrote in a spreadsheet box for data and comment, "but its prominence vis a vis the Trump administration I think establishes its importance."

Alt-right was part of a batch of drafts I sent to Steve Perrault. It was in there with *ball hawk*, an existing entry that I redid with a new sense, "a baseball fan who attends games in order to acquire baseballs hit or thrown by players, coaches, or other on-field personnel." And *kabaddi*, "a game originating in ancient India played between two teams (usually of seven players each) in which players taking turns cross into their opponents' half of a court or field and without taking a breath attempt to touch a member of the other team and return to their side without being pinned to the ground or pushed out of the field of play." And *GOAT*. And *alt-right*'s bedmates, *cuckservative* and *cuck*: "a Republican party official or voter whose beliefs or actions (especially on subjects such as immigration, race, or gender) are judged insufficiently conservative by far-right activists."

Ten months later, the OWL gained a modest 250 new words and definitions. "These terms have shown themselves to be fully established members of the language," Merriam said in a post, "some after hanging about on the fringes for decades, and others after proving themselves too useful to ignore in relatively short order." There was *troll*, which Emily Brewster had defined years earlier.

Froyo and *sriracha*. The *Internet of Things* and *cardioverter*, a medical device with which, thanks to a personal history of atrial fibrillation, I was familiar. *Pregame* as a verb meaning to drink before an event or party. A short shot in basketball called a *bunny*. And then: "With politics seeming to be ever-prominent in the public's mind, terms like *alt-right* and *dog whistle* are not surprising additions."

Yas! I clicked on the link. Perrault had done a substantial edit, and I couldn't blame him. *Alt-right* was a sensitive and critical entry, one that, as with any confusing, polarizing political -ism, was likely to enjoy a lot of clicks and potentially hate mail. He needed to closely vet the amateur's work.

alt-right *noun, less commonly* **alt right** : a right-wing, primarily online political movement or grouping based in the U.S. whose members reject mainstream conservative politics and espouse extremist beliefs and policies typically centered on ideas of white nationalism

I bowed to Perrault's fingers and wrote him a note of thanks. I was glad time had passed. The word was evolving, I decided; it needed to percolate. I sounded like an old-school disciple of Webster, Gove, and Morse, the last of whom told me he supported giving politically loaded words time to establish themselves. He had opposed entering *backdoor draft*, a term critical of the military during the Iraq War in 2003, and *partial-birth abortion*, which was coined by antichoice activists in the 1990s, when they were peaking in the media. "I don't like being the force multiplier for any kind of partisan position," Morse said. Merriam waited, and those terms eventually got in.

But maybe the dictionary was evolving, too. On Merriam's old calendar, two years—the length of time from *alt-right*'s reemergence to its enshrinement—might as well have been two days. The process with *alt-right* struck a balance: reflecting but not reacting to the news of the moment while protecting the scholarly distance the company so cherished.

12
social media

: forms of electronic communication through which users create online communities to share information, ideas, personal messages, and other content

In the long history of dictionaries, there is one reliable constant: the incessant bitching of offended readers. No book provoked more widespread and systematic upset than the *Third*, for its inclusion of *ain't*, its supposed laxity on *imply* versus *infer*, its alleged hastening of the death of proper English. But it's probably not an exaggeration to say that every day since 1961—or maybe 1847—Merriam has heard from readers about one perceived linguistic or grammatical perversion or another.

In a conference room adjacent to John Morse's office one day, I turned the pages of leather-bound binders stamped LETTERS that held copies—carbon and then photo—of Merriam correspondence dating to the early 1900s. Every fifth or so onion skin was a polite response to a reader asking the editors why a particular word wasn't in the dictionary or informing them that a definition was wrong. "We thank you for your letter of January 17th bringing to our attention the word 'moron', and shall at once refer it to our editors for investigation," a Merriam staffer wrote on January 22, 1913, to Dr. Mazyck P. Ravenel of the University of Wisconsin.

The common thread through the decades is an abject, though understandable, failure to comprehend the function and operation of a dictionary, that is, to cull from carefully edited publications evidence of the way words are actually used in written and spoken English. People focus on their individual beliefs. But lexicographers aren't concerned with what the Bible tells you, or your political convictions, or your opinion that, if only certain words were removed from the dictionary, the world would live as one. All they care about is portraying the meanings of words clearly and accurately based on the available evidence.

For a dictionary publisher, there's no winning. In the 1990s, the toy and game company Hasbro Inc. ordered Merriam to remove about two hundred words labeled *vulgar, offensive, disparaging,* etc., from the *Official Scrabble Players Dictionary*. In 2009, Merriam endured weeks of vile and vitriolic culture-war hate mail and coverage after Stephen Colbert on his Comedy Central late-night show, *The Colbert Report*, did a segment on a revision to the entry for *marriage*—made six years earlier for the print *Collegiate*—that added the sub-subsense "the state of being united to a person of the same sex in a relationship like that of a traditional marriage." ("That means gay marriage," Colbert's faux-conservative anchor said. "I'm beginning to think Merriam and Webster were conjugating more than just irregular verbs.") In the aftermath of the 2018 school massacre in Parkland, Florida, the right-wing website *The Federalist* asserted without evidence that Merriam had changed its definition of *assault rifle* "to one that matches what gun control advocates are pushing for." (In fact, the updated entry just added more detail about the weapon, based on citations.) And in 2023, a California man was sentenced to a year and a day in prison after sending and posting a series of violent anti-LGBTQ messages and threats against Merriam over its definitions of *girl*, *female*, and *woman* that forced the temporary shutdown of the company's offices in Springfield and New York.

To lexicographers, words are like abstract expressionist paintings, complicated and demanding of quiet contemplation and analysis. Their power lies in their existence, not their deployment. To others, though, words are armaments in an endless war, and the dictionary is the manufacturer. Two hundred years of marketing have pushed that idea—the American dictionary as influencer, authority, power. If you don't like a word, you know who to blame. "They didn't care about the mechanics of language change," former Merriam editor Kory Stamper wrote about the people outraged over the *marriage* edit, "they cared about the mechanics of culture change."

But for all of the things that have prompted red-faced readers to howl at Merriam—an entry, a definition, some bugaboo based in grammatical or lexicographic misunderstanding, ignorance about what dictionaries do and how they do it—no one could remember an illustrative quotation triggering a public-relations crisis.

"You did it for the first time," John Morse said.

I had started getting more words into the OWL. I was especially proud of identifying a new, sports-related sense for a very common word: *run*. After the verb *set* with a total of thirty-six senses, *run* is one of the longest entries in Merriam with thirty. But—accepts gold statuette and delivers gracious speech thanking everyone who made this moment possible—I added a thirty-first sense that generations of Merriam editors had missed: "*baseball* : to eject (a player, coach, or manager) from a game." My Oxford host Peter Gilliver spent nine months revising *run*—82 senses, 230 subsenses, 130 phrases—but, British or not, he also missed the sports-misbehavior sense, too.

I also drafted the entry for *N-word*—also *the N-word* or *the n-word*—illustrated with a quotation about a school district banning *Adventures of Huckleberry Finn* because of Twain's "overuse of the N-word." But neither *run* nor *N-word* caused any post-publication fuss. Instead, it was another, seemingly innocuous tally on my defining scorecard, which I learned about from a post by Merriam on Twitter: "Wake up! 'Sheeple' is in the dictionary now." I clicked on the link to see the entry. Steve Perrault had edited my draft only slightly.

sheeple *plural noun, informal* : people who are docile, compliant, or easily influenced : people likened to sheep

The serendipitous find was more thrilling than if Perrault had emailed me a heads-up. I dumped a bucket of Gatorade on myself on social media. Then my language friend Ben Zimmer emailed: *Sheeple* was blowing up.

I'd flagged *sheeple* while doomscrolling during Trump Part I. On the technology site *Recode*, below a nightmare-fuel closeup of Trump's hair, journalist Kara Swisher had criticized some Silicon Valley bigwigs—including the heads of Apple, Google, Microsoft, Amazon, and Facebook—for agreeing to meet Trump at his eponymous Manhattan office tower after the 2016 election. "The leaders of tech," she wrote, "should be ashamed of themselves for lining up like sheeple after all the numskull* attacks Trump has made on what is pretty much the United States' most important, innovative and future-forward business sector." (In 2025, some of those same execs sat behind Trump at his second inauguration.)

Sheeple didn't strike me as unusual. It's such a familiar portmanteau— *sheep* + peo*ple*—that I figured it must have been in the dictionary. But it wasn't in the *Unabridged* or the OWL. And it wasn't in New Words.

The *OED* did enter the word, with the delicate label *depreciative*: "People likened to sheep in being docile, foolish, or impressionable." It dated *sheeple* to 1945, with a citation from a journal called *The Musical Times and Singing Class Circular*: "The People, as ever (I spell

---

*The *Unabridged* favors this spelling, which dates to 1697. The OWL prefers *numbskull*.

it 'Sheeple'), will stand anything." The next cit was from a 1949 book called *The Old Hokum Bucket* by Atlanta newspaper columnist Ernest Rogers, who might have been the first to use the phrase "We the Sheeple."

For the next thirty years, *sheeple* popped up only sporadically: a Louisville forestry executive complaining in 1962 about "sheeple" who "can't see very far ahead and thus limit the success of forestry programs"; a reader in the *Winona* (Minnesota) *Daily News* in 1974 lamenting, "Sheeple working at things they can't possibly believe in, for money to spend on things they don't need."

Then it was discovered by the progun, antitax, antigovernment crowd, and the word's life arc changed. "To understand the American Patriots Association, you have to speak the language," the *Miami Herald* wrote in 1983. "Taxpayers are 'sheeple,' short for sheeplike people. Bureaucrats are 'bureau-rats.' Internal Revenue Service agents are 'tyrants and despots.' Dollar bills are 'Ferns,' which stands for Federal Reserve Notes (FRNS)." A 1984 *Wall Street Journal* story about live-free-or-die New Hampshire opened with an anecdote about a right-wing bookseller: "Mrs. Anderson begins every book sale with a lecture, and in this instance she derides taxpayers in general as submissive 'sheep people'—or 'sheeple' for short." In the 1990s, *sheeple* turned up in news stories about would-be bombers of the IRS, about the paterfamilias of the Ruby Ridge standoff against the feds, and about the homegrown terrorists who bombed the Oklahoma City federal building.

"As we become we the sheeple in this country, somebody's got to stand up and give Janet Reno the finger," lib-owning rocker Ted Nugent said in 1998 of the then U.S. attorney general. "I'm real proud to piss off the status quo and scare 'em." The status quo appeared unmoved by the singer of "Cat Scratch Fever" and "Wango Tango." But as far-right politics settled in the mainstream, *sheeple* began its upward march. Nexis hits cracked fifty in 2005, one hundred in 2007, two hundred in 2009, and three hundred in 2016.

"New York *Times* Demands Sheeple Wake Up and Quit Worshipping Breakfast," *New York* magazine wrote in a headline.

On the ironic left, *sheeple* got a boost from the webcomic *xkcd*. In 2009, its creator, Randall Munroe, published a panel titled "Sheeple" in which five stick figures on the subway each have the same thought bubble: "Look at these people. Glassy-eyed automatons going about their daily lives, never stopping to look around and *think*! I'm the only conscious human in a world of sheep." He followed in 2012 with "Wake Up Sheeple." A stick figure with a megaphone shouts: "Your government has turned against you! Corporations control your every thought! Open your eyes! WAKE UP, SHEEPLE!" Then a sheep-person holding a staff breaks through the earth, proclaiming, "TEN THOUSAND YEARS WE SLUMBERED. NOW WE RIIIIIIISE."

After amassing dozens of sample sentences, I submitted four to Steve Perrault: from Kara Swisher, Ted Nugent, a 1995 *New York Times* story about the Oklahoma City bombing, and a 2015 CNN review of an Apple phone case. He chose the latter two to accompany the definition.

The purpose of verbal illustrations (made-up sentences or fragments) and illustrative quotations (real-life ones), editorial operations director Madeline Novak's style guide explained, is to "help the user make sense of the definition." Editors were advised to keep it simple. Avoid quotations that include "irony, puns, striking originality, wit, etc." Avoid "narrative interest" that can distract a reader. Most of all, don't piss anyone off. "Knowing, as we do," the thirty-eight-page guide said,

> that people can be quick to take offense at real or imagined slights, and hoping, as we do, that people will find our dictionary entries helpful, we should do what we can to avoid offending people gratuitously. This means: Except in the illustrations of words relating to politics, religion, and other touchy topics, you

should avoid politics, religion, and other touchy topics. A person who gets upset at something that's mentioned in an illustration is a person who is unable to take in the information we're trying to convey to them. If the cause of the upset doesn't need to be there, why include it?

Sheeple obviously had political connotations. The bulk of the quotations I collected would annoy someone on either the left or the right. But its use wasn't always political. I thought Perrault made a sensible decision. The Swisher and Nugent quotes were directly political. The other two balanced *sheeple*'s history but seemed innocuous enough. The *Times* quotation reflected the word's cuckoo antigovernment roots: "James Nichols, who ran the family farm here, stamped dollar bills with red ink in protest against currency and told his neighbors that they were 'sheeple' for obeying authority like livestock." The CNN one displayed its more expansive modern attributes: "Apple's debuted a battery case for the juice-sucking iPhone—an ungainly lumpy case the sheeple will happily shell out $99 for."

Not for a millisecond did I think an old review of a phone case made by a company with annual revenue (at the time) north of $200 billion would inspire any reaction at all. But I didn't appreciate the cult of Apple, or the nature of discourse in the internet age.

One of the first commenters on Merriam's tweet anticipated what was about to unfold. "That second example sentence . . ." Then, amid the usual snark and tsktsking, came genuine outrage: "That's a low blow using Apple as an example. Just lost a little respect for Webster." "shouldn't you at least try not to use examples that might offend people?" "Wow! You put in a pejorative term, then used a specific group of people to illustrate it. Is Merriam-Webster used as an example for Idiotic?"

The Apple army stormed the *sheeple* entry. "This is disgusting, complete disrespect to people who use Apple's technology to enrich their lives and the ones around them," one reader hyperventilated. Another offered a multipart defense of the actual battery case. Media didn't miss this perfect viral story opportunity. "Apple Fans Are 'Sheeple': Merriam-Webster," *Fortune* magazine's website declared. The *San Francisco Chronicle*, CNET, BoingBoing, Gizmodo, Yahoo. "The dictionary takes a dig at one particular tech brand," NPR host Rachel Martin said on *Morning Edition*. The pro-Apple, anti-Merriam invective ("This is probably one of the most disgusting things I have ever seen") prompted a corresponding heap of anti-Apple schadenfreude ("Where is the safe space for the Apple users?" Safe space! Hah!).

During my time inside Merriam, my inner journalist and inner lexicographer battled constantly. I wasn't predisposed to the inoffensive, the way a seasoned definer would be. I thought a funny, cutting, sexy, or culturally relevant quotation could say more about how we use words than a vanilla sentence devoid of context. I wasn't mocking Apple lovers any more than I was taunting Ted Nugent. I thought I was choosing colorful examples of the word in action. Insta-outrage society disagreed.

The morning after the definition posted, I sent Perrault some of the tech-world reports. He already knew. Even though "this particular example captures the word's disparaging quality very effectively," he told me, the blowback was "a good illustration of why we generally try to avoid quotes that specifically criticize a named individual, company, etc. We're not looking to be provocative, despite what people may think."

The stories piled up. Even the animal-rights group PETA joined the fray, defending sheep as "gentle, social, and intelligent animals" who are "so smart that they listen to and watch the wisest, oldest leaders of the flock and follow them, a commonsense thing to do if you don't know the ropes." (PETA urged readers to boycott wool, not Merriam.) A handful of complaints arrived in Merriam's inbox, the social-media vitriol continued, and the walls closed in. Perrault reminded me that a quotation should illustrate use, keeping the reader's attention on the word, not what's happening in the quote. "And besides," he added, "we really don't need the grief."

I asked Perrault whether it was turning into a PR headache. It was.

"Unfortunately, the Apple quote wasn't doing its job very well, since everyone was focusing on the writer's criticism of the company and its customers," he emailed. "That was never our intention, of course, though in retrospect I probably should have realized that it was likely to happen sooner or later. So we removed the quote. We'll replace it somewhere down the road with another example."

Sheeple-gate was good for business. There were dozens of online stories about the kerfuffle, including translations into German, Greek, Turkish, Japanese, French, Czech *and* Slovak, Dutch, Portuguese, Vietnamese, Romanian, Italian, Russian, Hungarian, Hebrew, and Chinese. The "Wake up!" tweet, a nod to the millennials who read *xkcd*, elicited more than 1,300 likes and 2,100 retweets, five or six times the usual Word of the Day promo. All of the attention drove people to Merriam's website. And while I wasn't trying to be snarky when I picked that Apple quote, readers interpreted it that way for two reasons: because tech sheeple live in glass bubbles and because Merriam was earning a reputation as an online provocateur—a troll.

The *OED* traces the verb *troll*—"To move or walk about or to and fro; to ramble, saunter, stroll, 'roll'"—to German and French. Its earliest known use in English is in a 1377 Middle English poem by William Langland, *Piers Plowman*: "And thus hath he trolled forth this two & thretty wynter." Among many senses of *troll* over the centuries, the one from which the online arsonist meaning most logically derives is trailing a line in the water to attract fish, and its figurative offspring, "to entice, allure." The *OED* cites a 1639 play, *The Ladies Triall*, by John Ford: "I foster a decoy here, And she *trowles* on her ragged customer."

The *OED* entered noun and verb forms of the online *troll* in 2006. It traced first use to 1992, on a Usenet group, alt.net.folklore. Perrault added the noun to New Words in October 2009—"a person who tries to cause problems on an Internet message board by posting messages that cause other people to argue, become angry, etc." Emily Brewster drafted noun and verb senses—"Internet message board" didn't last far into the new decade—that were added to the *Unabridged* in 2014. Even before then, she had noticed that the verb form was becoming a straight synonym for *harass* or *antagonize*. By 2017, non-digital *trolling* was, Brewster said, "of course, everywhere and I keep meaning to draft a definition and get it on its way." She finally did and it entered the OWL later that year.*

Merriam itself became trollish gradually and then suddenly. For years after joining Twitter in 2009, the company's feed was as anodyne as this early offering: "Jolly Red-Suited Man Fact: 'Santa Claus' comes from the Dutch 'Sinterklaas,' which comes from 'Sint Nikolaas,' for 'St. Nicholas.'" The account shared words of the day and links to posts about linguistic tidbits. "Stuffy and scheduled and not interactive," Lisa Schneider told me. As Merriam's new head of digital, Schneider wanted to use social media to lure people to a revamped website. The dictionary's online presence, she said, didn't reflect "the personality of the company as represented by the people who work there, who were smart and funny and sassy."

To perform a personality makeover, Schneider hired Lauren Naturale, who had a master's in English literature from Cal-Berkeley and had taught English and worked in digital media. Soon after, Merriam's Twitter feed began highlighting words in the news, deploying emoji, and clapping back at commenters. Naturale quoted from *The Pickwick Papers* and zinged a blogger from a broey sports website.

---

* **troll** *transitive verb* **2 a :** to harass, criticize, or antagonize (someone) especially by provocatively disparaging or mocking public statements, postings, or acts

One tweet at a time, she created a persona for the oldster reference publisher: bookish and witty but also streetwise and cutting; "lol, smart," as one commenter wrote, but also able to burn, own, or, in internet lingo, pwn anyone or -thing that got in its face.* Who could win a war of words with a dictionary?

The 2016 presidential campaign, especially Trump's candidacy, made @MerriamWebster a celebrity. Naturale's first viral tweet was about Trump misspelling *honor* ("Wow, every poll said I won the debate last night. Great honer!") and, in one tweet, both *lightweight* and *choker* ("Lying Ted Cruz and leightweight chocker Marco Rubio teamed up last night in a last ditch effort to stop our great movement. They failed!"). Naturale drafted a tweet—as a joke, she told me—and turned around her laptop to show a colleague:

> **honer:** one that hones (http://merriam-webster.com/dictionary/hone)
> **leightweight:** We have no. idea.
> **chocker:** merriam-webster.com/dictionary/nope

"Is this okay?" Naturale asked.
"Do it, do it!"
She linked to one of Trump's tweets and published.
"The first fifty or a hundred retweets, we were happy," Naturale recalled. "Then we started to worry I was going to get fired."

Clicks were fine; unwanted controversy, not so much. But the post was liked and retweeted almost two thousand times apiece. The replies were nearly unanimous with appreciation: "a dictionary that talks smack is my favorite" . . . "Thank you, @MerriamWebster,

---

*Merriam entered the abbreviation *LOL* or *lol*—"laugh out loud; laughing out loud"—in 2009. The *OED* dates first usage to 1989 and includes a verb form ("I *lolled* and *lolled*"). Merriam added *pwn* in 2022: "to dominate and defeat : OWN, ROUT." *Pwn* is believed to have originated as a typo—because O and P are adjacent on the qwerty keyboard—and was popularized by online gamers. The *OED* dates first usage to 1999 ("Yeah, shiiit! I PWNED YO @zz!").

from copy editors and voters everywhere" . . . "Have I told you today how much I love you?" . . . "You are my favorite dictionary forevermore" . . . "The dictionary wins Twitter today, hands down." Dozens of media mentions followed, including articles by the *Washington Post*, CBS News, and *Huffington Post*.

Merriam's blog and social media campaign coverage was mostly uncontroversial: live-tweeting debates, reporting words that were spiking—*xenophobe, demagogic, locker-room, treason, deplorable*. But the pointed comments about Trump, his acolytes, and the political climate generated unprecedented online engagement and media publicity. On the eve of the election, Lauren Naturale and her colleagues changed Merriam's Twitter banner to the definition of *Götterdämmerung*—"a collapse (as of a society or regime) marked by catastrophic violence and disorder *broadly* : DOWNFALL"—over a picture of Max Brückner's set design from the final scene of Richard Wagner's opera of the same name.

When Trump tweeted "unpresidented" instead of "unprecedented," Naturale responded: "Good morning! The #WordOfTheDay is . . . not 'unpresidented'. We don't enter that word. That's a new one," and linked to the definition for *huh*. When Trump adviser Kellyanne Conway coined the Orwellian phrase "alternative facts," lookups for *fact* did indeed spike. Naturale wrote: "A fact is a piece of information presented as having objective reality." It earned 45,000 likes and 55,000 retweets in two days. And when lookups for *misogyny* jumped after Trump's victory, Naturale tweeted a link to a post about the word illustrated with a box of Tic Tacs, referring to the infamous *Access Hollywood* tape, on which Trump said, "I've got to use some Tic Tacs, just in case I start kissing her."

Was Merriam a "liberal" dictionary dumping on an illiberal administration? Was it, to quote Brewster's online sense of *troll*, behaving like "a person who intentionally antagonizes others online by posting inflammatory, irrelevant, or offensive comments or other disruptive content"? Merriam insisted no. At a time when words were central to the national discourse—post-truth and post-fact, to use two that hadn't been entered—Merriam was supplying information to help at least a large, frustrated, and left-leaning segment of the population sort through confusion, and dark humor to help it cope.

The dictionary's job is to be an unbiased arbiter of language and its evolution, one of the last apolitical authorities standing. Merriam was using a new medium and a provocative tone to defend the language against double-talk, ignorance, and newspeak—"propagandistic language marked by euphemism, circumlocution, and the inversion of customary meanings." And then, on the same medium favored by the new president, it was holding public figures accountable for their words. Pointing out the definition of *fact* when someone tries to co-opt facts wasn't subversive, it was journalistic. "Right now there are a lot of questions about what is true," the lexicographer Jesse Sheidlower said in one of the many profiles of Merriam during the 2016 campaign. "We want clear statements about what things are, and dictionaries provide that."

Merriam wasn't the first dictionary to serve as a fifth column of the fourth estate. Samuel Johnson defined *oats* as "a grain, which in England is generally given to horses, but in Scotland supports the people." The American writer Ambrose Bierce's satirical *The Devil's Dictionary*, published in 1911, defined *president* as "The leading figure in a small group of men of whom—and of whom only—it is positively known that immense numbers of their countrymen did not want any of them for President." More broadly, Noah Webster had a totally nationalist agenda—he wanted to *Americanize* the language, after all. And the Merriam brothers and their successors hitched the brand to patriotism and progress in what would become known as the American Century; not for nothing did the company add *International* to the name of its unabridged dictionary.

But modern Merriam wouldn't entirely own its new role, feigning snow-pure objectivity when asked about its more incendiary online behavior. "Why is it now that just copying and pasting a definition of a word—like *feminism*, like *fact*, like *complicit*—why is that viewed as a subversive act?" Peter Sokolowski, Merriam's usual media spokesperson, asked during an appearance on CBS This Morning. Why? Because, after all of the wink-winking, posting the definition of *Götterdämmerung* on the eve of an election in which one of the candidates is possibly a madman isn't just *viewed* as subversive, it actually is. (Schneider ordered the banner taken down the next morning, but the tweet lived on.) Because announcing that "We'll be tweeting the #debate. When you're a star, they let you do it" is funny and topical. But it's also another dig at the *Access Hollywood* tape.

Merriam was feeding a narrative about the Trump era. If you're even slightly, slyly rebellious, you're part of the opposition. If you're not, you're a collaborator. But while subtweeting the president enhanced the company's newfound popularity—Trump was a rising tide floating the ratings, pageviews, and subscriptions of all media boats—it also threatened to undermine its longstanding credibility. Actual trolls were always ready to pounce.

For business reasons, Merriam was right to capitalize on the fervor and ferment of the election. Unlike in 1961, when the stink bombs lobbed at Merriam after publication of *Webster's Third* were prompted by a deliberate misreading of the contents of the book—a cabal of permissive descriptivists is trying to destroy the language!—the dictionary's new image was grounded in its own marketing. "The year is 2017. America is a tire fire," one fan tweeted. "The resistance is led by Teen Vogue, Badlands National Park, and the Merriam-Webster dictionary."

Being part of the resistance means that every act is viewed as political, or a provocation, even when it's not. For a brand predicated on impartiality, objectivity, and trust, that was a risky place to venture; as Michael Jordan said, Republicans buy sneakers, too. By the time Trump took office in January 2017, Merriam's reputation as troller-in-chief was so entrenched that the dictionary was praised for being subversive even when it wasn't. "Merriam-Webster is at it again and we can't get enough," one site wrote in response to a blog post about the history of the word *blackmail* that made no reference to Trump or anything in the news.

In 2016, Merriam pushed out a scheduled tweet: "It's fine to use mad to mean 'angry'—even if doing so makes some people mad," and linked to a blog post on the topic. (Spoiler alert: Dictionaries have sanctioned *mad* for *angry* for more than 250 years.) A *Slate* editor, Gabriel Roth, wrote in a late-night mini-thread that Merriam was "turning into the 'chill' parent who lets your friends come over and get high."

> It's great at first, it's nice to have friends and a place to get high, but something about it starts to feel wrong.
>
> If no one's making rules for us, it means we're responsible for our own decisions, and we feel kind of ambivalent about that tbqh
>
> Sometimes we need totally arbitrary and unfair rules and fuck you mom no one ever died from smoking pot it's actually safer than alcohol

Roth told me at the time that he didn't mean you shouldn't use *mad* for *angry*, only that Merriam's "performative lexicographic wokeness, the 'Hi-we're-the-cool-descriptivist-dictionary' bit" was getting stale. It was fair criticism from a media professional.

The next morning, Naturale replied to Roth on Twitter: "No one cares how you feel." Roth's mentions became a cesspool. One person called him "an abjectly disgusting creature." Because he seemed to be making a call for authority, right-wing nuts showed up in his feed. "It was strange and it was not fun," Roth said. He wrote about the experience. In the past, brands like Merriam were "prevented by commercial imperatives from acting like a dick in public," Roth wrote. Not anymore. "It turns out that an aggressive, forward-looking brand—a venerable-but-staid brand that has turned to social media to add a bit of edginess to its image, perhaps—can indeed act like a dick in public, and will be rewarded with thousands of retweets, with celebratory gifs, with a BuzzFeed post chronicling its 'iconic drag.'"

Merriam never apologized to Roth. By choosing to be "authentic and quick and sassy," Schneider said the company ceded some image control to the vagaries of the internet. "This is a tradeoff that we've made as a business decision, as a company," she told me. "I think we have benefited so greatly from the authenticity and from being ourselves and answering things quickly that not everything is necessarily perfect." As for Roth, Schneider claimed that he had attacked Merriam's methodology, "and we take that very seriously." Naturale's tweet, she said, was "in the spirit of good fun." Naturale told me she was sorry that Roth was harassed online, but "I was not in the mood for straight white dudes"—Roth was an editor, writer, and author who worked for a major online magazine—"talking about the need for authoritarianism. You want the dictionary to discipline you, here's what discipline looks like."

For decades, Merriam attracted media attention when it published a new edition of a print dictionary, released a list of words added to the digital dictionary, or was dragged into a dustup over an entry. Now Merriam had a profile that was driving traffic: defender of democracy, check-and-balance on the language, five-tool smart-ass. It even won a Webby award in 2017 for best writing on social media. "Their Twitter account taught a master class in throwing shade," *New York Times* crossword puzzle editor Will Shortz said in presenting the award. "No one was safe from their, dare I say it, savage Twitter presence." Winners had to give five-word acceptance speeches. Lisa Schneider walked onstage brandishing a paperback

Merriam. "This," she said, pausing for dramatic effect, "is your secret weapon."

Privately, however, Schneider had doubts about Merriam's approach, especially after succeeding John Morse as publisher. She didn't like being labeled the "liberal" dictionary. She didn't like the media attention that branded Merriam as such. She also knew the Trump era wouldn't last forever. Her job was to ensure that Merriam did. Naturale would leave the company after sixteen months. Merriam backed off the sass.

But the company had achieved some goals. Media coverage skyrocketed.* More readers were clicking to the website from Twitter and Facebook. By 2025, Merriam was closing in on two million followers online, hundreds of thousands more than Oxford and Dictionary.com combined. Trump was good for clicks and then he wasn't essential, even during his political comeback. Merriam changed the banner on its social media pages to #WordsMatter, and then to a photo of the entry for *social media* from a new printing of the *Collegiate*.

When *sheeple*-gate broke, the dictionary was accused of malice aforetweet. "Hey look at that—a little bit of controversy and suddenly a 200 year old list of words is in the news again!" one commenter wrote, calling my choice of the iPhone case review quotation "clickbait." The news site Mashable labeled Merriam a "shade-master." NPR reminded readers that "The Merriam-Webster Dictionary Has Been Trolling Trump on Twitter for Months." Clickbait. Shade. Troll. *Sheeple* was post-politics confirmation of what the dictionary had become. Merriam, the tech blog Gizmodo wrote, "has been

---

*More than three hundred media outlets wrote about the following tweet, which is as trollingly scandalous as anything Merriam ever said about Trump: "Have a great #MemorialDayWeekend. The hot dog is a sandwich."

flirting with the thin line between cheekily relevant and irritatingly attention-seeking."

On the one hand, *sheeple* pushed people to the website, which was good for Merriam's bottom line. Every unique visitor mattered. On the other hand, the Apple quotation distracted from the definition, and arguably always would, reinforcing the idea promoted by its social media feeds that the dictionary was in the business of provocation as much as explanation. I was torn. Lexicographically, I understood that the quotation was imperfect, and I felt terrible that I had caused Steve Perrault editorial agita. Journalistically, I wanted Merriam to have my back—to explain to readers that quotations aren't selected to troll anyone—and not cave to the Apple stans.*

After the fuss ended, John Morse told me that making editorial changes in the face of controversy can encourage the idea that controversy will produce editorial changes. "You don't want to create the impression that the world gets to vote on what definitions are good and what definitions are bad." But having fought these fights before—all of the big word blowups had occurred on his watch—Morse understood that you had to pick your spots. "It's a tough enough time for dictionaries to mount defenses of all the things that have to be defended to find yourself defending a definition that, truth of the matter, your heart's not really in the defense."

Merriam later began supplementing example sentences collected by editors with ones auto-generated from online news sources. It added a warning label to those: "Any opinions expressed in the examples do not represent those of Merriam-Webster or its editors."

---

*Merriam added *stan* in 2019 as a noun, "an extremely or excessively enthusiastic and devoted fan," and a verb, "to exhibit fandom to an extreme or excessive degree : to be an extremely devoted and enthusiastic fan of someone or something."

13

news

: material reported in a newspaper or news periodical or on a newscast

In January 2017, more than three hundred word dorks, myself included, packed a hotel ballroom in Austin, Texas, to select the 2016 Word of the Year. Nearly half of the nominees were related to the president-elect: *post-truth, basket of deplorables, unpresidented, alt-right, fake news, locker-room banter, yuuuge.*

But the gathering seemed more a catharsis than a celebration of what for most people in the room was an annus horribilis.* These might not have been "the best words," which Donald Trump claimed to possess, but they were the most emblematic of the times. As we settled into our chairs, the vibe was ominous but not apocalyptic. It was pre-inauguration, pre-Charlottesville, pre-impeachments, pre-pandemic, pre–2020 election, pre–January 6, pre–felony indictments, pre–felony convictions, pre–assassination attempts, pre–2024 election, pre–DOGE: pre-everything.

"I'm waiting for someone to say *bigly*," WOTY emcee Ben Zimmer announced. Someone did, and the word was nominated for

---

*The *Unabridged* dates *annus horribilis*, "a disastrous or unfortunate year," to 1890, when it was used in an article in the *London Quarterly Review* to refer to the year 1870 and the formal adoption of the doctrine of papal infallibility.

WTF Word of the Year, a catch-all category of words that might cause offense.

"For most euphemistic, I'd go with *tiny hands*," Berkeley professor Geoffrey Nunberg said. In the 1980s, the smart and snarky *Spy* magazine dubbed Trump "the short-fingered vulgarian," and his Republican primary foe Marco Rubio had referred to his "small hands."

"I'm not sure of its lexical status," Zimmer replied.

"Would *pussy* count as a euphemism?" another attendee asked, referring to what Trump claimed on the *Access Hollywood* tape that he was free to grab.

During the debate over Political Word of the Year, Stanford linguistics professor John Rickford, a titan in the field, rose to address the room.

"I wanted to make a plug for *nasty woman*," he said of the phrase that Trump called Hillary Clinton at a debate, which had been adopted by some women as a slogan of honor. "I like its repurposing and the way it immediately came to . . ."

Rickford, a cheerful native of Guyana in his late sixties, was drowned out by a cascade of laughter. The lexicographer and public-radio language-show host Grant Barrett, who was typing commentary on an overhead screen, had made a double-entendre joke about the phrase.

Rickford looked up, chuckled, and didn't skip a beat. He mentioned an article by an African American Studies professor about "semantic inversion," in which *bad* became *baaaaad*, and was "repurposed and embraced." "So I think it's that spirit," Rickford said of *nasty woman*. "It has a wonderful linguistic element and I like the way it developed."

Fingers snapped in approval. Zimmer noted that Hillary Clinton's *basket of deplorables* remark about Trump supporters also was repurposed as a mark of pride. "One could say it may have had a large effect on the results of the election," Zimmer said. "It's a case where we see that words actually matter, whether for better or worse."

After the tumult of 2016 and the straight anxiety about 2017 and beyond, Word of the Year was a distraction and a lifeline, a way to scream: "YES! That's exactly what the year meant!"—and a eulogy for the twelvemonth past. WOTY promised closure, and everyone was looking for that. In the middle of the crowd, Dan Villareal, a linguistics postdoc, rose to his feet.

"Okay," Villareal said. "It's 2016. *Dumpster fire?*"

Earlier in the evening, the fire emoji, and also the trashcan and fire emojis used together to represent *dumpster fire*, won the emoji group. One of the older attendees had asked what *dumpster fire* meant. "It is used to describe an incredibly catastrophic situation," Zimmer explained. "Like some people think 2016 was one long *dumpster fire*."

Normalize, *post-truth*, and the fire emoji also got WOTY noms—the first time an emoji had made the list of finalists. Then John Rickford stood again. "Hold the screen stuff," he said. "*Woke*. Granted it's been around a while. But only if you stay woke can you put out the dumpster fire."

The house was brought down, and I figured it was game over. But then Nicole Holliday, a linguistics postdoc at the time, lobbied passionately against *woke*—"because it was appropriated from the Black solidarity movement in the 1960s and I think that we are so late to this game and last year was anything but woke," she said.

A chant rose: "Vote, vote, vote, vote!"

"Okay, how many votes for *dumpster fire* as Word of the Year for 2016?" Zimmer asked. One hundred twelve hands shot up. *Woke* trailed with seventy-four, followed by *normalize* with sixty, and *post-truth* with twenty-five. No word claimed a majority, so the two top vote-getters met in a runoff. Final score: *dumpster fire* 162, *woke* 129. Zimmer raced to write a press release. The rest of us headed to the hallway for wine and cheese.

The winner captured the spirit of the age. The runner-up's journey was only beginning.

In 1962, a young African American novelist named William Melvin Kelley published an essay in the *New York Times Magazine* headlined "If You're Woke You Dig It." The subheadline: "No mickey mouse can be expected to follow today's Negro idiom without a hip assist."

Woke doesn't appear in the essay itself. But it's in a sidebar chart by Kelley of "phrases you might hear today in Harlem or in any other Negro community." Among them were terms that would be appropriated in a short time by the wider (white-dominated) culture: *boss* (good), *bust* (to arrest, to be arrested, or an arrest), *dig* (to understand or to like), *hip* (well-informed, cool, up-to-date), *jive* (to exaggerate), *the man* (the police), *saying something* (meaningful, beautiful, good), *turn on* (to be initiated into, informed about), *woof* (to brag, boast, talk wildly). Other words on the list would not go mainstream: *burn* (to do something well, quickly or efficiently), *crack on* (to introduce (as evidence in a debate or argument)), *grays* (white people), *jump salty* (to become petulant), *ralph bunche* (to talk one's way out of a difficult situation). Kelley defined *woke* as an adjective meaning "well-informed, up-to-date." He included an example sentence: "Man, I'm woke."

Kelley's essay is less a political manifesto than a celebratory marking of cultural territory. It opens with an anecdote about a New York City subway poster that told riders, in twenty-one languages, "This is your train, take care of it." The eighteenth language was labeled "Beatnik": "Hey cats this is your swinging-wheels, so *dig it* and keep it boss!" Kelley noted that "if beatniks do exist (beatniks maintain that they do not exist) they would certainly explain that their language is a borrowed one." Borrowed from, he wrote, "the people who live in that area of New York referred to in 'No Strings'"—a musical with lyrics and music by Richard Rogers that had opened on Broadway earlier in 1962—"as 'uptown, way uptown,' or on Chicago's South Side, or any place where two Negroes pass the time of day."

By the time white America—beatniks included—adopted words like *cat*, *cool*, and *chick*, the lingo was "hopelessly out of date," Kelley wrote. Black Americans "guard the idiom so fervently they will consciously invent a new term as soon as they hear the existing one coming from a white's lips." Their "pride in this idiom is that of a man who watches someone else do ineptly what he can do well." Kelley, just twenty-four, was, for *Times* readers, most of whom resided in the Republic of Caucasia, an even-handed guide: bemused but not judgy. "I asked someone what they felt about white people trying to use 'hip' language," Kelley wrote. "He said, 'Man, they blew the gig just by being gray.'"

Kelley explained why African Americans adopted their own idiom (exclusion, secrecy, safety) and why doing so might be antithetical to social, political, and economic goals (acceptance, equality). But mostly he wanted readers to appreciate a language different from their own—and to understand why its existence mattered. "The American Negro feels he can, on the spur of the moment, create the most exciting language that exists in any English-speaking country today." As James Baldwin would write almost two decades later, also in the *Times*, "I do not know what white Americans would sound like if there had never been any black people in the United States, but they would not sound the way they sound."

Kelley went to Harvard, published four novels, and taught at the New School for Social Research and Sarah Lawrence College. So where did he find *woke*? A few years after his death in 2017, his wife and one of his daughters told journalist Elijah Watson that Kelley had "overheard someone use *woke* in Harlem." But that usage and Kelley's definition in the *Times* might have derived from earlier documented examples of the phrase *stay woke*. In his 1937 song "Scottsboro Boys," the blues singer and guitarist Lead Belly, born Huddie William Ledbetter, told the story of the group of Alabama teenagers falsely accused of raping a white woman and sentenced to death. "I advise everybody to be a little careful when they go along through there," Lead Belly said after recording the song for the Library of Congress in Washington, DC, in 1940. "Best stay woke. Keep their eyes open."

Writers have hypothesized that Lead Belly was approximating speech patterns, not coining a phrase. Either way, his words had the intended effect. In the 1972 play *Garvey Lives!* by Barry Beckham, about the Black civil-rights activist Marcus Garvey, *stay woke* took an explicit political context: "I been sleeping all my life. And now that Mr. Garvey done woke me up, I'm gon stay woke. And I'm gon help him wake up other black folk." *Stay woke* was a reminder to Black people to be aware of the unceasing threats they faced in America.

Standalone *woke* was around in the 1990s, "used exclusively by black people to refer to other black people," the journalist Damon Young, who is Black, wrote. "It was our word, because only we were mindful enough to recognize when that pro-blackness was a performance." In the 2000s, *woke* started to mean *liberal* or *virtuous* (in a socially liberal way); it was woke to recycle, or to tweet about the goodness of recycling, Young wrote. Another Black journalist, Michael Harriot, wrote, "By co-opting and transforming 'woke' into a beacon for self-congratulatory allyship, white *wokeness* had been reverse-engineered into the actual thing that Black people needed to stay woke about."

The phrase took off as a progressive anthem and social-media hashtag after R&B artist Erykah Badu sang it forty-five times in her 2008 track "Master Teacher" and then used it in a tweet about the jailed Russian band Pussy Riot in 2012. It exploded with the rise of the Black Lives Matter movement after the killing of teenager Trayvon Martin in Florida the next year and of Michael Brown in Ferguson, Missouri, the year after that. *Stay Woke* was the name of a 2016 documentary about BLM that aired on BET, Black Entertainment Television.

But use of *woke* was evolving. When she argued against the word at the WOTY vote, linguist Nicole Holliday had recently written that *woke* had been "sanitized for a mainstream audience" and "removed from its ties to black communities." It had been "lulled . . . into a complacent, apolitical slumber" and could "no longer perform the function of promoting and indexing black consciousness and liberation." For those who knew whence it came, *woke* was, in a word, dead. It had stopped being what made it powerful: a taut reminder to be alert to racism and its implications. Overuse had rendered it parodic, "levitating next to 'swag' and 'twerk' in the 'Words Ruined by White People' ether," Damon Young wrote. "What was a compliment just a few years ago has become, at best, an eye roll."

If only just an eye roll. White political commentators, and the public who read and listened to them, recognized that *woke* was an effective culture-war bludgeon—a four-letter distillation of what critics labeled overzealous progressive ideas and actions: opposing police brutality, supporting LGBTQ rights, taking a knee during the national anthem, promoting racial justice generally. "Wokeness Derails the Democrats," tenured white *Times* columnist Maureen Dowd wrote after the party stumbled in 2021 elections, approvingly quoting Bill Clinton–era strategist James Carville: "What went wrong is this stupid wokeness." Dowd's conservative colleague Bret Stephens wrote an entire column framing *woke* as a cultural threat.

Florida governor Ron DeSantis made a "war on woke" the leitmotif of his short-lived 2024 presidential campaign, and also a tenet of his governance. His administration named a law designed to squelch discussion of discrimination and equity in schools and workplaces the Stop WOKE (Wrongs to Our Kids and Employees) Act. In teleprompted stump speeches, DeSantis wielded the word like a preacher. He even nounified it. "We fight the woke in the legislature. We fight the woke in the schools. We fight the woke in the corporations," he said after winning reelection in 2022. "We will never, ever surrender to the woke mob. Florida is where woke goes to die."

DeSantis's benumbing repetition was akin to Senator Joseph McCarthy's insidious Cold War campaign against an imaginary red menace. *Woke* was cynically twisted into an existential threat against democracy—*woke mob* became a phrase all its own. But it was also a dog whistle to those who might oppose efforts to fight discrimination, promote voting rights, or teach students about the history of slavery in America. "It's now intended to be a racial slur and I think people should treat it as one, whatever that means for you," my *Slate* sports-podcast cohost Joel Anderson, who is Black, tweeted. After Supreme Court justice Stephen Breyer announced his retirement, Republican senator Josh Hawley of Missouri, who is very definitely not Black, asked on Twitter whether President Biden would "nominate someone who loves America and believes in the Constitution? Or will he continue to tear apart this country w/ a woke activist?" The Twitter account LOLGOP responded, "Hawley providing a classic example here of woke being said with a hard R."

William Melvin Kelley would have nodded in agreement. *Woke*'s mutation and migration from African American culture to the whiter world was predictable. But so was its deployment against the people who created it. *Woke* wasn't the only word that was lobbed back at Black America like a grenade. *Critical race theory* was a little-known academic field until it was redefined by conservatives as a pernicious movement to indoctrinate children and shame white people, and embraced by Fox News hosts scrabbling for a new front in their manufactured culture wars. Same for *cancel* meaning to shun for unacceptable behavior. *Cancel* was coined by the Black musician Nile Rodgers in a 1981 song and used by the screenwriter Barry Michael Cooper in the 1991 Black crime action film *New Jack City*. Rappers including 50 Cent and Lil Wayne used it. And then *cancel* was mutated into an entire *culture* of grievance. Going back further, to the tumult of the 1960s, *Black power* began as an in-group phrase of pride that was twisted to mean terrorism.

In linguistics, this is known as pejoration—"The development of a less favourable meaning or of less pleasant connotations for a word or expression," per the *OED*. It's not new, and not limited to words originating in Black America. *Miscegenation* was created in the 1860s by proslavery Democrats seeking to discredit Republican abolitionists. *Liberal* morphed into a sneering epithet starting in the 1980s. *Religious liberty* once meant, well, religious liberty; conservative Christians turned it into a catchphrase for their perceived persecution. *Groomer* had an unsavory second sense—Merriam: "someone who grooms a minor for exploitation and especially for nonconsensual sexual activity"—but was expanded to mean anyone who generally supported LGBTQ rights. Even *freedom* was cynically and clumsily co-opted—think "freedom fries" after 9/11 or the Trump II White House tweeting about Vice President JD Vance firing "freedom seeds" at a gun range.

Then there's *DEI*. The earliest example of the phrase "diversity, equity, and inclusion" that I found was in a display ad in Australia's *Sydney Morning Herald* newspaper in 1999: "BankWest seeks to embrace a culture of diversity, equity and inclusion." The abbreviation *DEI* began appearing in the early 2010s, usually in corporate or university job or program titles, but wasn't widely used until the end of the decade.* Then, during the 2024 presidential campaign, *DEI* was adopted by conservatives as a new cultural bogeyman. On Day 1 of his second term, Trump issued an executive order titled "Ending Radical and Wasteful Government DEI Programs

---

*Merriam entered *diversity, equity and inclusion* in October 2024, with two senses: "a set of values and related policies and practices focused on establishing a group culture of equitable and inclusive treatment and on attracting and retaining a diverse group of participants, including people who have historically been excluded or discriminated against" and "the state of having a diverse group of participants as well as policies and norms that are equitable and inclusive." *DEI* was added at the same time, cross-referenced to *diversity, equity and inclusion*.

and Preferencing" that mentioned *DEI* and *DEIA* ("accessibility") twenty-two times. Two days later, Trump issued another order about "illegal DEI" and "radical DEI."

Republican messaging—from the White House to new appointees to Fox News and other right-wing cable networks—was clear: *DEI* politically was the new *critical race theory* and idiomatically the new *woke*, a catch-all word implying that women, African Americans, and members of other minority groups were unqualified and undeserving. It, too, was intended as a slur. "No more DEI at @DeptofDefense," the new head of the department, Pete Hegseth, a former Fox News anchor, wrote on social media. Ten days into the new term, Trump, Hegseth, and Vance all attempted to blame DEI programs for the collision of a passenger jet and a helicopter in Washington, DC, that killed more than sixty people. The weaponization of *DEI* was stunningly rapid and sinister.

The twisting of language was never-ending. In my little corner of the world, the question was how the dictionary handled these changes in meaning and usage. The answer: as objectively as possible, but with a sense of urgency that didn't exist a generation or two earlier. *Cancel, cancel culture, critical race theory, Black Lives Matter*,[*] and *allyship* (defined as "such association with the members of a marginalized or mistreated group to which one does not belong")—all were new or updated entries in Merriam.

Woke had the most eventful trip. Merriam flagged *woke* in a 2016 blog post, calling it "a slang term that is easing into the mainstream" from African American Vernacular English, or AAVE, where *awake* was often rendered as *woke*, as in "I was sleeping, but now I'm woke." The post concluded, "The broader uses of *woke* are still very much in flux, and there are some who are woke to the broader implications of *woke*."

---

[*] Another term created by Black people for Black people and weaponized and co-opted by white people using spinoff terms like "All Lives Matter" and "Blue Lives Matter."

The word, in other words, needed time to settle. But the volume and prominence of use forced Merriam's hand. In 2017, the OWL entered *woke* as an adjective meaning "aware of and actively attentive to important societal facts and issues (especially issues of racial and social justice)." As the word's meaning got reshaped, a second sense was added in 2023 to reflect disparagement. Merriam attached the monitory label *disapproving*: "politically liberal or progressive (as in matters of racial and social justice) especially in a way that is considered unreasonable or extreme."

At the start of this book, I described how every new edition of every dictionary, from time immemorial, bragged about the tongue's astounding fecundity at that precise moment. Science! Technology! War! After observing the conveyor belt of words at Merriam, I was dubious that any one era was more productive than another. Glance at any year and you could spot incredible, indelible contributions to American English.

In fact, Merriam created a website doodad that allowed users to do just that. My birth year, 1963, bestowed upon the world *bobblehead doll*, *sicko*, *diddly-squat*, *call-waiting*, the verb *hotdog*, *delete key*, *zip code*, and *phat*, yet another word originating in AAVE. But it was no 2020, which was one of the most lexically intense years ever—because it was one of the most intense years ever, period. *Impeachment* enjoyed a surge when Trump was handed his first at the start of the year. *Defund*, *Black Lives Matter*, and *antiracism* (which dated to at least 1943) soared in use (and searches) after the killing of George Floyd.

Amid the subsequent protests, a twenty-two-year-old Black woman from Missouri, Kennedy Mitchum, emailed Merriam. Mitchum asserted that the dictionary's entry for *racism* didn't sufficiently describe the concept of institutional or systemic racism. That meaning arguably was conveyed in the entry's second sense:

"a doctrine or political program based on the assumption of racism and designed to execute its principles" or "a political or social system founded on racism." But it didn't specifically use the modern term; the first documented use of *systemic racism* in the *OED* is from 1968.

The lack of contemporary nuance wasn't surprising. The word *racism* dates to the early twentieth century. But it didn't appear in print much until the rise of fascism in Germany and Italy in the decades before World War II. *Webster's Second* in 1934 entered *racialism* but not *racism*. The early twentieth-century civil-rights activist and journalist Ida B. Wells used terms like *race prejudice* and *race hatred*.

Ben Zimmer discovered that a Merriam assistant editor named Rose Frances Egan flagged *racism* on a pink slip in 1938. Draft definitions that followed referred to "totalitarian ideology" and "the Nazi assumption of Teutonic superiority and attendant anti-Semitism." In 1939, *racism* was added to the Addenda of the *Second*, defined as "assumption of inherent racial superiority or the purity and superiority of certain races, and consequent discrimination against other races." The entry was overhauled for the *Third*, stripping allusions to Nazi Germany and breaking up individual belief and institutional policy into separate senses.

For the next six decades, the definition was untouched. When Mitchum contacted Merriam, editors already were reexamining a range of race-related terms, including *racism*. The entry for *systemic*, for instance, was updated with an illustrative quotation containing the phrase *systemic racism*. A Merriam editor who corresponded with Mitchum criticized the Gove-era definition, saying that while "our focus will always be on faithfully reflecting the real-world usage of a word, not on promoting any particular viewpoint," Merriam had concluded that "omitting any mention of the systemic aspects of racism promotes a certain viewpoint in itself. It also does a disservice to readers of all races." The editor went on, "This revision would not have been made without your persistence in contacting us about this problem. We sincerely thank you for repeatedly writing in and apologize for the harm and offense we have caused in failing to address the issue sooner. I will see to it that the entry for *racism* is given the attention it sorely needs."

When Mitchum's campaign went public, with widespread media coverage, Merriam pledged that the new definition would be less "opaque." "We will make the idea of systemic or institutional racism even more explicit in the wording of the definition," Peter Sokolowski said. And Merriam did. The second sense was rewritten as "the systemic oppression of a racial group to the social, economic, and political advantage of another; *specifically* : WHITE SUPREMACY." The entry was bolstered with a usage note and numerous quotations from writers of color including political activist and philosopher Angela Y. Davis, writer bell hooks, activist Bree Newsome, and Michelle Alexander, author of *The New Jim Crow*.

The dictionary was praised by some commentators for its sensitivity and awareness. Others, predictably, blasted it as woke, in the weaponized sense.

Politically and psychologically, the events that prompted these language bursts were tragic, traumatic, energizing, enervating. Lexically, though, it was fairly routine stuff, the shimmy and shake of English moving with the news, words enjoying a revival, a moment in the spotlight, a permanent slot in the starting lineup. Lexicographers could be patient, waiting to see how a word might be shaped and changed.

And then came *covid*.

Before February 11, 2020, *covid*, linguistically, did not exist. "I'll spell it," the head of the World Health Organization, Tedros Adhanom Ghebreyesus, said during a news briefing in Geneva, Switzerland, announcing the name of the disease caused by the novel coronavirus. "C, O, V, I, D hyphen one nine—COVID-19." It was an acronymic mashup of parts of two words: CO*rona*VI*rus* D*isease*, with the number representing the year of its emergence. Mutations appeared in media: *Covid-19, COVID, Covid, covid*. All were used as substitutes for the given name, which itself was clipped to *corona* and, colloquially, *'rona* and *the rona*.

What was lexically novel about the novel coronavirus was the speed with which it overtook the language, and the thoroughness with which it transformed it. In the spring, as the disease was beginning its horrific rampage, Oxford noted that *covid* cracked the top five most frequent nouns in its constantly updated corpus, alongside some of the most widely used words in English—*time, people, day,* and *year*. "That was like, wow," Kate Wild, an Oxford lexicographer, told me. "I'd never seen anything like that."

Oxford regularly produced a Top 10 list of words that appeared "significantly more frequently" in that corpus that month than they did in the corpus overall. In January 2020, *coronavirus, virus,* and *SARS* made the list, along with other words from the news: *bushfire, impeachment, Iranian, airstrike*. In February, eight of the ten were coronavirus-related. In March, April, May, and July, the list was all virus. (The U.S. antiracism protests dominated June.) For the first ten months of 2020, sixty-seven of Oxford's hundred trending words were covid-related.

At Merriam, it was almost instantly clear that *covid* wasn't a routine word-news story. In-house data showed a significant search for *coronavirus*—that word dates to 1968—on January 21, with a spike ten days later and steady upward climb. *Pandemic* spiked in February, *quarantine* in early March. Zeitgeisty words like *draconian, lockdown, martial law, xenophobia, apocalypse, calamity, pestilence,* and *Kafkaesque* all followed. But Merriam also was tracking failed searches—for words that weren't in the dictionary. *Covid, COVID-19, social distancing,* and *self-quarantine* topped that list. "People are asking the dictionary a question it can't answer," Peter Sokolowski said. That wasn't good, for people or for the dictionary.

To manage the flood of terms, editors created a spreadsheet of pandemic words. The initial plan was to blog about what was trending and hold off on the actual lexicography. But "it was becoming clear that these new entries should get included sooner rather than later," Joan Narmontas, Merriam's senior editor for life sciences, told me. The rapid spread of both the virus and the words being used to describe it prompted editors to do what just two years earlier was unthinkable, and also technologically unfeasible: an emergency update. The next window was in April, with a scheduled OWL update of several hundred new words.

Entries for *coronavirus disease 2019* and *COVID-19* were prepared first, followed by new entries or updates for *community spread, contact tracing, self-quarantine, social distancing, super-spreader,* and a few others. Not all of the terms were new. *Patient zero* dated to a 1987 book about the AIDS epidemic, *And the Band Played On,* by the journalist Randy Shilts. *Social distancing* was first used in 2003 and *community spread* way back in 1903, according to the *OED*, in an article in the *Australasian Medical Gazette* about a leper colony.

Even the April timeline was a rush, and not just because of Merriam's wait-and-see philosophy. Dictionary databases are complicated. Entries include lots of disparate parts: headword, pronunciation, cross-references, example sentences, etymology. Adding hundreds of words takes months of editorial and tech work. But Lisa Schneider, the digital director turned publisher, had persuaded Britannica to upgrade Merriam's data-processing system. The time required to add new entries had been shaved from weeks to hours. Now Merriam had an opportunity to flex, and to do something the dictionary had never done: act like a newsroom on deadline.

On March 9, the staff was informed about a special update of coronavirus words apart from the planned April rollout. A batch of twenty entries was keyed into a data file, proofread, and delivered to the tech department on March 12. "All entries got their usual review by editors specializing in cross-reference, dating, copyediting, etymology, and pronunciation," Narmontas said. On March 13, the entries were reviewed for digital display accuracy. The update went live at noon Eastern on March 16.

Less than five minutes after the button was pushed, before Merriam announced the update on its website or promoted it on Twitter, traffic spiked on the *COVID-19* entry. Editors had never seen anything like it. People were looking up the word constantly—and now Merriam had something for them to find, which was good for the dictionary's editorial credibility and for its pageviews. On the company's Slack channel, associate life sciences editor Chris Connor wrote, "clearly this information was in-demand!"

It had been just thirty-four days since the lexical item *COVID-19* was coined. Thirty-four days from creation to entry into the dictionary. On February 10, this particular string of English letters (and numerals) held no meaning whatsoever. A month later, it was known across the planet, by speakers and non-speakers of English alike.

Linguistically, that was astonishing. Lexicographically, it was, too. At thirty-four days, the addition was indisputably the fastest in Merriam history. The quickest before *COVID-19* was believed to be *AIDS*. The acronym first appeared in a major metropolitan newspaper in July 1982. A Merriam science editor named Roger Pease recognized the severity of the health crisis and the likely staying power of the term, and—at a time when it was normal for new words to take a decade or longer to make print—pushed for *AIDS* to be entered as soon as possible. It was added in the 1984 printing of the *Collegiate*.

As with *AIDS*, Merriam's action on *COVID* reflected the ability of and need for the dictionary to respond to a dire moment in human history. It also showed how, in the twenty-first century, dictionaries, including America's oldest and most lexicographically conservative one, were battling for speed, authority, and readers online. In that normal April update, Merriam added another bushel of pandemic-related words, including *self-isolate* (first known use 1925), *physical distancing* (1965), *WFH* (work from home, working from home; 1995), and *forehead thermometer* (1979).

And more important, Merriam's rapid reaction reflected how, in times of crisis, when people are confused, overwhelmed, and even frightened by the words in the news, the work of the dictionary matters. "We already think of dictionaries as authorities, so it's not all that surprising that, when people want clear information about something, they turn to them," former Merriam editor Kory Stamper told me. When people were trying to parse the difference between a *stay-at-home order* and a *shelter-in-place order*, between *quarantine* and *isolation*, words were "literally a matter of life and death."

Like everyone else, publisher Lisa Schneider was stunned by how the pandemic had overturned the world, and Merriam's little corner of it. "If you had asked us a few months ago if we'd agree to enter words after mere weeks, I expect we would have been awfully skeptical," she said. "I wouldn't anticipate other categories of words seeing this type of speed to entry. But unfortunately here we are, and we did what we thought was right and useful."

By the end of 2020, there were hundreds of pandemic-related terms to sift, new and old, some of which made dictionaries and others that just made you chuckle: *flatten the curve* (which peaked early in the pandemic, when it seemed like an achievable goal), *second wave*, *bubble*, *pod*, *hygiene theater*, *super-spreader*, *PPE*, *essential worker*, *face shield*, *Blursday*, *anti-mask*, *maskhole* (a person who refuses to wear a mask), *moronavirus*, *virtual happy hour*, *quaranteam*, *coronabro* (and scores of other *quaran-*, *corona-*, and *covid-* combiners). *Long-haulers* referred to people whose symptoms, including brain fog, fatigue, and chronic pain, persisted; it was coined on Facebook by a preschool teacher in Oregon, picked up by media, and stamped with approval at a Congressional hearing by none other than infectious disease pooh-bah Dr. Anthony Fauci.

The year-end Word of the Year selections reflected the ubiquity. Merriam and Dictionary.com went with *pandemic*. Collins picked *lockdown* and Cambridge *quarantine*. Macquarie of Australia tabbed *covidiot* as its people's choice. The Society of Austrian German's winner was *Babyelefant*, because the government used a cartoon of a baby elephant to demonstrate the recommended distance (in Austria anyway) that people should stand from each other to avoid spreading the virus: the length of one baby elephant, or about one meter.

Oxford decided it couldn't pick just one. Its editors and marketers produced what amounted to a covid language white paper. Titled "Words of an Unprecedented Year," the thirty-eight-page report cited the "phenomenal breadth of language change and development" wrought by the pandemic. Obscure scientific and medical terms became commonplace. Neologisms felt like lifelong friends. And all of it happened "at hyper-speed," Oxford wrote. The vocabulary altered our lives "in ways inconceivable in almost any other circumstances"—from what we do (*doomscrolling*) to how we do it (the retronym modifier *in-person*, as in *in-person voting*, *in-person classes*, or *in-person worship*). In *the before times*—which Oxford added to its free site—only the *online* versions of those words would have required distinction.

What stood out, Oxford said, was the interconnectedness of expression, how the pandemic touched everyone the same way across the English-speaking world. Normally, Oxford's data showed discrepancies in favored terms among Australia, the United States, the United Kingdom, East Africa, South Africa, India, Singapore, et al. Not this time. Despite a few expected localisms—*frontliners* for *essential workers* in the Philippines, *PUIs* (patients under investigation) in Malaysia—the shared experience of the disease resulted in a shared experience of language.

Kate Wild at Oxford said the breadth of lexicographic innovation during the pandemic reminded her of a project she worked on a few years earlier to update the *OED*'s World War I vocabulary. That's a humbling and depressing reality, but it made sense. Like the world wars, covid dominated the discourse, devastated the economy, and killed millions of people. Crisis requires new ways to express the horrors of the heretofore unknown. The covid pandemic was the first such truly global event of the digital age; the language to discuss and understand it was shareable across time zones and cultures. And lexicographers possessed the tools to decipher and define what was happening.

If language is like a shark—always moving lest it die—then 2020 was a great white. The year demonstrated how events shape language and language in turn shapes behavior. It showed how words in social and popular media spread as rapidly and widely as . . . well, "any of a large group of submicroscopic infectious agents that are usually regarded as nonliving extremely complex molecules, that typically contain a protein coat surrounding an RNA or DNA core of genetic material but no semipermeable membrane, that are capable of growth and multiplication only in living cells, and that cause various important diseases in humans, animals, and plants." That linguistic virality validated the demand for dictionaries; lookups, like cable-news ratings, skyrocket during times of trouble. And, at Merriam, it tested the company's willingness to jettison past protocol and activate all of its modern tools and behave like lexicographic frontliners.

As the year ended and a new one began, the pandemic's word stranglehold waned slightly, but only because of its doomscrolling twin, Donald Trump. Covid words vanished from Merriam's Top 10—who needed to look them up anymore?—replaced now by *insurrection, fascism,* and *impeach*.

But if language reflects life, maybe there was reason to hope.

For a few minutes one day in 2021—and not February 14—*love* cracked the Top 10.

14

artificial intelligence

: the capability of computer systems or algorithms to imitate intelligent human behavior

I met Erin McKean of Wordnik, the alt-dictionary that was trying to use computing power to find sentences that could substitute for definitions, back in 2018. At the time, she was adding more human-generated material to the site because the idea of training bots to write definitions was a pie-in-the-sky proposition; it was hard enough to get them to parse collocation, syntax, grammar, and intent in potential sample sentences. Having computers actually compose definitions—and consumers still wanted definitions, as dictionary website traffic demonstrated—remained, it seemed, a long way off.

McKean introduced me to Manuel Ebert, a cofounder of Summer.ai, the data firm that worked on Wordnik. I asked him about artificial intelligence, giant language databases, and their ability to write something like a dictionary-style definition. "When you define a word in the dictionary," Ebert said,

> you make assumptions about what humans know and what other words they know. Those assumptions are hard for AI. Meaning—making something meaningful—is still a very, very human problem domain. In general, I'm in the camp that says AI is just a tool,

like a power drill or a steam shovel. The point is to make things we do as humans faster, more reliable, quicker, whatever. I don't see AI replacing the jobs of lexicographers, unless it makes the work of just one editor at Merriam-Webster so efficient that you can fire other editors. You will always need the last editor.

McKean was confident that someday computers would be able to do what Noah Webster did at his circular desk surrounded by his sand-packed walls—and what his successors, hunched over their laptops, were still doing two hundred years later. "AIs don't work when things are super fuzzy," she said. It took decades, but programmers finally developed a bot that was able to beat a world champion at the ancient Chinese board game Go, "and that was the thing you weren't supposed to be able to teach a computer to do. So do I think computers could write definitions? Yes, I think they could."

And how long might that take?

"Since the Merriam model is so highly structured, I would not be surprised that sometime in the next fifteen years that someone could train an AI to do it."

In 2023, five years after we hung out, McKean, along with Will Fitzgerald, a machine-learning engineer at the software developer platform GitHub, presented a paper at ASIALEX, a biennial academic conference hosted by the Asian Association for Lexicography. The theme of the event, held in Seoul, was "Lexicography, Artificial Intelligence, and Dictionary Users." McKean and Fitzgerald's paper was titled "The ROI of AI in Lexicography." Fifteen years had shrunk by two-thirds. Using what are known as large language models, or LLMs, artificial intelligence could write dictionary definitions. Now that at least partial automation had arrived, the question was, what would it mean for the business and practice of lexicography?

artificial intelligence

The term *large language model* didn't even exist when I first met McKean. Merriam would enter it in the fall of 2023, defined as "a language model that utilizes deep methods on an extremely large data set as a basis for predicting and constructing natural-sounding text," with a first known use of 2019. (There's a link in the entry at *deep* to sense 8 of entry 1 of that word: "having or using many repetitions of algorithmic processing.") In the same OWL update, Merriam added *generative AI*, or "artificial intelligence that is capable of generating new content (such as images or text) in response to a submitted prompt (such as a query) by learning from a large reference database of examples."

Generative AI dated to 2012. But it roared out of Silicon Valley and into popular usage a decade later thanks to ChatGPT, the chatbot* created by the artificial intelligence firm OpenAI that overnight reordered our understanding of—and humanity's relationship with—language, science, work, creativity, insight, analysis, productivity, cheating, and more.

Lexicographers had long been early adopters of new tech. The *Random House Dictionary of the English Language* was organized with the help of a computer way back in 1966; it was "so far ahead of its time," McKean and Fitzgerald wrote, that no typesetter could create pages from its custom computer tape and the entire book had to be rekeyed for printing. Around the same time, Merriam created a digital version of the seventh edition of the *Collegiate* that was shared with researchers. IBM donated software to Oxford for the second edition of the *OED*, which came out in 1989, because it saw broader research applications in the development of the tools needed to create dictionaries. Merriam began capturing all new citations in digital form in the early 1980s. Putting the *Collegiate* online for free in the

---

*Merriam defined *chatbot* as "a bot that is designed to converse with human beings" (first known use 1994). The entry directed readers to sense 3 of the noun *bot* meaning "a computer program or character (as in a game) designed to mimic the actions of a person."

mid-'90s signaled the dictionary's willingness to boldly go where technology was leading.

AI was the newest, and potentially most disruptive, opportunity. The GPT in ChatGPT stands for generative pre-trained transformer—*generative* because of the LLM's ability to generate, in this case, sentences and paragraphs that sound like they were written by a human; *pre-trained* because it is trained on more than a trillion words from online sources; and *transformer* because that's the name of the neural network—a type of artificial intelligence—discovered by researchers at Google that can identify patterns in those huge datasets and spew out text by predicting the next word in a series, again and again.

Merriam-style dictionary definitions were a good candidate for AI because they are stylistically repetitive and replicable. For new words especially, AI could hoover up samples of usage and, with careful coaching, compose replaceable single-statement definitions, or full-sentence ones more useful for English learners. A large language model fed with enough example sentences, McKean told me in 2024, could generate a definition as good as "a middle-aged lexicographer with fifteen citations and a pressing deadline."

ChatGPT was released in late 2022. In the next year, a dozen or so papers and lectures examined the ability of it and other models, like Google's Bard (which would be renamed Gemini), to do the lexicographer's job. One lecture was ominously titled "The End of Lexicography?" Another answered the question: "The End of Lexicography, Welcome to the Machine."

The lexicographer, public-radio host, and Word of the Year celeb Grant Barrett named his presentation for a Dictionary Society of North America conference "Defin-o-Bots." Barrett asked ChatGPT-4 to create definitions, etymologies, and example sentences for a variety of new, not-new, common, complicated, offensive, and primarily British words. The word *mirusvirus*—a recently identified strain of virus that attacks plankton—was too new for ChatGPT-4's database, but that didn't stop it from offering to "imagine" that a *mirusvirus* "is a newly discovered computer virus that has a unique ability to mimic and replace existing software without detection." The bot also offered to define *virus* instead, and then plagiarized four dictionaries in the process. (Google Bard did better with that word.) ChatGPT-4 "hallucinated"—made up—quotations for a sense of *loo* meaning a summer wind in India, which Barrett chose because it's a term borrowed into an English dialect and also a homophone. The chatbots' brief etymologies for the football (soccer) slang *shithousery* were, Barrett wrote, "useless."

Other testers were more sanguine. Robert Lew, a professor at Adam Mickiewicz University in Poznań, Poland, asked ChatGPT to craft definitions for fifteen common verbs (*beg, argue, blame, suggest, recommend, insist*, etc.) written in complete sentences in the style of the Collins COBUILD dictionary for English learners. And then he did a blind taste-test, asking a bunch of experts to rate the COBUILD and ChatGPT definitions. "Our results indicate that ChatGPT is capable of producing dictionary definitions emulating COBUILD style that are *practically indistinguishable in quality* from those written by highly trained human lexicographers," Lew wrote (emphasis mine). "This is a ground-breaking finding, and one that challenges the centuries-long lexicographic orthodoxy that sees definition-writing as a rare elite skill that requires extensive training (and perhaps also unique inborn qualities)."

On the bright side, if you're composed of blood and bone, ChatGPT was again terrible at writing example sentences, a thread across the academic studies. But when Lew told ChatGPT about its shortcomings and fine-tuned his prompts, the engine returned sentences that were "authentic-sounding and accessible."

I wanted to see how I matched up with the silicon, metal, and ocean of water needed to cool the servers generating a thousand suns of environmentally calamitous heat so that an eleventh grader can avoid reading *Hamlet*. Had I wasted weeks laboring like Noah Webster with a quill pen over something AI could do as well or better, as some of the academics had concluded, in a split second? Even more dispiriting, was I worse at writing than a line of code?

I had AI take a crack at a handful of words that I had defined—a mix of old and new, verbs and nouns, serious and silly, widely used and not so much (looking at you, *sportocrat*). I started with *microaggression*. I asked Google Gemini to create a dictionary definition "in the style of Merriam-Webster." It ignored the "in the style of" part and returned, word for word, the published definition I had drafted (plus a few additional examples of affected groups). ChatGPT mashed up my Merriam definition and Dictionary.com's definition of *alt-right* and, to throw me off the plagiarism scent, pulled in some extra words often used online to describe the right-wing movement. Advantage, me.

For *pom-pom girl*, Gemini missed by decades on the emergence of cheerleaders, returning both "the early 20th century" and "the mid-1970s to early 1980s" as dates of origin for the term. When I probed about the outdated prostitute sense, ChatGPT categorically rejected the meaning. When I cited the entry in the online *Unabridged*, Gemini reported an "outdated and offensive slang definition" and cautioned: "You'll find this definition in some online dictionaries, but it's important to understand it's a derogatory and uncommon usage." One minute AI was telling me I was wrong. The next it was issuing warnings.

ChatGPT told me that *dogpile* was typically used "in the context of online searches or discussions." I questioned whether it wasn't also used to describe a celebration in sports. It said I was right, and then offered a separate definition reflecting that usage. I had to pry out the information. ChatGPT didn't come close to the *Unabridged*-style entry I created with five noun senses, two verb senses, and multiple subsenses.

But, again, its "work" took a second. Mine took days. I was the more complete researcher and writer. But ChatGPT was infinitely more efficient, and in most cases a reader wouldn't be able to distinguish its definition from mine. Still, as the academics concluded, the AI-generated definitions could be dense, wordy, reductive, or incomplete. If you knew something about the words, as I did, they read as if they were written by a computer. (*Thereby* appeared in one definition. Never use *thereby*.)

I signed off feeling that the bots required more or better information to produce dictionary-ready definitions completely on their own. That would come with more inputted language and inevitable programming advances. For now, just like us humans, they needed an editor.

Next: testing AI on a word I didn't define. Erin McKean suggested *cottagecore* as a good candidate: a newish word with limited use and almost no dictionary attention. The term appeared to have been coined on Instagram in 2014, gained some traction in 2018, and took off at the start of the pandemic in 2020 after the *New York Times* published the first mainstream story about the phenomenon: "Escape Into Cottagecore, Calming Ethos for Our Febrile Moment." The subhed read, "Small animals, calico tea cozies and not a lot of men."

I did my usual middle-aged-lexicographer-with-fifteen-citations due diligence. I collected example sentences, from the *Times* story, *Architectural Digest*, the *Washington Post*, and *Country Living*; from lifestyle websites with names like The Spruce and The Good Trade; from an academic article, "Crafting Cottagecore: Digital Pastoralism and the Production of an Escapist Fantasy." I spent a couple of hours marveling at pix of twentysomethings in Heidi dresses, bouquets of dried flowers positioned just so on distressed farm tables, and layer cakes designed to look like moss. I read the Wikipedia entry,

Google's "AI Overview" at the top of the search page for the term, and the only human-crafted dictionary definition I could find, from Dictionary.com.

But instead of then hunkering down to craft a definition as I'd done so many times, I fired up ChatGPT-3.5. "You are an etymologist and lexicographer," I told the chatbot, copying a prompt used by Grant Barrett. "Create a concise definition of the word 'cottagecore' written in the style of Merriam-Webster's online dictionary." One second later, the text scrolled:

> cottagecore (*noun*) \'kä-tij-ˌkȯr\
>
> : an aesthetic and lifestyle movement emphasizing a romanticized, idealized interpretation of rural and country life, characterized by simplicity, self-sufficiency, and a connection to nature
>
> *Example:* "Cottagecore enthusiasts often embrace activities like gardening, baking, and crafting as part of their idyllic rural fantasy."
>
> First Known Use: 2018
>
> Etymology: Derived from the word "cottage," referring to a small rural dwelling, and "core," a suffix used to denote an aesthetic or cultural movement.

Wordnik didn't include a definition of *cottagecore*, just a handful of citations added by users or discovered by the site's bots. So next I did what McKean and Fitzgerald did in their paper. I politely asked ChatGPT to craft a definition based on two of the Wordnik cits.

> Given the following two word-citations, please create a dictionary definition for the word "cottagecore" including a part of speech.
>
> "Aesthetically, cottagecore is women with long hair and long dresses holding wicker baskets, a warm berry pie resting on a

artificial intelligence

cloth served beside herbal tea in a thrifted china set, mason jars, foraged mushrooms, beeswax candles."

"The pandemic was all about cottagecore, an idyllic or avoidant retreat to country cutesiness, sourdough bread–making, and an allegedly simpler time."

ChatGPT needed a few more seconds this time before its digital teletype machine began clacking:

cottagecore (noun) \'kä-tij-ˌkȯr\
: an aesthetic and lifestyle movement that idealizes rural and pastoral life, often featuring elements such as long dresses, wicker baskets, homemade goods, and nature-inspired decor, and characterized by a nostalgic yearning for simplicity and self-sufficiency

The side-by-side results of the first ChatGPT definition and Dictionary.com's were revealing:

ChatGPT
: an aesthetic and lifestyle movement emphasizing a romanticized, idealized interpretation of rural and country life, characterized by simplicity, self-sufficiency, and a connection to nature

Dictionary.com
: an aesthetic or imagery inspired by an old-fashioned, rural lifestyle, characterized by rustic décor and fashion, a revival of traditional handicrafts, etc.

The brain cell–based definition is more fact-based. It consists of two sections: 1) what cottagecore is—"aesthetic" and "imagery"—and 2) some things that describe it. The definition totals a breezy twenty-two words (including "etc.") and uses four commas. ChatGPT describes cottagecore as not just an "aesthetic" but a "movement," which based on my admittedly brief research seems a tad overblown. Then it gets all judgy ("romanticized," "idealized"). The definition has the same two sections as Dictionary.com's and only two more words and one more comma, yet it feels like a run-on. Still, it's serviceable, a draft that, had I written it, Steve Perrault might have complimented before editing the hell out of.

The chatbot's second effort, based on the two Wordnik citations, is comprehensible, too. But it's a bloated, pause-to-breathe, five-comma, thirty-five-word stemwinder. One likely explanation: The cits on which I asked ChatGPT to craft its definition were crammed with specifics: wicker baskets, warm berry pies, thrifted china, mason jars, beeswax candles, sourdough bread. ChatGPT wrote like a panicky high schooler jamming in every detail in fear of leaving something out. When I gave the bot five citations to work with, the definition clocked in at thirty-eight words.

McKean and her partner used citations uploaded by Wordnik volunteers to generate definitions for similarly newish words, including *cheapfake*, *booksona*, and *boujetto*.* Overall, the authors concluded, the AI-generated definitions were "good" but sometimes "confused" and "over-specific." When ChatGPT was asked to rewrite some definitions (*careen*, *disgorge*, *screwball*, e.g.) for children ages seven to ten, the results were "stylistically inconsistent," "clunky," and "awkward." The bot wasn't bad at labeling words, but it was unreliable,

---

*Here's how ChatGPT defined those words:
   cheapfake (noun) A type of manipulated media that is created using easily accessible and low-cost technology, often with the intention of deceiving viewers
   booksona (noun) A representation of oneself as a book, reflecting one's reading preferences and personality
   boujetto (noun) A term used to describe a woman who embodies both hood and classy qualities
McKean and Fitzgerald noted that ChatGPT got the part of speech wrong for *boujetto*, a portmanteau combining *boujee* and *ghetto*. It's an adjective.

inconsistent, or just plain lousy at creating accurate pronunciations, writing coherent example sentences, and identifying first citations for words and quotations.

Human versus machine is an old story. John Henry driving railroad spikes in a matchup against a steam-powered drill in the 1800s. Chess champion Garry Kasparov taking on IBM's Deep Blue supercomputer in the 1990s. San Francisco 49ers placekicker Joe Nedney booting against a 14-inch-tall, 340-pound robot named Ziggy in 2010. The results are usually mixed: Henry outdrove the drill, but allegedly died trying; Deep Blue lost to and then beat Kasparov; Nedney was up and good from forty-five yards while Ziggy was not. No matter the outcome, humanity always expresses I-am-become-death awe at what it hath wrought. "I've been working half my life to do this thing," Nedney told reporters who had gathered to watch the Kezar Stadium showdown, "and this guy comes out here and builds a machine in a couple years and all of a sudden it can outkick a human being. Doesn't seem like it's an even playing field."

Even if Ziggy was trained to kick ninety-yard field goals, though, it wasn't going to displace one of my fellow pro kickers.* The existential threat of an AI Frankenstein's monster was just a *liiiiiittle* more portentous. In May 2023, just six months after ChatGPT debuted, the nonprofit Center for AI Safety released a statement reading, in full, "Mitigating the risk of extinction from A.I. should be a global priority alongside other societal-scale risks, such as pandemics and nuclear war." The scary sentence was endorsed by the heads of two of the leading AI companies, OpenAI and Google DeepMind, and two of the Turing Award–winning research godfathers of AI.

---

*I spent a summer as a training-camp placekicker with the Denver Broncos to write a book about life in the NFL, *A Few Seconds of Panic*. Ziggy would have beaten me.

In my lexicographic outpost of the revolution, extinction, if not on a planetary scale, was real. In the twenty decades since Webster's trembling hand composed the entry for *zygomatic*, wrapping up the 1828, the U.S. dictionary interstate has been strewn with roadkill: Worcester. Century. Funk & Wagnalls. Thorndike. Barnhart. American Heritage. Random House. Webster's New World. Thanks to digital licensing agreements, the work of some of those historic names endured. But they were zombie lexicons, preserved online but collecting pixelated dust, untended and un-updated by their owners, some of whom were long gone.

Could AI save lexicography? Or would it be its deathblow? There was no consensus on whether the proposition was binary. In any case, the discussion was speculative, because AI was in its infancy. AI was good at some things, bad at others, and, as of the publication of this book's first edition in late 2025, not a threat to upend the last gladiators of commercial lexicography. "It reinforces what you already know," Grant Barrett said. "It's a really eager intern who thinks it knows more than it does. It really wants to help you. But you really have to guide it."

Today's quibbles about wordy definitions, poor sense division, lousy example sentences, and imperfect pronunciations—or about AI's general utility/futility and power for good/evil—could be tomorrow's chuckles about the early days of the technology. (A computer program couldn't beat a chess grandmaster until the 1980s; today an app on a phone can.) Sources might be flagged to address copyright concerns. Plagiarism might be programmed away. Confabulation and hallucination—aka getting things wrong and making stuff up—could be eliminated, too. Writing could improve, as it does as we morph from children with developing brains to adults with mature ones. Perhaps most important, for this modest application of tech's latest disruptor, dictionary-makers might find ways to tailor large language model datasets, as they did with corpora, for their own purposes, figuring out how to use them in ways that improve a customer's word experience.

Or, generative AI might be too costly, suck up too much power, and not evolve enough to fully replace humans for tasks like lexicography, which can be handled by small and comparatively cheap staffs. Some experts were similarly pessimistic about the likelihood of AI revolutionizing the world's industrial and intellectual economies. "Human cognition involves many types of cognitive processes, sensory inputs, and reasoning capabilities," Daron Acemoglu, an MIT economist and author of *Power and Progress: Our Thousand-Year Struggle Over Technology and Prosperity*, said in 2024. "Large language models today have proven more impressive than many people would have predicted, but a big leap of faith is still required to believe that the architecture of predicting the next word in a sentence will achieve capabilities as smart as HAL 9000 in *2001: A Space Odyssey*. It's all but certain that current AI models won't achieve anything close to such a feat within the next ten years."

But lexicography isn't rocket science or heavy industry. On a purely process level, AI looked like it should pose a sky-is-falling, existential risk to human-generated lexicography. After all, in just a few months of existence, it was already writing competent definitions and performing other dictionary tasks. One lexicography software program, TLex, added an AI tool; with good prompt engineering, a chatbot could write an entire dictionary overnight.* Using large language models to do the creative work would "risk losing lexicography as a profession entirely," McKean and Fitzgerald said in their paper.

On the other hand, given the dwindling size of the industry and the glut of available information about words already, how much of a risk could AI really pose? Would the productivity gains from using

---

*Note: "Dictionary" isn't restricted to commercial databases and books. There are hundreds of smaller, niche lexicons out there that you or I will never stumble across.

AI to update dictionaries and create web content about language justify the expense and the reputational risk of fully automating your two-century-old business—especially if it's profitable, as Merriam has always been? Circumstances change, but if their corporate and intellectual philosophies endured, the word honchos in Springfield and Oxford weren't suddenly going to start publishing definitions without the traditional heavy vetting by trained pros.

And the threat of an internet flooded with fully automated AI dictionaries didn't seem especially scary. "Look at all the fucking dictionaries online now that aren't getting traffic, that aren't getting ad clicks, that went under," Barrett said. "We're going to have more dictionaries online? What kind of market are they taking? They're going to take that point zero zero zero one percent of traffic from WordHippo?" (WordHippo is an Australian word-search site.)

The biggest threat to lexicography wasn't a rogue AI dictionary or even the fear that the remaining publishers would replace their harmless drudges with scary chatbots. It was the reality that John Morse had identified when I started this project: that expertise was ceasing to matter, that institutions were growing suspect, that quality was becoming elastic. The chatbot revolution was just the latest manifestation, in lexicography as in life. "People are happy with good enough," Grant Barrett said. "And AI-based definitions are good enough."

As much as I wanted to romanticize Merriam and Oxford, it was possible they would succumb to the siren song of the perceived efficiency of the bots and inefficiency of the humans. And even if they didn't, Google probably would. It already had eaten at traditional publishers' online market share by posting licensed definitions at the top of its search pages, deterring readers from scrolling down and clicking on a commercial dictionary link. According to SEO expert Rand Fishkin, Merriam at one point was losing as much as 70 percent of available clicks because of Google's "knowledge boxes." If or when Google stopped licensing traditional dictionaries and started AI-ing definitions exclusively, poof, there goes more revenue from the business.

A linguist at the University of Ghent in Belgium, Gilles-Maurice de Schryver advised the profession to take a deep breath. Cameras didn't result in the end of painting, he wrote; calculators didn't replace mathematicians. "The same may be expected for the use of ChatGPT in lexicography. Just give it time, as we do not know yet how this revolution will pan out."

15
future

time that is to come; what is going to happen

"It's crack. It's like crack for people like us," Wendalyn Nichols said.

I was standing with the Cambridge University Press editor in a library at Indiana State University, surrounded by very old dictionaries. We were among a couple dozen lexicon lovers who had risen early one day during a Dictionary Society of North America conference at Indiana University in Bloomington and, like kids on a school field trip, bused to visit the big dictionary collection at the in-state rival in Terre Haute an hour away. The Cordell Collection of Dictionaries was named for an A. C. Nielsen TV-ratings company executive who began amassing dictionaries in the 1960s on a whim. By the time of his death in 1980, Warren Cordell had donated almost 4,000 books to his alma mater; the collection had since ballooned to more than 13,000.

Amid walls of dictionaries shelved high behind glass, librarians had arrayed a curated selection on a long wooden table. Some of the titles related to sessions at the DSNA conference, like *A Classical Dictionary of the Vulgar Tongue* (1785)—a copy of which Madeline Kripke had shown me in her apartment—and *Little Dictionary of*

Creole Proverbs (1885). Others were librarian faves, like *Orthographia dictionum e graecis tractarum*, which, dating to 1471, was the oldest work in the collection.

I gently examined a pristine copy of the 1828 and a small edition of Webster's *Compendious Dictionary* with its brief definitions, and explored a cardboard box containing the German publisher Langenscheidt's bilingual *Lilliput* dictionaries and other dollhouse-size miniatures. Wendalyn Nichols and Beth Young, a University of Central Florida professor who was working on a searchable version of Samuel Johnson's dictionary, read an eighteenth-century word list. Out loud.

Across the hall, in open stacks, a wall of Merriams faced a wall of Worcesters like rival gangs, reenacting their late nineteenth-century turf war. I even found in there the exact edition of my old *Webster's New World Dictionary*—wearing the shiny, colorful dust jacket I had ditched forever ago. I opened the book and smiled. The moment reminded me why I undertook this project in the first place. My love affair with words began with that childhood birthday gift, and it hadn't ended. Using words to explain news and tell stories became my career. Playing with words on a rack and a board—memorizing them, unscrambling them, competing with them—became the nexus of my personal and professional lives. (Sorry dictionaries, Scrabble will be in the lede of my obituary.)

And now here I was, a quasi-lexicographer at a full-fledged dictionary conference trying to understand and then explain what had happened to the industry that produced my *Webster's New World* in 1974 and where it was heading now. I felt as if I had learned a secret handshake, infiltrated a subculture that's esoteric and intellectually unconquerable (the academic stuff, anyway). And deeply serious; my lexicographer friends bore the burden of responsibility for the preservation and analysis of our most precious and indispensable tool, language. But also fun, because studying and talking about words was endlessly, enormously, incredibly fun.

Back in Bloomington, Ben Zimmer delivered a slideshow presentation on the removal of *fuck* from *Webster's Third*. I attended one talk about defining emoji and another about the first update in thirty years of a monolingual Slovenian dictionary. ("It's looking good, I have to say," a bald Slovenian lexicographer in rectangular black glasses said.) There was a reception in the Lilly Library to celebrate an exhibit installed for the conference: a selection from the nine tons of archives donated to Indiana by the family of Clarence Barnhart, whose bow-tied, septuagenarian son David was in attendance. The display of UNIVAC punch cards used to collate citation slips was fascinating.

One night featured the second known rendition ever of a musical puppet show written by Philip Gove's wife, Grace, with lyrics by the Goves' son, Norwood. "The Big Book" was originally performed in 1961 at the launch party for the *Third* at the Goves' farm. The entire Merriam staff was invited, plus spouses. (Company president Gordon Gallan, with whom Gove had tussled over *fuck*, declined to attend, saying, "It's your day.") Gove greeted the guests wearing bib overalls, a contrast to his stiff office demeanor, and handed out drinks from a bar on a hay wagon. After a dinner on the porch that included fresh organic vegetables from the garden, Gove and some colleagues staged "The Big Book," which poked fun at themselves and the production of the *Third*.

Directing the revival was Lindsay Rose Russell, the University of Illinois English professor. "Everything about musical puppet shows appeals to me and if you add dead dictionaries it just puts it over the top," she told the room. "You will enjoy it because it's weird and it's awkward and this is a conference of nerds."

It was in fact weird and awkward—and hilarious, too. The characters are Gove, Gallan, editor H. Bosley Woolf, and editor Anne Driscoll, who quit because Gove refused to give her the title she believed she deserved on the masthead of the *Third*. There are inside jokes about Gove's work habits, the dictionary's production schedule, and the staff's low pay, and foreshadowing of public-relations problems to come. ("We are the direct descendants of Noah Webster," the Gove character says, "aren . . . ain't we?") And, in the end, there's the passion that consumed the dictionary's creators. "Let them flower / Let them spawn," the cast sings in "We Love Words," "They'll be here / When we're gone."

Another night, about fifty conference-goers gathered for a screening of *The Professor and the Madman*, a film based on the book by Simon Winchester starring Mel Gibson as James Murray and Sean Penn as William Chester Minor, the murderous American who while incarcerated contributed tens of thousands of citations to the *OED*. Ben Zimmer introduced the movie with a discussion of other lexicography-centered films (there aren't many), including Howard Hawks's 1941 screwball comedy *Ball of Fire* (starring Gary Cooper as Bertram Potts, a grammarian researching slang, and Barbara Stanwyck as Katherine "Sugarpuss" O'Shea, a nightclub singer who schools the professor about language—and love!) and *The Great Passage* (a 2013 Japanese drama literally about making a dictionary).

The Professor and the Madman had been tied up in litigation—Gibson fought its release—and also was roundly panned by critics. We hooted at the leaden plot and over-the-top speechifying. ("You crazy, beautiful bastard!" Gibson screams at the lexicon.) Afterward, Zimmer discussed linguistic inconsistencies in the script—because, at this conference, what did you expect. The Murray character, he noted, mentions the *London Times* crossword puzzle, which didn't debut until 1930, fifteen years after Murray's death.

The dictionary society honored University of North Carolina linguist Connie Eble, who for forty-six years collected slang from students. "It's like getting an Oscar, only better!" Eble said. And it recognized Enid Pearsons, who worked at Random House for many, many years as a pronunciation editor—an orthoepist, to be precise. Stooped and caned at eighty-nine, smiling in a smart green jacket, Pearsons made her way to the front of the room. "I'm being rewarded here for doing something I just loved—putting together the intellectual monument we call a dictionary," she said. "It is an honor and such a pleasure to be among you."

But for all of the tunes and testimonials, the most meaningful, and most somber, event on the schedule was a keynote speech by the group's outgoing president, Steve Kleinedler. Until recently, Kleinedler had been executive editor of the *American Heritage Dictionary*. He talked about his career: linguistics grad school, freelance lexicography, hired by the *AHD* in 1997. He worked on that book's fourth (2000) and fifth (2011) editions.* The dictionary's publisher, Houghton Mifflin Harcourt, laid off two-thirds of the staff in 2018. Kleinedler was hired back as editor at large, working from his apartment.

Then, citing the "continuing decline in consumer demand for print dictionaries," Houghton axed the book's famed fifty-year-old usage panel of writers, editors, and intellectuals—the cudgel it used against Merriam in the 1960s. And it fired the last full-timers. Kleinedler took a job as a technical editor for a software company. But the dictionary still wanted him for freelance work—five hours a week. Along with the three other freelancers, that meant the *AHD*—formed a half century earlier to rival Merriam-Webster—employed about one-half of one full-time employee.

In a 2004 "On Language" column in the *New York Times Magazine*, Erin McKean guesstimated that, excluding scholarly dictionaries, there were around two hundred full-time working lexicographers in the United States; as I finished this book, the number was under fifty, probably closer to thirty. In 2005, the *Times* wrote about the "young, hip lexicographers" who "have already or may soon take

---

*When the fifth edition was published, a press release asked, "Will this be the last print dictionary ever made?" I thought that was marketing hyperbole. More than a decade later, it was in fact looking like the last print overhaul of a major American dictionary.

over guardianship of the nation's language"; twenty years later, of the five mentioned in the story—Grant Barrett, Steve Kleinedler, Erin McKean, Jesse Sheidlower, and Peter Sokolowski—only one, Sokolowski, still had a full-time dictionary job.

In his talk, Kleinedler compared the dictionary business to his hometown, Flint, Michigan, which had bled tens of thousands of automotive jobs. His parting advice to his dictionary fellow travelers: Stay sharp, keep in touch with colleagues, and learn new things because "you never know when you're going to need to transition." But also: Don't give up, because the mission is too important.

"I know many in this room do not have the job they had twenty years ago, often through no fault of their own. But yet we're still here, and that says a lot," Kleinedler said. "It would be so easy to throw up our hands and declare ourselves obsolete. We don't and we carry on."

Listening to Steve Kleinedler lament the wreckage of the stateside dictionary business, I wondered if there was a way out of the morass. The subject came up at dinner another night in Bloomington. "If your choice is going out of business or trying to create some new model for preserving the language," I asked a handful of dictionary editors and academics gathered around a long table at a downtown farm-to-table restaurant, "what do you do?"

"Wiktionary," Oxford's Katherine Connor Martin said, referring to the crowdsourced dictionary which, its website boasted, "aims to describe all words of all languages using definitions and descriptions in English."

"That is the worst thing in the world. Oh, it is awful," Michael Adams, the Indiana professor and Madeline Kripke collection curator, replied.

Martin defended Wiktionary's citations, its word lists, and some of its groundbreaking avocational antedaters, mentioning Hugo van

Kemenade, the Finn who spotted *selfie* in a post by a drunk guy of a photo of his split lip on a science forum on the website of the Australian Broadcasting Corporation in 2002, eleven years before Oxford chose *selfie* as Word of the Year.

Urban Dictionary came up. Martin considered the site less praiseworthy than Wiktionary. As a corpus for scholarly lexicography, the site was noisier, more erratic, less reliable. It had mutated over time from a welcome digital middle finger at slow-moving mainstream lexicography—an instantaneous, real-time archive of our constantly evolving slanguage—into another internet sandbox overpopulated with bigotry and performative outrageousness. The experts considered Twitter to be a better linguistic corpus.

"And this gets to the point of: Why do you want to institutionalize lexicography?" Martin said. "And the answer is: I, a professional lexicographer, can go to these [other] sources and tell whether they are good or not for a given entry. But the variability of quality from entry to entry is vast."

So if crowdsourcing on its own wasn't a viable solution for a serious archive of this language, and universities weren't reliable longterm publishers, and bots couldn't do all the work of the dictionary—not yet, anyway—what was a viable solution? The group talked it through.

"It's very clear that we're past the point where you could get the American government to sponsor," said Lynne Murphy, an American academic who studied the differences between British English and American English, "and there would be freedom of speech issues, too: 'Why is it English that they're funding?'"

Someone noted that Dictionary.com had been purchased by Dan Gilbert, the mortgage-industry billionaire owner of the Cleveland Cavaliers of the National Basketball Association, for no apparent reason other than that he was a fan of dictionaries. That was the benevolent, or at least curious, billionaire model—not unlike Jacqui Safra buying Britannica (and Merriam) decades earlier.

"That's the answer," Martin said. "Someone who cares about data and cares about information. You wouldn't need that big an endowment."

"You need the kind of person who is into data but who does realize that there does need to be a human element in its analysis," Murphy said.

"Create a nonprofit that had people who are institutionalized and put some of the burden on them," Martin said.

"That's called a language academy and we're not doing that in the United States," Adams countered.

"The Silicon Valley Language Academy!" Martin joked.

So a government-backed institution with a nationalist name—like France's Académie Française or Sweden's Svenska Akademien, which is charged with defending the "purity, strength, and sublimity of the Swedish language"—was a nonstarter. But another model came up at dinner, a long-forgotten project that Michael Adams had researched and loved, the *Dictionary of American English on Historical Principles*, or *DAE*.

When the first edition of the *OED* was put to bed at the end of 1927, the *New York Times* published a dispatch from London: "Oxford Dictionary Completed After 70 Years; Occupied 1,300 People; Has Cost $250,000." "The making of the Oxford dictionary is one of the romances of English literature," the *Times* wrote. "Before its vast scope it is declared that Dr. Samuel Johnson's effort pales into insignificance."

But one of the book's top editors wasn't in Oxford to celebrate. William A. Craigie was a small, shy Scotsman with a short, pointy goatee and tiny, oval glasses. He joined the *OED* in 1897 and, four years later, was named a third editor, alongside James Murray and a self-educated philologist named Henry Bradley, who was hired after writing an impressive review of the first installment. Craigie was a master of Celtic, older Scots, and Scandinavian languages (also fluent in Icelandic!).

A prolific definer, Craigie handled most of the *OED* entries for the letters N, Q, R, Si–Sq, U, V, and Wo–Wy. He would be knighted for his work. And he could be a pain, flouting Murray's editorial guidelines and complaining when called on it. After Craigie submitted bloated drafts for *railroad* and *railway*, Murray told him that "no part of my work is so onerous and unpleasant to me as that of looking through your copy. I should be infinitely glad to have done with it."

The length of the fascicles of the *OED*, and the time it took to produce them, was a running battle. The book's editors, including Murray, wanted to ensure completeness. The book's overseers—a group of academics who served as "delegates" of Oxford University Press—wanted to control printing costs and to publish new installments quickly to recoup expenses.

To restrain length, Murray decided to use G. & C. Merriam's 1864 dictionary as a benchmark for the number of pages allocated for each letter in the *OED*. The Webster scale, as it was called, started at five times the number of pages per letter in the 1864, grew to six, and then eight. All the editors were scofflaws, especially as the dictionary crawled toward the end of the alphabet. Murray's final letter, T, was more than twelve times as long as T in the 1864. Bradley routinely surpassed fifteen to one. He blamed the American book because "the extent to which the Webster of 1864 is incomplete differs enormously in different letters."

Craigie was the biggest rule-breaker of all. His work on R clocked in at nineteen to one. U demonstrated that Webster was "useless" as a standard, Craigie wrote to his superiors. It severely restricted entries of words starting with *un*, containing, for instance, just eleven words from *uncommunicativeness* to *unconcernedly*, where he had assembled more than a hundred. And, Craigie gleefully noted, Merriam had trimmed the *un* section from its 1847 edition to the 1864.

Craigie was indeed logorrheic, especially when it came to quotations (me, too). But he had a point about Webster, and he was stubborn. "I don't think [Craigie] has treated us very well—each Delegate in turn has hammered at him," one of the *OED*'s overseers wrote, "and he was formally asked to cut it down drastically, which he can't pretend he has done." The blowup led to a sabbatical. After compiling the slips for U, Craigie set off on a year-long, round-the-world trip to Romania, Greece, Egypt, India, China, Japan, and the United States. He returned to Oxford, fought for a couple more years with his bosses, and, in 1924, left to teach a summer course at the University of Chicago.

While in Chicago, Craigie was reading through his U proof pages and noticed two successive words for which all evidence after 1700 was solely American. He proposed a historical dictionary of American English. It was one of several potential period dictionaries Craigie had suggested (others included Middle English, older Scots, and modern Scots). The University of Chicago agreed to the project and hired him as a full professor. The *Chicago Tribune* put the news on page 1 with a famous (among lexicographers) headline: MIDWAY SIGNS LIMEY PROF. TO DOPE YANK TALK. Craigie's new colleagues had to explain the Americanisms to him. He found the words charming.

Craigie admitted he wasn't the first to suggest a dictionary of American words. "The American bonanza is in the hands of squatters; it is yet to be worked scientifically. That is impossible in Oxford; it must be done here," a German-born Boston pastor and journalist named Carl W. Ernst, who had contributed quotations to the *OED*, had declared a decade earlier. "It will take at least twenty-five years to gather the materials, and twenty-five years more to digest them properly. And neither dogma nor cash can help us; the thing needed is grace."

Actually, cash was in fact the thing needed, because cash, and the competition for it, had defined American dictionary-making since the Merriams made lexicography a profit-driven enterprise. In addition to the 1864, 1890, and 1909 unabridgeds, the end of the nineteenth and start of the twentieth centuries saw publication of the beautiful and voluminous *Century Dictionary and Cyclopedia* and of Funk & Wagnalls' *A Standard Dictionary of the English Language*, which also advertised aggressively in America and England. The American word biz was cutthroat.

Between 1936 and 1944, in short fascicles, Craigie and his colleagues in Chicago produced the *Dictionary of American English on Historical Principles*. The *DAE*'s installments were collected in four red leather volumes—*A* to *Corn Patch*, *Corn Pit* to *Honk*, *Honk* to *Record*, and *Recorder* to *Zu-zu*. The work totaled more than 2,500 pages. It wasn't a general dictionary. The goal, instead, was to collect English words and phrases that 1) originated in America from the time white people landed on its shores, 2) were used more or differently in America than in other English-speaking countries, and 3) possessed "a real connection with the development of the country and the history of its people," Craigie wrote in the preface to volume 1. Each entry included a part of speech, a brief definition, and a string of illustrative quotations. Occasionally there was an etymological note.

I got lost in the *DAE* one afternoon in the library at American University in Washington, DC. Craigie's writing in the front matter is turgid, and the design of the books is bland. But the entries are a picture window into American history. They illustrate fully Noah Webster's vision of an American language, and how the creation of that language occurred. The first settlers borrowed words from the indigenous locals and other European arrivals. They invented words for things they'd never seen—plants, animals, weather. And they twisted the mother tongue to their own stylings. Wrote one reviewer: "They deeded, tabled, notified, obligated, located, advocated, belittled, affiliated, and progressed, which no well-brought-up Englander had ever done."

I learned that *blizzard* to describe a snowstorm was first noted in an Iowa newspaper in 1870 (it was later antedated to Kansas in

1859). That *to save one's bacon* goes all the way back to 1666. That the political uses of *cabinet* (1801) and *campaign* (1809) are ours. That *call slip* (1881)—"A slip for noting the number, title, etc. of a library book desired by a borrower"—is as 'murican as *apple pie*, and many other *apple* words. "The importance of the apple in American life," Craigie wrote in volume 1, "is illustrated by *Apple-brandy, -butter, -jack, pie, -sauce, -toddy*, etc., as well as by *apple-corer* and *-parer*."

Unsurprisingly, there are five pages of *buffalo* words, the earliest dating to 1635.* *Immigrant* (1789) is American, defined as "One who has come from a foreign country to settle in the United States." So are *bet your life* (1872) and *not on your life* (1905). *Hoodlum*—"A street rowdy; a loafer; a gangster or criminal"—originated in San Francisco around 1870 but its derivation was unknown. *C.O.D., coldsnap, dingbat, greenback, hamburger, hell-raiser, highfalutin, skedaddle* (and its predecessor in meaning, *absquatulate*)—all of them all-American, too.

The *DAE* was a critical success. Newspapers lavished regular reviews on the release of its fascicles and volumes. (Who wouldn't review publications with titles like *Baggage Smasher to Blood*† and *Blood and Thunder to Butterfly*?) "As a bedside book there is no equal," the *New York Times* gushed one year; it "will rank with the great civilizing dictionaries of all time," the paper said another. The green, softcover fascicles were "such a hit with the general book-lifting public that vigilant librarians have taken to keeping them under lock and key."

When the final book appeared in 1944, the *Times* concluded: "Here in these four handsome volumes is not only a dictionary of the American language. Here is also what amounts to a cyclopedia of Americana and a history of the American mind." The price tag

---

* Among them: *buffalo beef, buffalo berry, buffalo clover, buffalo fish, buffalo grass, buffalo horse, buffalo moth, buffalo pecker, buffalo pistol, buffalo road, buffalo robe, buffalo soldiers, buffalo stamp, buffalo tongue,* and *buffalo wallow* ("A depression caused by the rolling or wallowing of buffalo").

† *Baggage-smasher* is in *Webster's Third*: "a person (such as a baggageman) who handles the baggage of others especially in a baggage car or steamship."

for the collected four volumes was a steep $100. But the first press run was "all but exhausted."

In the roots of the *DAE*, I imagined a way forward for the American dictionary in the twenty-first century and beyond.

Consider the model. The *DAE* was housed at a university, with a staff of young editors, some of whom would go on to lexicographic greatness.* The dictionary was, in part, crowdsourced; students at Chicago and other universities were enlisted to read books and gather citations, and Craigie put out calls for assistance to the general public. Funding came from multiple sources—from the university; from the General Education Board, a philanthropy started by the industrialist John D. Rockefeller; from the American Council of Learned Societies, a nonprofit composed of scholarly organizations in the humanities and social sciences; and from a private donor, a Mrs. R. S. Maguire.

For decades, that was a standard approach for dictionaries researched and written at universities, like the *Middle English Dictionary* at Michigan, the *Dictionary of Old English* at Toronto, and the *Dictionary of American Regional English* at Wisconsin. By the 1980s, though, funders such as the universities themselves and the National Endowment for the Humanities were getting, in the words of Indiana's Michael Adams, "dictionary fatigue." The projects just took too long to satisfy the grant-givers.

But those were "specialty" dictionaries. When it came to general-interest dictionaries, the academic/public formula never took root stateside. Not for lack of opportunity. After acquiring Webster's leftovers, George and Charles Merriam hired all those Yale professors to compile and edit their books for them. Without their services, *Webster's* might have died with Webster. But I found no indication

---

*One of them was Allen Walker Read, Madeline Kripke's mentor.

that the Merriams considered going into business with Yale—even during the Civil War, when financial times were brutal—or that Yale suggested teaming up.

Similarly, the first edition of *The Century Dictionary* in 1891 was edited by William Dwight Whitney, the Yale professor who had worked for the Merriam brothers on the 1864. Like the 1864, the *Century* relied on academics for the grunt work but was entirely a commercial enterprise. It was started by the Century Company of New York, a publisher of magazines and hymnals, and run from elegant offices on East 17th Street in Manhattan. The *Century* was celebrated as "the handsomest dictionary that ever was made" and, in a dig at the unfinished *OED*, "the best completed dictionary of the English language." And it was marketed aggressively, through subscriptions sold on installment (a first for books), a flashy display at the 1893 World's Fair in Chicago, and promotional campaigns in the book sections of department stores (another first). The publishers made a fortune.

Whitney was a founder of the American Philological Association. But the group didn't lobby to sponsor a *Lexicon totius Americanis* the way the learned men of England had called for a national dictionary and then turned to one of their most prestigious academic bodies to bankroll, headquarter, and create. Instead, the free market ruled. Publishers battled and sued and hustled to get their books to market. The *Century* was, by dictionary standards, a crash project. Thanks to a massive initial investment and drive for profit, it was completed in a decade.

Dictionary makers, regardless of their business model, historically benefited from competition—and the pressure to succeed. The Merriams were threatened by Joseph Worcester. James Murray was pushed by the Merriams and the *Century*. The *Third* was challenged by Random House's unabridged and the *American Heritage*. Today's technology revolution and SEO battle has forced the few commercial survivors to innovate and differentiate.

Oxford's sinecure didn't thwart its business ambitions or its desire to lead lexicography in new directions. With consistent support from the university, Oxford grew into a multilingual, worldwide publishing behemoth, employing the most lexicographers, developing the most modern tech systems, and producing the most comprehensive monolingual English dictionary in the world. On its website, the *OED* noted, almost proudly, that at "no period in its history" had it been commercially profitable. No matter. Oxford University Press "remains committed to sustaining research into the origins and development of the English language wherever it is spoken." As Oxford editor Peter Gilliver told me, "In theory, OUP could decide, 'Well, it's not in our interest to continue with this project.' Imagine the outcry."

History doesn't support the idea of an American university as the country's lexicographic sugar daddy. Yale didn't cut a deal with the Merriams in the 1860s; Chicago bailed on the *DAE* in the 1940s; Wisconsin let *DARE* founder in the 2010s. But commercial publishers haven't sustained their commitment, either; a Hall of Fame of marquee titles was resting in peace. Merriam-Webster was the happy outlier, and at the time we gathered in Bloomington, in 2019, it was reinventing itself for another new era.

A nonprofit model was working in some quarters of my chosen profession, journalism. Organizations like ProPublica, the *Texas Tribune*, and the *Baltimore Banner* were countering the traditional ads-and-subscriptions system that—thanks to Craigslist, Google, and Facebook, rapacious hedge-fund ownership, and other factors—had seen more than half of all U.S. newspapers disappear in the last two decades.

A hypothetical dictionary nonprofit might be bankrolled by a technology company with an interest in artificial intelligence, natural language processing, or even actual dictionaries. A university home base could provide talent for projects like corpora and dataset creation, online search tools, and edge technology. An assembly line of linguistics students could manage the automated collection of citations. A robust, full-time staff could be paid professional wages to define words by hand and edit definitions composed by chatbots, and also blog, tweet, podcast, and deploy whatever as-yet uncreated media to spread the word about words. The sale of corpora, language-learning tools, translation devices, subscription services, word lists, and other to-be-developed products could generate revenue.

The ultimate goal: ensuring the survival of the craft and purpose of lexicography, by whatever means necessary. And recognizing that a company like Merriam-Webster is more than a brand—not just a chronicler of the nation's language but a central character in the American story whose operator has a historical, cultural, and even moral obligation to find a way to preserve.

"When you say you want to save the American dictionary, you don't really mean a title," Katherine Connor Martin of Oxford had said at dinner. "You mean the notion of a group of colleagues who are working together in a coherent way with a specific methodology to record the language."

That was it right there: the centuries-old tradition and the immutable value of the dictionary. America had plenty of other problems, Michael Adams noted. So what if this wasn't health care or income inequality or race relations or democracy itself. The dictionary needed solving, too. "It has to do with what kind of America we want to be," Adams said. "The dictionary is just an emblem of that. The dictionary, though it may seem marginal to some people, is an icon of America."

16
end

: the point where something ceases to exist

Not long after boarding the dictionary carnival ride, I sought out Jesse Sheidlower to better understand the modern business. After studying classics and English at the University of Chicago and in the tiny Department of Anglo-Saxon, Norse & Celtic at Cambridge University—where he contributed citations to the *OED*—Sheidlower wound up at Random House in the 1990s. The print dictionary wars were hopping. The publisher had just released a new edition of its college lexicon that was dubbed the "politically correct dictionary" for its inclusion of *womyn*, *herstory*, *waitron*, and more.* The book included a two-page appendix titled "Avoiding Sexist Language." Suggestions included substituting *homemaker* for *housewife*, *synthetic* for *man-made*, and *humankind* for *mankind*.

When the book was done and publicity ran dry, most of the staff was let go, as the print dictionary publishing cycle prescribed. Sheidlower stayed on as new words editor and chief public talker. In one of his first interviews, he dissed Merriam's failure to include

---

*The entry for *womyn* noted that the alternative spelling for *women* was intended to "avoid the suggestion of sexism perceived in the sequence m-e-n." It wasn't the first attempt to redo the word. Noah Webster entered the phonetic *wimmen* in the *Compendious* in 1806 as the "primitive and correct orthography."

cyberpunk in the 1993 *Collegiate*—and noted that *dis* was exclusive to the Random House book, too. He was the project editor of the *Historical Dictionary of American Slang*. Building on that work, he edited a book titled *The F-Word*.

Sheidlower joined the OED as its North American editor. For more than a decade, he was more or less a public lexicographer: NPR "wordsmith" and go-to media quote, about whatever new word was in the news. But Sheidlower had left Oxford a few years before we met, not by choice. His ouster shocked the small community of definers, which wasn't accustomed to conflict or turmoil. An editor at another dictionary called it a sobering moment. It was also a canary in a coal mine.

These days, Sheidlower was working at an academic publisher and, on the side, writing an online science-fiction dictionary and vetting scripts for a TV show, *The Man in the High Castle*, an Amazon series based on a Philip K. Dick novel in which Japan and Germany win World War II and occupy the United States. Sheidlower was hired to ensure that the language in the show scanned with the time, 1962. It was right up his alley. But it wasn't lexicography. "The problem is there aren't other dictionary jobs," Sheidlower said. "There aren't any good options now."

Random House had stopped updating its college dictionary in 1999, while he was still there, and soon after abandoned dictionary-making altogether; the remnants of its operation were absorbed by Dictionary.com. My beloved *Webster's New World*, written and edited in Cleveland from its start in 1951, cycled through corporate owners until its last edition in 2014. The *American Heritage* was a shell of its once-robust self. At the end of a talk at a lexicography conference, Ben Zimmer posted a slide of a cruise ship labeled "USS Dictionary" heading for an iceberg labeled "Google."

In 2019, Oxford Dictionaries rebranded as "Oxford Languages," to emphasize that it did more than define words. Proclaiming itself a "language content provider," Oxford asked consumers "to think outside of the dictionary box and consider how our language data can power your research and products." If James Murray didn't weep, he at least stroked his long beard quizzically. Three years later, Oxford shuttered its free online dictionary, which it already had subcontracted to Dictionary.com and renamed Lexico, focusing instead on the *OED* and other products. Fellow Brit publisher Macmillan had announced in 2012 that it would no longer publish physical dictionaries. In 2023, it killed its online dictionary, thesaurus, and blog. Online-only Macmillan "didn't even turn a teenager," the academic Gilles-Maurice de Schryver wrote, "and now there is nothing left."

Digital tools had blown open new frontiers in linguistic inquiry, enabling greater understanding of the way that language works—how frequently a word is used, the specific contexts for an expression or idiom, "things people tend not to think about if you just think about what a word means," Sheidlower said. But the advances were strangling the business. Definitions, good and bad, were a click away, and most people didn't care or couldn't tell which was which: expert research, scraped data, zombie websites, whatever popped up in a search. John Morse once told me that legacy dictionaries like Merriam faced the same growing popular distrust of traditional authorities that media and government did. Once upon a time, the worrying phrase for publishers was "any old *Webster's* will do"; now it was "any old website will do."

On top of all that, the research needed to produce professional definitions was available to anyone with a laptop and a wifi connection—and this was before AI was even a glimmer in a lexicographer's eye. The exigent need for curated definitions was disappearing in the rearview mirror.

"Until very recently, in order to do dictionaries, you needed those citation files, and only dictionaries that have been collecting this for decades or centuries had that," Sheidlower said. "Now anyone has access to the same information. Not everyone is trained and most people can't be trained—lexicography is very hard—and being interested in it isn't enough. But the point is that anyone can do it. And this is a radical thing."

When Dan Gilbert acquired Dictionary.com and Thesaurus.com in 2018, his private-equity firm, Detroit-based Rock Holdings, announced the deal with a tongue-in-cheek, tryhard* statement that attempted to let the world know that it was buying, you know, websites filled with big words:

> From the genesis, we admit to invariable conjecture in the unmitigated competency of online mechanization to ameliorate the total sum of completed undertakings throughout our mortal existence. Cognition and discourse are conjointly associated. Whilst the cosmos that encompass us are invariably in flux, an aphorism has perpetually prevailed—the desideratum for efficacious articulation to connote doctrine, conjecture, et al. Comparatively we persevere, maneuvering a terrain glutted with permutation, crystal clear communication will always be the key to success. In addition, over the past two decades, these "raw materials" of language are in essence not only the "vessels" of all communication but at the same time they are also becoming the currency of the digital age . . . The stipulations of the procurement remain unavailable.

Groan. For the previous decade, Dictionary.com was owned by the media and internet company IAC Inc., which operated dozens of brands, including Match.com, The Daily Beast, and Ask.com. Dictionary.com's playroom-chic Oakland offices were as far from Merriam's plastic-covered-couch aesthetic as possible. When

---

*Dictionary.com entered *tryhard* as a noun ("an underskilled or untalented participant attempting to compensate with sheer effort in order to succeed") and a verb ("to make an obvious effort to excel, but achieve only moderate success, especially when measured against ambitious goals").

I visited, I saw lots of millennial goodies—brightly colored beanbag chairs; bowls filled with M&Ms and bocce balls; giant-screen iMacs; historic quotations painted on the hallway walls that made the words of twentieth-century Swiss linguist Ferdinand de Saussure sound like a Quote of the Day dumped into your inbox: "Without language, thought is a vague, uncharted nebula"—but nary a physical book in sight.

Typical for an online giant, search engine optimization, engineering, and ad sales lorded over content. Despite a lack of resources, Dictionary.com's small editorial staff innovated. Its verticals for slang, emoji, memes, and gender and sexuality were robust and topical. Its word-of-the-day videos were clever and authentic. Its periodic dictionary updates were trendy and substantial. It hosted a Halloween writing contest, a poetry challenge, and a March Madness word bracket. In the mid-2010s, the company boasted it was in the Top 500 for web traffic with more than five billion searches in one year alone, and it was largely profitable.

So the takeover by the lexicon-loving Gilbert seemed, with apologies to his PR team and to you, a fortuitous amalgamation of linguistic bemusement interfused with monetary wherewithal. Inside the company, the line was that Gilbert wanted "to own the English language." And he did seem genuinely interested in the work of the dictionary. "Every so often he would ask a question that a reader might ask," John Kelly, a longtime Dictionary.com editor, recalled. Gilbert was into extreme weather and had subordinates brief him on terms like *bombogenesis*.* When Rock Holdings' mortgage and financial companies went public in 2020, Dictionary.com remained privately held.

In 2023, Dictionary.com hired three full-time lexicographers, including Grant Barrett and Kory Stamper, as director and senior

---

*Merriam's definition: "rapid intensification of a storm caused by a sudden and significant drop in atmospheric pressure."

editor of lexicography, respectively, and put eleven freelancers on contract, including two voice actors to record pronunciations. The goal was to modernize the dictionary, which, like most dictionary goals, was a titanic one. Dictionary.com was based primarily on the Random House unabridged dictionary (first published in 1966, updated in 1987), which was based on *The Century Dictionary* (1891), which was based on *The Imperial Dictionary of the English Language*, also known as Ogilvie, after its editor, the Reverend John Ogilvie (1850). Some of the entries were more than a hundred years old.

The A-list lex team got right down to the nitty-gritty. The editors revised heavily viewed terms like *theory* and *hypothesis*, which generated lots of traffic at the start of the school year. They wrote pronunciations and etymologies, cleaned up declensions, added senses. They removed sexist and archaic language and diversified names in example sentences. ("*John went to school*," Barrett said. "Why not 'Juan' or 'Juanita' or 'Giannis'? This is a multicultural society.") Stamper cleaned up 47,000 entries in Thesaurus.com (which generated about twice as much traffic as the dictionary). They dumped lexicographese, substituting, for instance, "like" for "as" in definitions. "Let's write like human beings," Barrett said.

They created a data-driven reading program to flag emerging lexical items and turbocharge additions, which helped triple the volume of new words. A February 2024 rollout included *barbiecore*, *bed rotting*, *slow fashion*, *range anxiety*, and *enshittification*, which the American Dialect Society had chosen a month earlier as its 2023 Word of the Year; none of those had been entered by Merriam. They were building a database to quickly update entries and post them on social media, and were developing a synonym-based game. They were training wannabe lexicographers. They were getting media for Words of the Year (*woman* in 2022 because of the national conversation about gender and identity; the AI sense of *hallucinate* in 2023) and words in the news.

The goal wasn't to be or beat Merriam; Dictionary.com couldn't match its history or reputation. It was, instead, "to position ourselves to capture language at the pace of change," to be "hipper and more experimental, but also rigorous AF,"* John Kelly said. "You don't have to go far online to see that everyone's a linguist out there. Why do *demure* or *brat*"—which went viral in summer 2024—"pop off? Because we're all equally competent in a language sense."

The piecemeal efforts improved the dictionary's quality, reputation, and cool quotient. But the work also reminded Grant Barrett why he loved lexicography: He was surrounded by smart, hard-working, passionate, creative colleagues who cared about language and how it was presented to the world, verbally and visually. He used words like "vigorous," "vitality," and "pizzazz" to describe working at D dot com, as it's known. For a time Barrett could plug his fingers in his ears and tune out the sobering reality. "We went into a job at a volatile company that hadn't made money in [several] years and the dictionary business was crumbling—but they were paying dot-com bucks," he said. "So ride it till the wheels fall off. And the wheels fell off."

Not long after Rock Holdings took over, the dictionary business grew more challenging. Google's "knowledge box" hogged the top of search pages with definitions licensed from Oxford, with synonyms and antonyms, and, eventually and predictably, with AI-generated info. The proprietary clutter pushed traditional-dictionary links below the fold, to use newspaper lingo, and Dictionary.com's traffic declined steadily and significantly, by around 40 percent. At the same time, the pandemic drained advertising revenue. Dictionary.com tried to stanch the decline with

---

*Dictionary.com entered the slang abbreviation *af* or *AF*, "as fuck; to a great degree (a euphemistic initialism used as a general intensifier, without explicit vulgarity)." As of 2025, Merriam hadn't entered it.

more and more ads—which created a progressively worse user experience.

Dictionary.com rolled out a K–12 online tutoring service, an AI writing software, other education products. None of it jibed with a dictionary, and none of it worked, former employees said. The cherry on top, or the turd: As interest rates rose, revenue at publicly traded Rocket Companies, the parent of Rocket Mortgage, plunged from $15.6 billion in 2020 to $3.8 billion in 2023, when it posted losses of $400 million. While the dictionary's finances were couch change in the sprawling corporation, the pressure to make money and cut costs—to hit OKRs, objectives and key results, in bizspeak—was inescapable. Even for a benevolent billionaire who was in the dictionary business for the ego more than the profit, the bottom line mattered.

In April 2024, Rock Holdings sold Dictionary.com to IXL Learning, the owner of Rosetta Stone, Vocabulary.com, and other online ed-tech brands. "In a world brimming with countless words, Dictionary.com is a trusted guide that helps people navigate the English language and express themselves," IXL's founder and CEO, Paul Mishkin, said in a statement. Within two weeks, though, it laid off all of its full-time lexicographers and dumped most of the freelancers. Including non-lex editorial, tech, and others, Dictionary.com started 2024 with around eighty employees. After the sale, only a handful remained.

Barrett wasn't bitter, or surprised. Dictionary.com didn't aspire to be a fully staffed lexicon in the tradition of the books on which it was based. It didn't have Merriam's advertiser base, content backlist, or two-century-old core mission: to preserve, protect, and define American English. "This was never truly the thing that it was about," Barrett said. "And I understand that, because dictionary content is expensive. Just the cost of lexicographers—people are expensive and the output is low. It is very difficult to justify that just for the sake of completism. You will never have enough staff to keep up. People are too productive in the creation of language.

"It's a fool's game. Fools have tried and fools have failed—make that my blurb. The nobility of lexicography's cause is worn away by the crassness of commerce. That's the story of lexicography."

Amid the Sturm und Drang and doom and gloom, Merriam managed to rebound. Editors of color were hired. Staffers enjoyed raises. Pre-pandemic, the editorial floor received a modest makeover, reducing the ghost-town vibe of empty cubicles; my desk was among the disappeared. Post-pandemic, staffers mostly worked from home.

Merriam had traditionally been reluctant to exploit modern analytical tools, which had as much to do with a stubborn belief that its traditional defining methods were adequate as with its parsimonious parent. Now the company brought on a computational linguist. The new job was largely about developing products and features for Merriam's website and apps—"bridging the gap between definers and website," Peter Sokolowski said. The better the dictionary served users, the healthier the dictionary would be.

Just as the *New York Times* became a puzzle and recipe website that also delivered news—kidding!—Merriam goosed traffic by developing and acquiring games. In 2023, it bought Quordle, a variation on the box-office smash Wordle. Parent company Britannica in turn added Octordle and head-to-head Victordle. As of the summer of 2025, the Merriam site featured ten games, including The Missing Letter, a daily dictionary-based crossword, and Pilfer, a twenty-first-century version of the nineteenth-century word-stealing game Anagrams. A stable of word-related quizzes also kept users on the website—in front of rotating ads—for critical minutes at a time.

"We want to maintain the Merriam-Webster mission and level of lexicography and attention to detail and all of that. And also we're a business, so we have to do that in a way that makes money," publisher Lisa Schneider told me shortly before she left Merriam during the pandemic. "Lexicographers are not magical fairies going around doing magical lexicography. We're a company and we have to pay the rent and we have to pay the bills and we have to give our owners some money. That's how it works and there's nothing wrong with that."

Journalistically, the cutbacks I witnessed at Merriam were news: Vaunted Dictionary Confronts Vagaries of Algorithms and Advertisers in the Digital Age. Schneider pointed out that "it's not exactly unusual for a media company to have had layoffs sometime between 2008 and now," and she was right. The internet disrupted every word-driven industry. But non-print-publishing-cycle layoffs were unprecedented for Merriam-Webster Inc., and, in a shrinking business, portentous.

In any case, I was never rooting for that story, just chronicling it. As I told Schneider, I love Merriam. I love lexicography. I'm grateful that I was given a peek inside the bindings, and allowed to contribute in a tiny way to cataloging American English. I wanted Merriam to catalog American English as long as there was an American English to catalog. I was glad that clicks and revenue rebounded.

Schneider and Britannica modernized Merriam's tools, structures, and practices, and integrated its editorial, technology, and business operations. She hired coders and web designers, and an SEO specialist. She used jargon that likely would never make the dictionary, about moving from top-down "waterfall software development" to collaborative "agile software development," that is, editorial and technology staff working together to develop features that showcased the thrill of the language and appealed to user eyeballs and Google bots.

Merriam's clunky, old data systems got an upgrade. The new technology, based in the cloud and not on physical hardware, allowed it to upload a dictionary update in a couple of hours rather than a couple of weeks and let editors post content without the intervention of a geek squad. The emergency covid-words update showed that the dictionary could be a sprinter instead of a mall-walker. The systems also allowed Merriam to build a better and faster dictionary API—application programming interface—to license dictionary and thesaurus content and boost income. While Google made the search racket more challenging, SEO upgrades, new editorial content, and more mentions in traditional and social media helped the company fight back.

There were apps and an online store, where you could buy actual books—Merriam was still producing new editions of school, children's, and bilingual dictionaries, even a new printing of the eleventh edition of the *Collegiate*—and be-logoed and word-themed onesies, hoodies, jigsaw puzzles, greeting cards, mugs, phone cases, and more. And while Merriam's social media persona avoided politics—even as Trump was voted into the White House a second time—it still found ways to let people know where it stood. I particularly enjoyed a 2024 post featuring a multicolor image in the style of a popular social justice yard sign:

IN THIS HOUSE WE BELIEVE:

'LITERALLY' CAN BE USED TO MEAN 'VIRTUALLY'
'CONVERSATE' HAS BEEN A WORD FOR 200 YEARS
WHILE NONSTANDARD, 'IRREGARDLESS' IS A REAL WORD
IT CAN BE PRONOUNCED EITHER 'ESPRESSO' OR 'EXPRESSO'
YOU CAN END A SENTENCE WITH A PREPOSITION
'EMBIGGEN' IS A PERFECTLY CROMULENT WORD

Britannica also found surer footing. It rebranded as the Britannica Group—the word *encyclopedia* is scarce on the company's website now—and expanded into education software and generative AI tools. The company developed a chatbot based on its warehouse of information, and it applied artificial intelligence to create and edit content for the online encyclopedia. It was also using AI to update Merriam's thesaurus to answer queries about phrases in addition to individual words. In 2024, Britannica floated plans for an initial public offering that valued the company at $1 billion. "We have more users now than we've ever had," Britannica chief executive Jorge Cauz told the *New York Times*.

John Morse and the dictionary had been married a long time, but the business blips that coincided with his departure created an opportunity for changes designed to position Merriam for the digital present and future. But the work wouldn't stop with one up cycle. Like all digital publishers, Merriam would need to keep cat-and-mousing Google. It would need to constantly improve functionality and bolster content—lexicographic and otherwise—and find creative new ways to reach readers. It would need young, diverse, and aware staffers who, whenever possible, could plop the ancient brand smack in the middle of a news cycle. It would need to explore and invest in AI. It would need to draw on the past while imagineering* the future.

Above all, Merriam would have to sprint ever harder toward the bleeding edge of digital lexicography. Spitballing here: How about a daily feature about a rising new word spotted by a Merriam bot? Or adding info like date of entry, so people can see when a word was sanctioned by Big Dictionary. Or writing more colloquially, ditching the Govian replaceable single statement. Or deploying more visual gems like images of citation slips. Or incorporating the *Unabridged* into the OWL. The contents of the big book turned website—the direct legacy of Noah Webster; this mighty thing, to borrow the *Atlantic Monthly*'s description a century and a half ago—deserved to be released from behind the iron bars of the paywall, deserved to be used as more than just the source for the Scripps National Spelling Bee.

---

* The *OED* entered *imagineer* as both a verb—"To devise and implement (a new or highly imaginative technology, concept, etc.)—and a noun—"A person who devises . . ." The blend of *imagine* and *engineer* is commonly associated with the Walt Disney Co., but the earliest recorded usage is much older. More in the endnotes.

John Morse had told me that lexicography needed to do something like Merriam had done in 1864, when the Yalies overhauled Webster. A more modern parallel was the *Second* in 1934, which was stuffed with non-lexical matter. Those two old books demonstrated how lexicography at the beginning of the internet age—and we're still at the beginning of the internet age—had failed to conjure, let alone produce, a dictionary able to fully capitalize on the infinite bounties of the modern medium.

If you were to start from scratch, with no restriction other than a capacity for wonder, you wouldn't design a digital dictionary to look like any existing one, or like a print dictionary. You would build something far more inclusive. A natively digital dictionary—as opposed to a digitized print product—would be as freewheeling as Wordnik, spidering the web for undiscovered words, using photos, audio, video, historical evidence, journalism, and citation slips to create a 3D image of words and their place in popular culture. It would combine the power of computers with the discretion of lexicographers, distinguishing fully sanctioned entries from budding ones. Words previously stashed in New Words for staff eyes only could pass go—but with, say, the headword in a different color or font to flag that it was on probation. When promoted to full-fledged entry, balloons and champagne (the emoji kind, of course).*

Editors could sift reader submissions and tap interesting ones on the go. I had dozens of orphans that I never got around to typing into New Words: *ratfucking, sportswashing, rickroll, derp*. And more that I did but weren't picked up: *nothingburger, velo, testilying, failson*. In 2024, the *New York Times* explored the mainstreaming of *rawdogging*, which it explained "has historically been used to refer to sexual intercourse without a condom" but "has been adopted to describe almost any activity accomplished without the assistance of a buffer." In the

---

*In February 2025, Merriam debuted a "Slang & Trending" page featuring just these sorts of entries. See the endnotes for more.

months before that year's presidential election, the use of *sanewashing* exploded, mainly to describe media translating Donald Trump's gibberish into what appeared to be coherent thoughts.* ("On the one hand: god, what a time for American dictionary publishing to have pretty much collapsed," Kory Stamper wrote on social media. "On the other: god, what a relief not to be the lexicographer who has to deal with the entry for 'Gulf of Mexico.'")

I left Merriam not knowing if the upgrades, and the cozier relationship with Britannica, would be enough to endow it indefinitely. I also didn't know what distant-future model might work best, for any dictionary-maker. Getting swallowed by a tech giant or go-big-or-go-home digital upstart that expected hockey-stick growth had proven untenable. A billionaire willing to let the dictionary just be the dictionary—a self-sustaining company with a modest staff performing an outsize cultural job that might not always be profitable—looked less and less desirable. (See Dan Gilbert and Dictionary.com. Or, in other media industries, Jeff Bezos's stewardship of the *Washington Post*, or Elon Musk's and Mark Zuckerberg's of social media platforms. Not to mention the ever-present threat of strip-mining takeovers by private-equity vultures.) Maybe capitalism was the problem, not the solution. Maybe the answer was that bold collaboration among private, not-for-profit, and academic institutions, uniting multiple forces with an interest in ensuring that American English, its archives and its future, are shepherded by people who care, deeply and apolitically.

In the end, for whatever little I knew—after all, I was just a reporter cosplaying a lexicographer—I definitely knew this: Noah Webster invented the American dictionary. George and Charles Merriam reinvented it as a consumer product. And their twenty-first-century heirs needed to re-reinvent it for the digital future. The

---

*For the record, I wrote the two previous sentences before *rawdog* defeated *sanewashing* in a runoff to become the American Dialect Society's 2024 Word of the Year. I cast my ballot for the loser but still was irrationally excited to have crystal-balled the first- and second-place finishers. More on both words in the endnotes.

flow of words wouldn't stop. The need for a dictionary, human or robot, to steer it shouldn't, either.

I typed *sportocrat* into the Merriam-Webster.com search bar and hit return. "The word you've entered isn't in the dictionary."

I didn't expect that it would be. To check up on my old friend, I did one last database dive for citations. And look what I found: *sportocrat*, in a newspaper, in 1980—seventeen years before Nike boss Phil Knight uttered the word in the *Wall Street Journal*. "For months now Olympic 'sportocrats' have been slipping in and out of Greece," George Coats wrote in *The Guardian* after Greece's prime minister offered to host the games permanently near ancient Olympia. It was the perfect quote. My first sense—"an official of a large sports organization"—with the privilege that it implied. George Coats: journalism hero.

I scrolled through time. The Sportocrat was a "coat sweater"—$3.95 at Silverberg's in Scranton, Pennsylvania, in 1932—and a V-neck pullover sweater-shirt with two breast pockets made by Robert Reis & Co. of New York. In 1905, the *Seattle Star* published a column of sports tidbits with my word right there in the title: "Food For Sportocrats," implying sophisticated consumers of all things sport. 1905: Pretty good antedating.

None of that made *sportocrat* a lock for entry, just a more interesting linguistic foray. But then I found a few more-recent hits, including two by a theater reviewer for the *Financial Times* who in the span of five months used *sportocracy* ("The story itself is a predictable account of institutional sexism, thuggish *sportocracy*, and victim-blaming") and *sportocratic* ("Frantic yet pointless administrative toil allows them to ignore their dysfunctional romantic lives and the *sportocratic* inanity of US education"). I emailed the writer, Max McGuinness. He said he had picked up the word from his friend Christopher Hitchens. In a 2010 memoir, *Hitch-22*, Hitchens described a boarding-school jock as "a thick-necked sportocrat with the unimprovable name of Peter Raper."

"I very much hope you can get it into the dictionary," McGuinness said.

As I was ending my reporting inside Merriam, I checked in with Steve Perrault about the status of my words. Perrault said he had a soft spot for *sportocrat*. "I do find the question of the spelling and meaning really quite interesting," he said. And for some of my other words, too. My draft of *tweetstorm* just needed some tweaking, Perrault said. *Headbutt* was "a perfectly valid dictionary entry." *Dogpile*, too. The Canadianism *gong show*, meaning chaotic or out of control, which I researched for weeks, was "obviously something that should get in at some point." Perrault even seemed to be warming up to the farting sense of *Dutch oven*, or at least he didn't just laugh it off when I mentioned it one last time. And my new sense of *redshirt*—holding back a kid in kindergarten to gain a developmental leg up—was "potentially addable," he said.

"Everything is potentially addable," I joked.

"I think more of your words will eventually get into the dictionary," Perrault said. "As the process goes on, as we make further revisions, and look further for things we could enter, those are good things we could enter."

Perrault even acknowledged that the pronouns *xe* and *ze* stood a chance. They're "oddities," Perrault said, because their use in print typically was as an example of a neopronoun, not as an actual pronoun used by an actual person. Maybe, Perrault suggested, we could start by beefing up the entry for *gender-neutral* ("not referring to either sex but only to people in general") with a run-on for *gender-neutral pronoun* and some examples that included the pronouns, damn the old cross-reference rule that every word used in the dictionary, including words in quotations, needed to be defined in the dictionary.

Perrault admitted that he might not be best equipped to pass judgment about words like *xe* and *ze*, that maybe the imperatives of the modern dictionary business and the rapidity of social change demanded a new standard for the "National Standard," as Merriam described itself in 1880. "Let's face it, I'm an old white guy," he said. "It's possible my own attitudes are slow and I'm a little bit behind the world here. I have to be conscious of that possibility. I don't feel like I'm standing in the way of these kinds of words. I think I'm just trying to make reasonable decisions about what should get into the dictionary right now."

During my time at Merriam, I drafted more than ninety definitions of new words or senses. By the start of 2025, fourteen of them, by my count, had made the dictionary, including a few that Perrault had predicted would pass muster: *alt-right, burkini, dogpile, GOAT, headbutt, hot take, microaggression, N-word, overserve, posterize* ("to make a forceful and overpowering dunk shot over (an overmatched defensive player)"), my new sense of *run, safe space, sheeple,* and *tweetstorm*. Another fourteen terms I added to New Words eventually were defined by other editors: *adulting, bralette, bruh, chirp* ("to make sharply critical, complaining, or taunting remarks"), *deconflict,* the new sense of *jamoke* (which went in as "an ordinary, unimpressive, or inept person → typically used as a term of mild or joking disparagement for a man"), *meetup, pickleball, shitpost,* the baseball stats term *slash line, spear phishing* ("a targeted attempt to trick a specific person into revealing personal or confidential information that can then be used illicitly"), the secondhand-shopping sense of *thrift,* and *unbanked* ("not having money deposited in a bank").

For a rookie thrust into the bigs, it wasn't a terrible performance. As a writer, I wished I had been better at spotting dictionary-worthy words and composing their definitions. But Perrault had a tall to-do stack and, tbh,* I drafted a bunch of terms that lacked what folks in the biz call "lexical intensity." Still, Perrault was kind enough

---

*Merriam entered all-caps-only *TBH* as the abbreviation for *to be honest* in 2021. I prefer the lowercase variant, which the *OED* sanctions. Oxford dates first usage to the Usenet newsgroup rec.food.veg in 1991.

to fluff all of my finds. "A lot of these things we could add to the unabridged dictionary without much hesitation at all," he said.

But there was no unabridged dictionary. Or everything was an unabridged dictionary. Merriam had won, if that's the right word, the 200-year-long War of the Dictionaries and was the Last American Dictionary Standing. That wasn't necessarily good for Merriam—competition is healthy—or for American English either. "Dictionaries are like other works of human art. The differences matter," said Michael Adams, the Indiana professor. "The field is diminished when there's one type of monopoly. Even when that one type of monopoly is as revered as Merriam-Webster." Plus, Adams asked and answered, "Who's being trained as a lexicographer now? Almost no one." A millenniums-old craft was slowly dying.

Or maybe it was just evolving. Maybe Merriam would hum along successfully, generating revenue from ads and puzzles, cranking out periodic OWL Releases, staying true to its founders' mission. Or maybe it would staff up and embark on the full, romantic, historically respectful revision I anticipated when I first walked into the building, seizing the opportunity that technology had on offer. Or, flip side, maybe the chatbots would improve enough to reliably compose definitions and voice pronunciations and the human staff would be contracted—and in five or twenty or fifty years, Merriam-Webster would be nothing more than a red book in a Smithsonian display case alongside a *cathode-ray tube* and an *internal combustion engine*, two words that crashed the unabridged a century ago. Or maybe Merriam would be the last and best bot standing. No one could say for sure.

I thanked Perrault for editing and including as many of my words as he did.

"Even when you're finished with the book, I hope you won't necessarily forget us."

I could be like the guy whose distinctive citation slips, in stuttery, old-man scrawl, I kept finding in the citation files. I saw one just that morning, when I was researching the history of the baseball term *stuff.* It was a quotation attributed to Boston Red Sox broadcaster Dave Martin from a game on August 6, 1973, as heard on the Hartford, Connecticut, radio station WTIC. The slip was stamped on February 2, 1982, by a greenhorn named John Morse; reviewed by senior editor H. Bosley Woolf; and used in drafting the entry that would appear in the ninth edition of the *Collegiate* the following year.

"Mr. Conboy!" Perrault exclaimed when I showed him the slip. Robert W. Conboy was an editorial assistant on the *Third*. The book's front matter reported that he had a bachelor of arts from the University of Miami and a master of arts from Vanderbilt. Conboy worked at Merriam from 1952 to 1970. After retiring, he lived in downtown Springfield in the Hotel Charles, which had declined with the city into a dingy SRO—"a house, apartment building, or residential hotel in which low-income or welfare tenants live in single rooms," to quote the dictionary one last time. Mr. Conboy would record citations from radio and television—especially Red Sox games; many of his slips quoted Ned Martin, the team's play-by-play voice for three decades (no relation to Dave Martin, his boothmate for several seasons)—and deliver them to Merriam in boxes.

"They're all over the place," Perrault said. "They always said, 'Key words exact, rest may be approximate,' or something like that."

On the *stuff* cit, around his jagged handwriting, Conboy had typed "key words exact rest maybe paraphrased." But I preferred Perrault's rendering. *Key words exact, rest may be approximate.* It captured the soul of the dictionary, especially the modern one. The dictionary projects totality, but it's thwarted by missing or unknown or newly imagined strings of letters. The dictionary projects permanence, but the language is Jell-O, slippery and mutable and forever collapsing on itself. The dictionary projects ubiquity, but even the best AI hasn't figured out how to collect and define every collectable and definable word.

We humans might not be up to the task either but, for the sake of recorded history, here's hoping that we are, and still care enough to do it.

acknowledgments

: things done or given in recognition
of something received

The germ of this book dates to the summer of 2012 at the North American Scrabble championship, held that year in Orlando, Florida. Peter Sokolowski (who as part of his Merriam duties regularly attends the tournament) told me (who regularly competes in it) about the *Unabridged* revision. He also mentioned a new book about the controversy over the making of *Webster's Third*, David Skinner's *The Story of Ain't*. I read it and was hooked. I proposed a story about the past, present, and future of America's foremost lexicon to my editors at *Slate*. Merriam publisher John Morse talked it over with his bosses and staff and invited me up.

My trip was delayed again and again—other writing projects, general procrastination, life itself. When I finally made it to Springfield, in the summer of 2014, Morse packed my schedule: a guided tour of the old building, a roundtable lunch (sandwiches and chips) in a first-floor conference room, a parade of one-on-ones with editors. My 10,000-word story—plus a Q and A with the author; a video about the history of Merriam's all-time most-searched word, *pragmatic*; and interactive features—was published in January 2015. I got a book deal that spring and began traveling to Springfield in the fall. I visited regularly and then occasionally into 2018; I didn't want to surrender my monk-like days in the Merriam hush. I also kept finding more word events to attend, people to meet, ideas to explore. Reporting is fun, writing is hard. And, oh, there was a pandemic in there.

All of which is to say that this book was—to use a word so overused that a former colleague wrote a *New York Times* story about its overuse—a journey, one that required the support and help of many people.

I'll start with John Morse, whose trust and generosity made this possible. When I pitched the *Slate* story, John said he could count on one hand the number of times Merriam had allowed a writer inside 47 Federal Street. He made it happen. When I pitched the book, he said he knew I was going to ask about writing one. He made it happen. And when I pitched writing definitions, he made that happen, too. John spent countless hours while I was a fake Merriam staff member and in the years after ensuring I understood the company and lexicography—and got the details right. (But any mistakes are mine and mine alone.) John will be a unanimous first-ballot entry into the American Dictionary Hall of Fame and Museum that does belong in the building on the hill in Springfield.

Stephen Perrault had better things to attend to than my reportorial whims, like the "ceaseless seining of the endless river of words," to quote that Merriam corporate history, *Noah's Ark*. But he always treated me as if I belonged on the second floor. So did Madeline Novak, who deftly managed and patiently explained the logistical challenges of publishing the dictionary. Steve and Madeline retired during the pandemic. They'll no doubt be in that Hall of Fame, too.

After Morse's departure, Lisa Schneider kindly allowed me to continue my on-site reporting and sat for interviews. Also at Merriam, Emily Brewster and Peter Sokolowski were especially helpful. And thanks to current and former staffers Daniel Brandon, Serenity Carr, Chris Connor, Allison DeJordy, Joanne Despres, Matthew Dube, Jim Lowe, Meghan Lunghi, Joan Narmontas, Lauren Naturale, Jim Rader, Neil Serven, Ammon Shea, Mark Stevens, Emily Vezina, and the late E. Ward Gilman.

acknowledgments

Ben Zimmer has been a source, sage, sounding board, and supporter in all of my word-related endeavors, especially this one. I can't thank him enough. For schooling me about lexicography, I'm hella grateful to Grant Barrett, Katherine Connor Martin, John Kelly, Steve Kleinedler, Erin McKean, Lynne Murphy, Wendalyn Nichols, Jesse Sheidlower, and Kory Stamper. Lots more folks answered my emails, took my calls, or talked IRL, including David Barnhart, Dennis Baron, Genny Beemyn, Anne Bello, Charles Carson, Kirby Conrod, Anne Curzan, Mark Davies, Gilles-Maurice de Schryver, Paul Dickson, Stefan Dollinger, Manuel Ebert, Dan Greaney, Jack Grieve, Orin Hargraves, the late Robin Herman, Nicole Holliday, Joan Houston Hall, Sally Jenkins, Randall Kennedy, Ilan Kernerman, Sonja Lanehart, Charles Levine, Robert Lipsyte, Ruth Mazo Karras, Gretchen McCullough, John McWhorter, the late Allan Metcalf, Laura Mixon, Orión Montoya, Enid Pearsons, Michael Rundell, Lindsay Rose Russell, Hans-Jörg Schmid, Jon Simon, David Skinner, Jane Solomon, Kate Wild, Kelly Wright, and Beth Young. I'm sure I'm forgetting someone; thanks to them, too.

Madeline Kripke is no doubt holding court right now with Samuel Johnson, Noah Webster, James Murray, and Allen Walker Read, showing off some rare volume, racy pamphlet, or goofy tchotchke. Visiting her apartment was sense I.5.b of the *OED* entry for *trip*: "An experience, esp. a stimulating one." Thanks to Madeline's friends and fellow dictionary-lovers for reminiscing about her life, marveling at her passion, and detailing the fate of her collection: Michael Adams, Tom Dalzell, Jonathon Green, Barbara Minsky, John Morse, Rob Rulon-Miller, Jesse Sheidlower, and Peter Sokolowski.

Passing out some emoji: For my visit to Oxford, Raising Hands to Peter Gilliver and Beverley McCulloch. For my visit to Indiana University, Folded Hands to Michael Adams, Erika Dowell, and Joel Silver. For my visit to Dictionary.com, Thumbs Up to Liz McMillan, Rebekah Otto, and Jenny Davis. For my visit to Google, Flexed Biceps to Seth Lipkin and Jon Orwant. And a row of Heart Hands to

acknowledgments

Cliff McCarthy, Maggie Humbertson, and Guy McLain at the Wood Museum of Springfield History; Springfield historian Barbara Shaffer; Kelly Dyson and Chamisa Redmond at the Library of Congress; and the staff at the Beinecke Rare Book and Manuscript Library at Yale.

Josh Levin has been my editor, podcasting partner, and pal for two decades. He was there for me throughout my lexicographical—uh-oh, I'm gonna say it—journey. Josh deftly edited my original *Slate* story (and many other stories), immeasurably improved this book's manuscrpt, and listened to me whine in between. He's never failed to make my sentences and paragraphs better and, more important, to have my back. At *Slate*, Ben Blatt, Ayana Morali, John Swansburg, and Mike Vuolo worked on the original story package, and David Plotz and Julia Turner greenlit it.

In addition to several others already named, Kirby Conrod, Gene Demby, Charles Fishman, and Sam Masling read all or parts of the manuscript and offered helpful suggestions; Howard Gensler workshopped subtitles. David Plunkert designed the gorgeous jacket and Maisie Derlega drew the beautiful little dictionary separating text. My sister-in-law Cindy Fatsis shot the author photo; Marcia Philipson assisted and Bucks County Community College provided studio space and equipment. Thanks to them all.

Katie Benton-Cohen and Stacey Marien provided academic access to various reading materials. Annie Rosenthal transcribed. John and Leigh Rae let me crash at their home and eat their food during my visits to Springfield. Cabot Brown and Ingrid Jacobson and Jane Levin and Bob Rifkin hosted me during other reporting trips. For years of support, collegiality, advice, and friendship, bro hugs and fist bumps to Joel Anderson, Lampros Fatsis, Jonathan Hock, Robert Shepard, and Dan Wachtell. And a shoutout to the DC Writers Room, where I wrote most of this book, socialized with other humans, and lollygagged.

My two-time editor and all-time friend Eamon Dolan acquired this project for Houghton Mifflin and took it with him to Simon

& Schuster. Post-pandemic, we parted, amicably. I owe Eamon a career's worth of gratitude.

That led me to George Gibson at Grove Atlantic. George edited my first book near the end of the last century. He was willing to take a chance then on a young, crank-it-out, daily reporter with a niche idea—chronicling a start-up baseball league in the Midwest—but no clue how to write more than a couple thousand words at a time. And he was eager to stage a reunion now. George edited the old-fashioned way, with a No. 2 pencil and a sharp eye. I'm grateful for his intellect, his counsel, and, above all, his unwavering support and enthusiasm. So cool to do this together again.

It's humbling to join the roster of Grove Atlantic authors. Thanks to president and publisher Morgan Entrekin for putting me on the team. John Mark Boling, Emily Burns, Toni Burns Busot, Natalie Church, Sal Destro, RJT Green, Miranda Hency, Amy Hundley, Jisu Kim, Gretchen Mergenthaler, Joseph Payne, Sophie Pugh-Sellers, Mike Richards, and Rachael Richardson copyedited my words, turned them into a physical object, shepherded that object into the world, and tried to persuade people to buy and read it. High fives to them all.

My agent, David McCormick, negotiated these deals, tolerated my sloth, and boosted my spirits when I figured this was destined to be read in three-sentence chunks on social media. Thanks, David, for not letting me give up.

Finally: My wife, Melissa Block, saved me from dilating my pupils in the sun on page one of my last book and from improperly bearing arms in chapter 5 of this one. More important, she believed in this project from A to Z, when for most of the alphabet I did not. Our daughter, Chloe, was in middle school when I started this and is a college graduate now. While I was defining a few words and writing some more, she learned tens of thousands of them en route to Scrabble greatness. Unabridged love to them both.

endnotes

: notes placed at the end of the text

note

ix **His birthday, October 16:** "October 16," *National Day Calendar*, accessed December 14, 2024, https://www.nationaldaycalendar.com/october/october-16.

ix **titled *An American Dictionary of the English Language*:** The subtitle is pretty, um, thorough:

> Intended to Exhibit,
> I. The origin, affinities and primary signification of English words, as far as they have been ascertained.
> II. The genuine orthography and pronunciation of words, according to general usage, or to just principles of analogy.
> III. Accurate and discriminating definitions, with numerous authorities and illustrations.
>
> To Which are Prefixed, an Introductory Dissertation on the Origin, History and Connection of the Languages of Western Asia and of Europe, and a Concise Grammar of the English Language.

x **The 1847 edition was the first:** The word *abridged* and phrase "not abridged" had been used to refer to dictionaries as far back as 1699. But *unabridged* was new. Its use on the side of the 1847 dictionary, under "WEB-STER'S DICTIONARY," likely was meant to signal that the one-volume book contained the same amount of material as the 1828 edition, which was published in two volumes. An 1848 company poster referred to "WEB-STER'S DICTIONARY, ONLY UNABRIDGED EDITION." But the word would quickly become associated with Merriam dictionaries specifically, and then dictionaries generally. The *Oxford English Dictionary*'s second sense of *unabridged* is "A copy of the 'unabridged edition' of Webster's Dictionary." The definition was written around 1919, edited by William A. Craigie, who was the "title page editor" for the letter U (and who returns in chapter 15), and published in 1921 in an *OED* installment titled *U–Unforeseeable*. It is illustrated with a quotation from an 1860 book by Oliver Wendell Holmes Sr. (father of the Supreme Court justice), *The Professor at the Breakfast-Table*: "You small boy there, hurry up that 'Webster's Unabridged'!" That date indicates that *unabridged* was associated with Webster's before the word appeared in the book's title. Peter Sokolowski, "Why 'Unabridged'?" *Merriam-Webster*, January 14, 2013. https://web.archive.org/web/20150125164320/https://unabridged.merriam-webster.com/blog/2013/01/what-about-the-word-unabridged; Peter Gilliver, email message to author, January 13, 2025.

introduction

2 **This work made me:** Jonathon Green, *Chasing the Sun: Dictionary-Makers and the Dictionaries They Made* (New York: Henry Holt, 1996).

3 **But he also wanted to assemble:** The idea of an alphabetical dictionary itself required an explainer. "If thou be desirous (gentle Reader) rightly and readily to understand, and to profit by this Table," Cawdrey wrote, "then thou must learne the Alphabet, to wit, the order of the Letters as they stand, perfectly without booke, and where every Letter standeth: as (b) neere the beginning, (n) about the middest, and (t) toward the end." Robert Cawdrey, *A Table Alphabeticall*, Robert A. Peters, ed. (Gainesville, Florida: Scholars' Facsimiles & Reprints, 1966), https://extra.shu.ac.uk/emls/iemls/work/etexts/caw1604w_removed.htm.

3 **Samuel Johnson labeled:** Johnson's more famous characterization of the lexicographer as a "harmless drudge" was in his definition: "A writer of dictionaries; a harmless drudge, that busies himself in tracing the original, and detailing the signification of words." "lexicographer, n.s.," *Johnson's Dictionary Online*, accessed April 22, 2025, https://johnsonsdictionaryonline.com/1755/lexicographer_ns.

5 **Vast sociological and political:** David Guralnik here violated a core rule of dictionary-making. He printed a word in the dictionary, *unalienated*, that was not already entered in the dictionary.

5 **Noah Webster started writing:** Noah Webster, *An American Dictionary of the English Language* (New York: S. Converse, 1828), preface, https://archive.org/details/noahwebstersfirs00001webs/mode/2up.

6 **The fifth edition of G. & C. Merriam's:** This handsome book, a "Thin Paper" edition published in 1946, has a supple, pebbled cover featuring the company's signature interlocking MW colophon embossed in gold. I rescued it from my mother's apartment long after my father died when I was a teenager. The book's edges are frayed and faded; specks of leather and paper flake off at the touch. An inscription reads, CAPT. M. FATSIS. NEW YORK. OCTOBER. 1949. The M. was for *Michalis*, Michael once he settled in America. He had spent more than twenty years at sea, hence the honorific. He was a Greek citizen who joined the U.S. Merchant Marine during World War II and served thirty months on four vessels, including as chief mate on the SS *Jedediah S. Smith* ferrying troops, vehicles, and supplies during the June 1944 invasion of Normandy. Five years later, Capt. Michael would have been settling into his new landlocked life in New York. He would marry my mother in 1951, and they would have one son, then another, then,

endnotes 311

eight years later, when he was pushing sixty, a third (me). He would ride Metro North to Grand Central Station and the No. 4 train to Wall Street to manage cargo routes for shipowner relatives. He worked and socialized and counted the weekly donations at church with other Greeks, but he was in America now, so he needed a dictionary. I have no idea how much he used it. However much he did, he could have used it more. While my father's English was passable—he had sailed around the world and lived for a time in Scotland—his accent was heavy and his vocabulary light, and he preferred speaking Greek. I picture the dictionary sitting next to the rotary phone, oversize leather ledgers, and ashtray for his cigars on his office desk at 80 Broad Street. "No matter how much digital supplants print, the physical object will always hold a place, especially as a place where memories can reside," John Morse emailed when I told him about my heirloom. It happened be his favorite edition of the *Collegiate* "as a made object." "The trim size is right, it feels good in the hand, and the cover design is elegant. Hold on to that gem."

7 **The word *internet*, short for:** *Internet* was written at the start with a lowercase *i*, contrary to how it would be rendered for decades. Here's how a Merriam-Webster lexicographer would include an example of use of the word, known as a citation, in a draft of a definition: < . . . these same codes are used in the error field of the internet packet. —Vinton Cerf, Yogen Dalal, and Carl Sunshine, *Request for Comments*, "Specification of Internet Transmission Control Program," December 1974>

7 **The nation, H. L. Mencken:** H. L. Mencken, *The American Language; A Preliminary Inquiry into the Development of English in the United States* (New York: Alfred A. Knopf, 1919), 26.

9 **teen-talk or leetspeak:** As I wrote this, Merriam hadn't entered *leetspeak* or *leet speak*, but competitors Dictionary.com and the *OED* had. Here's the latter's definition: "An informal language or code used on the internet, characterized by its distinctive vocabulary and by a nonstandard system of spelling in which all or some of the standard letters are replaced by numerals, special characters, or other letters." *Leetspeak*, in leetspeak, is "1337sp33k." Merriam did enter at least one example of leetspeak in the *Unabridged*: *woot*, or *w00t*, "used to express joy, approval, or excited enthusiasm."

I
train

11 **When it opened in 1940:** "New Dictionary Building Open to Workers Tonight," *Springfield Daily Republican*, June 14, 1940.

11 **"This fine building:** "In every cultured home of the land there is or should be a copy of this book printed here in Springfield," the mayor, Roger L. Putnam, had told about fifty employees and government officials at the building's groundbreaking just eight months earlier. The new building, he said, "stands for the best in intellectual culture, for the best in architecture, and I know that it will typify the best of Springfield." "Merriam Building

Cornerstone Laid," *Springfield Sunday Union and Republican*, October 15, 1939.

12 **Another copy was choking:** Some other items placed in the cornerstone on a temperate Saturday in 1939: a copy of *Webster's Second New International Dictionary* (1934); the fifth edition of the *Collegiate* (1936); minutes of Merriam board meetings at which the building was approved; newspaper stories about a zoning kerfuffle over the site; and a penny from the building architect's office. "Merriam Building Cornerstone Laid."

14 **New hires needed the right:** Robert W. Blake, "The Not So 'Harmless Drudge' at the Linguistic Institute: Philip B. Gove on Lexicography," *The English Record* xix, no. 4 (1969), 82.

14 **The Black Books were:** At least a couple of copies of the Black Books endured. They are marvelous, for their manual-typewriter font, their absurd thoroughness, their academic rigor, and for Gove's general curiosity, disdain, and willingness to concede defeat to language's insoluble dilemmas. On page 313, in a section titled "SOME PROBLEMS ABOUT MEANINGS," Gove wrote:

> Rather grotesquely, after centuries of lexicography and language study of one sort or another, it appears that no one has answered the question of how we may know with sharp clarity and definitive exactness when a word has one meaning alone, with or without some secondary extensions, ramifications, and differences in application, and when it has two or more quite discrete meanings. In lexicography, at any rate, no one has mentioned the criterion or criteria he has used in making decisions . . . At this time, under the circumstances in which we are working, it is not feasible to go in for a lengthy philosophical semantic inquiry. All that can be done now is to proceed with a report which is frankly expedient and, with more or less rule-of-thumb procedure, seeks to arrive at satisfactory answers to some commonly raised questions.

15 **In any case, Perrault:** I spent a delightful afternoon interviewing "Gil" at his house. E. Ward Gilman started at Merriam in 1958 as a proofreader on the production of the *Third* and, until his retirement in 1997, held just about every editorial job, including director of defining. He edited and wrote most of the highly acclaimed, nearly thousand-page *Merriam-Webster's Dictionary of English Usage*; the Dictionary Society of North America honored him for "presenting objective data on usage in lieu of myth & shibboleth, persnickety pedants notwithstanding." In a remembrance after Gil's death at age ninety, John Morse wrote that "it is likely that more of his definitions have been seen by more people than that of any other lexicographer working in the twentieth century." He was, as Merriam editor Emily Brewster put it, "the warmest of curmudgeons, the humblest of smarty-pants." John Morse, "E. Ward Gilman: In Memoriam," *Dictionaries: The Journal of the Dictionary Society of North America* 44, no. 1 (2023), 141–48.

15 **I switched my font to Times New Roman:** For its print dictionaries, Merriam-Webster decades ago designed its own typeface with squat caps

and short tails to reduce the leading, or space between lines, in order to save space. It's based on Times New Roman and is known inside the company as the Merriam-Webster font. "Dipping Into the Mailbag: 'Yeet,' 'Typeface' vs. 'Font,' and 'Lo and Behold,'" *Merriam-Webster*, February 9, 2022, https://www.merriam-webster.com/word-matters-podcast/episode-75-yeet.

16 **The first time I opened:** The New Words spreadsheet had boxes for part of speech, editor's initials (mine: SMF), date, sample definition, citation, and supporting information. On that day, the list ran from *AAC* (*Advanced Audio Codec*, or *Coding*) to *Zumba* (capital Z because it's trademarked).

16 **"You're in the right place:** Emily Brewster didn't consider lexicography as a career until an adviser at the nearby University of Massachusetts Amherst, where she majored in linguistics and philosophy, suggested it. "Lightbulbs, buzzers, all those cartoon things going off in your head," she said. Brewster cold-called Steve Perrault and badgered him for a year until a job opened and she got it.

18 **In fact, I'd encountered:** Jason Collins's use of *big* also struck me as noteworthy. And then I discovered that Perrault already had defined it as the second nounal sense: "a big player : a center or forward whose large size and strength are used to control play near the basket." The first sense also was sporty, as in calling Major League Baseball *the bigs*. Jason Collins, "I'm Out," *The Players' Tribune*, November 20, 2014, https://www.theplayerstribune.com/articles/jason-collins-retires.

19 ***The New Yorker* wrote about:** Daniel A. Gross, "The Encyclopedia Reader," *New Yorker*, September 13, 2016, https://www.newyorker.com/books/page-turner/the-encyclopedia-reader.

20 **I smoked out this dialogue:** *The Sopranos*, season 5, episode 4, "All Happy Families . . . " written by David Chase and Toni Kalem, directed by Rodrigo Garcia, featuring Robert Iler, Steve Buscemi, James Gandolfini, and John Ventimiglia, aired March 28, 2004, on HBO.

20 **The *OED* added *fart*:** The first edition of the *OED* was published between 1884 and 1928 in periodic updates originally called Parts (more than 300 pages) and later Sections (64 or 72 pages). *Fart* appeared in a Section containing 897 main words from *fanged* to *fee*. "The section is remarkable for the almost complete absence of terms of modern science or other words of recent formation, and for the unusually large proportion of words that have a long history," Henry Bradley, who edited the letters E, F, and G, wrote. "OED Editions," *Oxford English Dictionary*, accessed May 6, 2025, https://www.oed.com/information/about-the-oed/history-of-the-oed/oed-editions/; Henry Bradley, "Fanged–Fee," in *Dispatches from the Front: The Prefaces to the Oxford English Dictionary*, ed. Darrell R. Raymond (Waterloo, Ontario: UW Centre for the New Oxford English Dictionary, 1987), https://s3.eu-west-1.amazonaws.com/com.idmgroup.oed100.sounds.prod/wp-content/uploads/Volume-IV-Fanged-Fee.pdf.

21 **In a profile of retired:** Greg Bishop, "Brett Favre," *Sports Illustrated*, July 6, 2015, 48.

21 **Wut?:** As of May 2025, no commercial dictionary entered the online shortening of *what*. The crowd-sourced Wiktionary noted that *wut* is used in place of the standard interjection "but especially as a response to an outrageous or unexpected statement."

22 **The journey took me to:** Exhibiting no restraint, I sent Steve Perrault a draft definition that totaled 788 words, including three alternate spellings (*pompom girl, pompon girl,* and *pom pom girl*); three senses (1. cheer or dance squad member; 2. booster, sycophant; 3. pickup, prostitute); eighteen illustrative quotations from 1948 to the present; and the supplemental information note, or SIN, below explaining the word's history. Alas, the entry was not updated to reflect my labors.

> ♦The phrase **pom-pom girl** dates to the early twentieth century. The "Pom-Pom Girls" was an all-female theatrical troupe in the 1910s and 1920s that traveled the United States performing musical comedy skits. Children dressed up as *pom-pom girls* for Halloween and women did the same at masquerade balls. The familiar modern sense of a *pom-pom girl*—a member of a group that cheers at a sports event waving colorful tufts of shredded paper—appears to have emerged in the western United States around 1940. The most curious sense of the phrase is World War II military slang meaning *prostitute*. This outdated usage may have arisen from various South Asian words for sexual intercourse or, like *pom-pom gun*, it may be imitative. Today, just as the activity of *cheerleading* has become the sport of *cheer*, *pom-pom girls* are likely to be members of a *pom squad* or *poms team*, and, like their earliest namesakes, their job is to dance. As one high-school dancer wrote in *The Gazette* (Cedar Rapids, Iowa) in 2015, "The *poms team* is there for the crowd's entertainment, not to get them pumped for the offense or defense."

23 **"Many a single word:** Richard Chenevix Trench, *On the Study of Words* (London: John W Parker and Son, 1851), 5, https://archive.org/details/bub_gb_w4PpZet2TRsC/mode/2up.

2
history

24 **"The business of the lexicographer:** Herbert C. Morton, *The Story of Webster's Third: Philip Gove's Controversial Dictionary and Its Critics* (New York: Cambridge University Press, 1994), 205.

24 **In the 1780s, a young Noah:** Emily Brewster "discovered" this sense of *a* used as an indefinite article—"*a* young Noah Webster." It's entered as sense 3, subsense f, "used as a function word before a proper noun to distinguish the condition of the referent from a usual, former, or hypothetical condition."

25 **Webster was just twenty-four:** Peter Martin, *The Dictionary Wars: The American Fight over the English Language* (Princeton, NJ: Princeton University Press, 2019), 29.

endnotes 315

25 **"Sir, we must:** Joshua Kendall, *The Forgotten Founding Father: Noah Webster's Obsession and the Creation of an American Culture* (New York: G. P. Putnam's Sons, 2011), 231. I am indebted in this entire section to Kendall's entertaining biography.

25 **A 700-plus-page:** The full title: *A Brief History of Epidemic and Pestilential Diseases; With the Principal Phenomena of the Physical World, Which Precede and Accompany Them, and Observations Deduced From the Facts Stated.*

25 **For $2,066.66, he bought:** To help decide whether to devote his life to compiling a dictionary, Webster drew up charts listing the ages at death of great writers from ancient Greece and Rome, continental Europe, and England. "It is probable," he wrote, "that the unusual proportion of learned men who live to a great age may be in part ascribed to their temperate habits of life—and to an original firmness of constitution." So he plunged in. Kendall, *Forgotten Founding Father*, 236, 260; 256–57.

25 **And then he embarked:** Jill Lepore, "Noah's Mark," *New Yorker*, November 6, 2006, 78.

25 **Pro-America Republicans:** Kendall, *Forgotten Founding Father*, 261.

26 **He lent some support:** Kendall, *Forgotten Founding Father*, 154–55.

26 **Webster's 1806 *Compendious*:** Kendall, *Forgotten Founding Father*, 279. The *Compendious* wasn't the first English dictionary written in America. *A School Dictionary*, a pocket book compiled by Samuel Johnson Jr. (no relation), was published in 1798, and Caleb Alexander's 550-page *Columbian Dictionary of the English Language* came out in 1800. Alexander's book advertised "many new words peculiar to the United States," such as *caucus*, *moccasin*, and *chipmunk*. Wrote one critic: "a disgusting collection." Martin, *Dictionary Wars*, 46–47.

26 **And while Webster wimped out:** Noah Webster, *A Compendious Dictionary of the English Language* (New Haven, CT: Sidney's Press, 1806), https://archive.org/details/compendiousdictionaryoftheenglishlanguage1806.

26 **He also included hundreds:** Martin, *Dictionary Wars*, 48.

26 **"the wildest innovator:** Martin, *Dictionary Wars*, 52.

26 **Even his own brother-in-law:** Kendall, *Forgotten Founding Father*, 283.

27 **"the lowest of all vulgar words:** Martin, *Dictionary Wars*, 54.

27 **"New words will be formed:** Noah Webster, *Letter to the Honorable John Pickering*, 1817, in Kendall, *Forgotten Founding Father*, 319. Thomas Jefferson also believed that language should promote national identity. "The new circumstances under which we are placed, call for new words, new phrases, and for the transfer of old words to new objects. An American dialect will therefore be formed," he wrote in 1813. The *OED* credits Jefferson with coining more than one hundred words. Martin, *Dictionary Wars*, 7.

27 **After packing the walls:** Kendall, *Forgotten Founding Father*, 291–92.

27 **Then one morning, he said:** Kendall, *Forgotten Founding Father*, 296.

27 **But the immediate effect:** Kendall, *Forgotten Founding Father*, 308–10.

27 **His manuscript, titled "Synopsis:** Fred Robinson, a Yale University professor and Old English scholar, wrote a paper about Webster's nonsensical manuscript. Fred C. Robinson, "Noah Webster as Etymologist," *Neuphilologische Mitteilungen* 111, no. 2 (2000), 167–74.

27 **Short of money, Webster:** Martin, *Dictionary Wars*, 56.

27 **"In the second story:** Emily Ellsworth Fowler Ford, *Notes on the Life of Noah Webster* (New York: privately printed, 1912), 116, https://archive.org/details/notesonlifenoah00skeegoog/page/n9/mode/2up?view=theater.

28 **"When I had come to the last:** Ford, *Notes on the Life of Noah Webster*, 293.

29 **"It is not only important:** Webster, *An American Dictionary*, preface.

29 **Webster's dictionary contained:** Kendall, *Forgotten Founding Father*, 342.

29 **Webster still lifted from his nemesis:** In a study published in 1962, Samuel Johnson scholar Joseph Reed found that about a third of the definitions in the letter L in Webster's 1828 dictionary were copied verbatim or barely changed from Johnson's 1755 dictionary, and Webster used two-thirds of Johnson's cited authors or quotations. Borrowing, however, wasn't uncommon in lexicography, and Webster's inclusiveness was groundbreaking. "By introducing matter previously limited to technical and professional books, Webster did more than perhaps any other lexicographer to initiate the encyclopedic dictionary," Reed wrote. Joseph W. Reed Jr., "Noah Webster's Debt to Samuel Johnson," *American Speech* 37, no. 2 (1962), 95–105.

29 **claimed he had written:** Martin, *Dictionary Wars*, 77.

29 **It added *jeopardize*:** Webster defined *jeopardize* as "To expose to loss or injury; to jeopard." His comment about the word's uselessness is the second citation in the *OED*. The first is from a 1646 sermon by an English minister, Nehemiah Barnet, "We doe . . . *Jeoperdize* our soules safety."

30 **and, yes, *Americanize*:** "Every nation must have its *isms* and its *izes*, to express what is peculiar to it," Webster wrote, arguing that if *Latinize* and *Anglicize* were words, *Americanize* should be, too. But he didn't invent the word. "I wish to see our People more americanized, if I may use that Expression," John Jay wrote twenty years earlier to John Trumbull, the painter known for the portrait of Alexander Hamilton on the $10 bill. Webster, *Letter to the Honorable John Pickering*, in Kendall, *Forgotten Founding Father*, 319; "From John Jay to John Trumbull, 27 October 1797," *Founders Online*, https://founders.archives.gov/documents/Jay/01-06-02-0288.

30 **Based on Webster's decade:** Publisher William Converse hired a polymath Yale grad named James Gates Percival to edit and proofread the pages. Percival, who had been studying the work of German linguists, clashed repeatedly with Webster over the flawed etymological theories. "I regret that I have ever engaged in this thing," Percival wrote. "It will be one of the miseries of my life to think of it." Webster fired him six months before publication. Martin, *Dictionary Wars*, 69–70.

30 **But this time Webster's work:** Kendall, *Forgotten Founding Father*, 346; Peter Sokolowski, "The Invention of the Modern Dictionary," in *The Whole*

World in a Book: Dictionaries in the Nineteenth Century, eds. Sarah Ogilvie and Gabriella Safran (New York: Oxford University Press, 2020), 176.

31 **Almost two hundred years:** "America's Oldest Brands," *Ranking the Brands*, 2012, https://www.rankingthebrands.com/The-Brand-Rankings.aspx?rankingID=268&year=502.

31 **It took eight years to sell:** Kendall, *Forgotten Founding Father*, 349.

31 **In 1831, three years after:** Printing and publishing was the family business. In 1798, the Merriams' father, Daniel, and an uncle, Ebenezer, started a printing company, E. Merriam & Co., in West Brookfield, Massachusetts. After George (born 1803) and Charles (1806) decamped to Springfield, their brothers William (1809) and Homer (1813) opened a bookseller and bindery, W. & H. Merriam, in Greenfield, Massachusetts, in 1838. A fifth brother, Lewis (1811), took over that business after Homer and William set up shop in Troy, New York, in 1842.

31 **A dictionary fit the model:** The Merriams' only family connection to Noah Webster was embarrassing. A few decades earlier, Daniel and Ebenezer "mistakenly," according to a company history, printed and sold Webster's Blue-Back Speller without permission.

32 **At a trade show in New York:** The Merriam store rules and the letter from George to Charles about buying the dictionary were discovered by the New York dictionary collector Madeline Kripke, who I write about in chapter 8.

32 **In early 1845, they reprinted:** The Merriams advertised the edition as "*without abridgment*" with "a SUPPLEMENT of several thousand words, prepared by the author, and first published in 1843, since his decease." "Dr. Webster's Dictionary," *Springfield Daily Republican*, January 10, 1845.

32 **But by shrinking the type:** The Webster family objected to the single volume and the price reduction, believing the moves cheapened the dictionary's reputation and disrespected Noah. They were wrong. Within a quarter century, the book would spin off a quarter million dollars to Webster's heirs.

32 **To bolster the brand:** John Morse, "Publishing the Dictionary: The Business Side of the Business," in *The Cambridge Handbook of the Dictionary*, eds. Edward Finegan and Michael Adams (Cambridge, England: Cambridge University Press, 2024), 598–99.

32 **whom the company praised:** I reflexively used *whom* here because it's technically accurate—"as the object of a following preposition," Merriam says—and because it's been one of my smarty-pants pet peeves. But Merriam notes that actual, unstilted, non-stickler usage of *who* and *whom* isn't much different now than in Shakespearian times, and we're still hung up about it because of rules inflicted on the public by 18th-century grammarians, whose main success was "to encourage hypercorrect uses of *whom*." I took out a stilted *whom* four endnotes up. Other *whoms* in this book are as the "object of a verb or a preceding preposition," as in "for whom the bell tolls," which remains normal.

33 **To subdue competitors:** The Merriams didn't mess around. In 1858, Joseph Worcester announced that his forthcoming dictionary would include

thousands of woodcut illustrations alongside definitions, a first in America. The Merriams rushed to update their 1847 book. The new Pictorial Edition, with an eighty-one-page section of woodcuts, beat Worcester to market by a few months, stealing publicity and sales. "Worcester after that fell comparatively harmless to the ground," Charles Merriam recalled. Martin, *Dictionary Wars*, 250–52, 255.

33 **In a letter to the Merriams:** Noah Porter to George and Charles Merriam, June 2, 1857, G. & C. Merriam Company Archive, General Collection, Beinecke Rare Book and Manuscript Library, Yale University, https://archives.yale.edu/repositories/11/resources/705.

33 **Porter agreed to lead it:** Reluctantly. "Dictionary making is not at all in my line of study or duty," Noah Porter wrote, "& I have had enough experience of it to be entirely decided that I neither wish, nor ought to have any thing more to do with it." Noah Porter to George and Charles Merriam, June 2, 1857, G. & C. Merriam Company Archive.

34 **Subject experts included:** William Dwight Whitney was paid $1.50 an hour. James Dana got $40 a month. Chester Lyman earned sixty cents an hour for science definitions, while musical terms, contributed by a John S. Dwight Esq. of Boston, fetched ten cents less. "Prices for Editing for 1864 ed.," undated, G. & C. Merriam Company Archive.

34 **They included Porter's wife:** Only one woman is mentioned by name in the preface to the 1864 dictionary: Mary Cowden Clarke, a nineteenth-century scholar whose concordances* were used to collect quotations from Shakespeare and Milton.

35 **they were a giant pain:** William Webster complained to the editors about altering some of his father's spellings: *imbitter* to *embitter*, *insnare* to *ensnare*, *intrust* to *entrust*, *mustache* to *moustache* (and others). "This will hardly do for a dictionary bearing the name of Webster," he sniffed about giving *practise* preference over *practice*. "I am anxious to have every modification made which can be done without ignoring the authority of my father & Mr G[oodrich]. But these are some changes proposed which seem to me uncalled for & inexplicable." All of those words, rightly or not, retained their 1828 spellings. William A. Webster to George and Charles Merriam, January 11, 1862, G. & C. Merriam Company Archive; William A. Webster to George and Charles Merriam, September 6, 1861, G. & C. Merriam Company Archive.

35 **"I sincerely wish I could find:** Noah Porter to George and Charles Merriam, February 3, 1861, G. & C. Merriam Company Archive.

35 **I read about this drama:** Some of the correspondence in the Beinecke files was transcribed long ago, judging by the typewritten pages. Some has been cited in other books about Noah Webster and the company. And some was scoured, parsed, and transcribed by Merriam senior editor Joanne Despres, whose research and advice were enormously helpful in writing about nineteenth-century Merriam.

---

* **concordance** *noun* : an alphabetical index of the principal words in a book or the works of an author with their immediate contexts

endnotes

35 **"It has involved an investment [footnote]:** George and Charles Merriam to Chauncey A. Goodrich, December 3, 1847, *G. & C. Merriam Company Archive.*

35 **thanking the publisher:** I also enjoyed this 1878 letter signed "R. Waldo Emerson": "On my return home from the seashore a few days ago, I found the stately gift you had sent me to my great delight. In my youth my father gave me Johnson's Dictionary; long after in Cambridge I became acquainted with Mr. Worcester, and bought his book. Meantime, I have learned from good judges the superiority of Webster's Dictionary, and am very greatful [sic] to you for the gift." Ralph Waldo Emerson to George and Charles Merriam, August 21, 1878, *G. & C. Merriam Company Archive.*

36 **Springfield in 1864 had:** I drew this portrait of Springfield from Donald J. D'Amato, *Springfield—350 Years: A Pictorial History* (Virginia Beach, VA: Donning Co., 1985), 69; Michael H. Frisch, *Town Into City: Springfield, Massachusetts, and the Meaning of Community, 1840–1880* (Cambridge, MA: Harvard University Press, 1972), 74–75, 59–60; and an interview with Guy McClain of the Wood Museum of Springfield History, May 13, 2016.

36 **"Still they come!":** "City Items," *Springfield Daily Republican,* March 5, 1864.

36 **"Such a book, of course:** The newspaper was blown away by the locally made product. "One cannot but be amazed at the vast amount of labor and learning incorporated into this magnificent volume," it gushed. "What research, what patience, what love of learning, what profusion of unseen toil, what minuteness of detail and vast sums of money have been expended in its preparation! . . . Then think of the hundreds of men employed upon it—authors, copyists, printers, proof-readers, binders, engravers, manufacturers of materials, electrotypers; the tons of printers ink used upon it; the vast piles of white paper necessary to publish even a small edition—and we begin to have a *faint* conception of what it has cost to produce such a volume. Perhaps at some future day—as there is no apparent limit to human improvement—some enterprising author and publisher may cast this book into the shade by another still better; but at present it unquestionably stands without a peer, the real, undisputed Monarch of Dictionaries, to whom all others must do homage . . . We look then to see the new edition quite speedily enter every well regulated household wherever the English language is spoken, and side by side with the Bible, begin its grand mission of elevating mankind by the diffusion of its store of inexhausted learning." The paper called the book's physical printing and appearance "faultlessly beautiful." "The New Unabridged," *Springfield Daily Union,* September 29, 1864.

37 **"The business guts of these guys:** Unlike Noah Webster, the Merriams got rich off of the dictionary. George and his family lived in a mansion on Chestnut Street, a couple of blocks from the original Merriam offices in a building known as the Old Corner Bookstore.

37 **Even their gardening:** "City Items," *Springfield Daily Republican,* September 18, 1865.

37 **sent a dozen to the Seneca Indians:** "City Items," *Springfield Daily Republican,* April 8, 1865.

37   **A Springfield bookstore:** "City Items," *Springfield Daily Republican*, July 4, 1865.

37   **The *Daily Republican* reported:** "How Dictionaries Are Made," *Springfield Daily Republican*, February 15, 1865.

38   **thirty-three senses in 1828:** Noah Webster was a "splitter," a lexicographer who divides a definition into many narrow senses, in contrast to a "lumper," who condenses meanings into a few senses. Like Webster, I was proving to be a splitter.

38   **In a letter to George and Charles:** William Webster to George and Charles Merriam, February 29, 1864, G. & C. Merriam Company Archive.

38   **They knew Webster's name:** Chauncey Goodrich once wrote that he thought lexicography "disgusting," but he stuck around out of respect for his father-in-law. Noah Porter whinged before taking on the 1864, but he remained as editor even as he became president of Yale. Webster, Goodrich, and Porter are buried in Grove Street Cemetery in New Haven. I visited each of their resting places: an obelisk for Webster, a tall headstone for Goodrich, a sarcophagus for Porter. None mentions the dictionary.

38   **They were careful not to connect:** Morse, "Publishing the Dictionary," 601.

39   **"The name of its founder:** Reviewing an 1879 printing of the 1864, with nearly five thousand new words, the *Atlantic Monthly* observed that the dictionary had evolved from the solo-act era: "the impetus which this concretion of scholarship has now obtained, together with all the material interests involved in its fortunes, gives us a right to regard the dictionary as an organic institution, with an interest for all Americans, quite freed from any petty considerations of partisanship." The writer complained about various missing obscurities used once by a Donne or an Emerson and about overlooked words that would become commonplace. "Why is *cent shop* here, and not *dollar store*? One might preach a sermon upon these two phrases, and trace the decadence of thrift in them. *Figuline* is given, but not its friend, if not substitute, *figurine*. *To go back on* occurs under *go*, but not the phrase *to go for*, with its curious double use in exactly antagonistic meaning. *Shebeen* is given, but not the more idiomatic *shebang*. *Launder* as v. t. is set down as obsolete, and reference made to Shakespeare; but the editor could have seen the word on street signs as he took his daily walk after working on the dictionary . . . We miss *fly* in its technical sense as employed by the vast army of base-ball players; and considering the fact that the game of base-ball generally occupies more space in the daily paper than the game of European politics and war, we think all its terms might find explanation." "Recent Literature," *Atlantic Monthly*, October 1879.

40   **"The greatest single volume:** David Skinner, *The Story of Ain't: America, Its Language, and the Most Controversial Dictionary Ever Published* (New York: Harper, 2012), 2.

40   **The 1934 marked the apex:** As work on the *Second* was wrapping up, Merriam president Asa Baker wrote a letter to the book's general editor, Thomas Knott. "We have just completed the reckoning of the number of man-hours

devoted to the Dictionary, and find that it is 588,000," he said. "Interpreted another way, at the rate of 8 hours a day, 40 hours a week, 2,000 hours to the year, it would take one man 294 years to finish the dictionary. If Noah Webster had been alive to undertake the task, it would have required 12 generations of him to finish the work." Baker suggested adding that info to the book's introduction. "How Long Did it Take to Write the Dictionary?" *Merriam-Webster*, undated, https://www.merriam-webster.com/wordplay/websters-second-how-long-did-it-take.

40 **The *Second* was enhanced:** Robert Keith Leavitt, *Noah's Ark, New England Yankees, and the Endless Quest* (Springfield, MA: G. & C. Merriam Co., 1947), 86.

40 **It was important to Merriam:** Morton, *Story of Webster's Third*, 53.

41 **Its editor in chief, Philip Babcock Gove:** The section about Gove's background and hiring at Merriam draws on Morton, *Story of Webster's Third*, 13–39 and 54–58.

42 **an editorial staff of seventy:** "The staff is in effect a faculty which specializes in different branches of knowledge much as a small college faculty does," Gove wrote. "Listed among the resident editors are a mathematician, a physicist, a chemist, a botanist, a biologist, a philosopher, a political scientist, a comparative religionist, a classicist, a historian, and a librarian as well as philologists, linguists, etymologists, and phoneticians whose speciality is the English language itself." Philip B. Gove, "Preface," *Webster's Third New International Dictionary of the English Language, Unabridged*, ed. Philip B. Gove (Springfield, MA: Merriam-Webster Inc., 1961), 4a.

42 **He lived on a working farm:** Morton, *Story of Webster's Third*, 72–73

42 **"I have declared violent war on all commas:** I found this May 5, 1958, letter from Gove to Audrey Duckert, an assistant editor on the *Third* from 1953 to 1956, in a filing cabinet in the Merriam basement. Duckert had left Merriam to get a PhD in linguistics at Harvard and then taught English at the University of Massachusetts Amherst for forty years. She contributed to the second edition of the *OED* and was an editor on the mammoth *Dictionary of American Regional English*, which I write about in chapter 7. Duckert died in 2007.

44 **Still, the *Third* couldn't be:** "The vocabularies of the Merriam-Webster dictionaries accumulated from the first one in 1828," Gove told an interviewer, "so that by the time we turned to this problem seriously in the 1950s, we found we could drop 250,000 words, and no one would know the difference until they were told." Gove noted that the biographical and geographical terms in the *Second* were included in the book's count of entries. "There are 600,000 entries in the *Second Edition*, and when they took those out, all those words disappeared," he said. "But of course, there were these other 250,000 obsolete words, completely obsolete. I can give you one concrete example. Somebody in California was very angry with us because he bet five dollars that he could spell *yodel* y-o-d-l-e, and sure enough in the *Second Edition* we did spell it *yodel* or *yodle*. But when we reexamined that claim to spelling it *yodle*, we found that Edna Ferber used it once in a novel, and somebody else had used it, and those were the only two instances that

we could find since the *Second Edition*, and none of any great standing before them. So we dropped it." Blake, "Not So 'Harmless Drudge,'" 81.

44 **He replaced the *Second*'s:** Gove sneered at his predecessors' fussiness, in particular over complaints about ditching the label *colloquial*. "You can't talk or think without using colloquial language," he said. "You can't write without using colloquial language, and in the face of such widespread misusage of the label—misunderstanding of it—we thought it would be better to take it out anyway . . . We don't have any idea when we write the definition how anybody is going to use the word." Gove also said that "things change so fast." He noted that *bathing beauty* was labeled *slang* in the *Second*. "Now, that makes that dictionary look ridiculous, and every time anybody looked at it, even then, the label probably made it look ridiculous." He roasted the editors of the *Second* for labeling as *slang* the baseball pitch *slider*. "If you're going to talk baseball, you've got to use baseball talk." Blake, "Not So 'Harmless Drudge,'" 78–79.

45 **Hanging in the Merriam lobby:** "A New Dictionary for a New President," *Merriam-Webster*, November 23, 2020, https://www.merriam-webster.com/words-at-play/jfk-dictionary-photo.

45 **one of his favorite words:** In an essay for *Sports Illustrated* after the 1960 election, Kennedy used *vigor* or *vigorous* nine times. John F. Kennedy, "The Soft American," *Sports Illustrated*, December 26, 1960, https://theleanberets.com/wp-content/uploads/2020/02/1960-JFK-The-Soft-American-SI-VAULT.pdf.

45 **In a January 1962 essay:** Wilson Follett, "Sabotage in Springfield: Webster's Third Edition," *The Atlantic*, January 1962, https://www.theatlantic.com/magazine/archive/1962/01/sabotage-in-springfield-websters-third-edition/658237/.

45 **Other critics railed:** Perhaps the most ironic fact was that *ain't*—which Merriam had touted in its press release for the *Third* and which became a locus of critical opprobrium—was also in the *Second*.

45 **"This development is disastrous:** "Webster's New Word Book," *New York Times*, October 12, 1961. When Kennedy in November 1961 said, "We have not finalized any plans," the *Times* wrote a news story *and* an editorial on the same day chastising the president. It also criticized his predecessor, Dwight Eisenhower, who said, "Soon my conclusions will be finalized," and the new "Webster's Third (or Bolshevik) Dictionary" for including the word. "In any case," the *Times* admonished JFK, "please be careful where you walk, because there may be some loose syntax lying about. Meanwhile, let's invite the cleaners in. They'll have the know-how to get the job finishized." "President Strikes Blow for 'Finalize' as English" and "Finalized?" *New York Times*, November 20, 1961.

45 **"It Ain't Right," *The New Republic*:** These articles, and an additional fifty-plus more, were collected in a 274-page book about the reaction to the *Third*. The editors said the book was designed as a curriculum for a freshman college English class, illustrating how deeply the furor over the *Third* penetrated popular culture. James Sledd and Wilma R. Ebbit, *Dictionaries and THAT Dictionary: A Casebook on the Aims of Lexicographers and the Targets of Reviewers* (Chicago: Scott, Foresman and Co., 1962).

46 **Maybe the uproar reflected:** For the full tale of the making of and backlash against the *Third*, see Skinner's engaging narrative and Morton's more academic work.

46 **In direct response to the *Third*:** Morton, *Story of Webster's Third*, 229–30.

46 **The debate dribbled into:** David Foster Wallace, "Tense Present: Democracy, English, and the Wars over Usage," *Harper's Magazine*, April 2001, https://harpers.org/wp-content/uploads/HarpersMagazine-2001-04-0070913.pdf.

47 **"I think that those who:** Anne Pence Bello, "Letters to a Dictionary: Competing Views of Language in the Reception of *Webster's Third New International Dictionary*," (PhD diss., University of Massachusetts Amherst, 2013), 214.

47 **Gove died at home:** "Dr. Philip B. Gove, 70, Is Dead; Editor of the Webster's Third," *New York Times*, December 17, 1972.

3
business

48 **In 1988, Merriam's then president:** Another unabridged had been assumed in-house long before William Llewellyn's memo. "We have started immediately on the *Fourth Edition*," Philip Gove said in 1969. Blake, "Not So 'Harmless Drudge,'" 72.

49 **My beloved *Webster's New World*:** Michael K. McKintyre, "With Publication of Webster's 'College 5' Dictionary, the Book That Defined Cleveland Editors' Work Is Closed," *Cleveland*, October 17, 2014, https://www.cleveland.com/tipoff/2014/10/with_publication_websters_coll.html.

49 **Llewellyn couldn't imagine:** "The history of the computer is one of storing more information in less space at lower cost, and that trend has no end in sight," Llewellyn wrote in his memo. "In 1961, *Webster's Third* could be the dictionary of record as a book alone. In 2001, *Webster's Fourth* cannot be the dictionary of record unless it is also a magnetic disc." Llewellyn announced that Merriam for the first time would build an electronic database for text management. "The move to an electronic format is so commonplace that we are using it as a cover story for work on this project. We have named the project 'Webster's A-Z Database' with the stated objective of merely converting *Webster's Third*." Love a little corporate subterfuge.

50 **A 1913 printing:** That book was uploaded to the web as part of Project Gutenberg, the first effort, begun in 1971 at the University of Illinois, to place works with expired copyrights on the internet.

50 **Merriam tried to secure the URL:** Merriam's definition of *URL*, short for *uniform* (or *universal*) *resource locator*, is a mouthful: "the address of a resource (such as a document or website) on the Internet that consists of a communications protocol followed by the name or address of a computer on the network and that often includes additional locating information (such as directory and file names)." Verbal illustration: "our site's *URL* is http://www.Merriam-Webster.com."

55 **When Noah Webster began:** Kendall, *Forgotten Founding Father*, 291.

55 **When Britannica in 1964:** The final price was $16.2 million, after the publisher McGraw Hill Inc., which had attempted to buy Merriam for more than a decade, was approached by some Merriam stockholders and made a late counteroffer. The *Times* reported that Britannica's president, Maurice B. Mitchell, "was bitter over the terms of the deal . . . Mr. Mitchell said it was deplorable that an 'opportunist' should plunge into a business agreement with an assertion that he would pay more than the agreed price." Imagine! Milton Esterow, "Britannica Buying Merriam-Webster," *New York Times*, September 11, 1964; Harry Gilroy, "Britannica Gains Merriam Control," *New York Times*, October 14, 1964.

56 **By the 1990s, if you were:** Critics of Britannica long predated the internet. A 1917 book by art critic Willard Huntington Wright titled *Misinforming a Nation* said the encyclopedia was filled with "misstatements, inexcusable omissions, rabid and patriotic prejudices, personal animosities, blatant errors of fact, scholastic ignorance, gross neglect of non-British culture, an astounding egotism, and an undisguised contempt for American progress." The novelist Aldous Huxley ripped Britannica in 1934. And in 1964 physicist Harvey Einbinder wrote a 390-page book, *The Myth of The Britannica: The Great Encyclopedia of the Western World—Reputation and Reality*. Einbinder took on Britannica after reading the Galileo entry in the 1958 edition, which asserted that the sixteenth- and seventeenth-century scientist dropped objects of different weights from the Leaning Tower of Pisa to prove they fell at the same speed, a story that had been debunked decades earlier. Einbinder called the encyclopedia "a makeshift substitute for learning." Willard Huntington Wright, *Misinforming a Nation* (New York: B. W. Huebsch, 1917), 12; Irving Kristol, "Answering Service," *New York Review of Books*, January 23, 1964; Lawrence Clark Powell, "The Target Is Large and the Fees Are Picayune," *New York Times Book Review*, February 2, 1964.

56 **In 1964, Britannica was selling:** Esterow, "Britannica Buying Merriam-Webster."

56 **In 1990, the number was still:** Shane Greenstein, "The Reference Wars: Encyclopædia Britannica's Decline and Encarta's Emergence," *Harvard Business School*, April 4, 2016, https://www.hbs.edu/faculty/Pages/item.aspx?num=50951; Edward Wyatt, "The High Road at a High Cost," *New York Times*, October 24, 1999, https://archive.nytimes.com/www.nytimes.com/library/review/102499encyclopedia-review.html.

56 **An investor group led by:** Greenstein, "Reference Wars."

56 **"the crown jewel of accumulated:** "Britannica sold by Benton Foundation," *The University of Chicago Chronicle*, February 4, 1996, http://chronicle.uchicago.edu/960104/britannica.shtml.

56 **The *Times* wrote that Britannica:** Barnaby J. Feder, "Deal Is Set for Encyclopaedia Britannica," *New York Times*, December 19, 1995. The popular view of Britannica's decline in the 1990s is of a Luddite company oblivious to the emerging digital age. Harvard Business School professor Shane Greenstein in a 2016 paper suggested a more nuanced story: that Britannica

was technologically advanced—it developed its first CD-ROM in 1989, registered the domain name eb.com in 1993, and debuted its first online encyclopedia in 1994—but made rational business decisions to protect its traditional business model. For instance, while Britannica was criticized for rebuffing startup Microsoft in 1985, the home computer market at the time was minuscule and Britannica book sales were still growing. Similarly, while Britannica was mocked for pricing its first CD-ROMs in the late '80s and early '90s at up to $1,200, it couldn't afford to cannibalize book income or alienate its 2,000-person sales force. When growth flattened during a recession, Microsoft in 1993 priced its Encarta CD-ROM encyclopedia at just $99. Britannica couldn't pivot fast enough. Greenstein wrote that the company faced "diseconomies of scope" that resulted in internal management conflicts between its old bookselling business and the new digital marketplace. "These conflicts hindered the commercialization of new technology and hastened [Britannica's] decline." Greenstein, "Reference Wars."

56 **And that was five years before:** In April 2025, Wikipedia contained almost seven million articles in English, and millions more in other languages. Britannica said its database held more than 130,000 articles.

56 **A former top Britannica editor:** Robert McHenry, "The Faith-Based Encyclopedia," *Tech Central Station*, November 15, 2004, https://web.archive.org/web/20060613214340/http://www.tcsdaily.com/article.aspx?id=111504A.

57 **The journal *Nature* published:** Jim Giles, "Internet Encyclopaedias Go Head to Head," *Nature* 438 (2005), 900–01, https://www.nature.com/articles/438900a.

57 **In 2012, Britannica finally:** After the company announced the end of print publication, the writer Roger Angell reminisced about reading as a boy about ships in Britannica's eleventh edition, published in 1911. Angell, who was on the far side of ninety at the time, found a broken-down Britannica set in the *New Yorker* library, went right to volume XXIV ("Sainte-Claire Deville to Shuttle"). "What's gone, and what I miss most," he wrote, "isn't the Eleventh Edition in type, or a grand document of the last days of maritime empire, but my careless, spongy twelve-year-old mind, which saw time stretching away endlessly ahead and plenty of room in it every day for something absolutely astounding." Roger Angell, "More Time With the Britannica," *New Yorker*, March 20, 2012, https://www.newyorker.com/books/page-turner/more-time-with-the-britannica.

57 **In the *Harvard Business Review*:** Jorge Cauz, "Encyclopædia Britannica's President on Killing Off a 244-Year-Old Product," *Harvard Business Review*, March 2013, https://hbr.org/2013/03/encyclopaedia-britannicas-president-on-killing-off-a-244-year-old-product.

57 **Safra bought Britannica because:** Jacqui Safra's media mentions have been few, and usually tied to the sale of assets: a Manhattan townhouse, a Napa Valley vineyard, an Old Master pen-and-ink, a fourteenth-century Hebrew Bible. In the early 2000s, Woody Allen accused Safra and his partner, Jean Doumanian, of cheating the director out of as much as $14 million while producing several of his films. (Safra is listed in credits as J. E. Beaucaire.

J and E are his first and middle initials; Beaucaire is a character, King Louis XV's barber, played by Bob Hope in the 1946 film *Monsieur Beaucaire*.) Safra took the stand but the case was settled before the judge could rule. Given his wealth and other business interests, from software to cement plants to stocks, and Britannica's struggles at the time, the encyclopedia initially seemed like an emotional investment. But former Britannica president Paul Hoffman described Safra as a quirky and unpredictable boss who "reversed my big decisions and micromanaged my small ones." "I hoped that one day Safra would wake up and see the wisdom of leaving me alone to rescue his company," Hoffman wrote. "I also wondered if his seemingly haphazard actions might be part of an arcane business strategy that somehow eluded me." Paul Hoffman, *King's Gambit: A Son, a Father, and the World's Most Dangerous Game* (New York: Hyperion, 2007).

58 **The *Washington Post* labeled Merriam:** Chris Cillizza, "Winners and Losers from the First Presidential Debate," *Washington Post*, September 26, 2016, https://www.washingtonpost.com/news/the-fix/wp/2016/09/26/winners-and-losers-from-the-1st-presidential-debate/.

59 **Between mainstream and social:** The attention included my magazine story about the project. Stefan Fatsis, "The Definition of a Dictionary," *Slate*, January 12, 2015, https://www.slate.com/articles/life/culturebox/2015/01/merriam_webster_dictionary_what_should_an_online_dictionary_look_like.html.

59 **Morse said he wasn't disappointed:** "It may not be under me, but I do think there is a place for a deeper dive into words than what you necessarily want to do on a popular website like Merriam-Webster dot com," John Morse said. "So I think at some point work is going to resume on something like the *Unabridged*—unless you just say, 'Work of that depth and scholarly interest can only be sustained by a university press. American capitalism simply can't afford to create products like that.' If I really thought that, then that would be real tough. Because since about 1828, American capitalism has been able to support the best lexicography that can be done. I just think there are seasons." Interview with author, December 2, 2015.

60 **"A never-ending adventure:** Leavitt, *Noah's Ark*, 93.

4
define

62 **a new sense of the transitive verb *verse*:** The quotation I used—"the Power is *versing* the Rangers"—is what's known as a verbal illustration, a made-up line to illustrate a word's meaning. (The Power was my daughter's rec soccer team, which I coached; the Rangers were a regular opponent.) I was sure *verse* as a verb was a millennial thing; I first heard it in the early 2000s spoken by my then preteen nephew, Mike. But of course I was wrong. Language sleuths had been investigating the "back-formation" of *versus* for decades. *American Speech* noted it in 1981 and the *New York Times* included *to verse* in a list of "New Yorkese of 1984," defined as "High school slang

meaning to compete against another school's team." (Other words in the *Times* story: *fern bar, to fedex, signage,* and *user-friendly.*) The 2016 entry in the *Unabridged* included a first known use date of 1956. After I mentioned it, the language writer and linguist Ben Zimmer began hunting in the database Newspapers.com for earlier examples, known as antedates. In a series of emails, Zimmer sent examples of *versed* or *versing* in local sports stories in 1950 (Georgia), 1949 (California), and 1948 (Louisiana). I replied with a *versing* in a story about softball in Kentucky in 1946. But Zimmer topped me with *versed* about a "Volley Ball" game in Oregon in 1941; a "deck tennis" game in Illinois in 1937; and, finally, a basketball game in Oklahoma in 1936: "Ralph Partrick's team versed Chas. Cox's, Jr. team No. 2 with a score of 25 to 4 in favor of Partrick." Completing the usurpation of the fifteenth-century word, the writer Mark Oppenheimer pointed out that many young people seem to believe that *v.* or *vs.* is an abbreviation of *verse,* not *versus.* Charles C. Doyle, "Verbifying *Versus,*" *American Speech* 56, no. 4 (1981), 277; Eric Pace, "Latest Word: New Yorkese of '84 Is Here," *New York Times,* February 20, 1984; "Basket Ball Players Mix Up for Amusement of All," *Carmen Headlight* (Carmen, OK), December 17, 1936; Mark Oppenheimer, "'Aesthetic' Does Not Mean What You Think It Does," *Oppenheimer,* February 5, 2025, https://markoppenheimer.substack.com/i/156525880/aesthetic-does-not-mean-what-you-think-it-does.

63 **Editing down the more expansive:** *Person-hour*—"a unit of one hour's work by one person"—is entered in both the *Unabridged* and the OWL, with a first usage date of 1975. *Man-hour* (1912) also is in both lexicons. But while the *Collegiate* definition of *man-hour* mimics the gender-neutral language of *person-hour,* the word escaped an effort to remove sexist defining language from the *Unabridged* database, and the *Webster's Third* definition from 1961—"a unit of one hour's work by one man"—lived on.

65 **my time inside 47 Federal Street:** For its address, the company was allowed to choose any odd number from 31 to 49. It picked 47 to honor the publication of the first Merriam dictionary in 1847.

65 **stood with the hoi polloi:** The *the* before *hoi polloi* is often taken to be redundant; *hoi polloi* is a transliteration from the Greek οι πολύ meaning *the many.* But a lengthy Merriam supplemental information note explains that *hoi* doesn't mean anything in English and that "most writers" use the *the.*

66 **In a story about Nike:** Roger Thurow, "Shtick Ball: In Global Drive, Nike Finds Its Brash Ways Don't Always Pay Off," *Wall Street Journal,* May 5, 1997, https://www.wsj.com/articles/SB862794440708525500.

66 **"Nike relished being:** Stefan Fatsis, "Nike Tackles Soccer, Nicely," *Wall Street Journal,* July 2, 1998; Letters, *The Daily Telegraph,* November 5, 1998; Daniel Engber, "Concussion Lies," *Slate,* December 21, 2015, https://slate.com/culture/2015/12/the-truth-about-will-smiths-concussion-and-bennet-omalu.html; Joshua Keating, "Our Favorite Villains of 2015," *Slate,* December 30, 2015, https://slate.com/culture/2015/12/greatest-villains-2015-taylor-swift-jonathan-franzen-and-ashley-madison.html; Colin McGowan, "FIFA finally gets one right in upholding Barcelona transfer ban," *Sports*

Illustrated, October 2, 2015, http://www.si.com/cauldron/2015/10/02/fifa-barcelona-transfer-ban-upheld; Nick Carroll, "An Argument for Inclusion," *Surfing Life*, June 18, 2015; Bryan Walsh, "Don't Let the IOC Ruin Ultimate Frisbee," *Time*, August 3, 2015, https://time.com/3982671/dont-let-the-ioc-ruin-ultimate-frisbee/.

67 **It was out there:** Shoutout to a related word that one of my sportswriting idols, Robert Lipsyte, loved the way that I love *sportocrat*. It's *jockocracy*, referring to athletes hired to call games on television. Lipsyte credited that meaning to bombastic ABC Sports announcer Howard Cosell, who used it in the 1970s and '80s to deride the networks' obsession with putting ex-jocks in the booth. "I think he always saw himself as an outsider, a Jew, an English major in the jockocracy, a kind of Lone Ranger," Lipsyte wrote in *An Accidental Sportswriter*. "He didn't feel like part of the team." Lipsyte said he first heard *jockocracy* spoken by the African American lawyer, feminist, and activist Florynce Kennedy, and passed it on to Cosell. Robert Lipsyte, *An Accidental Sportswriter* (New York: HarperCollins, 2011), 90-91.

67 **lexicographic nepo babies:** "The shortened form *nepo* was hitched to the denigrating term *baby* to refer especially to celebrities who had a parent (or two) who were also in the entertainment industry," Merriam wrote in a 2023 blog post about *nepotism*. It entered *nepo baby* in 2024. "Word of the Day," *Merriam-Webster*, September 27, 2023, https://www.merriam-webster.com/word-of-the-day/nepotism-2023-09-27.

67 **Perrault said to make sure:** My draft definitions, sans many illustrative quotations:

> **sportocrat** *also* **sporteaucrat** *noun* : an executive or bureaucrat with a large sports organization : a senior international sports official whose actions are viewed with suspicion or contempt
>
> **sportocracy** *also* **sporteaucracy** *noun* | : the governing body of a sport or group of sports : a large international sports organization (such as the International Olympic Committee)

68 **Of forty-six newies touted:** "Drunk Texts, Squad Goals, and Brewer's Droop: An Oxford Dictionaries Update," *Oxford Dictionaries*, February 23, 2017, https://web.archive.org/web/20170224213953/https://blog.oxforddictionaries.com/2017/02/dictionary-new-words/.

69 **chef's kiss (which Merriam:** Merriam defined *chef's kiss* as "a gesture of satisfaction or approval made by kissing the fingertips of one hand and then spreading the fingers with an outward motion." The entry notes that the phrase is "often used interjectionally," which is why I didn't use the article "a" before it.

69 **"This Is the Most Compelling:** Lauren Tousignant, "This Is the Most Compelling Vajazzle I've Ever Seen," *Jezebel*, August 22, 2024, https://www.jezebel.com/this-is-the-most-compelling-vajazzle-ive-ever-seen. That story is about a sculpture of a woman's hips, groin, and thighs by a Milwaukee artist, Niki Johnson, created from pieces of aluminum signs from five Planned Parenthood clinics shuttered after state defunding. The sculpture was part

of an exhibition near the Democratic National Convention in Chicago. "Atop her pubic mound is a mirrored vajazzle of our nation's capitol," a plaque said. "The mirror was purchased from Hobby Lobby, who won a landmark Supreme Court victory in 2014 allowing corporations to deny their employees birth control on religious grounds."

70 **I'd like to think fun inspired:** *The Simpsons*, season 7, episode 16, "Lisa the Iconoclast," written by Jonathan Collier, directed by Mike B. Anderson, aired on February 18, 1996, on Fox.

71 **The word appeared in 1884:** C. A. Ward, *Notes and Queries: A Medium of Intercommunication for Literary Men, General Readers, Etc.*, August 16, 1884, 135, https://www.google.com/books/edition/Notes_and_Queries_A_Medium_of_Inter_Comm/25bCMeP4UTQC.

73 **"What I do worry about:** Just before Election Day in 2024, John Morse told me:

> I remember all too well the days following 9/11, when *surreal* and *succumb* topped the list, and my great relief in seeing that we had defined those words well. And someone at MW should be feeling relieved, and maybe even proud, that MW covers *fascism* as well as they do, because it is topping the list just about every hour of every day recently. A central lesson I took from my time at MW is dictionaries are used by serious people with serious questions about serious words, and that is where our efforts should focus. And yes, by the way, that is also where most of the traffic is. The day I write a book about dictionaries, I'll be very tempted to title it *The Ubiquitous Paradigm and the Esoteric Epiphany*. Email with author, November 3, 2024.

73 **A former chief editor of the OED:** John Simpson, *The Word Detective: Searching for the Meaning of It All at the* Oxford English Dictionary (New York: Basic Books, 2016), 125.

5
corpus

77 **"You never say 'cause happiness':** I compared the phrases on Google Books Ngram Viewer. The frequency of "cause disaster" has indeed outpaced "cause joy" and "cause happiness" since the 1800s. But the gap has narrowed in the last century and, in a standard Google search in January 2025, both "cause joy" and "cause happiness" delivered more hits than "cause disaster."

77 **The categories for the corpus:** W. Nelson Francis and Henry Kučera, "Manual of Information to Accompany A Standard Corpus of Present-Day Edited American English, for Use with Digital Computers," Brown University, 1964 (revised 1979).

79 **At its last update, COCA:** Check out all of Mark Davies's corpora at English-Corpora.org.

79 **A coronavirus corpus compiled:** Davies's corpus contained articles with at least two references to *coronavirus*, *COVID*, or *COVID-19* or at least one

of the following words or letter strings in the title (the asterisk denotes any subsequent letters): *at-risk, cases, confirmed, contagious, containm*, coronavirus, covid*, curbside, curve, deaths, disinfect*, distanc*, epicenter, epidemic, epidemiol*, flatten*, flu, high-risk, hoard*, hospital*, hydroxychloroquine, infect*, influenza, isolat*, lockdown, lock-down, mask*, nursing, outbreak, pandemic, panic, patient*, pneumon*, preventative, preventive, quarantin*, re-open*, reopen*, respiratory, sanitiz*, self-isolat*, shelter*, shutdown, spread, spreading, stay-at-home, stay at home, stockpil*, testing, vaccine*, ventilator*, virus.*

79 **An academic used Davies's:** Dennis Baron, "Antonin Scalia Was Wrong about the Meaning of 'Bear Arms,'" *Washington Post*, May 21, 2018, https://www.washingtonpost.com/opinions/antonin-scalia-was-wrong-about-the-meaning-of-bear-arms/2018/05/21/9243ac66-5d11-11e8-b2b8-08a538d9dbd6_story.html.

80 **In 2018, former CIA director:** John Brennan's tweet mentioning *kakistocracy* continued: "As the greatest Nation history has known, we have the opportunity to emerge from this nightmare stronger & more committed to ensuring a better life for all Americans, including those you have so tragically deceived." Brennan was one of dozens of former Trump-administration officials whose warnings about reelecting Trump in 2024 millions of Americans ignored. John O. Brennan (@JohnBrennan), Twitter, April 13, 2018, https://twitter.com/JohnBrennan/status/984803286006951936.

80 **a corpus of almost 30 billion words:** That corpus was created and updated daily by the Jožef Stefan Institute, a scientific research organization in Slovenia that, go figure, is hot for computational lexicography. Katherine Connor Martin (@ kconnormartin), Twitter, April 13, 2018, https://twitter.com/kconnormartin/status/984816209333014531; "Jozef Stefan Institute Timestamped Web Corpus," *Sketch Engine*, https://www.sketchengine.eu/jozef-stefan-institute-newsfeed-corpus/.

82 **the baseball sabermetrics term VORP:** Created by Keith Woolner at the website Baseball Prospectus, VORP measures the number of runs produced by a player beyond what an average player at the same position would produce. VORP is used to gauge both a player's performance and their value.

82 **Instead of defining *bro hug*:** I gave *bro hug* the full treatment: noun, transitive and intransitive verbs, and a supplemental information note. I went simple on the definition—"a brief embrace between two men"—but got technical in the SIN. "While the term is usually applied generally," I wrote, "a *bro hug* can refer to a specific embrace, in which two men clasp right hands at a 90-degree angle, lean in toward each other, bump right shoulders, and pat each other's backs with their left hands." My quotations came from Barack Obama ("although I've got huge differences with Chris Christie, the fact that I gave him a bro hug or something right after his state had gone through this enormous disaster and we were trying to work together to help them, those things suddenly became weapons to be used") and another from *The Economist* ("the bro-hug should be both genuinely affectionate, and vigorous enough to prove that both men could still wrestle down an enemy if needed"). As of early 2025, it had not been added to the OWL.

83 published in the magazine *Science*: Jean-Baptiste Michel et al., "Quantitative Analysis of Culture Using Millions of Digitized Books," *Science* 331, no. 6014 (2010), 176–82. See also Erez Aiden and Jean-Baptiste Michel, *Uncharted: Big Data as a Lens on Human Culture* (New York: Riverhead Books, 2013).

83 the NPR program *Talk of the Nation*: Strawberry Saroyan, "In Land of Lexicons, Having the Last Word," *New York Times*, March 19, 2005, https://www.nytimes.com/2005/03/19/arts/in-land-of-lexicons-having-the-last-word.html.

83 After delivering a TED Talk: Erin McKean, "The Joy of Lexicography," *TED*, August 30, 2007, https://www.youtube.com/watch?v=J4VzuWmN8zY.

90 a few recent additions: Flora Graham, "Can We Inoculate Against Fake News?" *Nature*, November 4, 2024, https://www.nature.com/articles/d41586-024-03630-9; Rob Fisher, Maura Hodge, and Bridget Beals, "Greenwashing, Greenhushing, and Greenwishing: Don't Fall Victim to These ESG Reporting Traps," *ESG Today*, June 21, 2023, https://www.esgtoday.com/guest-post-greenwashing-greenhushing-and-greenwishing-dont-fall-victim-to-these-esg-reporting-traps; Bartleby, "How to Beat Desk Rage," *The Economist*, June 1, 2023, https://www.economist.com/business/2023/06/01/how-to-beat-desk-rage.

6
neologism

91 Ask a linguist and you'll get: As of early 2025, Merriam had not entered *sciencey* or *sciency*. The *OED* added both spellings in 2014: "Of a somewhat scientific or technical nature; (also) having an interest in or aptitude for science." Its first citation is from 1964.

92 The papers resulting: Jack Grieve, Andrea Nini, and Diansheng Gui, "Analyzing Lexical Emergence in Modern American English Online," *English Language and Linguistics* 21, no. 1 (2017), 99–127, and "Mapping Lexical Innovation on American Social Media," *Journal of English Linguistics* 46, no. 4 (2018), 293–319.

94 Survival of the fittest: The quotation is from Darwin's follow-up to *On the Origin of Species*. Charles Darwin, *The Descent of Man, and Selection in Relation to Sex* (London: John Murray, 1871), 62.

94 Data collection was a pain: Grieve identified a distinction between the rise of words mainly associated on Twitter with the South, including *baeless* and *fallback*, "many of which appear to come from African American English," and words mainly associated with the rest of the country, like *gainz* and *amirite*. Thanks to location tags, he was able to pin the popularity of words to specific regions: *Lordt* (a more emphatic "lord!") was big in Louisiana; *boolin* and *brazy* in Georgia; *cosplay* and *tbfh* ("to be fucking honest") on the West Coast; *litt* and *lituation* (alternate forms of *lit*, for something exciting or excellent) in New York.

95 **Schmid's group identified:** Daphé Kerremans, Jelena Prokić, Quirin Würschinger, and Hans-Jörg Schmid, "Using Data-mining to Identify and Study Patterns in Lexical Innovation on the Web: The NeoCrawler," *Pragmatics & Cognition* 25, no. 1 (2018), 174–200.

95 **Even some of NeoCrawler's:** Hans-Jörg Schmid shut down NeoCrawler. The researchers were amassing more data than they could analyze, and didn't have the financial support to keep the project going.

97 **In his book *The American Language*:** Mencken, *American Language*, 91–97.

97 **This is the guy who wrote:** H. L. Mencken, "As H. L. M. Sees It," *Evening Sun* (Baltimore), September 18, 1926.

97 **So his admiration for America's:** Merriam added *side-eye* or *side eye* in 2017: "a sidelong glance or gaze especially when expressing scorn, suspicion, disapproval, or veiled curiosity." But it's possible that Mencken would have come across the term—Merriam dated first usage to 1797.

97 **For his language research:** Mencken leaned equally on the work of language scholar Allen Walker Read, who unearthed the origins of scores of American locutions. According to research by Indiana University English professor Michael Adams, who was working on a biography of Read, Mencken cited Pound 106 times and Read 100 times in *The American Language* and supplements published in 1945 and 1948. More on Read in chapter 8 and other endnotes. Michael Adams, "Appendix B: Allen Walker Read and H. L. Mencken," *Allen Walker Read: A Biobibliography* (unpublished). Shared with author, November 16, 2024.

98 **I dug up Bolinger's first column:** For more on the history of "Among the New Words," including year-by-year highlights, see Benjamin Zimmer, Charles E. Carson, and Jane Solomon, "Seventy-five Years Among the New Words," *American Speech* 91, no. 4 (2016), 472–512.

99 **For a fiftieth-anniversary book:** John Algeo, *Fifty Years Among the New Words: A Dictionary of Neologisms, 1941–1991,* Cambridge University Press, New York, 1991. I bought a copy online. I love this book so much.

100 ***Thob* was coined in a 1926 book [footnote]:** Henshaw Ward, *Thobbing: A Seat at the Circus of the Intellect* (Indianapolis: Bobbs-Merrill Company, 1926), 7, https://archive.org/details/b29817298/page/n11/mode/2up. Reviewing Ward's "genial diatribe" against naiveté, denialism, and wishful thinking, the *New York Times* said the author (who published under Henshaw Ward or C. H. Ward) "went beyond the covers of Webster's unabridged" for the title. After gaining some mainstream usage, *thob* was added to *Webster's Second* in 1934, defined as "[*think* + *opinion* + *belief*] To think according to one's wishes; to rationalize one's opinions or beliefs. *Slang*." *Thobber* appeared in "Among the New Words" in 1959 in an article about "*-er* derivatives" that hadn't appeared in standard dictionaries. "Among the New Words" took its *thobber* definition from a 1945 *Time* magazine story. "All who use pseudo-science as a short-cut cure for troubles, especially mental ills," *Time* wrote, "are thobbers to some extent—e.g., those who apply to astrologers, numerologists, graphologists, self-styled psychologists with fake degrees

(Ps.D., Ms.D.), spiritualists, hypnotists, some beauticians and gymnasium proprietors and advice-to-the-lovelorn editors." *Thob* was among the tens of thousands of words axed for *Webster's Third* in 1961. Halsey Raines, "An Attack on 'Wishful Thinking,' *New York Times Book Review*, May 16, 1926; I. Willis Russell and Woodrow W. Boyett, "Among the New Words," *American Speech* 34, no. 2 (1959), 132; "Medicine: Life Among the Thobbers," *Time*, September 24, 1945, https://time.com/archive/6822761/medicine-life-among-the-thobbers.

100 **In 1990, members of the American:** The 1990 WOTY was the first Word of the Year *in English*. The government-sponsored Society for the German Language first picked a *Wort des Yahres* in 1971, when it went with *aufmüpfig*, meaning rebellious or defiant, a nod to the 1960s counterculture movement. "Word of the Year (Germany)," *Wikipedia*, accessed December 26, 2024, https://en.wikipedia.org/wiki/Word_of_the_year_(Germany).

100 **Word of the Year was a key party:** The premise of a *key party* was that men would place their car keys in a bowl and leave with whichever woman picked them. The phenomenon associated with the 1960s and '70s may or may not actually have occurred, but it's been depicted in the 1997 film *The Ice Storm* and TV programs including *That '70s Show* and *The Simpsons*. The term never appeared in "Among the New Words."

101 **Looking at the WOTY winners:** You can see all of the Words of the Year and nominees of the year on the American Dialect Society's website, https://americandialect.org/woty/all-of-the-words-of-the-year-1990-to-present/.

101 **"They should have picked *rizz*!":** While the American Dialect Society did not, Oxford did choose *rizz* as its 2023 Word of the Year, defined as "'style, charm, or attractiveness; the ability to attract a romantic or sexual partner." It noted that *rizz*, which emerged and blew up on the internet, was etymologically interesting because it comes from the middle part of another word—*charisma*—like *fridge* from *refrigerator* and *flu* from *influenza*. Merriam entered *rizz* in September 2023; as of May 2025, the OED had not added it. "Rizz crowned Oxford Word of the Year 2023," *Oxford University Press*, December 4, 2023, https://corp.oup.com/news/rizz-crowned-oxford-word-of-the-year-2023/.

101 **To juice web traffic:** Merriam included *woot* or *w00t* in one of the final Releases for the *Unabridged*. The OED traced *truthiness* to the nineteenth century but its modern sense dates to the television host Stephen Colbert, who first used it in 2005. Merriam added *truthiness* to the OWL in 2020 (and Colbert did a bit about it, pasting the definition into a print *Collegiate*). "At a time when truths of various kinds are under siege, and facts and news are put into constant question," Merriam wrote, "English speakers find it useful to have a special word for the kind of unproven and unprovable utterances that don't measure up to the standards of evidence and research that are required for consensus and understanding." "We Added New Words to the Dictionary for April 2020," *Merriam-Webster*, undated, https://www.merriam-webster.com/wordplay/new-words-in-the-dictionary-april-2020.

103 **WTF?:** Merriam added the initialism for *what the fuck*, "used especially to express or describe outraged surprise, recklessness, confusion, or bemusement,"

to the *Unabridged* in 2015 and ported it over to the OWL. It added *IRL*, for *in real life*, in 2017.

103 **That year, only one:** Trump used *schlonged* to describe Hillary Clinton's loss to Barack Obama in the 2008 Democratic presidential primary: "she was favored to win—and she got *schlonged*, she lost, I mean she lost."

103 **Trumpian words dominated:** The 2016 WOTY was *dumpster fire* (see chapter 13). *Fake news* won in 2017 and *tender-age shelter* in 2018 (a euphemism, for government-run detention centers used to house children of asylum seekers along the U.S.-Mexico border, that had no lexical legs).

103 **The suffix -*ussy* wore:** "The playful suffix builds off the word *pussy* to generate new slang terms," Ben Zimmer, chair of the American Dialect Society's New Words Committee and the WOTY festivities emcee, wrote in a news release. "The process has been so productive lately on social media sites and elsewhere that it has been dubbed *-ussification*."

103 **a ginormous Sheraton ballroom:** The portmanteau of *gi*gantic and en*ormous* is entered in Merriam with first usage dated to 1942.

104 **eminent octogenarian linguist:** How eminent? Dennis Preston's CV is fifty pages long. His 1969 dissertation is titled "Bituminous Coal Mining Vocabulary of the Eastern United States: A Pilot Study in the Collecting of Geographically Distributed Occupational Vocabulary." Linguistics is awesome.

106 **the *New York Times* didn't print:** Sam Corbin, "Among Linguists, the Word of the Year Is More of a Vibe," *New York Times*, January 15, 2024, https://www.nytimes.com/2024/01/15/crosswords/linguistics-word-of-the-year.html.

106 **When Beyoncé sampled:** David Mack, "The C-Word Is Everywhere Right Now—and Not in a Bad Way," *Rolling Stone*, May 15, 2023, https://www.rollingstone.com/culture/culture-features/c-word-is-everywhere-lgbt-tucker-carlson-1234735324/. In a report on the 2023 WOTY proceedings, Kelly E. Wright, an associate professor of language sciences at the University of Wisconsin–Madison, wrote that *cunty* "is a term that many currently find offensive—and with good reason!" She added: "We have to allow for multiple meanings to exist; this is the way of lexical development. We also have to allow people to meet language use in their own time and to employ lexemes without fully understanding their history . . . We must create space for users to describe the meaning of terms as they understand them." Kelly E. Wright, et al., "Among the New Words," *American Speech* 99, no. 3 (2024), 371–72.

106 ***Cunty* now meant *campy*:** Adam Aleksic, a young, Harvard-educated linguist with a big internet following, and the author of the 2025 book *Algospeak: How Social Media is Transforming the Future of Language*, said that *cunt* experienced a "context collapse" where "people see other people using a word, they don't understand that it's part of the vernacular of an in-group, they then replicate the word, and a bit of the meaning is diluted." He noted that *cunt* derivations were popular among fans of South Korean K-pop bands on social media: "[W]hen the K-pop fans are talking about their idols *giving cunt*, they're talking about expressing coolness or some campy expression of power. Less so about the original ballroom sense of, 'you're displaying femininity in

an extravagant way.'" Sam Reed, "When Did We All Get So Comfortable Saying the C-Word?" *Glamour*, April 15, 2025, https://www.glamour.com/story/when-did-we-all-get-so-comfortable-saying-the-c-word.

108 **It was coined by the writer:** Cory Doctorow, "Social Quitting," *Medium*, November 15, 2022, https://doctorow.medium.com/social-quitting-1ce85b67b456.

108 **artificial intelligence term** *stochastic parrot***:** The WOTY folks defined *stochastic parrot* as a "large language model that can generate plausible synthetic text without having any understanding." Created by University of Washington computational linguist Emily Bender in a paper published in 2021, the term combines *stochastic*, meaning "randomly determined," and the bird known for repeating what it hears. Bender and her coauthors described a large language model as "a system for haphazardly stitching together sequences of linguistic forms it has observed in its vast training data, according to probabilistic information about how they combine, but without any reference to meaning: a stochastic parrot." The term took off in the AI community. Bender lamented that it was being perceived as an insult by people in the field or, as she told Ben Zimmer, "an insult to the machines that they have anthropomorphized (and maybe identified with)." Ben Zimmer, "'Stochastic Parrot': A Name for AI That Sounds a Bit Less Intelligent," *Wall Street Journal*, January 18, 2024, https://www.wsj.com/arts-culture/books/stochastic-parrot-a-name-for-ai-that-sounds-a-bit-less-intelligent-789372f5.

108 **On the blog** *Strong Language***:** Nancy Friedman, "Enshittification," *Strong Language*, February 1, 2023, https://stronglang.wordpress.com/2023/02/01/enshittification/.

7
slip

110 **words typed in reverse order:** The Backward Index was created by Philip Gove. It was useful in identifying related terms that might be defined the same way, or particular groups of compounds, or words that rhymed. Merriam editor Peter Sokolowski reported that the index's 315,000 slips filled 129 file boxes. "In the pre-digital era," he wrote, "how else could we have ascertained that there are some 500 words in the dictionary that end in *-ology*? that the third English word ending in *-shion*, after *cushion* and *fashion*, is *fushion* (a rare variant of *foison*)? that *publicly* is the only adverb that now more commonly ends in *-cly* than in *-cally*? or that there is a third word in English ending in *-gry*?" In the *Unabridged*, that word is *anhungry*, an obsolete variant of *hungry*. Shakespeare used it in *Coriolanus*. The number of *-gry* words increased to four with the addition of *hangry* in 2018. Peter Sokolowski, "The Mystery of the Backward Index," *Merriam-Webster*, undated, https://www.merriam-webster.com/wordplay/backward-index-mystery.

111 **When James Murray took over:** Peter Gilliver, *The Making of the Oxford English Dictionary* (Oxford, England: Oxford University Press, 2016), 117.

111 **From the outset, readers:** Philological Society, *Proposal for the Publication of a New English Dictionary* (London: Trübner and Co., 1859), 10; K. M. Elizabeth Murray, *Caught in the Web of Words: James Murray and the Oxford English Dictionary* (New Haven, CT: Yale University Press, 1977), 179–80.

111 **The slips arrived at the Scriptorium:** K. M. E. Murray, *Caught in the Web of Words*, 174. The *OED*'s first sense of *scriptorium* explains why Murray was joking: "A room or area in a monastery set apart for writing, *esp.* one used by scribes copying and illuminating manuscripts; (hence) a particular school of scribes." Its second sense is self-referential: "In extended use: a room or place used for writing, research, storage of books, etc. *spec.* (usually with capital initial) with reference to either of the two purpose-built outbuildings in which parts of the first edition of the *Oxford English Dictionary* (1884-1928) were written (the first was built in 1879 in Mill Hill, Middlesex, where the chief editor, James Murray, worked; a replacement was later built in the garden of his Oxford home)."

111 **By the time the first edition:** K. M. E. Murray, *Caught in the Web of Words*, 136; Peter Gilliver, email with author, May 8, 2025. James Murray derided the couple million quotation slips collected by the Philological Society before he became editor. "With the exceptions of yours and a few others," he wrote to a volunteer contributor named Fitzedward Hall in 1899, "the original materials are bad enough, and rarely to be trusted, and, in point of fact, 5/6 of the quotations that we print, are taken from those collected under my supervision since 1879, and for which I can in some measure vouch." Charlotte Brewer, "Early Progress," *Examining the OED*, April 28, 2020, https://oed.hertford.ox.ac.uk/quotations/oed1-quotation-collection/early-progress/.

111 **"Paper to be written on one side:** Noah Porter to George and Charles Merriam, July 5, 1860, *G. & C. Merriam Company Archive*.

112 **When *Webster's Second* was published:** Gove, *Webster's Third*, 4a.

112 **The intent was to portray "language:** Skinner, *Story of Ain't*, 202.

112 **Under Gove, editors collected:** Gove said in 1969 that "whereas we used to gather [citations] at a rate of 80,000 a month, we are now gathering them at the rate of 10,000 a month or so, slowly building up again. But we have already 200,000 or 300,000 additional ones, new ones." Blake, "Not So 'Harmless Drudge,'" 72.

113 **a century-long scrapbooking:** Merriam dates the nouns *scrapbook* and *scrapbooker* to 1825 and 1928, respectively.

113 **makes them an irreplicable:** *Irreplicable* wasn't in Merriam, the *OED*, or any other standard dictionary. You could, however, find a definition in Wiktionary and other sources that comb Wiktionary, including Wordnik and YourDictionary.com.

114 ***Fuck* hadn't appeared:** The word made its dictionary debut in an Italian-English lexicon in 1598 as a synonym for the Italian word *fottere*. It next showed up in a 1671 dictionary of English etymology written in Latin. The English lexicographer Nathaniel Bailey put it in a 1730 book, while Samuel Johnson left it out, along with other vulgar words. The 1795 dictionary that

included *fuck* was the *New and Complete Dictionary of the English Language* by John Ash, first published in 1775. Ash defined it as "to perform an act of generation, to have to do with a woman," and labeled it "a low, vulgar word." The modern trailblazer was Britain's *Penguin English Dictionary* in 1965. In America, it was the *American Heritage* in 1969, with a substantial entry of five verb and two noun senses, plus adjective and adverb ones. Like the *Third*, the 1966 *Random House Dictionary of the English Language* was lambasted for its refusal to enter *fuck*. "The excuse here, no doubt, is 'good taste,'" a *New York Times* reviewer wrote, "but in a dictionary of this scope and ambition the omission seems dumb and irresponsible." *The F-Word*, Jesse Sheidlower ed. (New York: Oxford University Press, 2009), xxviii–xxxi.

116 ***Fuck* indeed was a topic of:** Herbert C. Morton, "Philip Gove's Formative Years," *Dictionaries* 13 (1991), 24.

118 **"Why this residual prudishness:** Mario Pei, "Ain't Is In, Raviolis Ain't," *New York Times Book Review*, October 22, 1961.

118 ***Hungarian Studies in English*:** Ladislas Országh, "Books Reviewed," *Hungarian Studies in English*, vol. 1 (1963).

121 **Stamper laid out her findings:** For a fuller treatment of *irregardless*, see Kory Stamper's fantastic memoir, *Word by Word: The Secret Life of Dictionaries* (New York: Pantheon, 2017), 52–67.

121 **The note cites similar:** The *irregardless* entry generated more than a thousand comments on Merriam's website. Predictably, many simply refused to accept the dictionary's findings. A sampling: "The dumbing down of the English language." "A once valued resource has now lost all credibility." "So you brought more inaccuracy to your product . . . your product is trash." "This is why they are not THE experts, the end-all-be-all voice for all things pertaining to the English language." "Just because people are, as a species, incredibly stupid does NOT mean the friggin DICTIONARY needs to pander to that stupidity. Shame on Merriam-Webster." "A pox upon everyone involved in making this happen."

124 **"It was sad," he said:** Jonathan Lighter handwrote most of the 115,000 three-by-five cards. "They smelled like cigarette smoke," said lexicographer Grant Barrett, who worked on the project at Oxford. Barrett used a check scanner to digitize the cards and Oxford typed them up for publication—and then canceled the project. Lighter didn't respond to an email. "Recalling the years I put in on *HDAS* has become so distasteful that it is hard for me to discuss the subject with equanimity or even maturity," he once said. Simon Winchester, "The Mongrel Speech of the Streets," *New York Review of Books*, March 8, 2012, https://www.nybooks.com/articles/2012/03/08/mongrel-speech-streets.

124 **That effort to chronicle:** *DARE*'s work would continue with small quarterly website updates done on a volunteer basis. In 2024, twenty-five words were added or revised, among them *milk gap*, "An opening in a pasture fence where cows are milked," from southern Appalachia; *ponny*, "To coast on a sled, esp by running and throwing oneself face down on it," from New York City and Long Island; and *cutering*, an adjective meaning

"crooked," with a figurative sense of "muddled up; bad-tempered," from New England. The entry for *cutering* includes a fantastic illustrative quotation from a 1911 book, *On Board the Mary Sands*, by Laura Elizabeth Howe Richards: "Many's the time I've got straightened out, when things has been a mite cuterin', just lookin' at the sun rise,—or set, as might be,—and takin' it by and large." Richards wrote more than ninety books and won a Pulitzer Prize in 1917 for a biography of her mother, Julia Ward Howe, the poet, abolitionist, and suffragist who wrote the lyrics to the "Battle Hymn of the Republic." Subscribe to *DARE* at https://www.daredictionary.com and read updates at https://dare.wisc.edu.

125 **"If anybody really wanted:** I supplemented my interviews with *DARE* editor Joan Houston Hall with printed sources including: Mark Johnson, "End of a 'Whoopensocker': UW's Famed Dialect Dictionary Closing after 54 Years," *Milwaukee Journal Sentinel*, October 28, 2017; Jesse Sheidlower, "The Closing of a Great American Dialect Project," *New Yorker*, September 22, 2017, https://www.newyorker.com/culture/cultural-comment/the-closing-of-a-great-american-dialect-project; Michael Adams, "The Lexical Ride of a Lifetime," *American Speech* 88, no. 2 (2013), 168–95.

125 **From 1968 to 1977, the OED:** Gilliver, *Making of the Oxford English Dictionary*, 482, 505.

126 **assistant named J. R. R. Tolkien:** When the *OED* entered *hobbit* in the late 1960s, Tolkien himself wrote most of the definition: "one of an imaginary people, a small variety of the human race, that gave themselves this name (meaning 'hole-dweller') but were called by others *halflings*, since they were half the height of normal men." Tolkien is quoted or mentioned in 344 *OED* entries. Other Tolkien words in the book: *orc, mathom, mithril*. Gilliver and two *OED* colleagues wrote a book about Tolkien and the dictionary. Peter Gilliver, Jeremy Marshall, and Edmund Weiner, *The Ring of Words: Tolkien and the Oxford English Dictionary* (Oxford, England: Oxford University Press, 2009).

126 **And then, from 1933 to 1957:** In those years, Oxford University Press did publish new editions of smaller dictionaries with names like the *Concise Oxford Dictionary* (which debuted in 1911), the *Pocket Oxford Dictionary* (1927), and the *Little Oxford Dictionary* (1930) edited by lexicographers working outside of Oxford. But World War II, internal strife, and financial concerns delayed plans to update the *OED*. "I expect the great work will stand for at least half a century," an Oxford University Press executive wrote in 1940. Preparations for a new supplement took shape in the early 1950s and lexicographic work began in 1957 with the hiring of an Oxford academic, Robert Burchfield, as editor. Gilliver, *Making of the Oxford English Dictionary*, 425-451.

128 **The original 1857 proposal:** Philological Society project backer Richard Chenevix Trench wrote that dictionaries had too few words, "maimed and incomplete" definitions, poor etymologies, inaccurate dating, and insufficient illustrative quotations. Trench believed the dictionary was obligated, and was failing, to recognize the sweep of the English language. "The maker, for example, of an English Dictionary," he wrote, "may not consider

'mulierosity,' or 'subsannation,' or 'coaxation,' or 'ludibundness,' or 'delinition,' or 'septemfluous,' or 'medioxumous,' or 'mirificent,' or 'palmiferous,' or 'opime,' or a thousand other words of a similar character which might be adduced . . . to contribute much to the riches of the English tongue; yet he has not therefore any right to omit them, as all these which I have just adduced, with a thousand more of like kind, have been omitted from our Dictionaries." Trench also lamented the absence from Johnson, Webster, and other dictionaries of words that sound like they were dreamt up by Lewis Carroll or Dr. Seuss: *hickscorner*—"the loose ribald scoffer at sacred things"—*titivillars, grimsire, jackstraw,* and *shewel*. Plus *lurry, privado, powldron, druggerman, chokepear,* and *palliard*. And this lovelyjumble quintet of out-of-favor compounds: *cankerfret, witwanton, rootfast, neednot,* and *woodkern*. Trench wasn't indiscriminately inclusive. Scientific, technical, and even grammatical terms were "hideous exotics," he wrote, "intruders and interlopers" in a general dictionary. His way forward was a thorough, modern dictionary produced by credentialed philologists and etymologists aided by an army of readers who would unearth "the innumerable words which have escaped us hitherto, which are lurking unnoticed in every corner of our literature." Work on what would become the *OED* wouldn't begin for more than a decade and wouldn't produce results for two more after that. Richard Chenevix Trench, *On Some Deficiencies in Our English Dictionaries* (London: John W Parker and Son, 1857), https://archive.org/details/onsomedeficiencio0trenrich/mode/2up.

128 Dr. William Chester Minor: W. C. Minor was one of the *OED*'s most prolific volunteer readers, contributing tens of thousands of illustrative quotations over three decades. "So enormous have been Dr. Minor's contributions during the past 17 or 18 years, that we could easily illustrate the last 4 centuries from his quotations alone," editor James Murray wrote in 1899. Murray had no idea that Minor was locked up at Broadmoor Asylum for shooting a man in London in 1872 in a state of delusional rage; based on Minor's return address, Murray thought he was a physician. Years earlier, as a medical student Yale, Minor was paid $500 to write definitions for the 1864 Webster's "in the following departments . . . Zoology, Natural History, Geology, Mineralogy, Botany, Chemistry, Anatomy, Surgery of all sorts." Minor was listed as an editor in the book's front matter. But his work was riddled with errors, and considered one of the few flaws of the 1864. Minor's mental health began deteriorating after he served as a frontline Union Army surgeon. He would spend four decades in Broadmoor before he was sent back to America. Joshua Kendall, "A Minor Exception: On W. C. Minor and Noah Webster," *The Nation*, April 4, 2011, https://www.thenation.com/article/archive/minor-exception-wc-minor-and-noah-webster/.

130 In those days, he said: Peter Gilliver could identify contributors by their handwriting. The penmanship of benefactor, quotation-gatherer, and proofreader Henry Hucks Gibbs sloped sharply to the right until, Gilliver told me, Gibbs shot off his right hand in a hunting accident. On a slip in front of us, lo and behold, Gibbs's post-shooting handwriting sloped to the left. Gilliver identified another slip—for *snobbishly*—as the work of Thomas Austin, a London-born brewer with a classical education who, with 165,000 quotations by 1888, was the biggest contributor to the first edition. The most prolific reader was Marghanita Laski, a London journalist, writer, broadcaster, and intellectual who submitted around 250,000 quotations from 1958 to 1986.

130 **"That's a correction I can make:** After apologizing for letting my earthshaking lexicographic discovery slip through the cracks, Gilliver in 2024 confirmed the spelling of *snitch'em's*. He changed the headword in the OED and replaced the 1798 quotation from *The Sporting Magazine* that I saw in the files with an earlier one from what he said "appears to be, essentially, the same article" in the October 1773 issue of the *Covent-Garden Magazine*. I'm an OED contributor! Looking forward to my knighthood.

131 **"Whether we would consider:** When the OED began computerizing the dictionary in 1984, Robert Burchfield was asked whether the quotation slips collected during creation of the four-volume supplement that he edited would be thrown out after the project was completed. "Never," Burchfield replied. "I don't trust this electronic equipment." Leslie Plommer, "Dictionary meets its Waterloo," *Globe and Mail* (Toronto), May 16, 1984.

133 **The writer Nicholson Baker:** Nicholson Baker, "Discards," *New Yorker*, April 4, 1994, 64–86. Adding a personal quest to buy and save from destruction old newspaper bound volumes, Baker expanded his story into a book, *Double Fold: Libraries and the Assault on Paper* (New York: Random House, 2001).

133 **The Library of Congress published:** Library of Congress, *The Card Catalog: Books, Cards and Literary Treasures* (San Francisco: Chronicle Books, 2017).

133 **An Oregon artist painted:** "WingedWorld," *Etsy*, accessed November 12, 2024, https://www.etsy.com/shop/WingedWorld. I bought a dozen cards from the artist, Vickie Moore. They're fantastic!

134 **A Massachusetts librarian asked:** Chris Shores, "GCC Librarian Saves Card Catalog," *The Recorder* (Greenfield, MA), May 31, 2013.

8
collection

139 **She and Read became friends:** Allen Walker Read was one of America's most prominent and fun-loving word scholars. He is best known for solving the mystery of OK. Read dated it to the *Boston Morning Post* of March 23, 1839, which wrote, "o.k.—all correct." (Elsewhere it was explained as a shortening of the playfully misspelled "oll korrect.") But he also traced the origins of *blizzard*, *Dixie*, *Podunk*, and much more. "No emanation of the human spirit is too vile or too despicable to come under the record and analysis of the scientist," Read wrote in *Lexical Evidence*, which was republished in 1977 as *Classic American Graffiti*. Kripke eventually owned four of the seventy-five original copies. One copy belonged to H. L. Mencken. Another was Read's personal copy, which turned up on eBay after his death, along with other papers and photographs, which Kripke of course showed me. Allen

Walker Read, *Lexical Evidence from Folk Epigraphy in Western North America: A Glossarial Study of the Low Element in the English Vocabulary* (Paris: privately printed, 1935); Douglas Martin, "Allen Read, 96, the 'O.K.' Expert, Is Dead," *New York Times*, October 18, 2002, https://www.nytimes.com/2002/10/18/nyregion/allen-read-96-the-ok-expert-is-dead.html.

139 **She could be ruthless:** Jonathon Green, editor of the definitive *Green's Dictionary of Slang*, told me that Kripke dropped him after he acquired a copy of an edition of Francis Grose's pioneering 1785 *A Classical Dictionary of the Vulgar Tongue* annotated by the author. Kripke already had one personal edition but wanted the entire set. "She could be quite hard. You could easily upset her, which I eventually did," Green said, pulling the volume off the shelf in his London apartment and showing it to me over Zoom. Kripke also showed me her copy.

142 **Pamphlets and articles about:** Joseph Worcester and the Merriams accused each other of plagiarism, "gross literary fraud," and lexicographic incompetence. An 1854 manifesto is titled "Have We a National Standard of English Lexicography? Or, Some Comparison of the Claims of Webster's Dictionaries, and Worcester's Dictionaries." In it, the Merriams attempted to debunk Worcester's boast that his dictionary contained more than 100,000 words. "How are these made up?" they wrote. "If we notice the *compound* words, we shall see that great multitudes are thus formed." They listed seventeen words starting with *short*: *short-armed, short-eared, short-horned, short-tailed, short-waisted*. "Now, what possible use is it to swell a Vocabulary in this way? How easy to enlarge the list indefinitely by prefixing the word *short* to half the words of the language." The Merriams also accused Worcester of padding his book with entries like *shopocracy, thawy, transcribbler, unsufficingness*, and *wegotism*. In fairness, Worcester did nail a bunch of words the Merriams mocked, including *squeezable, illiberalism, interestingly, transmogrification, harassment*, and *regularize*. Worcester published his last dictionary in 1860 and died in 1865.

143 **She knew something about every:** Kripke guided me through a stack of photographs of lexicographers. "Here's a guy who wrote something akin to the *OED* but only for words in English or Scotland or Wales that were dialect," she said about one photo. "This is a linguist I don't like. He's an arbiter of what's right and what's wrong. He's a stuffed shirt," she said about another.

144 **a neat and polite April 1849 letter:** Only the first issue of the *Brooklyn Freeman* survives so there's no record of Whitman's review. But in 1845 he wrote about the Merriam's first printing of Webster's dictionary in *The Brooklyn Eagle, and Kings County Democrat*, calling the book "not only an authoritative standard, but likewise a monument of patience and perseverance." The 1847 was Whitman's dictionary of choice while composing the poems in *Leaves of Grass*. He also followed the "War of the Dictionaries" between the Merriams and Joseph Worcester and was fascinated by the growth of American English. The letter to the Merriams is one of fewer than two dozen existing Whitman letters from before *Leaves of Grass*. Madeline

Kripke and Ed Folsom, "A Newly Discovered 1849 Whitman Letter to the 'Messrs. Merriam,'" *Walt Whitman Quarterly Review*, 38, no. 2 (2020), 118-125.

145 **"I wasn't admitting many people:** N. R. Kleinfield, "Enriched by His Friendship With an Agnostic, a Rabbi Finances a Storied Legacy," *New York Times*, May 9, 1997, https://www.nytimes.com/1997/05/09/nyregion/enriched-by-his-friendship-with-an-agnostic-a-rabbi-finances-a-storied-legacy.html.

145 **"Like an atomic bomb:** Kristin E. Holmes, "Friendship Investment Pays Off in Endowment," *Philadelphia Inquirer*, May 14, 1997.

145 **the seminary would get another:** Douglas Martin, "Rabbi Myer Kripke, Early Buffett Friend and Investor, Dies at 100," *New York Times*, May 3, 2014, https://www.nytimes.com/2014/05/04/us/rabbi-myer-kripke-100-early-buffett-friend-and-investor-dies.html.

146 **"If I magically had my druthers:** Daniel Krieger, "The Dame of Dictionaries," *Narratively*, August 15, 2013, https://narratively.com/the-dame-of-dictionaries/.

147 **The *Times* published a lengthy obituary:** Sam Roberts, "Madeline Kripke, Doyenne of Dictionaries, Is Dead at 76," *New York Times*, April 30, 2020, https://www.nytimes.com/2020/04/30/nyregion/madeline-kripke-dead-coronavirus.html.

147 **A remembrance in the journal:** David Jost, "Madeline Kripke, 1943-2020," *Dictionaries: The Journal of the Dictionary Society of North America*, 44-2, fall 2020.

148 **Indiana, which had recently acquired:** Indiana also boasted the largest collection of three-dimensional puzzles in the world, 33,000 in all. Crossword puzzle titan Will Shortz, who graduated from Indiana in 1974 with a degree of his creation dubbed enigmatology, pledged his papers to the school.

149 ***The Hobo's Hornbook*:** George Milburn was born in Native American territory in eastern Oklahoma. He wrote a series of joke books in his early twenties and then rode the rails and collected material for his book of hobo ballads, which came to the attention of H. L. Mencken, who published Milburn in the *American Mercury*, which led to work for *The New Yorker*, *Vanity Fair*, *Harper's*, and other magazines. Milburn also wrote short stories and novels about Oklahoma, and scripts for radio and television. He died in 1966 in New York. Larry O'Dell, "Milburn, George (1906–1966)," *Oklahoma Historical Society*, undated, https://www.okhistory.org/publications/enc/entry?entry=MI018.

149 **And *The Hobo Philosopher*:** The subtitle of this ten-cent pamphlet piqued my curiosity: "Why work six days a week when you can get your living by working one?" The author, Roger Payne, was a Cambridge University–educated lawyer who in 1939 published a 175,000-word book titled *Why Work?* (Author's note: Writing a 175,000-word book is a lot of work.) Payne "rode the rods" for years around America before living in furnished apartments in New York. In 1955, he was struck by a car while crossing Fourth

Avenue at 26th Street and died. "Hobo Writer, a Foe of Toil, Is Dead," *New York Times*, February 24, 1955.

152 **The replica would be:** "The replica was one of Madeline's favorite things. She objectified it, too—showed it off, a dictionary novelty," Michael Adams would write:

> Now, it's still a thing in a large room with boxes filled with things that have to be sorted through, organized, listed, processed, catalogued, and stored. Later on, visitors to the Lilly Library will request those things, and staff will retrieve and deliver those things in the reading room. Then, the books or whatever material will be, not mere objects, nor only objects of admiration, but objects of research. Among them all, the replica box of *Webster's Third* is an object by design.

Michael Adams, "Marketing Webster's Third: The Big Book as a Big Box," *Lilly Library*, April 12, 2023, https://blogs.libraries.indiana.edu/lilly/2023/04/12/marketing-websters-third-the-big-book-as-a-big-box/.

153 **an autographed copy of *Steve Allen's*:** From "Goldilocks and the Three Cool Bears":

> Shortly thereafter the downstairs door banged open and in walked three bears. "I smell Arpège," said the mama bear to her mate. "Gus, you've had a broad here." "You're out of your skull," said the papa bear, "although it does look as if somebody had eyes for soup over there." "I'm hip," said the mama bear. "And dig! The upstairs bedroom door is open."

Steve Allen, *Steve Allen's Bop Fables* (New York: Simon & Schuster, 1955).

154 **The childhood spelling records:** This George Merriam didn't go into the family business. After studying theology at Yale, he edited a magazine for the clergyman and abolitionist Henry Ward Beecher, wrote a biography of newspaper publisher Samuel Bowles, and authored eight other books about "life and conduct and the spiritual side of things." "George S. Merriam," *New York Times*, January 23, 1914.

154 **A 1966 issue of the men's magazine:** "What follows is the language of the hipster, the language of the marijuana smoker, the language of the streets in certain of our larger cities. It is a mixed bag full of the slang of junkies, of gangsters, of pushers, of pimps. It is an amalgamation of jazz argot, the jargon of the underworld, the vocabulary of the dispossessed and the words of the alienated." Among them were words that would be quickly absorbed into mainstream use, including *beat* ("exhausted, broke, down and out"), *boss* ("an adjective meaning great or good"), *cool* ("an all-purpose word indicating anything you like or any situation that is not 'hot' with the law"), *chick* and *fox* for a woman, and *grass* for marijuana. Allen Geller, "The Hippie's Lexicon," *Mr. Magazine*, April 1966, 8.

156 **Madeline Kripke, rest in peace:** By early 2025, Indiana had inventoried 13,000 items, or about two-thirds of the collection, not including manuscripts, ephemera, videotapes, and other non-lexical material. The library hoped to host its first Kripke Collection event in 2026.

9
slur

158 In September 1997: Michael A. Fletcher, "Furor Erupts Over a Racial Epithet," *Washington Post*, October 8, 1997, https://www.washingtonpost.com/archive/politics/1997/10/08/furor-erupts-over-racial-epithet/16a5c19b-8c49-42a4-bc70-975e59f990a1/.

159 In the first sentence: Randall Kennedy, *Nigger: The Strange Career of a Troublesome Word* (New York: Pantheon, 2002), 3.

161 In America, it's from 1619: Heather Andrea Williams, "Slavery, Rooted in America's Early History," *OUP Blog*, November 28, 2014, https://blog.oup.com/2014/11/slavery-american-history-vsi/.

161 Ignatius Sancho, a child of: Ignatius Sancho to Laurence Sterne, July 1776, in *Letters of the Late Ignatius Sancho, An African. In Two Volumes. To Which Are Prefixed, Memoirs of His Life, Vol. 1* (London: J. Nichols, 1782), 95, accessed in Documenting the American South on November 14, 2024, https://docsouth.unc.edu/neh/sancho1/sancho1.html.

165 I looked at that day's: "N.A.A.C.P. Leader Urges 'Violence,'" "Teachers' Ousting Stirs Little Rock," and "4 Whites Indicted in Rape of Negro," *New York Times*, May 7, 1959.

167 In 2005, a scholar: Ives Goddard, "'I Am a Red-Skin': The Adoption of a Native American Expression (1769–1826)," *European Review of Native American Studies* 19, no. 2 (2005), 1–20, https://repository.si.edu/handle/10088/31970.

168 A 1959 slip quotes: Philip Rahv's essay, "Paleface and Redskin," was published in *The Kenyon Review* in 1939, twenty years before the Merriam citation was stamped. "At his highest level the paleface moves in an exquisite moral atmosphere; at his lowest he is genteel, snobbish, and pedantic," Rahv wrote. "In giving expression to the vitality of the people, the redskin is at his best; but at his worst he is a vulgar anti-intellectual, combining aggression with conformity and reverting to the crudest forms of frontier psychology." In Rahv's estimation, almost all American novelists excepting Henry James and Nathaniel Hawthorne were "redskins to the wigwam born."

168 In 2002, a University of Iowa: Robert S. Wachal, "Taboo or Not Taboo: That Is the Question," *American Speech* 77, no. 2 (2002), 195–206.

169 In 1968, students at Dartmouth: Marty Ralbovsky, "An Indian Affair," *New York Times*, November 14, 1971.

169 The team's president: Dan Steinberg, "The Great Redskins Name Debate of . . . 1972?" *Washington Post*, June 3, 2014, https://www.washingtonpost.com/news/dc-sports-bog/wp/2014/06/03/the-great-redskins-name-debate-of-1972/.

173 Dan Jenkins's football novel: I asked Jenkins's daughter, *Washington Post* sports columnist Sally Jenkins, about *Semi-Tough*'s n-word-laced opening pages written in the voice of white Southern running back Billy Clyde Puckett. She noted that the book was part of an era of acidic political and cultural satire—movies like *M*A*S*H* and TV shows like *All in the Family*.

"In my dad's view, one effective way to tackle bigotry was to make fun of it—hilarious send-up fun, until it lost its power and became ridiculous," she said. "The opening is the first salvo in the guerrilla attack. My father was all about the urge to strip away pretension, to peel off the facades of certain things. He wanted to send up the holy pretensions of the NFL with a set of characters talking the crude way players really talked, doing the things they really did, most profanely." Email with author, March 22, 2016.

173 **"He really used it:** In addition to covering Ali for the *Times* in the early 1960s, Robert Lipsyte cowrote Dick Gregory's memoir. Lipsyte told me he suggested that Gregory use the word for the book's title. The inspiration came from a story Gregory had told him, about how Gregory fantasized about opening a restaurant in Chicago that would have one table, serve exquisite and expensive food, and have the same name as the book—on a big neon sign. "The publisher thought it was a bad idea," Lipsyte said of the title. "[Gregory's] eyes lit up, of course. This quixotic idea of busting the word—because this book was going to be such a bestseller that people were going to be saying it all over the place" and it would lose its epithetical power. Gregory dedicated the book to his mother: "Wherever you are, if you ever hear the word 'nigger' again, remember they are advertising my book." Interview with author, March 22, 2016.

173 **The slip for the citation:** The headline was a spin on Hunter Thompson's classic 1971 road trip/memoir *Fear and Loathing in Las Vegas*. It would be used again in the title of Thompson's book about the 1972 presidential election based on his *Rolling Stone* reporting, where the Dellums quotation also appears. (I still have the paperback edition I read in college.) Hunter S. Thompson, *Fear and Loathing: On the Campaign Trail '72* (New York: Warner Books, 1983), 73.

174 **the Capitol Hill press conference:** Ron Dellums first endorsed a presidential run by Shirley Chisholm, a Black member of Congress from New York, in December 1971 in Washington. Chisholm announced her candidacy in January 1972, in Brooklyn's Bedford-Stuyvesant neighborhood and later the same day on Capitol Hill. Dellums was onstage with her at both events. Frank Lynn, "New Hat in Ring: Mrs. Chisholm's," *New York Times*, January 26, 1972.

174 **Dellums used the word:** United Press International, "Dellums Says 'Niggerism' Hits All, Asks Unity," *Press-Democrat* (Santa Rosa, CA), March 19, 1972; Stephen Curwood, "In the News: Ronald Dellums," *Bay State Banner*, May 18, 1972.

174 **even baton twirlers:** Here's the citation: "People think you're a twit if you twirl. It's a prejudice of the unknowing. Twirlers are the niggers of a white university. Yes they are." Jane Martin, "The Revelations: Three Monologues for Actresses," *Esquire*, November 1982.

174 **(Not in the files: Yoko Ono:** After the song's release, Apple Records placed a half-page ad in the African American news and culture magazine *Jet* with a quotation in large type attributed to Ron Dellums: "I agree with John and Yoko. Women are the niggers of the world." Dellums told the magazine he hadn't said that. "Unfortunately, I appear to have been the victim of some overzealous promoting company's efforts to capture a portion of the Black

music market," he wrote in a letter to the editor. But Dellums also revealed that Lennon and Ono had sent him a copy of the single along with one of his quotations, which included "women" on his rhetorical list. "I have stated many times and I will state again here: In a white-dominated society that sees the role of women as bed-partners, broom pushers, bottle washers, typists and cooks, women are niggers in THIS society." Lennon defended the title and lyrics, which were praised by women's rights groups. But the song was all but banned by radio stations and sold poorly. Apple Records, advertisement, *Jet*, June 1, 1972, 61; Ronald V. Dellums, "Rep. Dellums Objects to Quote in Record Ad," *Jet*, June 15, 1972, 4; Anne Duston, "Lennon, Ono 45 Controversial," *Billboard*, June 17, 1972, 65.

174 **"Anybody can be a nigger:** "Dick Gregory: He Is Very Funny But Wasting Away," Philip Nobile, *Palm Beach Post*, January 2, 1972.

176 **A decade earlier, a Black reporter:** Terry E. Johnson, "The Sounds of Black History," *Philadelphia Inquirer*, February 13, 1983.

176 **Karen Russell, the daughter:** Karen Russell, "Growing Up With Privilege and Prejudice," *New York Times Magazine*, June 14, 1987, https://www.nytimes.com/1987/06/14/magazine/growing-up-with-privilege-and-prejudice.html.

177 **Instead of a boldface colon:** The boldface colon was added by Philip Gove for the *Third*, borrowed from the field of mathematical logic. The formation "—used . . ." had been house style for definitions of function words like *the* and *of*, for trademarks like *Kleenex*, and for pronunciation spellings like *coulda*, among other entries. Steve Perrault expanded its use to cover offensive terms.

178 **Before Merriam disabled:** In the first digital decades at Merriam, entries asked readers why they had looked up the word. Merriam removed the function for some offensive or otherwise sensitive words and then entirely.

178 **On the one hand, the lexicographer:** I interviewed Harvard Law School professor Randall Kennedy in 2020. Nearly two decades after publication of his book, Kennedy still felt that Merriam's bare-bones definition was adequate. But he also noted the word's cultural evolution and transformation. "Get granular then," he said. "I think it would be a nice thing. *Nigga* has become common usage in some communities as a term of endearment. It's winking ironically at the old usage, the racist usage. But we're using it ourselves in a defiant way. It truly has become a term of almost routine address."

178 **the linguist John McWhorter:** John McWhorter, *Nine Nasty Words: English in the Gutter—Then, Now, and Forever* (New York: Avery, 2021).

179 **"If you could choose one word:** Ta-Nehisi Coates, "In Defense of a Loaded Word," *New York Times*, November 23, 2013, https://www.nytimes.com/2013/11/24/opinion/sunday/coates-in-defense-of-a-loaded-word.html.

180 **the first slur to be redrafted:** The entry for *redskin* and other offensive words also received the new treatment:

> redskin *noun offensive* → used as an insulting and contemptuous term for an American Indian.

The arrow was a recent addition to Merriam's style toolbox, replacing the em dash in definitions that stress function over meaning, such as the offensive terms, pronouns, and interjections.

10
pronoun

For most of the historical examples cited in this chapter I relied on the work of University of Illinois professor Dennis Baron, especially "The Epicene Pronoun: The Word That Failed," *American Speech* 56, no. 2 (1981), 83–97; "The Gender-Neutral Pronoun: After 150 Years Still an Epic Fail," *The Web of Language*, August 2, 2010, https://blogs.illinois.edu/view/25/31097; and *What's Your Pronoun? Beyond He and She* (New York: Liveright, 2020). I also interviewed Baron.

181 In 1884, an Erie, Pennsylvania: C. C. Converse, "A New Pronoun," *The Critic: A Literary Weekly, Critical and Eclectic*, August 2, 1884, https://debaron.web.illinois.edu/essays/thonconverse.pdf.

182 A 1659 rant by a Quaker writer: The writer was Thomas Ellwood, an Englishman and friend of John Milton who was jailed for his Quaker beliefs, and his rant is something:

> Again, The Corrupt and Unfound Form of Speaking in the Plural Number to a Single Person (Y O U to One, instead of T H O U ;) contrary to the Pure, Plain and Single Language of T R U T H T H O U to One, and Y O U to more than One) which had always been used, by G O D to Men, and Men to G O D, as well as one to another, from the oldest Record of Time, till Corrupt Men, for Corrupt Ends, in later and Corrupt Times, to Flatter, Fawn, and work upon the Corrupt Nature in Men, brought in that false and senseless Way of Speaking, Y O U to One ; which hath since corrupted the Modern Languages, and hath greatly debased the Spirits, and depraved the Manners of Men. This Evil Custom I had been as forward in as others and this I was now called out of, and required to cease from.

Mark Liberman, "That false and senseless Way of Speaking," *Language Log*, July 1, 2016, https://languagelog.ldc.upenn.edu/nll/?p=26554.

182 In 1971, a group of Harvard: "Pronoun Envy," *Harvard Crimson*, November 16, 1971, https://www.thecrimson.com/article/1971/11/16/pronoun-envy-pto-the-editors-of/.

182 In 2008, Yale computer scientist: David Gelernter, "Feminism and the English Language," *Weekly Standard*, March 3, 2008, https://www.washingtonexaminer.com/magazine/2390774/feminism-and-the-english-language/.

182 Even in the third edition: E. B. White died in 1985. The editors of the fourth edition of *The Elements of Style*, published in 2000, modified his rigid message. They acknowledged that "many writers" find the generic *he* "limiting or offensive," and suggested ways around *he or she*, including *their*. In the foreword to a 2005 edition illustrated by cartoonist Maira Kalman,

Roger Angell, White's stepson, noted "a light redistribution of genders to permit a feminine pronoun or female farmer to take their places among the males who once innocently served him."

183 **Jane Austen deployed:** "Jane Austen and Other Famous Authors Violate What Everyone Learned in Their English Class," *Republic of Pemberley*, accessed December 20, 2024, https://pemberley.com/janeinfo/austheir.html.

183 **Shakespeare wrote:** Mark Liberman, "Linguistic Reaction at The New Yorker," *Language Log*, March 8, 2016, https://languagelog.ldc.upenn.edu/nll/?p=24504.

183 **"The *Masculine Person* answers:** Lynda Mugglestone, *The Oxford History of English* (Oxford, England: Oxford University Press, 2013), 323.

184 **But rules deemed inviolable:** I do still wince at the use of *they* instead of *it*, as in "the NFL could automate measurement if *they* really wanted to, but there is evidence that *they* have DELIBERATELY avoided it so that *they* can carry on with this brazenly crooked analog chain business," as my friend Drew Magary wrote. For historical and cultural reasons, though, I am more sympathetic to English football's use of the plural to refer to an individual team, though less so U.S. soccer's borrowing of the style. Drew Magary, "The Ongoing NFL Conspiracy You Don't Know About," *Deadspin*, September 22, 2016, https://deadspin.com/the-ongoing-nfl-conspiracy-you-don-t-know-about-1786951013/.

184 **John McIntyre, a copy editor:** John E. McIntyre, "Everyone Goes Their Own Way," *Baltimore Sun*, January 6, 2015.

184 **The Associated Press conceded:** Lauren Easton, "Making a Case for a Singular 'They,'" *Associated Press*, March 24, 2017, https://blog.ap.org/products-and-services/making-a-case-for-a-singular-they.

185 **Baron has chronicled:** "We want a new pronoun," Kansas businessman and politician Napoleon Bonaparte Brown wrote in 1878. "The need of a personal pronoun of the singular number and common gender is so desperate, urgent, imperative, that according to established theories it should long since have grown on our speech, as the tails grew off monkeys . . . I do not believe there is a writer in the country that is not hampered every time he—no, she—There! I've run against the old snag." Napoleon Bonaparte Brown, "The Contributors' Club," *Atlantic Monthly*, November 1878.

185 **In the next decade, a Philadelphia:** Also in 1871, Congress passed what came to be known as the Dictionary Act, which sought to clarify language confusion in government documents. "In all acts hereafter passed," it stated, "words importing the singular number may extend and be applied to several persons or things; words importing the plural number may include the singular; words importing the masculine gender may be applied to females . . ." The use of the generic *he* prompted legal cases over whether women could be seated in Congress or hold the office of president.

187 **The *Sacramento Bee* took action:** "'Hir' Will Be the Bee's Word for 'He or She,'" *Sacramento Bee*, August 14, 1920.

187 The *Bee* used *hir*: A couple of examples: "It is the patriotic duty of every individual in the United States to put up a bold fight in order to win this war and to know hir is fighting for a purpose." "The law provides that a married person can remarry when hir spouse has been absent and not known to such person for a space of five years." "Does No Good," *Sacramento Bee*, July 27, 1942; "Am I Married?" *Sacramento Bee*, July 14, 1941.

189 "It's about all of us: Here's the full quotation:
> The fight against gender oppression has been joined for centuries, perhaps millennia. What's new today, is that it's moving into the arena of open political activism. And nope, this is not just one more civil rights struggle for one more narrowly-defined minority. It's about all of us who are genderqueer: diesel dykes and stone butches, leatherqueens and radical fairies, nelly fags, crossdressers, intersexed, transexuals, transvestites, transgendered, transgressively gendered, intersexed, and those of us whose gender expressions are so complex they haven't even been named yet.

Riki Anne Wilchins, "A Note From Your Editrix," *In Your Face*, spring 1995, https://www.digitaltransgenderarchive.net/downloads/1831ckoof.

189 While trans people have existed: Some seventeenth-century medical texts used plural pronouns to refer to "hermaphrodites," people who now would be considered transgender. "Medical texts, thinking of them as a blend of two genders, called individuals 'them,'" former Merriam editor Kory Stamper wrote. "Legal and general texts often assigned the person the pronoun that best matched their outward gender appearance, but in cases where that wasn't clear, they were called 'it.'" Kory Stamper, "'They' Did It!" *Boston Globe*, September 9, 2018.

189 The American Dialect Society recognized: I voted for *they*, which won in a landslide over the previously noted *ammosexual, on fleek, ghost* ("abruptly end a relationship by cutting off communication, especially online"), and *thanks, Obama* ("sarcastic expression in which a person pretends to blame [Barack] Obama for a problem"). "2015 Word of the Year Is Singular 'They,'" *American Dialect Society*, January 8, 2016, https://americandialect.org/2015-word-of-the-year-is-singular-they/.

189 In 2019, Steve Perrault revised: My first thought was that the entry didn't go far enough. Missing was the increasingly common use of *they* with *any* singular antecedent, including those in which the gender of the referent is known.

190 "'Trans' cultists and their dogmatist: Laurie Higgins, "Merriam-Webster Dictionary and the 'Transing' of Language," *Illinois Family*, September 18, 2019, https://illinoisfamily.org/homosexuality/merriam-webster-adds-singular-genderless-they/.

190 A right-wing blogger said: The writer's website has since been deleted, but the Internet Archive Wayback Machine never forgets. Mark Pantano, "Merriam-Webster Adds Non-Binary Definition of 'They' to Dictionary," *Mark Pantano*, September 18, 2019, https://web.archive.org/web

/20200302235410/http://markpantano.com/index.php/2019/09/18/merriam-webster-adds-non-binary-definition-of-they-to-dictionary/.

190 **In 2020, the group picked:** *Singular they* defeated *meme* in a runoff, as well as *#BlackLivesMatter, climate, emoji, #MeToo, opioid crisis, selfie,* and *woke*. In the same vein, the group's 2019 WOTY was *(my) pronouns*, which, Ben Zimmer wrote in a news release, "speaks to how the personal expression of gender identity has become an increasing part of our shared discourse." Winning Word of the Year *and* Word of the Decade was like *Titanic* sweeping the Oscars. "2019 Word of the Year is '(My) Pronouns,' Word of the Decade is Singular 'They' as Voted by American Dialect Society," *American Dialect Society*, January 3, 2020, https://americandialect.org/wp-content/uploads/2019-Word-of-the-Year-PRESS-RELEASE.pdf.

190 **usual event-related spikes:** Two more spikes occurred after the dictionary addition. The singer Sam Smith adopted the pronouns *they/them*. And the American Psychological Association endorsed singular *they* because "it is inclusive of all people and helps writers avoid making assumptions about gender."

191 **ages-old indefinite pronoun use:** As in, to quote Merriam's made-up example sentences, "You know what *they* say" and "People can do what *they* want."

191 ***They*'s leg up was:** The fact that a pronoun is shifting at all is linguistically remarkable. *They* is younger than *I*, *we*, and *you*, but it still dates to circa 1175, according to the *OED*. The last big pronoun shift in English was *you* going singular in the late thirteenth century.

191 **In 2018, Kirby Conrod:** Other academic studies found a correlation between feelings about transgender people and acceptance of *they*. "Negative attitudes toward non-binary singular *they* were best predicted by prejudice against transgender people," one survey found, "while negative attitudes to generic singular *they* were similarly predicted both by . . . anti-transgender bias and by prescriptive grammar ideology." Lex Konnelly, Kirby Conrod, and Evan D. Bradley, "Non-Binary Singular *They*," in *The Routledge Handbook of Pronouns*, ed. Laura L. Paterson (New York: Routledge, 2024), 456–9.

191 **According to the Gender Census:** The survey, which reported more than 48,000 responses, asked the following question: "Supposing all pronouns were accepted by everyone without question and were easy to learn, which pronouns are you happy for people to use for you in English?" Participants could choose from fifteen answers. The top five responses: *They* with 75 percent approval, *he* (42 percent), *she* (36 percent), *it* (20 percent), and "avoid pronouns/use name as pronouns" (14 percent). The threefold growth of *it* in the previous decade reflected growing acceptance among people under 30. "Gender Census 2024: Worldwide Report," *Gender Census*, September 2024, https://www.gendercensus.com.

192 **number of schools had increased:** "Colleges and Universities that Allow Students to Have the Name and Pronouns They Use for Themselves on Campus Records," *Campus Pride*, July 27, 2024, https://www.campuspride.org/tpc/records/. Conservative reactions were sadly predictable. After Michigan enacted the change, one student chose "His Majesty." In response, another

tweeted: "I chose 'she' bc that's my ID. I didn't use the 'other' option to make fun of ppl bc then I would've had to put 'asshole.'" Under pressure from Republican legislators and the religious right, the University of Tennessee forced its Office of Diversity and Inclusion to remove from its website a list of alternative pronouns intended for gay, lesbian, and transgender students.

192 **New high-scoring, strategy-shifting:** The words would be new in North American Scrabble, that is. ZE already was in the international-English Scrabble lexicon, edited by the British publisher Collins, though XE was not. (Words are capitalized in Scrabble notation.)

192 **"It's time to realize that:** Stephanie Burt, "Kim, Caitlyn, and the People We Want to See," *New Yorker*, July 27, 2015, https://www.newyorker.com/culture/cultural-comment/kim-caitlyn-and-the-people-we-want-to-see.

193 **And, according to trans writer:** Wilkinson said that while *ze* was preferred to *they*, "possession was weird." "It was 'hir,' pronounced like 'here,' or 'zir'—'Ze walked into the room, is that hir bottle, or zir bottle? It was awkward. It was about asking people to navigate a secret language that most people didn't understand." Stamper, "'They' Did It!"

193 **In its 2014 obituary:** Bruce Weber, "Leslie Feinberg, Writer and Transgender Activist, Dies at 65," *New York Times*, November 29, 2014, https://www.nytimes.com/2014/11/25/nyregion/leslie-feinberg-writer-and-transgender-activist-dies-at-65.html.

193 **A remembrance of Feinberg:** Shauna Miller, "The Importance of Leslie Feinberg," *The Atlantic*, November 17, 2014, https://www.theatlantic.com/entertainment/archive/2014/11/the-importance-of-leslie-feinberg/382852/.

195 **"The way pronouns affect:** In *Steering the Craft*, a book about writing, Ursula K. Le Guin wrote:

> My use of *their* is socially motivated and, if you like, politically correct: a deliberate response to the socially and politically significant banning of our genderless pronoun by language legislators enforcing the notion that the male sex is the only one that counts. I consistently break a rule I consider to be not only fake but pernicious. I know what I'm doing and why.

Ursula K. Le Guin, *Steering the Craft: A 21st-Century Guide to Sailing the Sea of Story* (New York: Harper Perennial, 2015).

195 **Despite a push for:** Ian Spiegelman, "Why is the Term 'Latinx' Such a Loser Among Hispanic Voters?" *Los Angeles Magazine*, December 6, 2021, https://lamag.com/featured/why-is-the-term-latinx-such-a-loser-among-hispanic-voters; Miami Herald Editorial Board, "The 'Latinx Community' Doesn't Want to be Called 'Latinx.' Just Drop It, Progressives," *Miami Herald*, December 7, 2021, https://www.miamiherald.com/opinion/editorials/article256374737.html; Luis Noe-Nustamante, Gracie Martinez, and Mark Hugo Lopez, "Latinx Awareness Has Doubled Among U.S. Hispanics Since 2019, but Only 4% Use It," *Pew Research*, September 12, 2024, https://www.pewresearch.org/race-and-ethnicity/2024/09/12/latinx-awareness-has-doubled-among-u-s-hispanics-since-2019-but-only-4-percent-use-it/.

195 **Emerging in its place:** Marina E. Franco, "Latine is the New Latinx," *Axios*, April 11, 2024, https://www.axios.com/2024/04/11/latino-latinx-latine-hispanic-term-explainer.

195 **Because new pronouns:** Here's a counterexample from a different society. In Sweden, *hen* was among 13,000 words added to one of the Swedish Academy's official dictionaries in 2015. *Hen* was created in the 1960s for the same reasons English speakers have created pronouns. *Hen*, though, was a good fit in Swedish because it scanned nicely with *han* for *he* and *hon* for *she*. While its use was by no means widespread, and was still a subject of eye-rolling and even fist-shaking, "It can now be found in official texts, court rulings, media texts and books, and has begun to lose some of its feminist-activist connotation," AFP reported. "Sweden Adds Gender-Neutral Pronoun to Dictionary," *AFP*, March 24, 2015, https://www.theguardian.com/world/2015/mar/24/sweden-adds-gender-neutral-pronoun-to-dictionary.

197 **The Linguistic Society of America:** *Katie Wood et al v. Florida Department of Education et al*, 24-11239, "Brief of Amicus Curiae Linguistic Society of America in Support of Appellee," (11th Cir. 2024).

197 **Dua Saleh, a Sudanese American:** Dua Saleh (@doitlikedua), Twitter, October 11, 2020, https://twitter.com/doitlikedua/status/1315366612598480897; Lou Delaney, "Dua Saleh Talks Transmuting Dysphoria Into Spellbinding Music," *Complex*, June 8, 2022, https://www.complex.com/music/a/loudelaney/dua-saleh.

198 **The University of Texas student newspaper:** Alyssa Weinstein, "Peers for Pride Celebrates 10-Year Anniversary," *Daily Texan*, April 10, 2019, https://web.archive.org/web/20190411135654/https://www.dailytexanonline.com/2019/04/10/peers-for-pride-celebrates-10-year-anniversary.

199 **a 2014 drama by Taylor Mac:** In 2023, the *New York Times* called *Hir* one of the "most influential works of postwar queer literature." In it, a transgender character uses the pronouns *ze* and *hir*. The *Times* writer noted the choice parenthetically and moved on. "When, at the play's end, ze approaches hir helpless father with a gesture of care, *Hir* dares to hope that truly radical change may yet walk hand in hand with tenderness." Compare that with a 2015 story in the *Times Magazine* by Dashka Slater about a trans teen named Sasha who was set on fire while riding a bus. The story included an elaborate explanation about pronouns. "Telling Sasha's story also poses a linguistic challenge, because English doesn't offer a ready-made way to talk about people who identify as neither male nor female. Sasha prefers 'they,' 'it' or the invented gender-neutral pronoun 'xe.' The *New York Times* does not use these terms to refer to individuals." Slater explained to the paper's public editor, Margaret Sullivan, that her editors rejected her original approach to use Sasha's preferred pronoun, *xe*, so she wrote the piece using no pronouns. Still, change at the newspaper hasn't been complete. The *Times* caught flak in 2022 for a story that mentioned but didn't use the pronouns—*e*, *eir*, and *em*—preferred by Maia Kobabe, the author of the bestselling graphic memoir *Gender Queer*. Sara Holdren et al, "The 25 Most Influential Works of Postwar Queer Literature," *New York Times Style Magazine*, June 22, 2023, https://

www.nytimes.com/2023/06/22/t-magazine/queer-postwar-books-plays-poems.html; Dashka Slater, "The Fire on the 57 Bus in Oakland," *New York Times Magazine*, January 29, 2015, https://www.nytimes.com/2015/02/01/magazine/the-fire-on-the-57-bus-in-oakland.html; Margaret Sullivan, "The Times and Transgender Issues (Part 1 of 2): On Pronouns," *New York Times*, February 11, 2015, https://archive.nytimes.com/publiceditor.blogs.nytimes.com/2015/02/11/the-times-and-transgender-issues-part-one-of-two-on-pronouns/; Alexandra Alter, "How a Debut Graphic Memoir Became the Most Banned Book in the Country," *New York Times*, May 1, 2022, https://www.nytimes.com/2022/05/01/books/maia-kobabe-gender-queer-book-ban.html.

199 **With editing help from Emily:** I cut one quotation—from a poem by José Edmundo Ocampo Reyes, "The Origin of the Specious," published in *The Hudson Review* in 2005—that asks the reader to do too much work but is lovely. "Tomorrow, new specimens will be discovered: / perhaps the gender-neutral pronoun / that has eluded us, or tenses and cases / to account for time travel's permutations."

199 **I also wrote a usage note:**

♦ Since the dawn of the English language, the absence of a third-person singular pronoun of common gender has posed a problem: What's the best way to refer to a singular noun antecedent that can apply to either the male or female gender? Despite the wails of some grammarians, the plural pronouns *they, their, them,* and *themselves* have been used this way since the 14th century. But beginning at least in the late 1800s, people have coined third-person singular replacements for *he* or *she*—such as *ou, se, hiser, e, ne, ve, thon,* and dozens more. These efforts centered on antecedent agreement. More recently, the discussion shifted to gender, or the indistinctness or fluidity thereof; some people choose not to be identified as male or female. Writers, activists, colleges and universities, government agencies, and transgender, genderqueer, or nonbinary individuals have adopted, suggested, or required the use of various gender-neutral, or nonbinary, pronouns. While their use in mainstream media remains limited, the most frequently used and discussed gender-neutral pronoun substitutes for *he/him/his* and *she/her/hers* have been *ze/hir/hirs* and *xe/xem/xyr*.

199 **But as of 2025, they hadn't been added:** "*Ze* I'm afraid seems to be languishing," Emily Brewster told me. "It's just not used frequently without commentary in running text. I keep checking and it's just not there yet."

200 **When it was time to trim:** *Thon* hung around thanks in part to periodic lobbying by a music and theater critic and Brandeis University professor, Caldwell Titcomb. In 1955, Titcomb wrote a letter to the *New York Times Magazine* responding to an essay by Albert H. Morehead about gaps in the English language. "For the clumsy 'he or she' (and the attendant 'his or her'), deplored by Mr. Morehead, I see no reason for not adopting the century-old word 'thon,' designed for precisely this purpose." Twenty-three

years later, *Times* columnist Tom Wicker, who had written about the "His or Her Problem," said that Caldwell had explained *thon* to him "with considerable erudition." Albert H. Morehead, "English at a Loss for Words," *New York Times Magazine*, September 11, 1955; Caldwell Titcomb, "He, She and 'Thon,'" *New York Times Magazine*, October 2, 1955; Tom Wicker, "He or She or What?" *New York Times*, April 18, 1978; Tom Wicker, "More About He/She and Thon," *New York Times*, May 14, 1978.

200 **a Harvard first-year:** Colleges and universities were slowly replacing the gender-specific *freshman* with the gender-neutral *first-year*. Merriam editor Serenity Carr added it to New Words, noting that it was used at the women's college she attended. It made the dictionary in 2023, with a first-use date of 1986.

200 **If young Americans were:** I found a perfect representation of the changing acceptance in a (since-deleted) Twitter post by a college student in 2017: "My 12 yr old sister wanted to know what the pronoun 'Ze' meant. I said well some people don't consider themselves 'She' or 'He' so . . . There is this new pronoun 'Ze'! and she said 'that's cool' and THAT WAS THAT."

200 **If defining a particular word:** If I've learned anything reporting on pronouns, it's that people will never stop having Strong Opinions about them—and also never stop inventing them. When the linguist John McWhorter wrote a *Times* column endorsing singular *they*, the paper was flooded with letters from readers pro and con, and also convinced they'd solved the centuries-old dilemma. "The most natural coinages would be those that form a set with 'she' and 'he' such as 'que' ('kwee'), 're' and 'xe,'" Simon Marcus of Oakland, California, wrote. "Could anything be closer to the heart of the L.G.B.T.Q. community than the first of those?" John McWhorter, "Gender Pronouns Are Changing. It's Exhilarating," *New York Times*, September 24, 2021, https://www.nytimes.com/2021/09/21/opinion/gender-pronouns-they.html; "Singular 'They' and Alternatives," *New York Times*, October 10, 2021, https://www.nytimes.com/2021/10/09/opinion/letters/gender-neutral-pronouns.html.

11
entry

202 **"the most modern electrical:** "New Dictionary Building," *Springfield Daily Republican*.

202 **a cone of silence:** I drafted a definition with my new sense, "an imposed state of silence." and the existing scientific one, and submitted three illustrative quotations: <"I have nothing to say, obviously," Jeffrey Kessler, a lawyer for the players association, said on his way out of the meeting. "We're in a *cone of silence*." —Howard Fendrich, Associated Press, 19 Feb. 2011> <Disney said that the *cone of silence* around characters' out-of-costume identities is part of the park's charm. —Sarah Kaplan, *Washington Post* (online), 9 June 2015> <Historically, police chiefs in L.A. and elsewhere have been part of the *cone of silence* in cases of deadly use of force. —*Los Angeles Times*, 12 Jan. 2016>

I also wrote a supplemental information note:

♦ The term **cone of silence** (sense 1 above) descends from a running gag on the U.S. television spy spoof *Get Smart* (1965-1970). The Cone of Silence was a clear plastic dome that descended from the ceiling and covered a desk to enable characters to talk privately; it usually malfunctioned. Before *Get Smart*, sound-canceling cones of silence were featured in a 1955 episode of the U.S. television series *Science Fiction Theatre* (1955-1957) and in the science-fiction novel *Dune*, which was serialized from 1963-1965. Today, a *cone of silence* usually refers to an enforced silence stemming from an order, agreement, or conspiracy to stay quiet.

203 **I helped Emily Brewster:** "A New Meaning of 'Liftoff,'" *Merriam-Webster*, undated, https://www.merriam-webster.com/wordplay/liftoff-meaning-by-federal-reserve. The new senses had not made the dictionary as of early 2025.

204 **Seventy-five years earlier:** "In days such as these," a local paper wrote, "it is comforting to know that Springfield is as well known for its dictionary as for its rifle!" "New Home of Webster's," *Springfield Sunday Republican*, June 16, 1940.

204 **I considered myself a *smashmouth*-ologist:** Stefan Fatsis, "Smash-Mouth: Sick of the Term? Sorry, There's No Stopping It," *Wall Street Journal*, February 16, 2001, https://www.wsj.com/articles/SB982273416933786092.

204 **I'd also reported that:** The OED labeled this sense of *smash-mouth*—"passionate kissing"—as rare. It included just one citation, from the *Wisconsin State Journal* in 1965, which reported that the term *making out* "gave way among the cute set to 'kissy face' a few years ago, but today's students are calling it 'smash mouth'."

205 ***Smashmouth* turned up in:** *Smashmouth* already was in the OWL and *Unabridged*—"characterized by brute force and an absence of finesse or trickery : HARD-NOSED"—but without any illustrative quotations. William Safire cited little ol' me in his "On Language" column a month after my *Journal* story. And a month after that, my colleague Joe Flint and I used the word in an autopsy of a violence-obsessed new league, the XFL. "At a time when TV is stooping for viewers ... the XFL fit right in," we wrote. "It promised 'smashmouth' football and extra-sexy cheerleaders." The OWL recorded 1975 as the first known date of use. I found two newspaper articles from 1971, in Toronto and Lompoc, California. Ben Zimmer antedated the first known use to a 1968 story in the *El Paso* (Texas) *Herald-Post*, "Football-osophy of George Hummer, Arizona State Center: 'The Name of the Game is Smash Mouth.'" William Safire, "Smashmouth," *New York Times Magazine*, March 25, 2001, https://www.nytimes.com/2001/03/25/magazine/the-way-we-live-now-3-25-01-on-language-smashmouth.html; Stefan Fatsis and Joe Flint, "How the XFL Football League Became One of the Biggest Flops in TV History," *Wall Street Journal*, April 23, 2001, https://www.wsj.com/articles/SB987984355871235792; Ben Zimmer, "Pigskin Parlance," *New York Times Magazine*, January 28, 2011, https://www.nytimes.com/2011/01/30/magazine/30FOB-onlanguage-t.html.

206 **But it dated to at least the 1970s:** Dorothy Storck, "Thomas Tryon Refuses to Play Just One Role," *Philadelphia Inquirer*, November 17, 1977;

Ben Zimmer, "Roots of the 'Safe Space' Controversy," *Wall Street Journal*, November 13, 2015, https://www.wsj.com/articles/roots-of-the-safe-space-controversy-1447429433.

207 **The author of the Thomas Tryon:** Dorothy Storck, "Of Rage and Invaded Space," *Philadelphia Inquirer*, February 27, 1981.

207 **The first seemingly explicit:** Jane See White, "Hope for the Hopeless," *Associated Press*, May 17, 1981.

208 **an October 1969 speech:** Gerry Raker, "Pierce Offers Understanding of Black Youth in Education," *Poughkeepsie Journal*, October 30, 1969.

208 **Pierce explained the term further:** Chester Pierce, "Offensive Mechanisms," in *The Black Seventies*, ed. F. Barbour (Boston: Porter Sargent, 1970), 266. The *OED* dated the earliest use of *micro-aggression* to Pierce's 1970 book. The antedating to the 1969 speech was reported by Yale Law School librarian and *Yale Book of Quotations* editor Fred R. Shapiro on the American Dialect Society's discussion board. Fred R. Shapiro, "Antedating of 'Microaggression,'" *American Dialect Society Mailing List*, January 19, 2025, https://listserv.linguistlist.org/pipermail/ads-l/2025-January/166419.html.

208 **"Well, *microaggression* is where:** Allison Keyes, "Travelers Prep for TSA Frisks," *Tell Me More*, NPR, Washington, DC, November 23, 2010, https://www.npr.org/2010/11/23/131542054/travelers-prep-for-tsa-frisks.

209 **"A '*microaggression*,' in case:** James Taranto, "Ivory Sour," *Wall Street Journal*, January 6, 2015, https://www.wsj.com/articles/ivory-sour-1420582049.

211 **I added *fashy* [footnote]:** <An articulate and well-dressed former football player with prom-king good looks and a "*fashy*" (as in fascism) haircut—long on top, buzzed on the sides—Spencer has managed to seize on an extraordinary presidential election to give overt racism a new veneer of radical chic. —Josh Harkinson, *Mother Jones* (online), 27 Oct. 2016>. Over the next year, the number of Google News hits for *fashy* more than doubled, with mentions in the *Washington Post*, *The Guardian*, *The Tennessean*, *The Atlantic*, the Southern Poverty Law Center website, and many others.

212 **Spencer told reporter David Weigel:** David Weigel, "'Cuckservative'—The Conservative Insult of the Month, Explained," *Washington Post*, July 29, 2015, https://www.washingtonpost.com/news/the-fix/wp/2015/07/29/cuckservative-the-conservative-insult-of-the-month-explained/.

212 **"The Breitbart alt-right:** Ben Shapiro, "The Breitbart Alt-Right Just Took Over the GOP," *Washington Post*, August 18, 2016, https://www.washingtonpost.com/posteverything/wp/2016/08/18/the-breitbart-alt-right-just-took-over-the-gop/.

213 **And *alt-right*'s bedmates:** *Cuck* already was in Merriam as a truncation of *cuckold*, "a man whose wife is unfaithful." A new sense later was added, explaining how use expanded from the narrowly political to a more generic insult: "a weak or submissive man → often used as an insulting and contemptuous term for a man who has politically progressive or moderate views."

215 **The process with *alt-right*:** In early 2021, just after the January 6 insurrection, *alt-right* was in the top 7 percent of Merriam lookups. By 2024, it was still

popping up in news stories but had vanished as a distinct movement—or had gone mainstream: "What was once the alt-right . . . is now Trump's Republican Party." Becca Rothfeld, "'Black Pill' Is a Disturbing Look at How 'Meme Magic' Captured the GOP," *Washington Post*, July 10, 2024, https://www.washingtonpost.com/books/2024/07/10/black-pill-elle-reeve-review/.

12
social media

216 **"We thank you for your letter:** Mazyck Ravenel, a professor of bacteriology and preventive medicine, was concerned about the sense of the word that Merriam today labels *dated, now offensive*, first used in 1910, of "a person affected with mild intellectual disability." A modern usage note explains that *moron*, as well as *idiot* and *imbecile*, "were formerly used as technical descriptors in medical, educational, and regulatory contexts." The first use of the colloquial sense of "a foolish or stupid person" is attributed to the humorist Robert Benchley, who referred to a "high class moron" in *Vanity Fair* in 1917.

217 **In the 1990s, the toy and game:** The expurgation began when a reader complained about the inclusion of *jew*, defined as "to bargain with," in the Scrabble dictionary. After a letter-writing campaign led by the Anti-Defamation League, Hasbro, which owns Scrabble and licenses Merriam to publish the Scrabble dictionary, ordered the removal of around two hundred "offensive" words. Scrabble players howled, and Hasbro allowed Merriam to publish a list of words, including the naughty ones, without definitions for use in club and tournament play. In 2020, one of the organizations that oversees competitive Scrabble in North America removed from its word list words deemed slurs.

217 **In 2009, Merriam endured:** The first sense of *marriage* in the OWL was later revised to remove any mention of gender or sexual preference: "the state of being united as spouses in a consensual and contractual relationship recognized by law." A usage note explained that the "understanding" of *marriage* "continues to be highly controversial" and "is not an issue to be resolved by dictionaries." Rather, Merriam said, the act of marriage (not the definition) "involves cultural traditions, religious beliefs, legal rulings, and ideas about fairness and basic human rights." The note cited the Supreme Court's 2015 decision in *Obergefell v. Hodges* legalizing gay marriage and, to quiet those ready to scream at the lexicon anew, concluded: "The definition of *marriage* shown here is intentionally broad enough to encompass the different types of marriage that are currently recognized in varying cultures, places, religions, and systems of law." For more on the *marriage* incident, see Stamper, *Word by Word*, 230-54.

217 **In the aftermath of the 2018:** Bre Payton, "Merriam-Webster Online Dictionary Changes Definition Of 'Assault Rifle' To One That Matches Gun Control Pushers," *The Federalist*, March 31, 2018, https://thefederalist.com/2018/03/31/merriam-webster-online-dictionary-changes-definition-assault-rifle/.

217 **And in 2023, a California man:** "I am going to shoot up and bomb your offices for lying and creating fake definitions in order to pander to the tranny mafia. Boys aren't girls, and girls aren't boys," the man wrote in one message. "California Man Sentenced for Threatening Merriam-Webster with Anti-LGBTQ Violence," *United States Attorney's Office, District of Massachusetts*, April 14, 2023, https://www.justice.gov/usao-ma/pr/california-man-sentenced-threatening-merriam-webster-anti-lgbtq-violence.

218 **"They didn't care about:** Stamper, *Word by Word*, 248.

218 **But—accepts gold statuette:** Full disclosure, I wasn't the first lexicographer to notice this use of *run*; it's the seventh sense in Paul Dickson's authoritative baseball dictionary. Ben Zimmer and I hunted for earliest usage. Zimmer found this headline about a 1908 game between Argenta and Poplar Bluff of the Arkansas State League: "Poplar Bluff Captain Run From Game." ("Captain Kelly of Poplar Bluff became obstreperous during the furious fire from the Argenta bats, and was ousted from the game by Umpire Camphor.") I found a 1905 quote attributed to Pittsburgh Pirates owner Barney Dreyfuss, about catcher Heine Peitz: "Well, the very first day he worked for me the umpire ran him off the line just as soon as he opened his mouth." But I think the inclusion of *off* negates the stand-alone usage of *run*, so 1908 it is, for now. Paul Dickson, *The Dickson Baseball Dictionary, Third Edition* (New York: W. W. Norton, 2009), 724; "Easy Picking for Shamrocks," *Arkansas Democrat* (Little Rock, Arkansas), April 29, 1908; "Afraid of 'Hey Barney' Signs," *Sunday Star* (Washington, DC), November 5, 1905.

For another lexicographic toughie, *go*, I proposed adding a twenty-first intransitive verb sense: the hockey term meaning to fight. <"Bobby got cold-cocked right at the start of the fight. Down he went to his knees. He was helped to the penalty box, got in the penalty box, then, as soon as he got out, wanted to *go* again." —Don Cherry, *Hockey Stories, Part 2*, 2011>. As of early 2025, it hadn't been added.

219 **I'd flagged *sheeple* while doomscrolling:** *Doomscrolling* appears to have been coined around 2016 but didn't get wide use until early in the pandemic in 2020. Merriam added it in 2023: "to spend excessive time online scrolling . . . through news or other content that makes one feel sad, anxious, angry, etc."

219 **"The leaders of tech:** Kara Swisher, "As Trumplethinskin Lets Down his Hair for Tech, Shame on Silicon Valley for Climbing the Tower in Silence," *Vox*, December 12, 2016, https://www.vox.com/2016/12/12/13917982/trump-hair-tech-summit-shame-silicon-valley.

219 **"The People, as ever:** "Anything," in this instance, was the BBC tolerating an announcer whose speech included the "intrusive R"—the British habit of inserting the /r/ sound in certain words before a vowel sound, as in "*lawr* and order."

220 **The next cit was from a 1949 book:** Ernest Rogers used *sheeple* in his newspaper column two years earlier: "I call 'em 'sheeple.' There's no use thumbing through your dictionary because the word isn't there . . . With

someone else to do their thinking they have nothing to do but to follow blindly and this they do with a fervor befitting a better fate. That leaders are not always to be trusted never enters their feeble minds. That they may be betrayed is a probability that never disturbs their equanimity. They know nothing but to follow and to accept such crumbs as may be tossed to them from the master's table." He added: "The 'sheeple' pay the bills and form the audience for strange prophets who prey on their gullibility. The German and Italian 'sheeple' made Hitler and Mussolini possible." Ernest Rogers, "Maybe You Should Know More About 'Sheeple,'" *Atlanta Journal*, March 4, 1947.

220 **Then it was discovered:** Michael Browning, "Patriots' Push for Tax Revolt," *Miami Herald*, February 21, 1983; Bob Davis, "In New Hampshire, 'Live Free or Die' Is More than a Motto," *Wall Street Journal*, February 27, 1984; L. Kent Wolgamott, "Motor City Madman at Z-92's Anniversary Bash," *Lincoln Star Journal* (Neb.), August 14, 1998; Clint Rainey, "New York *Times* Demands Sheeple Wake Up and Quit Worshipping Breakfast," *Grub Street*, May 23, 2016, https://www.grubstreet.com/2016/05/nyt-breakfast-hit-piece.html; Randall Munroe, "Sheeple," *xkcd*, July 15, 2009, https://xkcd.com/610/; Munroe, "Wake Up Sheeple," *xkcd*, February 6, 2012, https://xkcd.com/1013/.

223 **"The dictionary takes a dig:** Rachel Martin, "Merriam-Webster Adds 'Sheeple' As An Official Word," *Morning Edition*, Washington: NPR, May 1, 2017, https://www.npr.org/2017/05/01/526349470/merriam-webster-adds-sheeple-as-an-official-word/1000.

225 **a blogger from a broey sports website:** Merriam added *bro-ey* or *broey* in 2018, an adjective meaning like a *bro*, "a young male who is part of a group of similar male friends stereotypically characterized as hearty, athletic, self-confident, party-loving, etc."

228 **post-truth and post-fact:** My draft of *post-fact*:

> **post-fact** *adjective* : of or relating to a condition in which objectively demonstrable assertions, statements, or information are ignored, disputed, or dismissed

And some illustrative quotations:

> <... [Trump and Putin] have constructed and now inhabit *post-fact* worlds, in which truth is malleable and disposable. In this subjective arena you can continue to assert that, say, thousands of Muslims in New Jersey celebrated the attacks of September 11th, 2001, or that Russian troops did not invade Ukraine, despite overwhelming evidence to the contrary. —*The Economist*, 23 March 2016> <How can America answer a set of generational challenges when the leadership class is dysfunctional, political conversation has entered a *post-fact* era and the political parties are divided on racial lines—set to blow at a moment's notice? —David Brooks, *New York Times*, 12 July 2016> <"We seem to be in a *post-fact* era, you know." "*Post-fact*—how about no facts?" —Joy Behar and Whoopi Goldberg, *The View*, 29 June 2016>

228 **"Right now there are:** Katherine Rosman, "Move Over, Wikipedia. Dictionaries Are Hot Again," *New York Times*, February 11, 2017, https://

www.nytimes.com/2017/02/11/fashion/merriam-webster-dictionary-social-media-politics.html.

228 More broadly, Noah Webster: Morse, "Publishing the Dictionary," 627.

229 "The year is 2017: Kitty Chandler (@mightybattlecat), "The year is 2017. America is a tire fire," Twitter, January 24, 2017, https://twitter.com/mightybattlecat/status/824023324720328704.

229 as Michael Jordan said: After years of denial and debate, Jordan in the 2020 documentary *The Last Dance* confirmed saying "Republicans buy sneakers, too." "I don't think that statement needs to be corrected because I said it in jest on a bus with [teammates] Horace Grant and Scottie Pippen," Jordan said. "It was thrown off the cuff." Laura Wagner, "'Republicans Buy Sneakers, Too,'" *Slate*, July 28, 2016, https://slate.com/culture/2016/07/did-michael-jordan-really-say-republicans-buy-sneakers-too.html; Tim Bontemps, "Michael Jordan Stands Firm on 'Republicans Buy Sneakers, Too' Quote, Says It Was Made in Jest," *ESPN*, May 4, 2020, https://www.espn.com/nba/story/_/id/29130478/michael-jordan-stands-firm-republicans-buy-sneakers-too-quote-says-was-made-jest.

230 "Merriam-Webster is at it: Madison Medeiros, "Merriam-Webster Twitter Rolls Out History of Blackmail, Confirms Superior Shade Status," *Refinery29*, May 15, 2017, https://www.refinery29.com/en-us/2017/05/154573/merriam-webster-trolls-trump-blackmail-tweet.

230 linked to a blog post: "Is It OK to Use 'Mad' to Mean 'Angry'? *Merriam-Webster*, undated, https://www.merriam-webster.com/grammar/can-mad-mean-angry.

231 In the past, brands like Merriam: Gabriel Roth, "No One Cares How I Feel, According to Merriam-Webster," *Slate*, September 8, 2016, https://slate.com/human-interest/2016/09/merriam-webster-dictionary-tweeted-no-one-cares-about-how-you-feel.html.

233 It added a warning label: In 2016, a year before my *sheeple* controversy, Oxford landed in a similar public-relations mess. A Canadian grad student named Michael Oman-Reagan noticed and tweeted screenshots of verbal illustrations for some words in his Apple look-up, based on the *New Oxford American Dictionary*, that were sexist: "a rabid feminist"; "the rising shrill of women's voices"; "a nagging wife"; "I will never really fathom the female psyche." Taking a page from Merriam's snarky social media ops, Oxford replied, "If only there were a word to describe how strongly you felt about feminism . . ." and defended itself by saying the snippets came from "real-world use." After the spat went viral, Oxford apologized and promised to review the example sentence for *rabid*, noting that "rabid fan" had the highest frequency in its corpus. But, like *Slate*'s Gabriel Roth, Oman-Reagan was harassed online, while "men's-rights" activists defended Oxford. The larger questions were more consequential than with the *sheeple* quote: Should the dictionary always reflect the most popular usage, even if it's offensive? Should it ignore offensive usage completely? Or should it mark certain uses of words like *shrill*, *rabid*, or *hysterical* as pejorative? As we saw with the n-word, dictionaries have revised entries for racist language, and they've updated standards for gendering in definitions and example sentences. *Rabid* was another reminder of the need for vigilance in monitoring the language. "We need to know that the dictionary, as an institution, has a cultural power beyond the sum of its parts," Oxford's Katherine Connor Martin told *The New Yorker*. "And that does carry with it a responsibility to realize that we exist within that tension, and to not always hide behind the idea of descriptivist lexicography." Nora Caplan-Bricker, "Should Dictionaries Do More to Confront Sexism?" *New Yorker*, February 23, 2016, https://www.newyorker.com/books/page-turner/should-dictionaries-do-more-to-confront-sexism.

13
news

237 **In 1962, a young African American:** William Melvin Kelley, "If You're Woke You Dig It," *New York Times Magazine*, May 20, 1962.

237 *ralph bunche* **("to talk one's way:** Ralph Bunche was a diplomat and civil rights leader who played a central role in the creation of the United Nations after World War II and in subsequent U.N. decolonization and peacekeeping efforts. He was the first African American to receive the Nobel Peace Prize, for mediation work in Israel in the 1940s. The idiomatic use of his name also appeared in *The Third Ear: A Black Glossary*, a 1971 book by a Black Chicago school principal, Hermese Roberts, published by the English-Language Institute of America. On three-by-five index cards, Roberts collected thousands of examples of Black slang, which she culled to around four hundred, including now-familiar terms like *do rag*, *kick one's butt* ("to floor or baffle; e.g. That test sure *kicked my butt*."), and *wasted* for drunk. The *Chicago Tribune Magazine* reported that the Institute commissioned the glossary so companies could "help . . . executives and supervisors communicate with their black employes." But in her book's introduction, Roberts revealed a more humanistic intent. She explained that *third ear* was used by African storytellers to encourage listeners to pay attention. "Why would anyone need a 'third ear'? Could it be that we have used our two ears to listen to the communication-network variety of English for so long we have unconsciously shut ourselves off from hearing, understanding, appreciating, and enjoying the colorful language varieties minted and used by specific groups of people?" *New York Times* columnist Russell Baker crafted his own "White Glossary." Baker defined *Ralph Bunche* as "One of the few persons of any race you can think of who could move in next door without lowering real-estate values." Good lord. Hermese E. Roberts, *The Third Ear: A Black Glossary* (Chicago: English-Language Institute of America, 1971); Tom Hall, "Black Talk," *Chicago Tribune Magazine*, September 20, 1970; Russell Baker, "White Glossary," *New York Times*, November 22, 1970.

238 **"The American Negro feels:** The illustrations accompanying Kelley's *Times* essay were by Carl Rose, who drew for *The New Yorker* and other publications. "That was *my* fox, man, and you were copping my taste and

grit," one guy says to another, who replies, "Don't jump salty on me." Looking on, with a quill in his right hand and his left scratching his forehead, is none other than Noah Webster. Carl Rose, BTW, drew one of the most famous cartoons in *New Yorker* history. The 1928 panel shows a mother and daughter at dinner. "It's broccoli, dear," the mother says. "I say it's spinach, and I say the hell with it," the girl replies. The caption was written by E. B. White. "I say it's spinach"—or the full phrase, or just "spinach"—entered the popular vernacular, used by Irving Berlin in a Broadway song and by the writers Alexander Woolcott, S. J. Perelman, and others.

238 **As James Baldwin would write:** James Baldwin, "If Black English Isn't a Language, What Is?" *New York Times*, July 29, 1979, https://www.nytimes.com/2010/09/26/opinion/eq-baldwin.html.

238 **Kelley went to Harvard:** For more about William Melvin Kelley's life and career, see Kathryn Schulz, "The Lost Giant of American Literature," *New Yorker*, January 22, 2018, https://www.newyorker.com/magazine/2018/01/29/the-lost-giant-of-american-literature.

238 **A few years after his death:** Elijah C. Watson, "The Origin Of Woke: William Melvin Kelley Is The 'Woke' Godfather We Never Acknowledged," *Okay Player*, December 6, 2022, https://www.okayplayer.com/originals/what-does-woke-mean-history-origins-william-melvin-kelley.html.

239 **"I advise everybody to be:** "Lead Belly—'Scottsboro Boys,'" Smithsonian Folkways Recordings, YouTube, accessed October 21, 2024, https://www.youtube.com/watch?v=VrXfkPViFIE. The first known example of this sense of woke in print is believed to be an article in the March 1943 issue of *The Atlantic* by J. Saunders Redding, who was the first African American faculty member in the Ivy League. In an essay about about an "awakening" among Black workers in the South to the right to equal treatment, he wrote: "They mean what a Negro United Mine Workers official in West Virginia told me in 1940: 'Let me tell you, buddy, waking up is a damn sight harder than going to sleep, but we'll stay woke up longer.'" J. Saunders Redding, "A Negro Speaks for His People," *The Atlantic*, March 1943, https://www.theatlantic.com/magazine/archive/1943/03/a-negro-speaks-for-his-people/657170/.

239 **Standalone *woke* was around:** Damon Young, "In Defense of 'Woke,'" *New York Times*, November 29, 2019, https://www.nytimes.com/2019/11/29/opinion/woke-impeachment-trump.html.

239 **Another Black journalist:** Michael Harriot, "Weaponizing 'Woke': A Brief History of White Definitions," *The Root*, November 12, 2021, https://www.theroot.com/weaponizing-woke-an-brief-history-of-white-definitions-1848031729.

240 **When she argued against:** Nicole Holliday, "How 'Woke' Fell Asleep," *Oxford Dictionaries*, November 16, 2016, https://web.archive.org/web/20161227055631/http:/blog.oxforddictionaries.com/2016/11/woke/.

240 **"Wokeness Derails the Democrats":** Maureen Dowd, "Wokeness Derails the Democrats," *New York Times*, November 6, 2021, https://www.nytimes.com/2021/11/06/opinion/sunday/democrats-elections.html.

endnotes

240 **Dowd's conservative colleague:** Bret Stephens, "Why Wokeness Will Fail," *New York Times*, November 9, 2021, https://www.nytimes.com/2021/11/09/opinion/social-justice-america.html.

241 **"It's now intended to be:** Joel D. Anderson (@byjoelanderson), Twitter, January 9, 2022, https://twitter.com/byjoelanderson/status/1480219618706804742. Nikole Hannah-Jones, the Black journalist and author of *The 1619 Project*, another stalking horse for right-wing media, said this about *woke* on NPR's *Fresh Air* in 2021: "What does it mean? What are we saying when we say that? Are we saying that being anti-racist is bad? Are we . . . talking about Black people asking and fighting for justice as a bad thing, but we can't say that, so we use woke as this kind of catchall phrase? To me it's to really try to silence or diminish racial justice claims, people who are asking for racial justice. So I think many, many Black people hear it as a slur. One, we know that this is a term that was co-opted from Black people, that this is something that Black people were using. It became co-opted by conservatives in a way that is disparaging. I don't think that journalists should be using it. And I think when politicians and others use it, we should ask them to define what they mean, because when we're using terms like that, we are expecting people to fill in the blanks, and we're using terms like that because we don't want to be explicit about what it is that we're saying. And journalists should not be letting people get away with that. So I think it can be taken as a racist slur, yes." Terry Gross, "'1619 Project' Journalist Says Black People Shouldn't Be an Asterisk in U.S. History," *Fresh Air*, Philadelphia: WHYY, November 17, 2021, https://www.npr.org/transcripts/1056404654.

241 ***Woke's* mutation and migration:** By early 2025, *woke* entered what the linguist John McWhorter labeled a third phase with *woke right*, which emerged around 2022 and was largely confined to conservative online discourse. *Woke right* referred to beliefs, tactics, and, under the second Trump administration, policies centering on the purported victimization of straight, white Christians, mostly men. "Rather than applying specifically to the concerns of the left, 'woke' is now being used to refer more generally to a conspiracy-focused and punitive orientation to social change," McWhorter wrote. John McWhorter, "The Twisting Tale of 'Woke' Is the Story of the English Language," *New York Times*, February 20, 2025, https://www.nytimes.com/2025/02/20/opinion/the-long-strange-trail-of-woke.html.

241 ***Cancel* was coined by:** Clyde McGrady, "The Strange Journey of 'Cancel,' from a Black-Culture Punchline to a White-Grievance Watchword," *Washington Post*, April 2, 2021, https://www.washingtonpost.com/lifestyle/cancel-culture-background-black-culture-white-grievance/2021/04/01/2e42e4fe-8b24-11eb-aff6-4f720ca2d479_story.html.

242 ***Miscegenation* was created:** Bruce Handy, "On the Political Weaponization of Words: From 'Miscegenation' to 'Groomer,'" *LitHub*, September 15, 2022, https://lithub.com/on-the-political-weaponization-of-words-from-miscegenation-to-groomer/.

242 **Even *freedom* was cynically:** Dan Brooks, "American Freedom," *Defector*, April 8, 2025, https://defector.com/american-freedom.

243 Merriam flagged *woke*: "Stay Woke," *Merriam-Webster*, undated, https://www.merriam-webster.com/wordplay/woke-meaning-origin.

244 My birth year, 1963: Despite what you might read online, *phat* is not an acronym of "pretty hips and thighs," "pretty hot and tempting," or "pussy, hips, ass, and tits." Merriam defines *phat* as "highly attractive or gratifying : EXCELLENT" and the *OED* as "Of a person, esp. a woman: sexy, attractive" and "Esp. of music: excellent, admirable; fashionable, 'cool'." Its first cit is a 1963 *Time* magazine article about Black slang: "*Mellow, phat, stone, boss.* General adjectives of approval." "Beyond Greys," *Time*, August 2, 1963, https://time.com/archive/6807935/americana-beyond-greys/.

245 Ben Zimmer discovered: Ben Zimmer, "The Evolution of *Racism*," *The Atlantic*, September 4, 2020, https://www.theatlantic.com/culture/archive/2020/09/how-racism-made-its-way-into-dictionary-merriam-webster/615334/.

245 The editor went on: According to news reports, Kennedy Mitchum corresponded with a Merriam editor named Alex Chambers, whose emails were quoted at length in the *New York Times* and elsewhere. I'd never heard of an editor with that name—because none existed—so I asked a Merriam staffer about it. To protect the privacy of editors, especially in controversies that went public, Merriam had for a decade signed reader correspondence with a gender-neutral pseudonym; "Lee Goodrich" was another. Because having fake employees quoted in the *Times* might damage Merriam's credibility, "that policy ended yesterday," the staffer told me.

246 When Mitchum's campaign: Christine Hauser, "Merriam-Webster Revises 'Racism' Entry After Missouri Woman Asks for Changes," *New York Times*, June 10, 2020, https://www.nytimes.com/2020/06/10/us/merriam-webster-racism-definition.html.

246 "I'll spell it": "WHO Director-General's Remarks at the Media Briefing on 2019-nCoV on 11 February 2020," *World Health Organization*, February 11, 2020, https://www.who.int/director-general/speeches/detail/who-director-general-s-remarks-at-the-media-briefing-on-2019-ncov-on-11-february-2020; Ben Zimmer, "'Covid': The New Coinage That Defined 2020," *Wall Street Journal*, December 24, 2020, https://www.wsj.com/articles/covid-the-new-coinage-that-defined-2020-11608830903.

248 The rapid spread of both: I wrote about Merriam's fast addition of *covid* and other pandemic words, first in *Slate* right after the emergency update and later in the Dictionary Society of North America's journal. I also delivered a slideshow talk at the DSNA's 2021 conference, which was held virtually. Stefan Fatsis, "How COVID-19 Led Merriam-Webster to Make Its Fastest Update Ever," *Slate*, March 26, 2020, https://slate.com/culture/2020/03/coronavirus-merriam-webster-emergency-update.html; Stefan Fatsis, "Thirty-Four Days: Inside Merriam-Webster's Emergency Coronavirus Update," *Dictionaries: Journal of the Dictionary Society of North America* 42, no. 2 (2021), 45–56, https://muse.jhu.edu/article/843057.

248 *community spread* way back in 1903: I also found *community spread* in a 1945 journal article about . . . airborne disease transmission. The author, a Harvard scientist named William Firth Wells, discovered that tuberculosis could be transmitted via respiratory droplets. William Firth Wells, "Sanitary Ventilation by Radiant Disinfection," *Scientific Monthly* 60, no. 5 (May 1945), 332.

249 **The acronym first appeared:** The *OED* dated the first known usage of *AIDS* in print to an August 8, 1982, article in the *New York Times*. While reading the manuscript of this book, my friend and colleague Josh Levin alerted me to its use in a page-one story in the *Boston Globe* twelve days earlier. Antedating sleuths on the American Dialect Society's discussion board previously had unearthed the *Globe* citation and an even earlier one, in a letter from a doctor to a San Francisco gay newspaper in April 1982. After reading this note, *OED* editor Peter Gilliver updated the *AIDS* entry with the antedating. Robin Herman, "A Disease's Spread Provokes Anxiety," *New York Times*, August 8, 1982; Loretta McLaughlin, "New Illness Spreading, Officials Say," *Boston Globe*, July 27, 1982; Robert K. Bolan, M.D., "Poppers Clarification," *Bay Area Reporter*, April 8, 1982.

250 *Long-haulers* **referred to:** Ben Zimmer, "'Long-Hauler': When Covid-19's Symptoms Last and Last," *Wall Street Journal*, January 1, 2021, https://www.wsj.com/articles/long-hauler-when-covid-19s-symptoms-last-and-last-11609524809.

251 **Its editors and marketers produced:** "Word of the Year 2020," *Oxford Languages*, undated, https://languages.oup.com/word-of-the-year/2020/.

251 **Kate Wild at Oxford said:** Oxford posted an article about World War I words, with a timeline featuring one hundred of them, including the verb *machine-gun, war effort, shell shock, over the top, camouflage, air raid, trench coat, home front, lost generation* (attributed to Gertrude Stein, first used by Ernest Hemingway on the title page of *The Sun Also Rises* in 1926), and *cooties* meaning body lice and, starting in the 1950s, "an imaginary germ said to have infected a person of the opposite sex or someone considered socially undesirable." "The language of World War I," *Oxford English Dictionary*, undated, https://www.oed.com/discover/the-language-of-world-war-1.

252 **Covid words vanished:** Merriam in early 2021 added another batch of covid-related terms, including *long-hauler*; *wet market*, "a market that sells perishable items (such as fresh meat and produce) and sometimes live animals which are often slaughtered on-site" (because the virus was believed to have originated in one in China); and new senses of *bubble*, including "an area within which sports teams stay isolated from the general public during a series of scheduled games so as to prevent exposure to disease and that includes accommodations, amenities, and the location at which the games are held." The Wikipedia entry for the end of the National Basketball Association's regular season and playoffs is titled "2020 NBA Bubble." The Los Angeles Lakers beat the Miami Heat, four games to two, to win the bubble title. "We Added New Words to the Dictionary for January 2021," *Merriam-Webster*, undated, https://www.merriam-webster.com/wordplay/new-words-in-the-dictionary-january-2021.

14
artificial intelligence

254 Now that at least partial: Not long ago, the idea of digitally automated dictionaries seemed much more remote. "Will There Be Lexicographers in the Year 3000?" an esteemed computational linguist and computer scientist asked in a paper presented at a lexicography conference in 1998. "Paper still has a long life in front of itself, and as long as things are printed we will need the reasoned condensations that only lexicographers provide," he wrote. Gregory Grefenstette, "The Future of Linguistics and Lexicographers: Will There Be Lexicographers in the Year 3000?" EURALEX, 1998.

255 it was "so far ahead: Erin McKean and Will Fitzgerald, "The ROI of AI in Lexicography," *Lexicography: Journal of ASIALEX* 11, no. 1 (2024), 7–27.

256 In the next year, a dozen: Gilles-Maurice de Schryver, "Generative AI and Lexicography: The Current State of the Art Using ChatGPT," *International Journal of Lexicography* 36, no. 4 (2023), 355–87.

256 The lexicographer, public-radio host: Grant Barrett, "Defin-o-Bots: Challenging A.I. to Create Usable Dictionary Content," Dictionary Society of North America, DSNA 24, Boulder, Colorado (2023).

257 Robert Lew, a professor: Robert Lew, "ChatGPT as a COBUILD Lexicographer," *Humanities and Social Sciences Communications* 10 (2023), 704.

258 ChatGPT mashed up: The bot also was off by a year on the first known date of use for *microaggression*. And it invented example sentences and attributed them to mainstream publications including the *New York Times* and *The Guardian*.

259 after the *New York Times* published: Isabel Slone, "Escape Into Cottagecore, Calming Ethos for Our Febrile Moment," *New York Times*, March 10, 2020, https://www.nytimes.com/2020/03/10/style/cottagecore.html.

262 The bot wasn't bad at: Asked for the first citation of *edutainment*, the bot got the year (1984) and source (*New York Times*) correct, but it invented a quotation from the newspaper. Separately, when asked three different times who said the made-up quote "A family is an organization that is controlled by its most insane member," ChatGPT replied George Bernard Shaw, George Santayana, and George Carlin. Why not George Merriam?

263 "I've been working half my life: "Ziggy v. Joe Nedney," posted April 20, 2010, by BotJunkie, YouTube, 4:36, www.youtube.com/watch?v=rcnsTU8GFlQ; Priya Ganapati, "Human Beats 340-Pound Robot in Football Kick-off," *Wired*, April 28, 2010, https://www.wired.com/2010/04/human-beats-340-pound-robot-in-football-kick-off/.

263 In May 2023, just six months: Kevin Roose, "A.I. Poses 'Risk of Extinction,' Industry Leaders Warn," *New York Times*, May 30, 2023, https://www.nytimes.com/2023/05/30/technology/ai-threat-warning.html.

264 Confabulation and hallucination: Here's a 2024 headline from the tech site *The Verge*: "Google promised a better search experience—now it's telling us to put glue on our pizza." Closer to home, during a long conversation about *sportocrat*, Gemini correctly said that I had written *Word Freak* and *A*

Few Seconds of Panic. Incorrect: that the former book was published in 2008 (it was 2001) and that the latter is a "memoir about Fatsis's experience as a high school athlete and his attempt to qualify for the Boston Marathon." Also not true: that I wrote *Paddle Your Own Kayak*, "A book about the ethics of amateur sports and the pressure to win at all costs" (there is a how-to book about kayaking by that name) and the completely made-up titles *The Longest Win* ("about the history of the Major League Baseball season and how it has changed over time") and *Horace and the Demon of the Midway* ("a biography of Horace Stoneham, the longtime owner of the New York Mets baseball team"; Stoneham actually owned the New York/San Francisco Giants). On the other hand, Gemini said my writing "is known for its wit and ability to make complex topics accessible and enjoyable for a broad audience." Chatbots 4ever!

265 **"Human cognition involves:"** Allison Nathan, "Interview with Daron Acemoglu," *Top of Mind*, Goldman Sachs Global Investment Research, June 25, 2024, 5, https://www.goldmansachs.com/images/migrated/insights/pages/gs-research/gen-ai—too-much-spend%2C-too-little-benefit-/TOM_AI%202.0_ForRedaction.pdf

266 **According to SEO expert Rand Fishkin:** The chief executive of the online market-research company SparkToro was quoted in 2024 saying that Merriam "lost 30-70% of their available clicks when Google expanded Definition Boxes in its SERPs," or search engine results pages. The post appeared to have been later edited to remove the information. In an email, Fishkin told me he obtained the Merriam data before the pandemic. Separately, Fishkin in 2024 reported that only 36 percent of U.S. Google searches resulted in clicks on non-Google sites. For dictionaries, that demonstrates how people looking up a word might be satisfied by a Google box and not scroll down to click on a link to Merriam or another dictionary. "Give me Merriam-Webster any day," Fishkin wrote. "Sadly, they'll never have a chance." Dan Taylor, "How To Recover From a Google Update (A Checklist)," *Search Engine Journal*, May 22, 2024, https://www.searchenginejournal.com/how-to-recover-from-a-google-update/516034/; Rand Fishkin, "2024 Zero-Click Search Study: For Every 1,000 EU Google Searches, Only 374 Clicks Go to the Open Web. In the U.S., It's 360," *SparkToro*, July 1, 2024, https://sparktoro.com/blog/2024-zero-click-search-study-for-every-1000-us-google-searches-only-374-clicks-go-to-the-open-web-in-the-eu-its-360/; Rand Fishkin, "The Dirty Secret to Ranking #1 on Google (part 1 of 3)," *SparkToro*, June 28, 2020, https://sparktoro.com/blog/the-dirty-secret-to-ranking-1-on-google-part-1-of-3/.

267 **A linguist at the University of Ghent:** de Schryver, "Generative AI," 380.

15
future

268 **We were among a couple dozen:** With its acquisition of the Kripke Collection, Indiana University probably has the largest dictionary collection

in the world, ahead of Oxford, the New York Public Library, the Library of Congress, Yale, and Indiana State (not necessarily in that order). Indiana should change its state motto from Crossroads of America to Land of Lexicons.

268 By the time of his death in 1980: "Collecting old dictionaries is not too serious a crime, although my family and friends have had moments of doubt about my sanity," Cordell wrote. Warren N. Cordell, "Remarks," *Catalog of Dictionaries, Word Books, and Philological Texts, 1440–1900; Inventory of the Cordell Collection, Indiana State University*, ed. David E. Vancil (Westport, Conn.: Greenwood Press, 1993).

270 a selection from the nine tons: From the 1930s until after his death in 1993, Clarence Barnhart and his family produced dozens of general and niche dictionaries, under the family name and in collaboration with other publishers. Among them were the Thorndike-Barnhart series for children; the *World Book Dictionary*, a supplement to the encyclopedia of that name; and the *Barnhart Dictionary of New English*, which covered new words.

270 the second known rendition: Morton, *Story of Webster's Third*, 5-6; Skinner, *Story of Ain't*, 13–14.

271 The dictionary society honored: Connie Eble amassed more than 20,000 examples of college slang, providing first citations in the *OED* for *wuss* and *wuss out* (1976), *lose one's shit* (1983), *freakazoid* (1984), *walk of shame* (1990), and more. *Green's Dictionary of Slang* includes more than a thousand first cits from Eble's students: *weird out* (1972), *talk to Ralph on the big white telephone* (vomit, 1977), *tightie-whities* (1985).

272 "It is an honor: I talked to Enid Pearsons later that evening. She attended Queens College, for free, where her favorite class was an introduction to phonetics taught by Arthur Bronstein, who wrote a textbook called *The Pronunciation of American English*. After graduating in the early 1950s, Pearsons responded to a newspaper want ad for a pronunciation editor on a revision of Random House's *American College Dictionary* (originally edited by Clarence Barnhart). "I ran down and I looked at all the other people waiting for interviews and thought, 'Get the hell away from my job,'" Pearsons told me. She made some suggestions on how to improve pronunciations, and was hired. Most of the definers were men and pronunciation editors were women, she said. Pearsons worked at Random House until the dictionary department was shuttered in the 1990s. She freelanced afterward, writing the occasional definition or usage note well into her eighties. "You get paid for doing this!" Pearsons marveled. "It was just incredible!"

272 In a 2004 "On Language" column: Erin McKean, "Lexicographer," *New York Times Magazine*, November 14, 2004, https://www.nytimes.com/2004/11/14/magazine/lexicographer.html.

272 In 2005, the *Times* wrote about: Saroyan, "In Land of Lexicons."

274 *selfie* in a post by a drunk guy: "Um, drunk at a mates 21st, I tripped ofer [sic] and landed lip first (with front teeth coming a very close second) on a set of steps. I had a hole about 1cm long right through my bottom lip. And sorry about the focus, it was a selfie." Simpson, *Word Detective*, 337.

endnotes

274 **As a corpus for scholarly lexicography:** Urban Dictionary might not be scholarly but it's often entertaining. Featured words for the week I was typing this included *owo* and *twatching*. *Owo* was first posted in 2017, "an emoticon used in chat rooms similar to o.o but the 'w' is supposed to make it cute," and meant "a blank stare." The word was eventually added to Collins's online dictionary (and to Scrabble's international-English lexicon). *Twatching* was added in 2019, defined as "the act of experiencing an ongoing television show or event via live twitter monitoring, while avoiding the actual show or event," which I used to do all the time.

275 **When the first edition of the OED:** "'Zyxt' is the last word in words—the final word in the final volume of the Oxford English Dictionary, now completed and in the printer's hands," the *Times* story began, noting that *zyxt* "is a very old Kentish word, meaning thou seest." It added: "Other words in the last volume include 'wush,' meaning to make a soft rushing sound; 'wifle,' meaning to wave, to swing; 'whutter,' the sound of flapping wings; 'woop,' meaning a convulsive sobbing, and 'zooid,' which is something resembling an animal but not one." "Oxford Dictionary Completed After 70 Years; Occupied 1,300 People; Has Cost $250,000," *New York Times*, January 1, 1928.

275 **William A. Craigie was a small:** Gilliver, *Making of the Oxford English Dictionary*, 254; "W. A. Craigie Dies; A Lexicographer," *New York Times*, September 3, 1957.

275 **He joined the OED in 1897:** James Murray died in 1915 and Henry Bradley in 1923. When the OED wrapped, the top editors were William Craigie and Charles T. Onions.

276 **After Craigie submitted:** Gilliver, *Making of the Oxford English Dictionary*, 299.

276 **To restrain length, Murray:** During my visit to Oxford, archivist Beverley McCulloch assembled for me a box of correspondence and other documents relating to Merriam and the OED. I based this section about the Webster scale on this material and Gilliver, *Making of the Oxford English Dictionary*, 339–52.

277 **After compiling the slips:** Gilliver, *Making of the Oxford English Dictionary*, 352–54.

277 **While in Chicago, Craigie:** William A. Craigie, "Sidelights on the Dictionary of American English," *Essays and Studies by Members of the English Association* (Oxford, England: Clarendon Press, 1945), 100.

277 **The *Chicago Tribune* put:** "Midway Signs Limey Prof. To Dope Yank Talk," *Chicago Tribune*, October 18, 1924.

277 **"The American bonanza:** Craigie, "Sidelights," 101; Peter Gilliver, "Biographical information on individuals connected with the First Edition of the OED and the 1933 Supplement," *Oxford English Dictionary*, undated, https://www.oed.com/information/about-the-oed/history-of-the-oed/contributors-to-the-oed/biographical-information-about-contributors/.

278 **The American word biz:** The Oxonians were freaked out by their American rivals. James Murray mobilized friends to tell London critics that *The Century Dictionary* had pilfered material from the OED. When they saw marketing

materials for a new British edition of Merriam's unabridged in 1921, *OED* officials freaked out even more. Merriam's claim to be the "supreme authority" on English was "impudent," an Oxford University Press executive wrote in a letter to *OED* editor Henry Bradley. Bradley responded: "I am indignant now! The thing is scandalous, and the London publishers have made themselves responsible for the outrageous lies." Henry Bradley to Robert Chapman, November 24, 1921, Oxford University Press archives.

278 **"They deeded, tabled, notified:** L. H. Robbins, "Language Made in the U.S.A.," *New York Times Magazine*, October 6, 1940.

279 **"As a bedside book:** A. Dilworth Faber, "American English," *New York Times*, August 22, 1937; Peter Monro Jack, "A Dictionary of American English," *New York Times*, November 29, 1936.

279 **The green, softcover fascicles:** Robbins, "Language Made in the U.S.A."

279 **When the final book appeared:** Horace Reynolds, "A New Language Comes of Age," *New York Times*, January 23, 1944.

280 **But the first press run:** There was a second printing of the *DAE* but no subsequent editions. Office politics played a role. The staff grew so sick of Craigie's derision and egomania—he shrank the names of editors in print and downgraded their titles—that Chicago University Press wouldn't sponsor a revision. Plus, one of the dissed editors, Mitford M. Matthews, "wanted a dictionary with his name on it," said Michael Adams, who has researched the history of the *DAE*. Matthews edited *A Dictionary of Americanisms on Historical Principles*, which was published by Chicago in 1951. Limited to words and phrases originating in the United States, a narrower standard than the *DAE*'s, that book contained 50,000 entries, from *A* ("1. Abbreviation for Adultery (or Adulterer, Adulteress) formerly branded on those convicted of this crime, or ordered worn by them as a badge. Now *hist*.") to *zwieback* ("A form of bread made in small loaves, cut into small pieces and toasted until quite brown and crisp"), spread over 1,911 pages. Chicago published new editions in 1956 and 1966. For background on the making and politics of the *DAE*, I relied on Michael Adams, "Credit Where It's Due: Authority and Recognition at the *Dictionary of American English*," *Dictionaries: Journal of the Dictionary Society of North America* 19 (1998), 1–20.

281 **Similarly, the first edition:** Richard W. Bailey, "Centennial Celebration of *The Century Dictionary*," *Dictionaries: Journal of the Dictionary Society of North America* 17 (1996), 1–16.

282 **On its website, the *OED*:** The online *OED* revision started at the beginning of the twenty-first century with a commitment of at least $55 million. It would go on regardless of how many, or how few, people subscribed to the dictionary or clicked on its entries. "History of the OED," *Oxford English Dictionary*, first captured by *Internet Archive Wayback Machine* on September 18, 2012, https://web.archive.org/web/20120918020806/http://public.oed.com/history-of-the-oed/. The information about the *OED*'s profitability and funding appears to have been removed from Oxford's website during a 2018 redesign.

282 **more than half of all U.S. newspapers:** Zach Metzger, "The State of Local News: The 2024 Report," *Northwestern Medill Local News Initiative*, October

23, 2024, https://localnewsinitiative.northwestern.edu/projects/state-of-local-news/2024/report/.

16
end

284 **Suggestions included substituting:** The reaction to this dictionary was far less widespread but only slightly less wrongheaded than the one to the *Third* thirty years earlier. In an effort to stand out in a competitive marketplace by emphasizing progressive entries and advice, Random House was asking for it. A writer for the *Boston Globe* called the dictionary "a 1,567-page, 180,000-entry ABC of the newest pieties and the latest danger-zones in the realm of offensive speech" that has "gone absolutely whole hog on what is now called 'sensitivity.'" But the dictionary wasn't, in hindsight, wrong in cautioning against using *girl* in place of *woman*—"many women today resent being called girls," it noted—or in adding entries that have stood the test of time like *bumrush*, *mall rat*, and *def*, which the *Globe* writer mocked. "This was not a radical feminist tract," Jesse Sheidlower told me. Mark Euro, "The latest word: A dictionary that keeps up with the buzz," *Boston Globe*, June 29, 1991; Richard Bernstein, "Nonsexist Dictionary Spells Out Rudeness," *New York Times*, June 11, 1991, https://www.nytimes.com/1991/06/11/news/nonsexist-dictionary-spells-out-rudeness.html.

284 **In one of his first interviews:** "That was really a bad decision," Sheidlower said of Merriam's *cyberpunk* slight. "Cyberpunk really has enormous currency. It's not just a marginal word." John Blades, "com-pe-ti-tion," *Chicago Tribune*, December 2, 1993. Merriam eventually entered *dis* as "to treat with disrespect or contempt : INSULT." It noted that *dis* as a slang shortened form emerged from African American Vernacular English, particularly rap music, in the 1970s. "The word has had a meteoric rise, moving within a few decades from highly regionalized to global use." "'Dis': From Early Rap to Academic Journals," *Merriam-Webster*, undated, https://www.merriam-webster.com/wordplay/dis-from-early-rap-to-academic-journals.

285 **Proclaiming itself a "language content:** "Why have we changed from Oxford Dictionaries to Oxford Languages?" *Oxford Languages*, undated, https://languages.oup.com/why-has-oxford-dictionaries-changed/.

286 **Online-only Macmillan "didn't:** de Schryver, "Generative AI," 357.

287 **When Dan Gilbert acquired:** Jer Staes, "Dan Gilbert Just Bought the Dictionary," *Daily Detroit*, November 15, 2018, https://www.dailydetroit.com/dan-gilbert-just-bought-the-dictionary/.

289 **A February 2024 rollout:** Dictionary.com's definitions:

> **barbiecore :** an aesthetic or style featuring playful pink outfits, accessories, decor, etc., celebrating and modeled on the wardrobe of the Barbie doll
>
> **bed rotting :** the practice of spending many hours in bed during the day, often with snacks or an electronic device, as a voluntary retreat from activity or stress

slow fashion : a movement among clothing producers and consumers that emphasizes eco-friendly, well-made clothing, maintenance and repair of garments to extend their lifespan, and a general reduction of one's consumption of new clothing items

range anxiety : the apprehension or fear that an electric vehicle's battery will run out of power before reaching one's intended destination or a charging station

Victoria Bisset, "Barbiecore? Bed Rotting? Greedflation? Dictionary.com Adds New 2024 Words," *Washington Post*, February 13, 2024, https://www.washingtonpost.com/style/2024/02/13/dictionary-com-new-words-2024/.

290 **Why do *demure* or *brat*:** *Demure* exploded thanks to a thirty-eight-second TikTok video by a beauty influencer named Jools Lebron: "See how I do my makeup for work? Very demure, very mindful." Lebron said she used the word tongue-in-cheek to reflect her status as a plus-size trans woman. *Brat* and the phrase *brat summer* had a moment after the release of an album by Charli XCX with the one-word title. The pop singer defined *brat* on TikTok: "You are just that girl who is a little messy and maybe says dumb things sometimes, who feels herself but then also maybe has a breakdown but parties through it."

291 **In April 2024, Rock Holdings sold:** "IXL Learning Acquires Dictionary.com and Thesaurus.com," *PR Newswire*, April 1, 2024, https://www.prnewswire.com/news-releases/ixl-learning-acquires-dictionarycom-and-thesauruscom-302104315.html.

291 **"In a world brimming with:** A few months after the acquisition, I asked IXL how it planned to use the dictionary and whether it would be revised regularly by professional lexicographers. A spokesman, Eric Bates, replied that the company was "still in the process of figuring out how to best improve the platform" but was "prioritizing meaningful investments in Dictionary.com, and our existing team of experienced linguists will keep the dictionary updated." In August 2024, IXL posted a job listing for a lexicographer. Previous experience in the field was "a plus" but not required. In a discussion about the job in the Dictionary Society of North America's Facebook group, Grant Barrett, Kory Stamper, and others who had worked for word sites previously acquired by IXL said the company had a history of replacing experienced language writers and editors with younger, lower-salaried people, and that in this case it wasn't clear yet who would train a newbie. Barrett wrote that "every company sucks in some way" but "if someone wants a lexicography job, anyone interested in the field should jump at this and see if it's right for them."

291 **After the sale, only a handful:** John Kelly was laid off, too. A content creator, Nick Norlen, posted on LinkedIn, "My time at Dictionary.com is ending, so I'm announcing my professional availability in the standard way, with a 1,400-word diss track showcasing the vast superiority of my word skillz over AI." A sample:

> I got wordplay for 24-hour periods
> Myriad synonyms: infinite, inexhaustible

Neverending like a pasta bowl
Topped with possible meat
I mean we've got beef
I'm posterizin' imposters asleep
Preposterously you say you're AI, but I say you're Ty Lue
Bots are boastin' new thoughts, but that's a lie, too

Obligatory sports explanation: In Game 1 of the 2001 NBA Finals, after hitting a step-back jump shot, Allen Iverson of the Philadelphia 76ers emphatically stepped over Tyronn Lue of the Los Angeles Lakers, who had fallen down. Norlen is punning on the two AIs—Allen Iverson and artificial intelligence.

293 **I was glad that clicks and revenue:** According to the data analytics firm Similarweb, Merriam in January 2025 was the top-ranked commercial online dictionary worldwide with 62.5 million monthly visits, four times as many as Dictionary.com (and 30 percent more than Britannica.com). That was up from 50 million five years earlier but well off a peak in that period of 79 million in March 2023 (which saw a spike in lookups for *indict* after a New York grand jury indicted Donald Trump in the Stormy Daniels hush-money case in which he would be convicted on thirty-four felony counts). Merriam users averaged 2.4 pages per visit and stayed on the site an average of two and a half minutes, the data showed. "merriam-webster.com Website Analysis for January 2025," *Similarweb*, accessed February 6, 2025, https://www.similarweb.com/website/merriam-webster.com/#overview.

294 **I particularly enjoyed a 2024:** Merriam-Webster (@MerriamWebster), X, July 11, 2024, https://x.com/MerriamWebster/status/1811435384758321246.

294 **The company developed a chatbot:** Michael J. de la Merced, "Britannica Didn't Just Survive. It's an A.I. Company Now," *New York Times*, December 20, 2024, https://www.nytimes.com/2024/12/20/business/dealbook/britannica-artificial-intelligence.html. Britannica chief executive Jorge Cauz and Merriam president Gregory Barlow did not respond to multiple recent requests to be interviewed.

295 **In 2024, Britannica floated plans:** Bloomberg reported that the company was seeking to raise more than $450 million to repay existing debt of Jacqui Safra unrelated to Britannica. It said that the capital raise could delay taking Britannica public. Hannah Boland, "Encyclopedia Britannica Plots $1bn Stock Market Listing," *The Telegraph*, March 18, 2024, https://finance.yahoo.com/news/encyclopedia-britannica-plots-1bn-stock-192516647.html; Carmen Arroyo, Ellen Schneider, and Amy Or, "Encyclopaedia Britannica Seeks Capital to Repay Safra's Debt," *Bloomberg*, June 5, 2024, https://www.msn.com/en-us/money/companies/encyclopaedia-britannica-seeks-capital-to-repay-safra-s-debt/ar-BB1nHJOS.

295 **The *OED* entered *imagineer* [footnote]:** A blog post credited the aluminum company Alcoa with coining *imagineering* in advertisements during World War II, and noted a one-off citation for *imagineer* in an automobile magazine in 1920. I also found *imagineer* in an Australian newspaper in 1921: "A girl told me . . . about the old lady who filled in a form for her absent son, who

was an engineer, and the old dame wasn't too good on spelling, and she put him down as an 'imagineer,' and I suppose there is a good deal of that about me." Ernie Smith, "Social Imagineering," *Tedium*, May 22, 2022, https://tedium.co/2022/05/20/disney-imagineering-word-history; "About Literature," *Sydney Stock and Station Journal*, May 6, 1921, https://www.newspapers.com/article/the-sydney-stock-and-station-journal-ima/162439713.

295 **Or incorporating the *Unabridged*:** By 2025, the only link to the dictionary that first drew me to Springfield was an all-caps line of text at the bottom of Merriam's home page.

296 **In February 2025, Merriam debuted [footnote]:** The slang entries were structurally similar to those in Dictionary.com's "Language and Culture" verticals, which were added in 2018. Merriam's sixty-five initial entries included casually written definitions, histories, and usage notes; examples from traditional and social media; and drawings or photos. Featured rollout words included the previously noted *skibidi* ("A nonsense Internet term connected to an absurdist YouTube show about evil toilets"); *situationship* ("When you're more than friends but less than official"); and *mog* ("To look or perform far better than someone else"). Others ranged from *almond mom* ("A mother who pushes her daughter to be skinny, through diet") to *neckbeard* ("Unattractive facial hair around the neck; a slovenly computer nerd; a misogynistic Internet troll") to *zoomies* ("A burst of frenetic running in dogs and cats; a bout of agitation or animation"). Some of the words arguably could have gone straight into the OWL. Siloing them created a fresh section for users to browse—the words weren't findable through Merriam's search bar—while preserving the sanctity of the traditional dictionary. ("Calm down, everyone, it's already out of date," Rebecca Shapiro, a linguist at the City University of New York, commented on Merriam's announcement. "The kids and their language are still able to hide from the olds.") Aided by Merriam's likely high rating as an "authority," the content immediately impressed Google's bots. The *skibidi* entry was the first hit in Google searches for both "skibidi" and "skibidi meaning," while the *mog* and *zoomies* pages topped searches of those words plus "meaning." "Slang & Trending," *Merriam-Webster*, accessed February 5, 2025, https://www.merriam-webster.com/slang; Rebecca Shapiro (@rebeccashapiro.bsky.social), Bluesky, February 5, 2015, https://bsky.app/profile/rebeccashapiro.bsky.social/post/3lhhaokq5mk2s.

297 **For the record, I wrote [footnote]:** *Rawdog* and *sanewashing* were linguistically interesting Word of the Year nominees. *Rawdog* is a dysphemism—"the substitution of a disagreeable, offensive, or disparaging expression for an agreeable or inoffensive one," per Merriam—a taboo term whose use is adapted and eventually becomes acceptable, like *sucks*, *scumbag*, or *screwed*. It appears to have emerged from the British slang *dogging*, meaning to have sex in public, with the *raw* appended with the sense of "in the natural state," with a first mention on Urban Dictionary in 2002. (*Green's Dictionary of Slang* notes a 1985 mention of *raw dog* meaning "to humiliate horribly, to treat someone with utter contempt.") *Rawdog*'s "semantic bleaching" dates to as early as 2012 and expanded around 2019. "Now, you can rawdog the flu by refusing medication;

you can rawdog cooking by not using a recipe; you can even rawdog life, by being sober," the *New York Times* wrote. *Sanewashing* appears to have been first used in 2007 by rhetorician Dale Carrico in a blog post titled "Sanewashing Superlatively" that I could not in a million years understand. The word was recoined in a 2020 Reddit thread explaining how far-left terms like *defund the police* and *antiwork* were reframed for popular palatability. With its nod to *whitewashing* and *brainwashing*—and its place among new *-washing* terms like *sportswashing* and *greenwashing*—plus the state of American political life, *sanewashing* had stick-around potential. At the WOTY vote, in Philadelphia, University of Delaware PhD student Vincent Mariani seemed to speak for both words when he nominated *rawdog*, saying it "represents going into a year without knowing what the hell is going to happen." Not everyone on social media was thrilled by the choice. "People were annoyed, but not because *rawdog* had a naughty meaning," Nancy Friedman wrote on her language Substack. "Nope: They were annoyed because it had a new, *non-naughty* meaning. A word that they had assumed meant one thing was now purported to mean something else! Was that even allowed?" Jessica Roy, "A Wildly Obscene Term's Path to Mainstream Usage," *New York Times*, July 17, 2024, https://www.nytimes.com/2024/07/17/style/rawdog-flights-term.html; Nancy Friedman, "Word of the Week: Sanewashing," *Fritinancy*, September 9, 2024, https://fritinancy.substack.com/p/word-of-the-week-sanewashing; "2024 Word of the Year Is 'Rawdog,'" *American Dialect Society*, January 10, 2025, https://americandialect.org/2024-word-of-the-year-is-rawdog; Nancy Friedman, "Word of the Week: Rawdog," *Fritinancy*, January 13, 2025, https://fritinancy.substack.com/p/word-of-the-week-rawdog.

297 **"On the one hand:** Kory Stamper (@korystamper.bsky.social), Bluesky, February 19, 2025, https://bsky.app/profile/korystamper.bsky.social/post/3lilaku3bes2z.

298 **In 1905, the *Seattle Star*:** The column's subhed changed based on available space. The longest: "A Little Whirl Around the Busy Circuit With a Few Short Stops at Different Stations—All the News That's Worth While in the Many Fields of Sports." The best: "A Bill of Fare for Hungry Fans That Hits the Spot These Balmy Spring Time Days." The last one in the database carried a byline: "Fresh From the Fields of Recreation—Chatterings of Sports—By Len Hunt."

299 **The Canadianism *gong show*:** The OED entered *gong show* not long after I drafted my definition. I also wrote 3,664 words about the word that I cut from this book but promise to publish somewhere, someday. Meantime, here's my draft definition and supplemental information note:

> **gong show** *noun, plural* **gong shows** *informal, chiefly Canadian* **1 :** something (such as an event, place, person or circumstance) marked by chaos, incompetence, or unprofessionalism **2 :** an amateur talent show
>
> ♦ The phrase **gong show** derives from the American television series "The Gong Show" (1976-1980). The satirical variety program, hosted by Chuck Barris, featured amateur musicians, comedians, and other performers, usually of negligible talent, who were judged by a panel

of celebrities. The program often devolved into chaos involving the host, panelists, performers, and audience. "Gong shows" became a staple of high school, corporate, and community events. The phrase "a gong show" meaning something chaotic or out of control dates to the late-1980s in Canada, where, by the mid-1990s, it was often used in ice hockey and politics. It's not clear why *gong show* became a common Canadianism, though Barris sometimes ushered failed acts offstage with a hockey stick.

299 **Perrault even seemed to be:** Serendipitous bookend to Steve Perrault's spotting *Dutch oven* in *Sports Illustrated* while I was drafting a definition: As my colleague Josh Levin was reading the manuscript of this book, he heard *Dutch oven* in an episode of the HBO series *Somebody Somewhere*. In the scene, Sam gives Brad and Joel a Dutch oven as a housewarming present. Here's the dialogue:

Brad: I still can't get over that Dutch oven you gave us. That was too generous.

Sam: Yeah, well, saw the name, I had to. It cracked me up.

Brad: What's funny about a Dutch oven?

Sam: What's funny about . . . Well, it's when, you, you trap a fart under the covers and you make the other person smell it. You've never heard of that?

Brad: No, I didn't know you could do that.

Sam: Yeah, I just did, except I was the only one there.

Brad: That'll be a fun trick to try out.

Somebody Somewhere, season 3, episode 2, "Dinky Dinkies," written by Lisa Kron, directed by Robert Cohen, featuring Tim Bagley and Bridget Everett, aired November 3, 2024, on HBO.

301 **voice pronunciations:** Go to Merriam-Webster.com, type *Meyer lemon* into the search bar, and click on the audio icon. That's me.

acknowledgments

303 **at the North American Scrabble championship:** I placed thirteenth in Division 2, my highest numerical finish in seventeen nationals. But I misplayed the Z in a critical endgame and blew a chance to finish in the top five. Not that I still think about it.

304 **to use a word so overused:** Lisa Miller, "When Did Everything Become a 'Journey'?" *New York Times*, May 13, 2024, https://www.nytimes.com/2024/05/13/well/health-journey.html.

bibliography

: the works or a list of the works referred to in a text or consulted by the author in its production

Adams, Michael. "Credit Where It's Due: Authority and Recognition at the *Dictionary of American English.*" *Dictionaries: Journal of the Dictionary Society of North America* 19 (1998).
Adams, Michael. "The Lexical Ride of a Lifetime." *American Speech* 88, no. 2 (2013).
Aiden, Erez, and Jean-Baptiste Michel. *Uncharted: Big Data as a Lens on Human Culture.* New York: Riverhead Books, 2013.
Algeo, John. *Fifty Years Among the New Words: A Dictionary of Neologisms, 1941–1991.* New York: Cambridge University Press, 1991.
Asim, Jabari. *The N Word: Who Can Say It, Who Shouldn't, and Why.* New York: Houghton Mifflin, 2007.
Bailey, Richard W. "Centennial Celebration of *The Century Dictionary.*" *Dictionaries: Journal of the Dictionary Society of North America* 17 (1996).
Baker, Nicholson. "Discards." *New Yorker.* March 27, 1994.
Baker, Nicholson. *Double Fold: Libraries and the Assault on Paper.* New York: Random House, 2001.
Baron, Dennis. "The Epicene Pronoun: The Word That Failed." *American Speech* 56, no. 2 (1981).
Baron, Dennis. *What's Your Pronoun: Beyond He & She.* New York: Liveright, 2020.
Barrett, Grant. "Defin-o-Bots: Challenging A.I. to Create Usable Dictionary Content." Dictionary Society of North America, DSNA 24, Boulder, Colorado (2023).
Bello, Anne Pence. "Letters to a Dictionary: Competing Views of Language in the Reception of *Webster's Third New International Dictionary.*" PhD diss., University of Massachusetts Amherst, 2013.
Blake, Robert W. "The Not So 'Harmless Drudge' at the Linguistic Institute: Philip B. Gove on Lexicography." *The English Record* XIX, no. 4 (1969).
Boswell, James. *The Life of Samuel Johnson.* London: Penguin Books, 1986.

Cauz, Jorge. "Encyclopædia Britannica's President on Killing Off a 244-Year-Old Product." *Harvard Business Review*, March 2013.

Coates, Ta-Nehisi. "In Defense of a Loaded Word." *New York Times*, November 23, 2013.

Craigie, William A. "Sidelights on the *Dictionary of American English*." *Essays and Studies by Members of the English Association*. Oxford, England: Clarendon Press, 1945.

D'Amato, Donald J. *Springfield—350 Years: A Pictorial History*. Virginia Beach, VA: Donning Co., 1985.

de Schryver, Gilles-Maurice. "Generative AI and Lexicography: The Current State of the Art Using ChatGPT." *International Journal of Lexicography* 36, no. 4 (2023).

de Schryver, Gilles-Maurice, and David Joffe. "On how ChatGPT can take over all of the dictionary maker's tasks." YouTube, March 1, 2023. Video, 1:35:50. https://youtu.be/watch?v=mEorwoyefAs.

Dickson, Paul. *The Dickson Baseball Dictionary, Third Edition*. New York: W. W. Norton, 2009.

Fatsis, Stefan. "The Definition of a Dictionary." *Slate*, January 12, 2015. https://www.slate.com/articles/life/culturebox/2015/01/merriam_webster_dictionary_what_should_an_online_dictionary_look_like.html.

Fatsis, Stefan. "How COVID-19 Led Merriam-Webster to Make Its Fastest Update Ever." *Slate*, March 26, 2020. https://slate.com/culture/2020/03/coronavirus-merriam-webster-emergency-update.html.

Fatsis, Stefan. "Thirty-Four Days: Inside Merriam-Webster's Emergency Coronavirus Update." *Dictionaries: Journal of the Dictionary Society of North America* 42, no. 2 (2021).

Follett, Wilson. "Sabotage in Springfield: Webster's Third Edition." *The Atlantic*, January 1962.

Ford, Emily Ellsworth Fowler. *Notes on the Life of Noah Webster*. New York: privately printed, 1912.

Francis, W. Nelson, and Henry Kučera. *Computational Analysis of Present-Day American English*. Providence, RI: Brown University Press, 1967.

Francis, W. Nelson, and Henry Kučera. "Manual of Information to Accompany A Standard Corpus of Present-Day Edited American English, for use with Digital Computers." Providence, RI: Brown University, 1964 (revised 1979).

Frisch, Michael H. *Town Into City: Springfield, Massachusetts, and the Meaning of Community, 1840–1880*. Cambridge, MA: Harvard University Press, 1972.

G. & C. Merriam Company Archive. General Collection, Beinecke Rare Book and Manuscript Library, Yale University.

Giles, Jim. "Internet Encyclopaedias Go Head to Head." *Nature* 438 (2005).

Gilliver, Peter. *The Making of the Oxford English Dictionary*. Oxford, England: Oxford University Press, 2016.

Gleick, James. "Cyber-Neologoliferation." *New York Times Magazine*, November 5, 2006.

Goddard, Ives. "'I Am a Red-Skin': The Adoption of a Native American Expression (1769–1826)." *European Review of Native American Studies* 19, no. 2 (2005).

Gove, Philip B., ed. *The Role of the Dictionary*. Indianapolis: Bobbs-Merrill Co., 1967.

Green, Jonathon. *Chasing the Sun: Dictionary-Makers and the Dictionaries They Made*. New York: Henry Holt, 1996.

Greenstein, Shane. "The Reference Wars: Encyclopædia Britannica's Decline and Encarta's Emergence." *Harvard Business School*, April 4, 2016. https://www.hbs.edu/faculty/Pages/item.aspx?num=50951.

Grieve, Jack, Andrea Nini, and Diansheng Gui. "Analyzing Lexical Emergence in Modern American English Online." *English Language and Linguistics* 21, no. 1 (2017).

Grieve, Jack. "Mapping Lexical Innovation on American Social Media." *Journal of English Linguistics* 46, no. 4 (2018).

Hoffman, Paul. *King's Gambit: A Son, a Father, and the World's Most Dangerous Game*. New York: Hyperion, 2007.

Johnson, Samuel. *A Dictionary of the English Language*. 1755, 1773, edited by Beth Rapp Young, Jack Lynch, William Dorner, Amy Larner Giroux, Carmen Faye Mathes, and Abigail Moreshead. 2021. https://johnsonsdictionaryonline.com

Jost, David. "Madeline Kripke, 1943–2020." *Dictionaries: The Journal of the Dictionary Society of North America* 44, no. 2 (2020).

Kelley, William Melvin. "If You're Woke You Dig It." *New York Times Magazine*, May 20, 1962.

Kendall, Joshua. "A Minor Exception: On W. C. Minor and Noah Webster." *The Nation*, April 4, 2011.

Kendall, Joshua. *The Forgotten Founding Father: Noah Webster's Obsession and the Creation of An American Culture*. New York: Berkley Books, 2012.

Kennedy, Randall. *Nigger: The Strange Career of a Troublesome Word*. New York: Pantheon, 2002.

Kerremans, Daphé, Jelena Prokić, Quirin Würschinger, and Hans-Jörg Schmid. "Using Data-mining to Identify and Study Patterns in Lexical Innovation on the Web: The *NeoCrawler*." *Pragmatics & Cognition* 25, no. 1 (2018).

Kleinfield, N. R. "Enriched by His Friendship With an Agnostic, a Rabbi Finances a Storied Legacy." *New York Times*, May 9, 1997.

Konnelly, Lex, Kirby Conrod, and Evan D. Bradley. "Non-Binary Singular They." In *The Routledge Handbook of Pronouns*, edited by Laura L. Paterson, 450–464. New York: Routledge, 2024.

Krieger, Daniel. "The Dame of Dictionaries." *Narratively*, August 15, 2013, https://narratively.com/the-dame-of-dictionaries/.

Landau, Sidney I. *Dictionaries: The Art and Craft of Lexicography*. New York: Cambridge University Press, 1989.

Leavitt, Robert Keith. *Noah's Ark, New England Yankees, and the Endless Quest*. Springfield, MA: C. & G. Merriam Co., 1947.

Lepore, Jill. "Noah's Mark." *New Yorker*, November 6, 2006.

Lew, Robert. "ChatGPT as a COBUILD Lexicographer." *Humanities and Social Sciences Communications* 10 (2023).

Library of Congress. *The Card Catalog: Books, Cards and Literary Treasures*. San Francisco: Chronicle Books, 2017.

Macdonald, Dwight. "The String Untuned." *New Yorker*, March 10, 1962.

Martin, Peter. *The Dictionary Wars: The American Fight over the English Language*. Princeton, NJ: Princeton University Press, 2019.

McCulloch, Gretchen. *Because Internet: Understanding the New Rules of Language*. New York: Riverhead Books, 2019.

McDavid, Raven I., and Audrey R. Duckert. *Lexicography in English*. New York: New York Academy of Sciences, 1973.

McHenry, Robert. "The Faith-Based Encyclopedia." *Tech Central Station*, November 15, 2004, https://web.archive.org/web/20060613214340/http://www.tcsdaily.com/article.aspx?id=111504A.

McKean, Erin. "The Joy of Lexicography." *TED*, August 30, 2007, https://www.youtube.com/watch?v=J4VzuWmN8zY.

McKean, Erin, and Will Fitzgerald. "The ROI of AI in Lexicography." *Lexicography: Journal of ASIALEX* 11 (2024).

McWhorter, John. *Nine Nasty Words: English in the Gutter—Then, Now, and Forever*. New York: Avery, 2021.

Mencken, H. L. *The American Language; A Preliminary Inquiry into the Development of English in the United States*. New York: Alfred A. Knopf, 1919.

Metcalf, Allan. *Predicting New Words: The Secrets of Their Success*. Boston: Houghton Mifflin, 2002.

Michel, Jean-Baptiste et al. "Quantitative Analysis of Culture Using Millions of Digitized Books." *Science* 331 (2010).

Micklethwait, David. *Noah Webster and the American Dictionary*. Jefferson, NC: McFarland & Co., 1999.

Morse, John. "E. Ward Gilman: In Memoriam." *Dictionaries: The Journal of the Dictionary Society of North America* 44, no. 1 (2023).

Morse, John. "Publishing the Dictionary: The Business Side of the Business." In *The Cambridge Handbook of the Dictionary*, edited by Edward Finegan and Michael Adams, 592–628. Cambridge, England: Cambridge University Press, 2024.

Morton, Herbert C. *The Story of Webster's Third: Philip Gove's Controversial Dictionary and Its Critics*. New York: Cambridge University Press, 1994.

Mugglestone, Lynda. *The Oxford History of English*. Oxford, England: Oxford University Press, 2013.

Murphy, Lynn. *The Prodigal Tongue: The Love-Hate Relationship Between American and British English*. New York: Penguin Books, 2018.

Murray, K. M. Elizabeth. *Caught in the Web of Words: James Murray and the Oxford English Dictionary*. New Haven, CT: Yale University Press, 1977.

Philological Society. *Proposal for the Publication of a New English Dictionary.* London: Trübner and Co., 1859.

Read, Allen Walker. *Lexical Evidence from Folk Epigraphy in Western North America: A Glossarial Study of the Low Element in the English Vocabulary.* Paris: privately printed, 1935.

Reed, Joseph W., Jr. "Noah Webster's Debt to Samuel Johnson." *American Speech* 37, no. 2 (1962).

Roberts, Sam. "Madeline Kripke, Doyenne of Dictionaries, Is Dead at 76." *New York Times*, April 30, 2020, https://www.nytimes.com/2020/04/30/nyregion/madeline-kripke-dead-coronavirus.html.

Roth, Gabriel. "No One Cares How I Feel, According to Merriam-Webster." *Slate*, September 8, 2016, https://slate.com/human-interest/2016/09/merriam-webster-dictionary-tweeted-no-one-cares-about-how-you-feel.html.

Rundell, Michael. "Automating the Creation of Dictionaries: Are We Nearly There?" Proceedings of the 16th International Conference of the Asian Association for Lexicography: "Lexicography, Artificial Intelligence, and Dictionary Users" (2023).

Saroyan, Strawberry. "In Land of Lexicons, Having the Last Word." *New York Times*, March 19, 2005, https://www.nytimes.com/2005/03/19/arts/in-land-of-lexicons-having-the-last-word.html

Shea, Ammon. *Reading the OED: One Man, One Year, 21,730 Pages.* New York: Perigee, 2008.

Sheidlower, Jesse. "The Closing of a Great American Dialect Project." *New Yorker*, September 22, 2017. https://www.newyorker.com/culture/cultural-comment/the-closing-of-a-great-american-dialect-project.

Sheidlower, Jesse, ed. *The F-Word.* New York: Oxford University Press, 2009.

Simpson, John. *The Word Detective: Searching for the Meaning of It All at the* Oxford English Dictionary. New York: Basic Books, 2016.

Skinner, David. "Philip Gove and 'Our Word.'" *The American Scholar*, November 10, 2023, https://theamericanscholar.org/philip-gove-and-our-word.

Skinner, David. *The Story of Ain't: America, Its Language, and the Most Controversial Dictionary Ever Published.* New York: Harper, 2012.

Sledd, James, and Wilma R. Ebbit, eds. *Dictionaries and THAT Dictionary: A Casebook on the Aims of Lexicographers and the Targets of Reviewers.* Chicago: Scott, Foresman and Co., 1962.

Sokolowski, Peter. "The Invention of the Modern Dictionary." In *The Whole World in a Book: Dictionaries in the Nineteenth Century*, edited by Sarah Ogilvie and Gabriella Safran, 168–89. New York: Oxford University Press, 2020.

Srinivasan, Amia. "He, She, One, They, Ho, His, Hum, Its." *London Review of Books*, July 2, 2020, https://www.lrb.co.uk/the-paper/v42/n13/amia-srinivasan/he-she-one-they-ho-hus-hum-ita.

Stamper, Kory. *Word by Word: The Secret Life of Dictionaries.* New York: Pantheon, 2017.

Trench, Richard Chenevix. *On the Study of Words*. London: John W Parker and Son, 1851.

Trench, Richard Chenevix. *On Some Deficiencies in Our English Dictionaries*. London: John W Parker and Son, 1857.

Wallace, David Foster. "Tense Present: Democracy, English, and the Wars over Usage." *Harper's Magazine*, April 2001.

Watson, Elijah C. "The Origin Of Woke: William Melvin Kelley Is The 'Woke' Godfather We Never Acknowledged." *Okay Player*, December 6, 2022, https://www.okayplayer.com/originals/what-does-woke-mean-history-origins-william-melvin-kelley.html.

Winchester, Simon. "The Mongrel Speech of the Streets." *New York Review of Books*, March 8, 2012.

Winchester, Simon. *The Professor and the Madman: A Tale of Murder, Insanity, and the Making of the Oxford English Dictionary*. New York: HarperCollins, 1998.

Wright, Kelly E., et al. "Among the New Words," *American Speech* 99, no. 3 (2024).

Wright, Willard Huntington. *Misinforming a Nation*. New York: B. W. Huebsch, 1917.

Zimmer, Benjamin, and Charles E. Carson. "Among the New Words: The Prospects and Challenges of Short-Term Historical Lexicography. *Dictionaries: Journal of the Dictionary Society of North America* 39, no. 1 (2018).

Zimmer, Benjamin, Charles E. Carson, and Jane Solomon. "Seventy-five Years Among the New Words." *American Speech* 91, no. 4 (2016).

index

: a list of items (such as topics or names) treated in a printed work that gives for each item the page number where it may be found

A

Abbey, Edward, 22
Abraham, Delphine, 158, 159
Acemoglu, Daron, 265
Adams, Michael, 94, 283
   Read and, 332
   DAE and, 275, 280, 370
   on importance of differences among dictionaries, 301
   Kripke collection and, 147, 148, 151–53, 343
   on Wiktionary, 273
African American Vernacular English (AAVE), 237–44, 371
AIDS, 248, 249, 365
ain't, 45, 322
Aleksic, Adam, 334
Algeo, Adele, 99
Algeo, John, 99
Ali, Muhammad, 173
Alligator Times, 171
alt-right, 211–15, 234, 258, 356–57
The American Bibliopolist, 183
American Dialect Society, 97–98, 100–9, 189, 190, 289, 297
An American Dictionary of the English Language
   1828 edition of, ix, 12, 27–31
   1845 printing of, 32
   1847 edition of, x, 32–33
   1864 edition of, x, 33–39, 318, 319
American English
   AAVE, 237–44
   American character and, 97
   cits as history of, 12, 111, 113, 120–23, 165, 168
   DAE, 275, 278–80
   Native American words in, 29–30
   Webster on importance of dictionary of, 29
   Webster's Second as rulebook for, 41, 44
American Ethnological Society, 118
The American Heritage Dictionary of the English Language, 46, 49, 50, 77–78, 82, 86, 89, 119, 123, 272, 285
Americanize, 30, 316
The American Language (Mencken), 97
American Speech, 13, 97–98, 151, 165, 184
"Among the New Words" (Algeo and Algeo), 99
"Among the New Words" (Bolinger), 98
"Analyzing Lexical Emergence in Modern American English Online" (Grieve), 93
Anderson, Joel, 241
Anderson, Steve, 86
And the Band Played On (Shilts), 248
Angell, Roger, 325, 348
Anthony, Susan B., 186–87

index

artificial intelligence (AI)
  ChatGPT, 255–63
  cottagecore and, 259–62
  definitions written by, 254, 256, 258–59, 263–67
  making something meaningful and, 253–54
  Merriam's thesaurus and, 295
  as threat to lexicographers, 263–67
  words defined by author and, 257–59
The Associated Press, 184, 207
Atlanta Braves, 167
Atlantic Monthly, 39, 320
Aviance, Kevin, 106

B

Backpfeifengesicht, 64–65, 206, 340
Backward Index, 110, 335
Badu, Erykah, 239
Baker, Asa, 320–21
Baker, Nicholson, 133, 340
Baker, Robert, 185
Baldwin, James, 238
Ball of Fire (film), 271
Barnhart, Clarence, 100, 148, 270. 368
Barnhart, David, 100, 270
Baron, Dennis, 184–85, 187–88, 192
Barrett, Grant
  AI definitions and, 256–57, 260, 264, 266
  at Dictionary.com, 288–91
  at *Historical Dictionary of American Slang*, 337
  on lexicography jobs, 272
  WOTY and, 84
  and Word of the Year, 107, 235
Beckham, Barry, 239
Beemyn, Genny, 194
Bender, Emily, 335
Bender, Harold, 122
Benton, William, 56
Bethel, John, 122, 164
Beyoncé, 106
Bierce, Ambrose, 228
"The Big Book," 270–71
Bjorkman, Bronwyn, 198
Black Books, 14–15, 312

Black Lives Matter movement, 239
The Black Seventies (Pierce), 208
Black Thunder, 167
Blue-Back (or Blue-Backed) Speller, 25, 27, 317
Boland, Edward, 45
Bolinger, Dwight L., 98
Bornstein, Kate, 193–94
Boston Recorder, 185
Bradley, Henry, 275, 276, 313, 369, 370
Bradley, Milton, 36
Brennan, John, 80, 330
Brewster, Emily
  author drafting entries and, 206
  basic facts about, 16, 19, 58, 313
  blog posts by, 203–4
  discovery of use of *a* as an indefinite article, 314
  gender-neutral pronouns and, 188, 189, 190–91, 192, 199, 200
  troll in *Unabridged*, 214, 225, 227
  on usage notes and offensive words, 177
bro, 81–82
broey, 225, 359
bro hug, 330
Brown University Standard Corpus of Present-Day American English, 77–78
Brunette, Joyce C., 170–71
Buffett, Warren, 145
Burchfield, Robert, 125–26, 152, 340
Burt, Stephanie, 192

C

Calepino, Ambrosius, 2, 140, 144
Canning, Dominique, 108
card catalogs of libraries, 132–34
Carville, James, 240
Cauz, Jorge, 57, 59, 295
Cawdrey, Robert, 3, 310
Center for AI Safety, 263
The Century Dictionary, 33, 39, 86, 278, 281, 289
Chance (Conrad), 168
Charli XCX, 372
ChatGPT, 255–63, 366
Chaucer, Geoffrey, 20–21

chef's kiss, 328
Chicago Sun-Times, 45
Chicago Tribune, 186, 277
Chisholm, Shirley, 174, 345
cits (citations)
  for *American Heritage Dictionary*, 123
  collection of, for early Merriam dictionaries, 111-12
  collection of, under Gove, 112
  color coding of, 169, 170
  creation of, 16, 112
  current number of, 112
  for *DARE*, 125
  definitions as at mercy of, 22
  file sets of, 22
  as history of American English, 12, 111, 113, 120–23, 165, 168
  importance of physical cards, 131–32
  New Files, 22, 172, 178, 205
  for *OED*, 111, 125, 127–31
  preservation of, 134
  for *Webster's New World*, 124
Clark, Mary Cowden, 318
Clavijero, Francisco Javier, 30
Clinton, Hillary, 235
CNN, 221, 222
Coates, Ta-Nehisi, 179
Coats, George, 298
COBUILD corpus, 78, 257
Cohen, David X., 72
Colbert, Stephen, 217
Collection of Essays and Fugitiv Writings (Webster), 26
College "Standard" Dictionary of the English Language (Funk & Wagnalls), 5
Collegiate (dictionary)
  acknowledgment of lexicographers in, 19
  AIDS in, 249
  basic facts about, x, 8
  definitions in, 63
  first edition of, 39, 142
  fifth edition of, 6, 310
  front matter of, 20
  fuck/fuck up in, 119, 120
  Gove and, 47, 119
  internet in, 7
  Irregardless in, 123
  last edition of, 8, 13
  Madeline Kripke and, 137
  n-word in, 173
  online, x, 50, 255–56
  redskin in, 167, 172
  sales of, 49
  squaw in, 157
Collins, Billy, 134
Collins, Jason, 18
community spread, 248, 364–65
A Compendious Dictionary of the English Language (Webster), 12, 25–27, 269, 284
computational lexicographers, 75–76
computational linguistics, 77–78, 91–96, 292
Conboy, Robert W., 302
cone of silence, 202, 354–55
Connor, Chris, 249
Conrad, Joseph, 168
Conrod, Kirby, 189, 191, 197
Consolidated Files. *See also* cits (citations)
  contents, 22, 110, 112–13
  historical value of, 111, 113, 120, 132, 134
Converse, Charles Crozat, 181–82, 185
Converse, William, 28, 316
Conway, Kellyanne, 227
Cooper, Barry Michael, 241
Copeland, Robert, 54, 119
Cordell, Warren N., 268, 368
corpora
  Brown University Standard Corpus of Present-Day American English, 77–78
  COBUILD, 78, 257
  Davies and, 78–79
  definition writing and, 80, 212–13
  Hargraves and, 75–77
  Oxford, 80, 81
  structure of, 81
  of Twitter posts, 92
Corpus of Contemporary American English (COCA), 78–79

Corpus of Early Modern English, 79
Corpus of Founding Era American English, 79
Cosell, Howard, 328
cottagecore, 259–62
COVID-19 language, 246–52, 329–30, 365
Cowan, John, 193
Craigie, William A., 275–78
cromulent, 70, 71, 72, 73
cunty, 106–8, 334–35
"Cunty (The Feeling)," 106

D

Dalzell, Tom, 140, 147, 154
Dana, James, 34, 318
Davies, Mark, 78–79
Dawes, Thomas, 26–27
decleat, 18
definitions
  AI-generated, 254, 256, 258–59, 263–67
  in *Collegiate*, 63
  corpora and, 80, 212–13
  crafting, 17–18, 34, 37–38, 42–44, 64
  effect of controversy on, 233
  "free-range," 86
  Google-licensed, 266–67
  internet and, 22
  legal use of, 196–97
  as at mercy of cits, 22
  in OWL, 63
  problems presented by, 85–86
  quality and good-enough, 266
  quotations used in, 223–24, 360–61
  rewriting of Webster's original, 34
  usage notes and, 177
definitions, author's. *See also Backpfeifengesicht, cone of silence, decleat, dogpile, Dutch oven, fluffer, headbutt, go, gong show, microaggression, pom-pom girl, post-fact, run, safe space, sheeple, sportocrat*
  added to OWL, 215, 218–19, 300–01
  AI's versus, 257–59
  drafting of, 16, 17, 21–23, 210–11, 213–14

number drafted, 300–301
Perrault on adding, 299, 300–301
Perrault's editing of, 66–67, 210–11, 215, 219, 221
Perrault's nixing of, 65–66
DEI (diversity, equity and inclusion), 242–43
Dellums, Ron, 173–74, 345, 346
Demakopoulos, Steve, 153
DeSantis, Ron, 240–41
de Saussure, Ferdinand, 288
de Schryver, Gilles-Maurice, 267, 286
The Devil's Dictionary (Bierce), 228
dictionaries. *See also* specific dictionaries
  academic/public formula for specialized, 280
  addition of words and comprehensiveness of, 44
  as authorities, 40, 84, 228, 250, 286
  competition among, 39, 46, 49, 281
  complaints about, 216–18, 222–24
  Cordell Collection of Dictionaries, 268–69
  crowdsourcing, 273–74
  early, 2–4
  extinct, 264
  function and operation of, 217
  importance of, in times of crisis, 250
  importance of differences in, 301
  inclusion of gender-neutral pronouns in, 198–99
  legal use of definitions in, 196–97
  "low-frequency words" and, 83
  natively digital as opposed to digitized print product, 296
  need for, in era of search engines, 83
  need to stay up to date, 60
  online presence of, 49–50, 51–52, 266
  possibility of nonprofit, 282–83
  as profit-driven enterprise, 277–78, 281, 297
  as unbiased arbiters of language and its evolution, 5–7, 84–85, 228
  as validators of way people tend to think about words' authenticity, 84

as windows on culture, 152, 153, 196
WOTY and, 101
Dictionary Act, 348
Dictionary.com, 50–51, 53, 199, 261, 274, 287–91, 371, 372
Dictionary of American English on Historical Principles (DAE), 275, 278–80, 282, 370
Dictionary of American Regional English (DARE), 124–25, 282, 337–38
A Dictionary of the English Language (Johnson), 3–4, 25, 27
Dictionary Society of North America (DSNA), 205, 268
"Discards" (Baker), 133
Doctorow, Cory, 108, 109
dogpile, 16, 205, 258, 299, 300
doomscrolling, 7, 219, 251, 252, 358
Dowd, Maureen, 240
Dowell, Erika, 150–51
Driscoll, Anne, 123, 270–71
Duckert, Audrey, 321
Duke, David, 173
dumpster fire, 236
Dutch oven, 20–21, 299, 376
Dwight, John S., 318

E

Ebert, Manuel, 253–54
Eble, Connie, 271, 368
editors. *See* lexicographers
Egan, Rose Frances, 245
Elements of Style (Strunk and White), 182–83
embiggen, 70–72, 73
Emerge (African American affairs magazine), 158, 159
Emerson, Ralph Waldo, 36, 319
Encyclopædia Britannica Inc. *See also* Merriam-Webster Inc.
  history of, 55–56, 324
  purchase of Merriam, 55, 324
  relationship with Merriam, 53, 55, 58–60, 248, 292, 293–95
  business fortunes of, 55–58, 324–25, 373
The English Record, 13

Ernst, Carl W., 277
enshittification, 108, 289
Eveleth, George Washington, 192

F

fart, 20–21, 313
Fatsis, Michael, 310–11
Fauci, Anthony, 250
Favre, Brett, 21
Feinberg, Leslie, 193
Fierro, Daniel, 50
FIFA, 66–67
finalize, 45, 322
Financial Times, 298
Fisher, Ann, 183
Fishkin, Rand, 266, 366
Fitzgerald, Will, 254, 255, 260, 262, 265
fluffer, 16, 66, 68, 74
Follett, Wilson, 45, 46
Ford, Emily Ellsworth Fowler, 27–28
Fortune, 223
Francis, W. Nelson, 77
Franklin, Benjamin, 26
"free-range" definitions, 86
Friedman, Nancy, 108–9
Fuchs, Edward, 164
fuck/fuck up, 114–20, 270, 336–37
Funk & Wagnalls, 6, 39, 162, 186

G

G. & C. Merriam Company. *See also* Merriam, George and Charles, and Merriam-Webster Inc.
  citation slips of, 111–12
  during Civil War, 36–37
  founding of, ix, 31
  headquarters of, 11, 201, 311
  history of, 31, 142–44
  innovations and marketing by, 39
  nineteenth-century archives, 35
  OED's use of 1864 dictionary of, 277
  street address of, 327
  Webster's *American Dictionary* and, 32–35, 36–39, 141
Gallan, Gordon J., 115, 117–18, 270
Garvey Lives! (Beckham), 239
Gates, Ed, 164–65, 205

Gelernter, David, 182
Gender Census, 191, 196, 350
gender-neutral pronouns
   attitudes of lexicographers and, 299–300
   in colleges and universities, 191–92, 198
   Converse and, 181–82
   "duo-personal pronouns," 186
   gender as binary and, 188, 189
   he as, 182–83, 187
   hen, 352
   hiser, 185–86
   late nineteenth century proposals, 185–86
   Latinx, 195
   meaning of absence of, 185
   Perrault on, 18, 299–300
   they/their/them/themselves, 183–84, 189–91, 196, 350
   thon, 181, 185, 186
   twentieth century proposals, 187–88, 192, 198
   usage note by author, 353
   xe/xy/xim, 192, 196, 197, 199
   you singular as, 182
   ze/hir, 192–96, 198, 199, 299, 351, 352, 353
genderqueer, 188–89
generative AI, 255, 256
Ghebreyesus, Tedros Adhanom, 246–47
Gibson, Mel, 271
Gilbert, Dan, 274, 287, 288
Gilliver, Peter, 125–28, 130, 131, 282, 339–40, 365
   run and, 218
Gilman, Daniel, 33–34
Gilman, E. Ward "Gil," 15, 119–20, 171, 312
Gilman, Emily, 34
Gilman, Maria, 34
The Girl Must Die (Lopez), 194
Gizmodo, 232–33
go, 358
gong show, 299, 375–76
Goodrich, Chauncey, 32, 34, 320

Google, 51–53, 82, 258, 266–67, 290
Gove, Philip B.
   basic facts about, 41–42, 47, 118
   and boldface colon, 346
   collection of cits under, 112
   as descriptivist, 114
   fuck/fuck up and, 113–20
   performance of "The Big Book" and, 270–71
   training of lexicographers and, 13–14
   use of monitory labels, 114, 122–23, 165–66, 322
   Webster's Third and, 5–6, 42–48, 321
   wording of definitions and, 42–44
Granville, Wilfred, 152
Greaney, Dan, 71, 72
The Great Passage (film), 271
Green, Jonathon, 147, 341
Gregory, Dick, 174, 345
Grieve, Jack, 91–94, 96, 331
The Guardian, 298
Guralnik, David B., 4–5, 310

H

Hall, Joan Houston, 125
Hannah-Jones, Nikole, 363
Hargraves, Orin, 75–77
Harper's Weekly, 186
Harriot, Michael, 239
Harris, William T., 40
Harvard Business Review, 57
Hasbro Inc., 217, 357
Hawley, Josh, 241
headbutt, 18–19, 66, 299, 300
he as gender-neutral pronoun, 182–83, 187
Hegseth, Pete, 243
hiser, 185–86
Historical Dictionary of American Slang, 124, 175, 178, 285, 337
Hitch-22 (Hitchens), 298–99
Hitchens, Christopher, 298–99
hoi polloi, 327
Holliday, Nicole, 105–6, 236, 240
Holt, Lucius, 163
Hoopes, Joshua, 193

Hopkins, Dan, 170
Houghton Mifflin/Houghton Mifflin Harcourt, 46, 272
Howe, Hezekiah, 28
Hungarian Studies in English, 118

I

imagineer, 295, 373–74
The Imperial Dictionary of the English Language, 289
Indiana University, 148, 150–56, 342, 343
internet. *See also* social media; *Merriam-Webster Unabridged* (online dictionary)
   death of print dictionaries and, 285–86
   determining definitions and, 22
   dictionaries' presence on, 49–50, 51–52, 255–56, 266
   Encyclopedia Britannica and, 56–57
   finding new words on, 91–93, 94–95
   free Oxford dictionary on, 69–70, 286
   Google, 51–53, 82, 258, 266–67, 290
   Merriam's social media posts, 219, 225–32
   natively digital as opposed to digitized print product on, 296
   need for dictionaries in era of search engines, 83
   OED on, 68–69
   SEO and, 51–52
   SERP and, 53
   traffic for online dictionaries, 266
   Urban Dictionary, 86
   URLs, 50, 51
   Webster's Third on, 58–59
   Wiktionary, 86
   word, added to dictionaries, 7, 311
   Wordnik, 83–84, 86–90, 253, 260, 262, 296
In Your Face, 189
irregardless, 121–23, 337
iWeb corpus, 79
IXL Learning, 291, 372

J

J. S. & C. Adams, 31, 32
Jefferson, Thomas, 315
Jenkins, Dan, 173, 344
Jenkins, Sally, 344–45
jeopardize, 29, 316
jockocracy, 328
joggle, 205
Johnson, Samuel, 3–4, 25, 27, 111, 228, 310
Johnson, Terry, 176
Jordan, Michael, 229, 360

K

Kariger, Brian, 50
Karras, Ruth Mazo, 194
Kay, Mairé Weir "Miss Kay," 122–23, 170, 171
Kelley, William Melvin, 237–38
Kelly, John, 288, 290, 372
Kennedy, John F., 45, 168, 322
Kennedy, Randall, 159–60, 178, 346
Kent, James, 30–31
key party, 333
Kleinedler, Steve, 272, 273
Knight, Phil, 66
"knowledge boxes," 266
Kripke, Dorothy, 137, 145
Kripke, Madeline
   Adams and, 151–52
   Read and, 139, 340–41
   basic facts about, 137–38, 145–47, 154
   collection of, 135–37, 138–41, 145–56, 340, 341, 343
   history of G. & C. Merriam Company and, 142–44
Kripke, Myer, 137, 145
Kripke, Saul, 138, 146, 147
Kučera, Henry, 77

L

Lanehart, Sonja, 105, 160–61
language
   dictionaries as unbiased arbiters of language and its evolution, 5–7, 84–85, 228

language (*continued*)
  history of, 98–99
  most frequently words searched online, 51–52, 53
  percent of English, undocumented, 82–83
  processes of word formation, 93
  weaponization of, 105, 240–44
  writings about, 8–9
language, addition of words to, 7–8
  from African American usage, 105, 236–41, 243–44
  AIDS, 249
  during Civil War, 37
  comprehensiveness of dictionaries and, 44
  COVID, 246–52
  factors in success of permanence of, 93–96
  Native American, 29–30
  nouns, 95
  processes of, 91
  reaction to, 45–46
  reasons for, 187, 189, 195
  reasons for including, in dictionaries, 73, 74
  social media and, 69, 92–93
  as subversive act, 229
  Trump and, 9, 95, 103
  in 2020, 244, 252
  by writers of *The Simpsons*, 70–71
large language models (LLMs), 254–55, 256, 265
Latinx, 195
Leavitt, Robert Keith, 60
Lebron, Jools, 372
Ledbetter, Huddie William "Lead Belly," 238–39
leetspeak, 9, 311
Lerps, Art, 113–16
Lew, Robert, 257
Lexical Evidence from Folk Epigraphy in Western North America (Read), 139, 340
Lexico, 286
lexicographers. *See also* specific individuals
  AI as threat to, 263–67

as detectives, 18–19
  early, 2–3
  films about, 271
  gender-neutral pronouns and attitudes of, 299–300
  as "humble drudge" or "harmless drudge," 3–4, 310
  inability of, to keep up with new words, 292
  job market for, 285
  new technology adopted by, 255
  number of full-time, 272–73
  power of words to, 218
  public acknowledgment of, 19
  training of, 13, 14–15
  Webster on role of, 24
lexicography
  citation-based, 79
  corpus-based, 75–80
  percent of English undocumented, 82–83
  repetitive nature of, 75
  use of analytical software in, 75–76
"Lexicography, Artificial Intelligence, and Dictionary Users" (McKean and Fitzgerald), 254, 255, 264
Lexicon Book Publishing Record, 77
Life magazine, 45
Lighter, Jonathan, 124, 337
Linguistic Society of America, 102, 197
Linkinen, Tom, 194
Lipsyte, Robert, 173, 328, 345
The Lives of Transgender People (Beemyn and Rankin), 194
Llewellyn, William, 48–49, 126, 323
Locke, M. J., 194, 195
long-hauler, 250, 365
Lopez, Erika, 194
Los Angeles Magazine, 195
Lowe, Jim, 54–55
Lyman, Charles, 34, 318

M

Mac, Taylor, 199, 352
Macdonald, Dwight, 45–46, 118
Mahn, Carl August Friedrich, 33

index

The Making of the Oxford English Dictionary (Gilliver), 125
Maledicta, 171
Manchester Guardian Weekly, 118
"Mapping Lexical Innovation on American Social Media" (Grieve), 93
marriage, 217, 218, 357
Marshall, George Preston, 167–68
Martin, Dave, 302
Martin, Katherine Connor, 69–70, 80, 81–82, 273, 274, 275, 283, 361
Martin, Rachel, 223
"Master Teacher" (Badu), 239
Matthews, Mitford, 370
Maugham, W. Somerset, 169
McCulloch, Beverley, 128, 129, 130
McGuinness, Max, 298, 299
McIntyre, John, 184
McKean, Erin
   on AI, 254, 255
   basic facts about, 83
   cottagecore as AI test, 259
   on dictionaries as gatekeepers of language, 84–85
   on LLMs, 256, 265
   on number of full-time lexicographers, 272
   on problems presented by definitions, 85–86
   Wordnik and, 83–84, 86–88, 89–90, 253, 260, 262
McNamee, Roger, 84
McWhorter, John, 178–79, 354, 363
Mencken, H. L., 7–8, 97, 332, 340, 342
Merman, Ethel, 44
Merriam family members, 154, 317, 343
Merriam, George and Charles. See also G. & C. Merriam Company
   basic facts about, 31–32, 35–39
   competitiveness of, 33, 37, 317–18
Merriam, Homer, 142–44
Merriam-Webster.com
   author's definitions added to, 218
   basic facts about, x, 50–53, 62–63
   entries from *Unabridged* in, 63
   fuck in, 120
   genderqueer in, 188
   generative AI in, 255
   history of, 50–53
   irregardless in, 121
   large language model in, 255
   n-word in, 179–80
   they in, 190
   traffic to, 50, 53, 266, 367, 373
   woke in, 244
Merriam-Webster Inc.
   author at, 12–13
   Clinton-Trump presidential debate, 58
   G. & C. Merriam Company renamed as, x
   layoffs at, 53–54, 57, 58, 59
   offices, 11–14, 201–3
   post-pandemic revitalization of, 248, 292–94
   relationship with Encyclopedia-Britannica, 53, 55, 57–60, 248, 292, 293–95
   Slang & Trending page, 296, 374
   social media posts, 219, 225–28, 229–33
   threat against, 217, 358
   typeface, 312–13
   website data, 373
Merriam-Webster's Collegiate Dictionary. See *Collegiate*
Merriam-Webster Unabridged (online)
   addition of words to, 71
   entries from, put on OWL, 63
   Mx. in, 200
   subscription deficit, 58–59
   troll in, 225
   updating, 19, 62, 63–64, 160
Metcalf, Allan, 100, 108–9
Miami Herald, 118, 195, 220
microaggression, 207–11, 258, 356
Milburn, George, 149, 342
Mill, John Stuart, 185
The Miller's Tale (Chaucer), 20–21
Minor, William Chester, 128, 271, 339
Minsky, Barbara, 140, 146
Mish, Frederick C., 20, 176, 204
Mishkin, Paul, 291
Mitchum, Kennedy, 244–46, 364

Mixon, Laura J., 194–95
Montoya, Orión, 84
Morse, John
   on addition of new words, 73, 74, 215, 329
   author and, 2
   basic facts about, 12, 59, 204, 302
   on definition of *n-word*, 158–59
   on effect of controversy on definitions, 233
   layoffs at Merriam and, 53, 57, 58
   on dictionary publishing, 326
   at Lowe's retirement, 54–55
   on Madeline Kripke, 146
   on Merriam brothers, 37
   number of cits and, 112
   online presence of dictionaries and, 50, 51–52
   on retention of cits, 132
   retirement of, 59–61
   on *Webster's Second* as rulebook for American English, 41
Morton, Herbert C., 116
Munroe, Randall, 221
Munroe, Robert C., 203
Murphy, Lynne, 274, 275
Murray, James, 19, 111, 271, 275, 276
Mx., 200
My Gender Workbook (Bornstein), 193–94

N

Narmontas, Joan, 248
Naturale, Lauren, 225–27, 230–232
Nature, 57
Nedney, Joe, 263
Neilson, William Allan, 41
NeoCrawler, 94–95
neologisms. *See also* language, addition of words to
   factors in success of permanence of, 93–96
   Grieve and, 91–94, 96
   processes of, 91, 93
   Schmid and, 94–96
   social media and, 92–93
   WOTY and, 100–109

neopronouns. *See* gender-neutral pronouns
nepo baby, 328
New Files, 22, 172, 178, 205
A New Grammar With Exercises in Bad English (Fisher), 183
Newman, Edwin, 8
The New Republic, 45
Newton, Fred, 186
New Words
   author's additions to, 16, 20, 65–66, 206, 211–13, 300
   format of, 313
   gender-neutral pronouns added to, 192, 200
   natively digital dictionaries and, 296
   Perrault's additions to, 225
   purpose of, 16
New-York Commercial Advertiser, 185–86
The New Yorker, 19, 45–46, 118, 133, 192
New York magazine, 221
New York Times, 45, 55, 56, 58, 88, 165, 169, 193, 221, 222, 238, 259, 272–73, 275, 279, 296
New York Times Book Review, 118
New York Times Magazine, 20, 237, 272
Nexis, 65–66, 67, 81, 200, 212, 214, 220
Nichols, Wendalyn, 80, 268, 269
nigga, definition and labeling of, 176
Nike, 66, 298
Noah's Ark, New England Yankees, and the Endless Quest (Leavitt), 60
nonstandard, use of, 122, 123
Norlen, Nick, 372–73
Notes and Queries: A Medium of Intercommunication for Literary Men, General Readers, Etc., 71–72
Novak, Madeline, 13, 15, 19, 53, 221–22
Nugent, Ted, 220, 221, 222
Nunberg, Geoffrey, 73, 235
n-word, definition and labeling of, 158–63, 164–65, 166, 172–80, 218

O

Oakes, Edward F., 162–63
Oakley, Bill, 71
Official Scrabble Players Dictionary, 54, 217

Ogilvie, John, 289
Oman-Reagan, Michael, 360
Online Webster's Lexicon (OWL). See Merriam-Webster.com
Ono, Yoko, 174, 345
Orwant, Jon, 134
Oxford corpora, 1, 80
Oxford English Dictionary (OED)
  addition of words to, 71
  author at, 125–30
  basic facts about, 282
  fart in, 20–21
  first edition, 275–77, 369
  free Oxford online dictionary compared to, 69–70
  genderqueer in, 188–89
  internet in, 7
  Minor and, 271
  n-word in, 178
  offices, 127
  online revision of, 126, 127, 370
  quotation slips for, 111, 125, 127–31, 336
  reaction to Merriam dictionaries, 370
  Scriptorium/*scriptorium*, 111, 127, 336
  second edition, 130–31
  sheeple in, 219–20
  singular *they/their/them/themselves* in, 183
  troll in, 224–25
  use of 1864 Merriam dictionary in, 277
  use of technology, 255
  waggle dance in, 73
  Webster scale for, 276
  ze/hir in, 199
Oxford online dictionary, free, 68–70, 71, 82, 286
Oxford University Press, 125, 125, 276, 282, 338, 370

P

paradigm, 52, 53, 329
Partridge, Eric, 152
Payne, Roger, 149, 342–43
Pearsons, Enid, 271–72, 368
Pease, Roger, 249
Pei, Mario, 118
Percival, James Gates, 316

Perrault, Stephen
  on adding author's definitions, 299, 301
  author's definitions edited by, 66–67, 210–11, 215, 219, 221
  author's definitions nixed by, 65–66
  basic facts about, 13, 17, 19, 72
  on definition and labeling of n-word, 176, 180
  definitions in OWL and, 63
  on gender-neutral pronouns, 189–90, 198–99, 299–300
  layoffs at Merriam and, 53
  at Lowe's retirement, 54, 55
  as master lexicographer, 17, 18, 20–21, 63, 72
  on quotations used in definitions, 223–24
  on retirement of Morse, 59
  on *sportocrat*, 299
  they/their/them/themselves and, 189–90
  troll and, 225
  on writing definitions, 15
phat, 244, 364
Philadelphia Inquirer, 176, 206
Phillips, McCandlish, 110
Phrenological Journal and Magazine of Moral Science, 33
Pierce, Chester, 207–8
The Players' Tribune, 18
Polk, James Knox, 33
pom-pom girl, 21–23, 258, 314
Porter, Mary, 34
Porter, Noah, 33, 34–35, 37–39, 40, 111, 320
post-fact, 228, 359
Pound, Louise, 97–98, 332
Preposition Project, 76
Preston, Dennis, 104, 334
The Professor and the Madman (book), 128
The Professor and the Madman (film), 271
A Pronouncing Dictionary of American English, 202
pronouns, 189. See also gender-neutral pronouns
"Pure/Honey" (Beyoncé), 106

R

R. R. Donnelley & Sons, 113–14
racism, 244–46
Rahv, Philip, 168, 344
ralph bunche/Ralph Bunche, 237, 361
Random House college dictionary, 284, 371
Random House Dictionary of the English Language: The Unabridged Edition, 46, 50, 289
Rankin, Susan, 194
Ravenel, Mazyck, 217, 357
rawdog/rawdogging, 296–97, 374–75
The Razor's Edge (Maugham), 169
Read, Allen Walker, 139, 340–41
reading and marking, 16
Redding, J. Saunders, 362
redskin, 167–72, 346–47
Reed, Joseph, 316
Rickford, John, 235, 236
rizz, 101, 333
Roberts, Hermese, 361
Rodgers, Nile, 241
Rogers, Ernest, 220, 358–59
Rolfe, John, 161
Rolling Stone, 106
Rose, Carl, 361–62
Roth, Gabriel, 230–31
run, 218, 358
Russell, Karen, 176
Russell, Lindsay Rose, 117, 270

S

"Sabotage in Springfield" (Follett), 45
Sacramento Bee, 187
safe space, 206–7, 210
Safire, William, 8, 20, 54, 355
Safra, Jacob E. "Jacqui," 56, 57, 134, 325–26
Saleh, Dua, 197
Samqua, Bert M., 171
Sancho, Ignatius, 161
sanewashing, 297, 374–75
San Francisco Chronicle, 223
Scalia, Antonin, 79
Schmid, Hans-Jörg, 94–95, 96
Schneider, Lisa, 59, 225, 231–32, 248, 259, 292–93
Schwandes, AV, 197
Science, 82–83
"Scottsboro Boys" (Lead Belly), 238–39
Scrabble, 12, 19, 192, 203, 217, 269, 303, 351, 357, 369, 376
search engine optimization (SEO), 51–53
search engine results page (SERP), 53
Seattle Star, 298
selfie, 88, 92, 274, 350, 368
Serven, Neil, 19
Shea, Ammon, 146, 147
sheeple, 219–21, 222–24, 232–33, 358–59
Sheffield, A. D., 121
Sheidlower, Jesse, 135–36, 146, 147, 228, 284–85, 286–87, 371
Sherman, Talia, 107
Shilts, Randy, 248
Shortz, Will, 231, 342
Silver, Joel, 154–55
Similarweb, 373
Simpson, John, 73
The Simpsons (television program), 70–71, 73
Sketch Engine, 76
Skibidi Toilet/*skibidi*, 104, 374
Sleeth, Charles R., 114
slurs, defining and labeling
  n-word, 158–63, 164–65, 166, 172–80, 218
  offensive label, 165–66
  redskin, 167–72
  squaw, 157–58
  in *Webster's Second*, 161–62, 163
smashmouth, 204–5, 355
snitch'em's, 130, 340
social media, 69, 92–93, 219, 225–28, 229–33
sociolinguistics, 93
Sokolowski, Peter
  on adding words as subversive act, 229
  on Backward Index, 335
  basic facts about, 1, 19, 273
  on importance of cis, 12
  on job of computational linguist, 292

on *joggle*, 205
obscene words file and, 117
on *racism*'s definition, 246
on words not in dictionaries, 247
Somebody Somewhere (television program), 376
The Sopranos (television program), 20
Spencer, Richard, 211–12
Spillane, Mickey, 44
sportocrat, 66–67, 258, 298–99, 328
Sports Illustrated, 22, 66, 173, 322
Springfield Daily Republican, 32, 36, 37, 201
Springfield Daily Union, 36
Springfield, Massachusetts
  as home of Merriam-Webster, 11
  in 1864, 36–37
squaw, 157–58
Stamper, Kory
  on dictionaries as authorities, 250
  at Dictionary.com, 288–89
  on Gove, 118
  on Merriam archives, 132, 134
  on *irregardless*, 121
  on revision of *marriage* entry, 218
Stephens, Bret, 240
Stevens, Mark, 19
stochastic parrot, 108, 335
Storck, Dorothy, 207
Strong Language (Friedman), 108–9
Strunk, William, Jr., 182–83
"Studies in Lexicography as a Science and an Art: Style Book esp. for Copy Editors, Proofreaders, & Other Interested Editorial Folks" (E. Gilman), 15
stuff, 301–2
Summer.ai, 253
Sunday Star, 45
Surfing Life, 66–67
Swisher, Kara, 219, 221, 222
systemic racism, 245, 246

T

A Table Alphabeticall (Cawdrey), 3, 310
they/their/them/themselves, 183–84, 189–91, 196

Thompson, Hunter S., 173–74, 345
thob, 100, 332–33
thon, 181, 185, 186, 199–200, 353–54
Thurow, Roger, 66
Tolkien, J. R. R., 126, 338
Transgender Warriors (Feinberg), 193
Trench, Richard Chenevix, 23, 338–39
troll, 224–25
Trump, Donald
  addition of words to English and, 9, 95, 103
  "best words" claim by, 234
  DEI and, 242–43
  Merriam's social media posts about, 226–28, 229–30, 232
  WOTY and, 103, 234–35
truthiness, 101, 333
Tryon, Thomas, 206
tush push, 104
Twaddell, W. Freeman, 41–42
Twitter, 91–92, 94, 219, 225–28, 231, 232

U

Unabridged. See *Merriam-Webster Unabridged* (online)
unabridged, defined, ix, 309–10
unabridged dictionaries, history of, ix–x
Up Against It (Locke), 194, 195
Urban Dictionary, 86, 274, 369

V

vajazzle, 69, 328–29
van Kemenade, Hugo, 88, 273–74
van Pelt Bryan, Frederick, 118
VerbNet, 76
verse (verb), 62, 326–27
Villareal, Dan, 236
VORP (Value Over Replacement Player), 82, 330

W

Wachal, Robert S., 168
waggle dance, 73
Wallace, David Foster, 46
Wall Street Journal, 66, 204, 209, 220, 298

Ward, C. A., 71–72
Ward, Charles Henshaw, 100, 332–33
"War of the Dictionaries," 33, 142, 341
Washington Post, 58, 184, 211–12, 297
Watson, Elijah, 238
Webster, Noah, Jr.
  American Dictionary and, 27–31
  basic facts about, ix, 24–25, 27, 31, 315
  Blue-Back (or Blue-Backed) Speller and, 25. 27, 317
  copying definitions from Johnson, 27, 316
  Compendious Dictionary and, 12, 25–27, 284
  goals of, 25–27, 29, 228
  on how to judge dictionaries, 60
  n-word and, 161
  reason for writing first dictionary, 5
  on role of lexicographer, 24
  spelling and, 26, 284
Webster, William, 34, 38, 318
Webster's Collegiate Dictionary. See Collegiate
Webster's Fourth New International Dictionary, Unabridged, 48–49, 323
Webster's International Dictionary, Unabridged (1890), x, 17, 39
Webster's New International Dictionary of the English Language (1909), x, 17, 112
Webster's New International Dictionary of the English Language, Second Edition, Unabridged (1934). See *Webster's Second*
Webster's Third New International Dictionary of the English Language, Unabridged (1961). See *Webster's Third*
Webster's New World dictionaries, 1, 4–5, 49, 101, 124, 269, 285
Webster's Second
  basic facts about, 39–40, 320–21
  cits created for, 112
  editors, 40–41
  in-house name for, x
  irregardless in, 122
  as prescriptive, 41, 44

racism added to Addenda of, 245
redskin in, 168
slurs in, 161–62, 163
thon in, 199–200
usage notes in, 40
Webster's Third
  basic facts about, 1–2, 47, 113
  "The Big Book" and, 270–71
  cits created for, 16, 112, 336
  definitions in, 42–44
  denotation of slurs in, 165–66
  as descriptive, 42
  fuck/fuck up in, 114–19, 120, 270
  in-house name for, x
  irregardless in, 122–23
  last printing of, 13
  n-word in, 173–74
  pom-pom girl in, 21–23
  preface of, 5–6
  racism in, 245
  reaction to publication of, 45–46
  size constraints, 44
  staff, 13, 19, 41–42, 271, 201, 302, 321
  they/them/their/themselves in, 184
  thon and, 200
  total number of words, 8
Weigel, David, 212
Wells, Ida B., 245
What's Your Pronoun? Beyond He and She (Baron), 184–85
White, E. B., 182–83, 347–48, 362
Whitman, Walt, 144, 341–42
Whitney, William Dwight, 33, 281, 318
who/whom, 317
Wiktionary, 86, 273–74
Wilchins, Riki, 189
Wild, Kate, 247, 251
Wilkinson, Karen, 176
Wilkinson, Willy, 193
Williams, Edward Bennett, 169–70
Williams, Kathryn, 158
Winchester, Simon, 271
Winona (Minnesota) *Daily News*, 220
Wittgenstein, Ludwig, 15
woke, 105, 236–41, 243–44, 362, 363
Wood, Katie, 197
Woolf, H. Bosley, 119, 122–23, 270, 302

Worcester, Joseph, 33, 36, 37, 317–18, 319, 341
Wordnik, 83–84, 86–90, 253, 260, 262, 296
Word of the Year (WOTY), 100–109, 190, 234–36, 251–52, 289, 333, 350
Words, 98
World Publishing Company, 1
Wright, Kelly E., 334
Wright, Milton C., 162
The Writer: A Monthly Magazine for Literary Workers, 186
WTF, 103, 333–34
wut, 21, 314

X

xe/xy/xim, 192, 196, 197, 199

Y

Yellowtail, Bill, 169
you (singular), as gender-neutral pronoun, 182
Young, Beth, 269
Young, Damon, 239, 240
Young, Ella Flagg, 186

Z

ze/hir, 192–96, 198, 199, 299, 351, 352, 353
Zimmer, Ben
  on state of dictionary business, 285
  fuck and, 270
  Historical Dictionary of American Slang cits and, 124
  obscene words file and, 117
  The Professor and the Madman and, 271
  racism and, 245
  run and, 358
  sheeple and, 219
  smashmouth and, 355
  verse and, 327
  WOTY and, 107, 234–35, 236, 350
zygomatic, 28